PSYCHOLOGY AND LAW

PSYCHOLOGY AND LAW,
A Critical Introduction

ANDREAS KAPARDIS

WITHDRAWN

 CAMBRIDGE
UNIVERSITY PRESS

PUBLISHED BY THE PRESS SYNDICATE OF THE UNIVERSITY OF CAMBRIDGE
The Pitt Building, Trumpington Street, Cambridge CB2 1RP, United Kingdom

CAMBRIDGE UNIVERSITY PRESS
The Edinburgh Building, Cambridge CB2 2RU, United Kingdom
40 West 20th Street, New York, NY 10011–4211, USA
10 Stamford Road, Oakleigh, Melbourne 3166, Australia

First published 1997

Printed in Hong Kong by Colorcraft

Typeset in Baskerville 10/12 pt

National Library of Australia Cataloguing in Publication data
Kapardis, Andreas.
Psychology and law: a critical introduction.
Bibliography.
Includes index.
ISBN 0 521 55738 0 (pbk.).
ISBN 0 521 55321 0.
1. Law – Psychological aspects. 2. Psychology, forensic.
3. Judicial process. I. Title.
340.019

Library of Congress Cataloguing in Publication data
Kapardis, Andreas.
Psychology and law: a critical appraisal / Andreas Kapardis.
p.   cm.
Includes bibliographical references and indexes.
ISBN 0-521-55321-0 (hb: alk. paper). – ISBN 0-521-55738-0
(pbk.: alk. paper)
1. Law Psychological aspects. 2. Psychology, Forensic.
3. Insanity – Jurisprudence. I. Title.
K487.P75K36   1997
340'.01'9–dc21   96–40439

A catalogue record for this book is available from the British Library

ISBN 0 521 55321 0 hardback
ISBN 0 521 55738 0 paperback

Contents

Tables

Foreword

Psychology and Law is an expanding field throughout the world. Research and knowledge in this area increased dramatically in North America and Great Britain in the 1970s and is now mushrooming in Europe (especially in the Netherlands, Germany and Spain). The recent formation of the European Association of Psychology and Law and the several major European conferences on Law and Psychology are both symptoms of current expansion and catalysts for further expansion. Given the common concerns of psychologists and lawyers with trying to understand and predict human behaviour, it seems clear that much can be gained by applying the theories and methodology of psychology to key issues arising in law and legal processes. This is primarily what this book is about.

I am very happy to welcome Andreas Kapardis' book, which is a detailed, wide-ranging, up-to-date text on psychology and law. Despite the clear need for such a book for undergraduate and graduate students, no comparable modern text with such an international focus exists, so this book clearly fills an important gap in the literature. It covers classic topics such as eyewitness testimony, the psychologist as an expert witness, children as witnesses, jury decision-making and sentencing, as well as other important topics such as detecting deception and psychology as applied to law enforcement.

The author, Andreas Kapardis, is extremely well-qualified to write such a book. He completed interesting Masters and PhD theses under my supervision at Cambridge University (on jury decision-making and sentencing) about fifteen years ago. Since leaving Cambridge he has been very active in teaching and research in the area of legal and criminological psychology in Australia. His chapters reveal his excellent and wide-ranging knowledge of psychology and law. I was very happy that he was able to complete his book while visiting Cambridge (and incidentally teaching my classes for me!).

Psychology and law have not always been happy bedfellows. The pioneering forensic psychologist, Lionel Haward, once described the witness box as 'an abattoir of sacred cows' for a psychologist. Nevertheless, the interest, respect and appreciation of psychologists and lawyers for each other have grown dramatically in the past twenty years, showing the great need for an up-to-date review of what is known about psychology and law. I am very happy to welcome Andreas Kapardis' book as a scholarly, but readable and accessible, introduction to this subject.

DAVID P. FARRINGTON
President of the European Association of Psychology and Law
Professor of Psychological Criminology, Cambridge University

Acknowledgements

I decided to write this book encouraged over the years largely by my students at La Trobe University. There were already a number of books dealing with psychology and law. However, I felt that none of them had covered such a broad range of areas in the one volume. I have tried to draw on European and Australian work as well as on more traditional North American sources, and to give sufficient of the legal framework to provide a proper context for the psycholegal research that is discussed. Inevitably, the book reflects my own background and interests in psychology, legal studies, criminology and law enforcement. I hope it will be used as a textbook and will be of interest to undergraduate and graduate students, as well as to professionals in psychology, law enforcement and social work.

As the manuscript goes to print, a sense of gratitude goes to my parents who taught me early on in life that where there is a will there is a way. While working on different parts of the manuscript I benefited from discussions with David Farrington, Roger Douglas, Austin Lovegrove and Stephen Schembri. I wish to thank D. Warren, K. Volenta and M. Hyslop of La Trobe University's library at Bundoora campus for tracking down at very short notice numerous invaluable references. I consider myself fortunate to have enjoyed the excellent facilities and helpful assistance of the staff at the Radzinowicz Library, Institute of Criminology, Cambridge University. I wrote a large part of the final draft of the manuscript while on a Visiting Fellowship at Clare Hall, Cambridge. I could not have wished for a more conducive environment. A special thanks goes to Phillipa McGuinness and Lee White for their editorial comments. Of course, none of the individuals or institutions is responsible for any weaknesses, mistakes or opinions expressed in this work.

Finally, this book would not have been possible without the tremendous support and patience of my wife Maria. In appreciation, I dedicate this book to her and to our children, Kostandinos Raphael, Elena and Dina.

ANDREAS KAPARDIS

Chapter 1

Psycholegal Research: An Introduction

- *Tracing the development of the psycholegal field.*
- *Bridging the gap between the two disciplines.*
- *Remaining difficulties.*
- *Grounds for optimism.*
- *Psychology and law in Australia.*
- *The book's structure, focus, and aims.*

'In the recent past psychologists' claims to knowledge and fact finding ability were altogether too forceful, and lawyers' reluctance to use psychological evidence, insights and sophisticated techniques altogether too irrational.' (Clifford and Bull, 1978:19)

'However relevant they may be to each other, the offspring of the relationship between psychology and law is still an infant and doubts are still cast upon its legitimacy.' (Carson and Bull, 1995a:3)

Introduction: Development of the Psycholegal Field

The plethora of applications of psychology to law can be differentiated in terms of what has been termed:[1] (a) 'psychology in law'; (b) 'psychology and law'; and (c) 'psychology of law'. According to Blackburn (1996:6), *psychology in law* refers to specific applications of psychology within law: such as the reliability of eyewitness testimony, mental state of the defendant, and a parent's suitability of child custody in a divorce case. *Psychology and law* is used by Blackburn (1996) to denote, for example, psycholegal research into offenders (see Howells

1

and Blackburn, 1995), lawyers, magistrates, judges and jurors. Finally, *psychology of law* is used to refer to psychological research into such issues as to why people obey/disobey certain laws, moral development, and public perceptions and attitudes towards various penal sanctions. As far as the term *forensic psychology* is concerned, Blackburn (1996:6) argues convincingly it should only be used to denote the 'direct provision of psychological information to the courts, that is, to psychology *in* the courts' (see also Gudjonsson, 1996).

Psycholegal research involves applying psychology's methodologies and knowledge to studying jurisprudence, substantive law, legal processes and law breaking (Farrington et al., 1979b:IX). Research into, and the practice of, legal psychology has a long tradition exemplified since the beginning of this century by the work of such pioneers[2] as Binet (1905), Gross (1898), Jung (1905), Münsterberg (1908) and Wertheimer (1906). In fact, Münsterberg has been called 'the father of applied psychology' (Magner, 1991:121).[3] The psycholegal field has been expanding at an impressive rate since the mid 1960s, especially in North America, since the late 1970s in the United Kingdom and in Australia since the early 1980s. In fact, on both sides of the Atlantic research and teaching in legal psychology has grown enormously during the last two decades (Lloyd-Bostock, 1994). More recently, the field of psychology and law has also been expanding in Europe, especially in the Netherlands, Germany and Spain (see Lösel et al., 1992a:509–53; Davies et al., 1996:579–601). As the chapters in this volume show, since the 1960s psychology and law has evolved into a single applied discipline and an often-cited example of success in applied psychology. In this context, Haney (1993) points to psycholegal researchers having tackled some very crucial questions in society and, *inter alia*, been instrumental in improving the ways eyewitnesses are interviewed by law-enforcement personnel; the adoption of a more critical approach to the issue of forensic hypnosis evidence in the courts; psychologists contributing to improving the legal status and rights of children; and, finally, generally making jury selection fairer (p. 372ff). Furthermore, the impact of legal psychology has not just been one way (Davies, 1995:187).

Despite such early works as Brown's (1926) *Legal Psychology*, and while most lawyers would be familiar with forensic psychology, traditionally dominated by psychiatrists, it was not until the 1960s that lawyers in the United States came to acknowledge and appreciate psychology's contribution to their work (see Toch, 1961, *Legal and Criminal Psychology*; Marshall, 1969, *Law and Psychology in Conflict*).[4] Since the 1970s a significant number of psycholegal textbooks have appeared in the US,[5] in England,[6] and some have been written by legal psychologists on continental Europe (Lösel et al., 1992a; Wegener et al., 1989). In addition, following Tapp's (1976) first review of psychology and law in the *Annual Review of Psychology*, relevant journals have been published, such as *Law and Human Behaviour* which was first published in 1977 as the official publication of the American Psychology-Law Society (founded in 1968) and is nowadays the journal of the American Psychological Association's Division of Psychology and Law. Other journals are: *Behavioural Sciences and the Law*; *Expert Evidence*; *Law and Psychology Review*; *Criminal Behaviour and Mental Health*. New psycholegal journals continue to be published. The first issue of *Psychology, Crime and Law* was published in 1994 and those of *Legal and Criminological Psychology* and *Psychology, Public Policy, and Law* in 1996 in the UK and the US respectively.

Despite the fact that in the UK lawyers and psychologists have been rather less ready than their American colleagues to 'jump into each other's arms', enough push by prison psychologists and increasing interest in the field (for example, at the Social Science Research Centre for Socio-Legal Studies at Oxford, the Psychology Departments of the University of East London [previously North-East London Polytechnic], the London School of Economics and Political Science and Nottingham University, as well as at the Institute of Criminology at Cambridge) had gathered enough momentum by 1977 for the British Psychological Society to establish a Division of Criminological and Legal Psychology. By the early 1980s empirical contributions by legal psychologists at Aberdeen University added to the momentum. Annual conferences at the Oxford Centre formed the basis for Farrington et al.'s (1979a) *Psychology, Law and Legal Processes* and Lloyd-Bostock's (1981a) *Psychology In Legal Contexts: Applications and Limitations*, 'established a European focus for collaboration between the two disciplines, attracting scholars from many different countries' (Stephenson, 1995:133) and paved the way for the more recent annual European Association of Psychology and Law Conferences. These two publications, together with Clifford and Bull's (1978) *The Psychology of Person Identification* and other British works published in the 1980s and early in the 1990s, have established psychology and law as a field in its own right in Britain, despite the fact that in 1983 the Social Science Research Council, under a Conservative government, ceased funding conferences for lawyers and psychologists (King, 1986:1). Psychological associations outside the UK also set up relevant divisions, for example, in the US in 1981 and in Germany in 1984 (see Lösel, 1992). In 1981 the American Psychological Association founded Psychology and Law as its 41st Division (Monahan and Loftus, 1982).

Besides a spate of international conferences on legal psychology that have been held in the UK and on continental Europe, there now exist both undergraduate and post-graduate programs in legal psychology

(Lloyd-Bostock, 1994:133). Finally, a number of universities on both sides of the Atlantic have recognised the importance of legal psychology by dedicating chairs to the subject (Melton et al., 1987). It must not be forgotten, however, that while by the beginning of the 1980s in the US one-quarter of graduate programs offered at least one course and a number had begun to offer forensic minors and/or PhD/JD programs (Freeman and Roesch, 1992), few psychology departments offered courses in psychology and law prior to 1973 (Diamond, 1992).

1 Bridging the Gap Between Psychology and Law: Why It has Taken so Long

In his book, *On The Witness Stand*, Münsterberg (1908:44–5) was critical of the legal profession in the US for not appreciating the relevance of psychology to their work.

However, Münsterberg was overselling psychology and his claims were not taken seriously by the legal profession (Magner, 1991). The rather unfortunate legacy left by Ebbinghaus (1885) and his black-box approach to experimental memory research – best exemplified by his use of nonsense syllables – contributed to the state of knowledge in psychology at the time and was one significant factor that negated the success of Münsterberg's attempt. Fortunately, the dominance of the black-box paradigm in experimental psychology came to an end with the publication in 1967 of Neisser's futuristic *Cognitive Psychology* book.

In the ensuing six decades, whilst behaviourism on the one hand and the experimental psychologists' practice on the other of treating as 'separate and separable' perception, memory, thinking, problem solving and language (Clifford and Bull, 1978:5) permeated and limited psychological research greatly, the early interest in psycholegal research fizzled out. However, by the late 1960s, as psychology matured as a discipline and, amongst other developments, social psychology blossomed in the US, the experimental method came to be applied to problems not traditionally the concern of psychologists. Psychologists began turning their attention to understanding deception and its detection, jury decision-making, the accuracy of eyewitness testimony and sentencing decision-making as human processes. Most of the early psycholegal researchers with a strong interest in social psychology focused on juries in criminal cases, those with an affinity to clinical psychology concerned themselves with the insanity defence, while cognitive psychologists examined eyewitness testimony. These same areas continue to be of interest to psycholegal researchers today but the questions being asked are more intricate and the methods used to answer them are more sophisticated (Diamond, 1992:VI). However, the somewhat narrow focus of psycholegal research caused enough concern to Saks (1986) as to remind such researchers that 'the law does not live by eyewitness testimony alone' and to urge them 'to explore under-represented areas of the legal landscape' (Diamond, 1992:VI). It is comforting for psychologists to know that, with the general growth and maturity of their discipline, major industrialised society has come to realise the wide-ranging benefits of psychology (McConkey, 1992:3).

Why, then, has it taken so long for the field of psychology and law to develop when, as some authors would argue,[7] psychologists and lawyers do have a lot of common ground? Both disciplines focus on the *individual* (Carson, 1995a). Yarmey (1979:7) wrote that 'both psychology and the courts are concerned with predicting, explaining and controlling behaviour', while according to Saks and Hastie (1978:1): 'Every law and every institution is based on assumptions about human nature and the manner in which human behaviour is determined'. In fact, Diamond (1992:VI–VII) states that 'on grandiose days, I think that law should be characterised as a component of psychology, for if psychology is the study of human behaviour, it necessarily includes law as a primary instrument used by society to control human behaviour. Perhaps this explains why laws are such a fertile source of research ideas for psychologists'. Similarly, Crombag (1994) argues that law may be considered a branch of applied psychology because the law mainly comprises a system of rules for the control of human social behaviour. Listing law as a component of psychology, however convincing the arguments put forward for it might be, is not a suggestion that will endear psycholegal researchers to lawyers.

While the law relies on assumptions about human behaviour and psychologists concern themselves with understanding and predicting behaviour, both psychology and law accept that human behaviour is not random. More specifically, research in psychology relates to various aspects of law in practice (Lloyd-Bostock, 1988:1). As in other countries, the legal profession in Australia, justifiably, perhaps, has been rather slow to recognise the relevance of psychology to its work. Compared to law, psychology is, chronologically speaking, entering its adulthood and, given a number of important differences between the two disciplines, it comes as no surprise to be told that there is tension, conflict between the two disciplines (see Marshall, 1966) that persists today (Carson and Bull, 1995b; Diamond, 1992:VIII). Bridging the gap between the two disciplines on both sides of the Atlantic, in Australia, New Zealand and Canada, as well as, for example, in Spain and Italy (see Garrido and Redodo, 1992; Traverso and Manna, 1992) has not been easy. In fact, there is a long way to go before the remaining ambivalence about psychology's contribution to academic and practising lawyers and ethical issues of such a function will be resolved (Lloyd-Bostock, 1988). Admittedly, 'Different psychologists have different ideas about what psychology should be about' (Legge, 1975:5) and 'Law, like happiness, poverty and good music, is different things to different people' (Chisholm and Nettheim, 1992:1). The simple fact is that there are significant differences in approach between psychology and law. To illustrate, the two disciplines operate with different models of man. The law, whether civil or criminal, generally emphasises individual responsibility in contrast to the tendency by a number of psychological theories to highlight 'unconscious and uncontrollable forces operating to determine aspects of individuals' behaviour' (King, 1986:76). In addition, 'The psychologists' information is inherently statistical, the legal system's task is clinical and diagnostic' (Doyle, 1989:125–6). As Clifford (1995) has put it: 'the two disciplines appear to diverge at the level of value, basic premises, their models, their approaches, their criteria of explanation and their methods' (p. 13).

In a submission to the Australian Science and Technology Council in the context of its investigation into the role of the social sciences and the humanities in the contribution of science and technology to economic development (see McConkey, 1992:3) it is stated that:

> Psychology discovers, describes and explains human experience and behaviour through the logic and method of science. Psychological research and application is based in a logical, empirical and analytical approach, and that approach is brought to bear on an exceptionally wide range of issues.

Law, on the other hand, as Farrington et al. (1979b:XIV) put it: 'is a practical art, a system of rules, a means of social control, concerned with the solving of practical problems'. Furthermore:

> The law is based on common-sense psychology which has its own model of man, its own criteria ... its own values. Common-sense explanation in the law is supported by the fact that workable legal processes have evolved under constant close scrutiny over many centuries. It is in this sense 'proven'. But this is quite different from explanation in terms of psychological theory backed by empirical evidence of statistically significant relationships. (p. XIII)

Finally, whereas the image of human beings projected by American social psychologists is that of the 'nice person', the law, and especially the criminal law, is characterised by a more cynical view of human nature and this view tends to be adopted by those who work within and for the legal system (King, 1986:76).

· Psycholegal researchers (for example, in eyewitness testimony) have utilised a variety of research methods including incident studies, field studies, archival studies and single case studies (see Clifford, 1995: 19–24; Davies, 1992). Many psychologists rely a great deal on the experimental method, including field experiments, to test predictions and formulate theories that predict behaviour and are sceptical of lawyers' reliance on common-sense generalisations about human behaviour based on armchair speculation, however ratified by conceptual analysis (Farrington et al., 1979b:XIII). A feature that unifies a lot of psychological research is their preference for subjecting assertions to systematic empirical research and, where possible, testing them experimentally. This will often involve randomly allocating persons to different conditions who, at the time, are normally not told the aim of the experiment. Clifford (1995) provides an excellent account of contemporary psychology's premises and methods. Many psychologists who favour experimental simulation tend not to also consider the issue of values in psychological and psycholegal research in general, and in particular whether psychologists can indeed avoid value judgements by demonstrating the 'facts'.

Theoretical models of man espoused by experimental psychologists have involved man as a black box, a telephone switchboard and, more recently, man as a computer. These models, which are different from the lawyer's notion of 'free will', have been rejected by cognitive psychologists because they do not take into account man as a thinking, feeling, believing totality (Clifford and Bull, 1978:5), as someone who interacts with the environment in a dynamic way.

For many a psychologist, a great deal of information processing is done without people being aware of it; the lawyer, on the other hand, operates a model of man as a free, conscious being who controls his/her actions and is responsible for them. What the law, based on a lot of judicial pronouncements, regards as 'beyond reasonable doubt' is rather different from the psychologist's conclusion that an outcome is significant at a 5 per cent level of statistical significance. One interesting aspect of this, for example, is the lawyer's reluctance to quantify how likely guilt must appear to be before one can say that such doubt as exists is not reasonable. The lawyer in court is often only interested in a 'yes' or 'no' answer to a question asked of a psychologist who is appearing as an expert witness, while, at best, the psychologist may only feel comfortable with a 'maybe' response. It should be noted, however, that the answers of interest to a practising lawyer might vary according to whether it is examination in chief or cross-examination. In the former, the lawyer is interested in a story, whereas in the latter, the lawyer is interested in questions that require a 'yes' or 'no' answer (see Chapter 8). Also, lawyers look at the individual case they have to deal with and highlight how it differs from the stereotype, they try hard to show in court that one cannot generalise, whereas psychologists talk about the probability of someone being different from the aggregate.

In addition to significant differences between psychology and law (see Carson, 1995b), there is the fact that the approaches of various branches of psychology differ in the degree to which they are based on what might be called scientific experiments. Furthermore, some psychologists have cast doubt on the practical utility of findings from controlled laboratory experiments that reduce jury decision-making, for example, to a few psychology undergraduates reading a paragraph-long, sketchy description of a criminal case and making individual decisions on a rating scale about the appropriate sanction to be imposed on the defendant (see Bray and Kerr, 1982; King, 1986; Konečni and Ebbesen, 1992). Rabbit (1981) pointed out that 90 per cent of the studies quoted in standard textbooks on the psychology of memory available then only tested recognition or recall of nonsense three-letter syllables. More recently, Konečni and Ebbesen (1992:415–16) have argued that: 'It is dangerous and bordering on the irresponsible to draw conclusions and make recommendations to the legal system on the basis of simulations which examine effects independently of their real-world contexts' (that is, on the basis of invalidated simulations or those that are not designed to examine the higher-order interactions). More recent research on the jury (see Chapter 5) includes protocol analyses, in-depth interviews with jurors after they have rendered verdicts in real cases, elaborate simulations involving video-taped trials and juror respondents, and even randomised field experiments (see Heuer and Penrod, 1989). Similarly, eyewitness testimony researchers have been making increasingly greater use of staged events and non-psychology students as subjects, as well as utilising archival data (see Chapters 2 and 3).

King (1986) has also criticised legal psychologists' strong reliance on the experimental method, arguing that there is a tendency to exaggerate its importance; that treating legal factors as 'things' and applying to them experimental techniques and statistical methods gives rise to at least four problems, namely, inaccessibility, external validity, generalisability and completeness (p. 31). King has also argued that exclusive reliance on experimental simulation also encourages legal psychologists to focus on inter-individual behaviours without taking into account the social context to which they belong (p. 7); that Karl Popper's (1939) refutability has been shown by philosophers of science to be a questionable criterion for defining whether a theory is scientific. Furthermore, King contends that the real reasons for legal psychologists' continued use of the experimental method as the prime or sole method for studying legal issues is: (a) a belief by psychologists that using the experimental method enables them to claim they are being 'scientific' in carrying out their research; (b) a need felt by psychologists for recognition and acceptability; and (c) a belief by psychologists that they are more likely to be accepted and recognised as 'experts' if they are seen to be 'scientific'. Finally, neo-Marxist critics of the use of the experimental method (see Wexler, 1983) 'see the failure to pay attention to the context of social behaviour as a political act perpetrated by psychologists in order to obscure the true form and content of social interaction' (King, 1986:103). King has advocated a shift 'away from the restrictive and self-aggrandising notions of what constitutes "scientific" research which have tended to serve as a starting point for much of what passes for legal psychology' (p. 82). No doubt many psychologists would disagree both with Wexler's (1983) picture of them as involved in a political conspiracy informed by a particular ideology and with King's (1986) push to get them to use the experimental method less in favour of ethnomethodology as their preferred method of enquiry.

Highlighting the dangers inherent in studying eyewitness testimony under rather artificial conditions in the laboratory, Clifford and Bull (1978) reminded their readers that such research could lead psychologists to advance knowledge that is, in fact, the reverse of the truth, as in the case of the influence of physiological arousal on recall accuracy. A theory of recall, or any other psychological theory for that matter, arrived at on the basis of grossly inadequate research could hardly be expected to be taken seriously by lawyers.[8]

According to Hermann and Gruneberg (1993:55), in the 1990s memory researchers no longer presume that a laboratory procedure will or will not extrapolate to the real world because the ecological validity issue in memory research has largely been solved. Hermann and Gruneberg propose that: 'It is time now to move beyond the ecological validity issue ... to the next logically appropriate issue – applied research'. In so doing legal psychologists in the late 1990s should heed Davies' (1992) words that:

> no one research method can of itself provide a reliable data base for legislation or advocacy. Rather, problems need to be addressed from a number of perspectives, each of which makes a different compromise between ecological validity and methodological rigour. (p. 265)

Another reason why problems arise when psychology and law meet is that, as Lösel (1992:15) points out, for the psychologist the plethora of theories and perspectives in the discipline is a matter of course. In law, however, the main goal is uniformity and the avoidance of disparity. Consequently, lawyers regard the numerous viewpoints in psychology as contradictory. Taking the psychological literature on bystander intervention and using good samaritanism (that is, intervening to assist or summon assistance for people in urgent need of such assistance – see Kidd, 1985, for a review) as an example, we find two conflicting decision-making models. On the one hand, experimental simulation studies of the phenomenon (see Latane and Darley, 1970) have given rise to a cognitive decision-making model. This model assumes that people are rational decision-makers who resolve to intervene directly or indirectly in an emergency after a series of decisions: whether an incident is an emergency, whether one has personal responsibility to get involved and, finally, whether the benefits outweigh the costs of intervention. On the other hand, there exists another model of bystander intervention, partly based on experimental studies (see Piliavin et al., 1981) and partly on interviews with individuals who had heroically intervened in real-life crime situations and comparisons with 'non-interveners' (see Houston, 1980), which depicts intervention as 'impulsive' and not as comprising a series of rational decisions. A basic assumption in law (see Luntz and Hambly, 1992) is that helping behaviour is the result of rational decision-making. The relevant psychological literature, however, provides conflicting views regarding the validity of this assumption for bystander intervention, a situation that does not help those who advocate introducing failure-to-assist provisions into the criminal law of jurisdictions like those of England and Australia which do not have such laws (see Geis, 1991).

Greer (1971) drew attention to the fact that many psychologists attempting to investigate questions of legal relevance on their own have had a rather limited view of legal objectives and, as a result, in the case of eyewitness testimony, for example, 'they failed to appreciate the intricacies and complexities of legal procedures for eliciting testimony ... [and] tended to oversee the legal implications of their work and seemed to expect their findings to be regarded as virtual saviours of the integrity of the legal profession' (p. 142). Greer's comment applies twenty-six years later to a significant amount of psycholegal research, as later chapters in this volume demonstrate.

Lloyd-Bostock (1981b) has also drawn attention to another problem besides that of extrapolating from the laboratory to real life, namely, in applying general psychological principles in the individual case. She has argued that: 'It is important to distinguish between application to particular cases on the one hand, and more general applications in policy formation on the other. Applications in individual cases (and hence expert evidence) are far more hazardous' (p. 17). Lloyd-Bostock has also maintained that while developments in the psycholegal field have paralleled more general developments within psychology, the relatively fast pace at which psychological knowledge changes and well-accepted theories are superseded detracts from the practical utility of psychological findings. As already mentioned, the prevailing legal model of man entails a conscious mind. As Lloyd-Bostock (1981b) rightly pointed out, this model is unlikely to be shifted in the face of psychological knowledge. Furthermore, even some psychologists themselves (for example, King, 1981) have opposed such a shift because the very question of 'whether the legal model should be shifted at all is a value judgement not a question of whether psychology or law is on an empirically sounder basis' (Lloyd-Bostock, 1981b:19).

Another explanation as to why it has taken a long time for psycholegal research to be embraced by both psychologists and lawyers lies in the fact that, as psychologists present themselves as experts in the courtroom, they find they have to deal with ethical dilemmas regarding, for example, the confidentiality of their clients (see Haward, 1981a). Toch (1961:19)[9] in his book, *Legal and Criminal Psychology*, warned of the danger of overselling psychology, similar to that which has happened with psychiatry (see Szazz, 1957). Of course, there is the additional danger of psychologists peddling their expertise and producing a favourable opinion for a client in a legal case to whoever would pay their fee. The US experience has shown that the field of the expert psychologist in court (see Chapter 7) can be a real money-spinner.

2 Remaining Difficulties

Interestingly enough, however, as Lösel (1992:11–12) reminds us: 'Despite the generally encouraging development of recent legal psychology, a number of problems still remain'. *Inter alia*, Lösel highlights the importance of the following factors:

2.1 The Internal Situation of Legal Psychology

Lösel identifies a great imbalance in the interest shown in various topics within legal psychology. For example, psycholegal researchers have focused on eyewitness testimony and ignored issues in civil law or custody law, cross-cultural comparisons or more multinational research.

2.2 The Position of Legal Psychology within Psychology

It would appear that only a small percentage of practising psychologists in western countries work in the field of legal psychology. This is, perhaps, not surprising in view of the fact that, as Lösel (1992:13–14) points out, legal psychology does not yet belong to the big areas of applied psychology and topics that concern legal psychologists are rather heterogeneous.

2.3 Legal Psychology's Relation to Legal Science and Practice

Lösel (1992:15) also rightly argues that how legal psychology will develop in the long run will depend on its relationship with the discipline of law and, above all, the legal profession. As this chapter makes clear, this relationship is inevitably not without conflict (see King, 1986; Melton et al., 1987). Of course, the situation differs from country to country. To illustrate, unlike Australia, the US seems readier to include legal psychology in law faculties and has even established chairs in legal psychology. In the UK, for a number of years there has existed an independent Division of Criminological and Legal Psychology within the British Psychological Society. In Australia, however, the College of Forensic Psychologists of the Australian Psychological Society, with its orthodox adherence to clinical psychology training as the prerequisite for anybody who might want to call themselves a forensic psychologist, has not, until recently, provided strong encouragement for the development of criminological and legal psychology as a field in its own right. It could be argued that such a myopic attitude towards psychology and law excludes, for example, cognitive and social psychologists as well as lawyers who have a lot to contribute to legal psychology, it discourages the teaching of legal psychology at both the undergraduate and postgraduate level and, finally, can be said to have almost stifled the development of the field in Australia. Fortunately, the pace of the discipline's development has accelerated in the last few years and looks likely to continue to do so.

2.4 New Psychological Findings vs. Long-Term Establishments in Law

The wheels of law turn very slowly when it comes to change and, not surprisingly, it often takes a long time for new and established findings by psychologists to be enshrined in statute or to be taken account of by judges in their case law (Lösel, 1992:16).

2.5 Empirical Experimentation vs. Principles of Equal Treatment and Fixed Jurisdiction

Finally, Lösel draws attention to a major constraint imposed on psychologists by the law: because of the emphasis on equal treatment of like cases and fixed jurisdiction in the justice system, some field experiments which psychologists might wish to carry out are not possible (p. 16). Examples of such field experiments are in the sentencing of criminal defendants or in the reaction to child abuse (p. 16).

Another problem that still remains is the strong tendency by legal psychologists to be method- rather than phenomenon-orientated and to lack first-hand knowledge of the legal issue they investigate. Such first-hand knowledge could be obtained by means of participant observation, fieldwork, and/or interviews with the main protagonists over a sufficiently long period of time. Instead, most legal psychologists rely on experimental simulation as a short-cut to knowledge (King, 1986:91). Finally, the results of psycholegal research would be more likely to be accepted by members of the legal profession, academic lawyers and policy-makers alike if psychologists show greater familiarity with both common law and statutory provisions relevant to their research, as well as with different theoretical stances in contemporary legal theory (see Davies, 1994) instead of a myopic perception of a legal issue. As shown in Chapter 5, there is more to the jury debate for academic and practising lawyers than simply the nature of the decision-making processes that underpin jury verdicts. Furthermore, utilising their research findings, psychologists should encourage 'constructive debate of basic jurisprudential issues of lively interest in the community' and not, rather conveniently, leave it to politicians to judge the significance of psycholegal research (Stephenson, 1995:136).

3 Grounds for Optimism

Despite differences between psychology and law, differences that have been exacerbated by the lack of communication between the two professions and the concomitant absence of collaborative research (Farrington et al., 1979b), it is comforting, perhaps, to know that the scope of psycholegal research has widened significantly beyond its early concern primarily with criminal law topics in general and with eye-witness testimony and other procedures in the courtroom in particular (Lloyd-Bostock, 1981a:ix). As Lösel (1992:10) informs us, in recent years there has been an important increase in psycholegal research into, for example, the honesty of tax-payers (see Hessing et al., 1988) and social cognition of tort law (Wiener and Small, 1992). In addition, it is nowadays well accepted that legal psychology does not have to be, as it often is, an applied field (Lloyd-Bostock, 1981b, 1988); in other words, the value of psycholegal research can be both theoretical and practical, of interest to both the practitioner and the academic psychologist and lawyer. Diamond (1992) argues, in fact, that the truly challenging, intellectual questions psychologists should be asking about law require them not to yield to the temptation to equate success with recognition by lawyers, a temptation that is the more understandable given the power of law and lawyers in society.

Raising questions about what psychology can contribute to law and the difficulties and ethical questions that occur does not mean that difficulties should be exaggerated (Lloyd-Bostock, 1981b:21). Similarly, while 'identifying and dwelling on difficulties may seem unduly pessimistic, exposing problems in a joint enterprise is not incompatible with a belief in its value' (Farrington et al., 1979b:xiii). Writing in 1981 Lloyd-Bostock pointed out that: 'Current topics of research in psychology and law are so diverse and sprawling that it is not possible even to offer an exhaustive list, let alone any idea of the type of work being done on each' (p. 2). Psycholegal research has continued to expand in both quantity and range, and to a significant degree in quality, too.

The interested reader would be forgiven for coming to the view that the available textbooks on psychology and law contain material on such a range of topics as to render psycholegal research an applied field and to depict psychologists as only interested in questions of direct practical interest to the legal fraternity. However, a number of textbooks (for example, Brewer and Wilson, 1995; Bull and Carson, 1995; Lösel et al., 1992a; Kagehiro and Laufer, 1992; Ross et al., 1994; Davies et al., 1996), including this volume, contain chapters addressing questions of interest to practising and academic lawyers as well as law-enforcement personnel that do have immediate policy implications. As Diamond (1992) puts it, the psycholegal field 'encompasses questions about how people exercise social control and how responsibility, resources, and risk are allocated. The capacity for basic research in psychology and law has not been fully explored'.

As we approach the 21st century, some feel that the full potential of the psycholegal field will only be realised with the development of a distinctly psycholegal jurisprudence (Small, 1993). To some extent a feeling of frustration still characterises both legal psychologists and lawyers (Pennington and Hastie, 1990:103). Psychologists are appalled when lawyers continue to ignore what the psychologists consider good empirical research results and, consequently, fail to resolve issues in law. For their part, the lawyers wish the psychologists would try harder to make their work more useful by ensuring that it is more relevant to actual legal contexts and 'less convoluted' (p. 104). Legal psychologists can, nevertheless, look back on a century of existence and take pride in their achievements. The research that is considered in the following chapters provides enough evidence for the belief that, by going a considerable way in bridging the gap between psychology and law, psycholegal researchers have provided us with knowledge the total of which is more than the sum of its parts. This realisation provides, perhaps, the best basis for optimism about legal psychology's future.

The wide range of topics dealt with in this and other textbooks does not mean that psychology and law is a field comprising a loose collection of topics – psychology and law is a recognisable field. Psychology has a unique perspective – its concern with the *individual* in a social context – and a unique contribution to make to law. In this regard, psycholegal research differs from such related fields as sociology of law in the way it addresses issues as well as in the methodology it uses. We can now take it for granted that psychology has a contribution to make to law; indeed, as the contents of this volume and others like it attest, psychology has been and is making a significant contribution in a number of ways. While not forgetting the narrower focus of a lot of psycholegal research alluded to above, the evidence is overwhelming that psychologists offer a unique perspective on law and have shown themselves capable of transcending the narrow boundaries of early psycholegal research to also address issues of the macro-sociological level, since the vast majority of psychologists today consider behaviour to be a function of both the individual and the environment. 'Boundaries [in psychology and law] are thus seen as providing contours and emphases rather than erecting walls' (Diamond, 1992:VIII). Lösel (1992:16–17) concludes his overview of legal psychology that there is justification for optimism as far as the future of legal psychology is concerned: 'In both law and psychology ... there is a growing understanding for the possibilities, peculiarities and idiosyncrasies of the other side ... recent legal psychology seems to be one of those fields in which psychology's relationships to neighbouring disciplines has developed relatively successfully'.

In pondering the future of psychology and law and deciding how best to move forward into the next century, psycholegal researchers should consider their position on a number of concerns raised by Haney (1993:376ff). They include: that, generally speaking, psycholegal research has not been well received by appellate courts; the discipline of psychology and law appears to have abandoned its sense of shared purpose – its mission of legal change; psycholegal researchers have a strong tendency to accept the legal status quo, thus precluding attempts to change it; researchers continue to give the impression that psycho-legal research is value free and, consequently, are in no position to debate values and lack a 'coherent framework' around which to organise their research; and that the focus is on fine-tuning procedures in the legal system to make them fairer and not on the outcomes of the procedures, and thus psychologists contribute to perpetuating social inequalities and injustices.

There can be no doubt that the experimental method has a number of merits. It must not be forgotten, however, that it also has its limitations and often, in order to understand, explain adequately and predict a particular psycholegal phenomenon, the experimental method needs to be supplemented by other methods. As the chapters that follow show, there has been a general tendency for researchers in the psycholegal field to be reluctant to combine different research methods, instead relying excessively on experiments of often questionable external validity and, furthermore, failing to locate their work in a contemporary critical sociolegal context. Without ignoring the constraints under which university-based psycholegal research often has to be conducted, a first step in making good these deficits and advancing psychology and law further as a discipline in its own right internationally would be a conscious effort by psychologists to increasingly use representative samples of the wider community as subjects where this is appropriate and under forensically-relevant conditions, to invest more time in the field relevant to their specific research interest, familiarising themselves with actual situations, as observers, utilising archival material, and talking with practitioners. Finally, legal psychologists have also neglected public education, thus rendering themselves almost impotent in the political arena when it comes to translating their knowledge into social and legal change. The main thrust of Haney's (1993) position is that psycholegal researchers should adopt a more critical perspective on the legal issues they study (p. 386) in order to 'confront several conceptual stress points that remain in our discipline' and to resolve the conflict and confusion that still exists about professional values (p. 392).

Carson (1995b) suggests that the way forward for psychology and law is primarily through 'collaboration focused upon change' (p. 38). Carson and Bull (1995b) are more specific about what the way forward for psychology and law should be about when they advocate 'finding ways in which psychology's product can appropriately and always questioningly and critically aid, and question, legal processes and goals' (p. 645).

4 Psychology and Law in Australia

Psycholegal research in Australia has not flourished to the extent it has done so on both sides of the Atlantic; it still involves a limited number of psychologists who tend to be relatively isolated from each other. Not surprisingly, in addition to Australian psycholegal research published internationally, there has been a small number of publications in Australian psychology journals or Australian books on such topics as: eyewitness testimony (for example, Thomson, 1981, 1984, 1991; McConkey and Roche, 1989; McConkey and Sheehan, 1988; Naylor, 1989; Tucker et al., 1990; Vernon, 1991), forensic hypnosis (Evans and Stanley, 1994), the psychologist as expert witness (Cattermole, 1984; Freckelton, 1987, 1996; Freckelton and Selby, 1993; Moloney, 1986; Wardlaw, 1984), confidentiality in the psychologist–client relationship

(McMahon and Knowles, 1995), recovered memories (Freckelton, 1996; Magner, 1995; Thomson, 1995b) and psychology and policing (Brewer and Wilson, 1995).

Since 1980 the main focus for Australian and New Zealand psycholegal researchers has been the annual congress of the Australian and New Zealand Association of Psychiatry, Psychology and Law (see Greig and Freckelton, 1988, 1989, 1990; Freckelton, Greig and McMahon, 1991; Freckelton, Knowles and Mulvaney, 1992). In addressing the second such congress in 1981 Justice Michael Kirby stated that 'one of the constant themes of the Law Reform Commission has been the need to bring together various specialised disciplines, particularly in the design of new laws', and, 'in an age of science and technology, this interdisciplinary communication useful at any time, becomes imperative'. The publication in 1994 of the *Psychiatry, Psychology and Law* journal in Australia and the March 1996 special issue on forensic psychology of *Australian Psychologist*, 31(1) are significant steps in formally establishing psycholegal research in Australia as a field in its own right. The fact remains, however, that, in addition to the vastness of the Australian continent, the relatively small number of prison psychologists and small number of practising and academic forensic psychologists, the situation in Australia has really been no different from that in the UK where there is 'a deep-rooted suspicion and scepticism among both lawyers and psychologists about the value of such interdisciplinary work' (King, 1986:1). This is not surprising, perhaps, in view of the very little contact and exchange of ideas between the thousands of psychologists and lawyers in Australia.

Australia has a population of approximately 17.5 million and thirty-nine universities, two of them private. According to the Australian Psychological Society (APS), in June 1996 there were twenty-three universities offering four-year degree courses accredited for the purpose of associate membership of the Society, forty-seven university campuses were offering psychology courses consisting of an approved sequence of three years, thirty-nine universities were offering approved fourth-year courses and, finally, master's courses accredited for membership were being offered by thirty universities. At the same time, twenty-seven university campuses were offering accredited LL.B degree courses. Postgraduate degrees in forensic psychology (Masters and PhD) are only offered by the Psychology Department of Edith Cowan University in Western Australia. The large number of psychology and law courses, as well as the development of the discipline of Legal Studies with its focus on law in context and an increasing number of publications by Australian law reform bodies,[10] have no doubt helped to increase awareness of the relevance of social sciences in general and legal psychology, in particular to law scholars and practitioners. Tremper's (1987a) assessment that on both sides of the Atlantic and on continental Europe 'The current state of legally oriented social science research is a mixture of success and unfulfilled promise' (p. 267) still applies, albeit to a lesser degree. It is hoped that, as psycholegal research in Australia gathers momentum, interested psychologists and lawyers will become better organised and will be able to contribute to Royal Commissions and Law Reform bodies and to the work of the courts, as their counterparts have done in the US[11] and in Britain.[12]

5 Conclusions

As legal psychology's maturity as a discipline continues, the arguments presented lead to the cautious conclusion that the late 1990s marks the dawn of a new era in legal psychology, characterised by a certain amount of healthy tension within psychology itself as well as between psychology and law. This multifaceted tension can be said to provide both the impetus and the focus necessary for the further maturity of this rather interesting field.

Those working in psychology and law can look back with a sense of pride to their discipline's development, albeit occasionally a chequered one, and its various achievements, especially regarding court procedures. They can also look forward to the discipline's promising future. At the same time, it is nice to know that the impact of psychology and law has been a two-way process (Davies, 1995). Recognising psychology's limitations regarding, for example, the external validity of a lot of experimental psycholegal research, and utilising more than one research method to study a particular phenomenon, as well as mistakes made in the effort to bridge the gap between the two disciplines (for example, overselling psychological research findings to the legal profession), and learning from them would seem to be imperative if, in Carson and Bull's (1995b) words, psycholegal researchers are to increase the legitimacy of the infant offspring of the relationship between the two disciplines. Psychology and law is by now an established discipline on both sides of the Atlantic, on continental Europe, and in Australia. One of its main pillars has been eyewitness testimony, the subject of the next chapter.

6 The Book's Structure, Focus and Aims

This book is intended to provide students at undergraduate and postgraduate level with a general overview of a number of important specific topics from the perspectives of different countries (US, UK, Australia, New Zealand, and Canada). The topics surveyed are inevitably only part of the interface between psychology and law. The author's intention is not to provide a complete overview of psychology and law. Consequently, other areas such as psychological research into people's perceptions of decisions about justice (see Mellers and Baron, 1993), confidentiality in psychological practice (see McMahon and Knowles, 1995), clinical approaches to working with offenders (see Davies et al., 1996; Hollin, 1995, 1996; Howells and Blackburn, 1995), psychological evaluations for the courts (see Heilbrun, 1992) including competency, criminal responsibility and violence prediction, and 'psychology of the law' literature, all of which deserve and have received book-length treatment of their own, are not included and the book is not concerned with civil law.

In the remainder of the book the first six chapters, which some authors might classify under 'psychology and courts', fall within Haney's (1980) '*psychology in law*' category: eyewitnesses – key issues and event characteristics; eyewitnesses – the perpetrator and interviewing; children as witnesses; the jury; sentencing as a human process; and the psychologist as an expert witness. The remaining four chapters (persuasion in the courtroom; detecting deception; witness recognition procedures; and psychology and the police) are examples of Haney's '*psychology and law*' category, also known in the literature as 'psycholegal studies', where the concern is with 'behaviour within the legal system as an arena of legal interaction' (Blackburn, 1996:6).

In each specific area the book aims to provide a comprehensive up-to-date survey of the published literature, drawing upon European and Australian work as well as more traditional North American sources, also giving sufficient of the legal background to provide a proper context for the psychological research. Appropriately, for a textbook, the present author is content to let the major protagonists in the literature speak for themselves. For a number of years now, there has been no comprehensive treatment of such a broad range of areas at the interface between psychology and criminal law. The present book is intended to remedy this.

Chapter 2

Eyewitnesses: Key Issues and Event Characteristics

- *Locating eyewitness testimony in a legal context.*
- *Human attention, perception, and memory.*
- *Merits and defects of different research methods.*
- *Extrapolating from controlled eyewitness research to real life.*
- *The need for psychologists to utilise a variety of research methods.*
- *A taxonomy of eyewitness testimony variables.*
- *The importance of 'event' variables.*

'Testimony to personal identity is proverbially fallacious.' (William James, 1890:97)

'Although such testimony is frequently challenged, it is still widely assumed to be more reliable than other kinds of evidence. Numerous experiments show, however, that it is remarkably subject to error.' (Buckhout, 1974:23)

'Human memory is a fragile and elusive creature. It can be supplemented, partially restructured, or even completely altered by post-event inputs. It is susceptible to the power of a simple word. This is not to imply that all memories are changed and no original memories remain intact.' (Loftus and Ketcham, 1983:168–9)

'Nowhere are the problems of generalizability and reliability of research findings more acute than in the study of eyewitnessing.' (Davies, 1992:265)

'It is important not to exaggerate the fallibility of human memory. Memory is often wonderfully detailed and accurate.' (Lindsay and Read, 1994:293)

Introduction

The above quotes reflect the concern over the years with the limitations of eyewitness testimony, the more recent acceptance of the fact that the whole process of observing and recalling faces and events is a complex, interactive and dynamic one and, finally, that we should not overlook the fact that such testimony can be accurate.

Eyewitness testimony is of crucial importance for both crime investigators and lawyers. Not surprisingly, therefore, within the psycholegal field, testimony, especially eyewitness testimony, has attracted a lot of attention over the years. Memory issues permeate the law and psycholegal studies of eyewitness testimony constitute one of the pillars of legal psychology. As the content of this and the next chapter indicates, more empirical studies have been reported in this area of forensic psychology than in any other area. Furthermore, assumptions about human memory are inherent in both substantial and procedural rules without which the legal system could not function (Johnson, 1993:603).

1 Legal Aspects of Eyewitness Testimony

The great importance of eyewitness testimony in criminal law can be seen in a number of different ways (Narby and Cutler, 1994:724): the various safeguards in law to protect defendants from wrongful conviction on the basis of mistaken identification; in the evidence that eyewitness testimony influences the outcome of trials (Cutler et al., 1990; Visher, 1987); as with all evidence, the prevailing practice by courtroom lawyers to discredit the other side's witnesses in order to win (Berman et al., 1995) and, finally, the very strong interest shown in testimony by psycholegal researchers and law reform bodies alike (see Cooney, 1994, for a sociologist's analysis of the social origins of evidence).

The courtroom procedure followed in US, Australian, British, Canadian and New Zealand courts and in other countries with a common law system is known as the 'adversary system'. This basically means that different sides to a dispute fight it out in court in order to obtain a favourable judgement (McEwan, 1995; Waight and Williams, 1995:2–17). This is based on the belief that the 'truth' is most likely to be discovered when the disputing parties each present their version of the facts in question to a magistrate (lay or stipendiary) or to a judge or to a judge and jury. So strong is this belief that until the US Supreme Court ruled in the case of *Maryland v. Craig* (1990) 497 US 836, a defendant's absolute right to confront his/her accuser/s face-to-face was, in fact, guaranteed by the Sixth Amendment of the Constitution. Unlike Royal Commissions in the UK, Canada, New Zealand and Australia, or Senate

Committees, House of Representatives Committees, Presidential Commissions or Grand Juries in the US, for example, which follow an 'inquisitorial' procedure, a court of law in common law jurisdictions may not call its own witnesses or carry out its own investigation into the case before it; it simply arrives at a decision on the basis of the evidence and arguments put before it by the two parties according to the rules of evidence and procedure which are intended to ensure a fair trial (see Jackson, 1995; McGinley and Waye, 1994; Waight and Williams, 1995).

A widely known rule, the *hearsay rule*, enables a court in common law countries to exclude statements by persons who are not witnesses and who, therefore, cannot be cross-examined (Gillies, 1987). In common law jurisdictions, a criminal or civil case often involves, then, a contest between two parties in which the party initiating the proceedings wants to convince the court that the defendant incurred criminal or civil liability. Typically, in non-guilty plea cases the different parties will disagree about material facts of the case, and the prosecutor in a criminal case or the plaintiff in a civil case will lead evidence to convince the court as to the existence and nature of those facts. The defendant has the choice of also 'adducing' evidence. Parties to a dispute can attempt to prove material facts by direct or circumstantial evidence. 'Direct evidence is that which goes directly to prove a material fact. Circumstantial evidence requires the fact finder to draw inferences other than that the witness is correctly reporting what their senses registered' (McGinley and Waye, 1994:9). There is a presumption that evidence should be given to a common law court in oral form (Magner, 1995:25). Therefore, oral evidence is an important feature of most trials and legal disputes in general. As Leippe (1994) rightly points out, the existence of an eyewitness is of importance in the investigation of a crime, the decision to prosecute a suspect and at trial where a confident witness could sway the jury (p. 385).

According to Doyle (1989:128–9): 'It is an article of faith among lawyers that cross-examination represents "[T]he greatest legal engine ever invented for the discovery of the truth" (Wigmore, 1974, Sec.1367)'. A wealth of judicial opinions assert that whatever problems may exist with the eyewitness testimony, cross-examination is their solution. Each party has a right to cross-examine the other side's witnesses, to question them in order to discover other facts or in order to cast doubt on the importance the court should place on the evidence already provided by the other side's witnesses (see Chapter 8). If the cross-examination discovers some new fact, then the first party may re-examine. It is up to the magistrate or the judge, as the case may be, to decide whether the evidence being led by a particular party is admissible on the basis of existing law of evidence. Of course, cross-examination of witnesses does not guarantee that there will be no wrongful convictions due to false identification. As the extensive literature cited in this chapter shows, there is indeed an 'eyewitness identification' problem. Unfortunately, some authors (for example, Wells, 1993:554) take a rather narrow view and write about this problem as if it were synonymous with witness error in identifying a suspect in an identification parade/line-up, a task that does not confront the great majority of witnesses in criminal investigations and prosecutions.

Psycholegal researchers run the risk of exaggerating the practical importance of their studies if they are unaware, for example, that the great majority of criminal defendants plead guilty (Willis, 1995) and, consequently, all material facts are not in dispute. Also, most criminal cases in western common law English-speaking countries are not decided by a jury and, finally, eyewitness testimony plays but a very minor role in crime detection. The last point is brought home by a study of burglary and violence offenders in Nottingham, England, by Farrington and Lambert (1993). They found that: (a) victim descriptions of suspects accounted for 2 per cent of burglary and 14.7 per cent of violence offenders arrested; and (b) witnesses' descriptions contributed 6.7 per cent and 13.3 per cent to burglary and violence arrests respectively. Also, many experimental psychologists seem to have overlooked the fact that a trial under the adversary system is not a search for ultimate truth but a means of settling disputes. Lawyers are, first and foremost, interested in winning their case in court, not in being impartial – as psychologists researching witness testimony might wish them to be. Furthermore, experimental psychologists reporting studies of the reliability of eyewitness testimony have generally failed to locate their work in a truly psycholegal context by relating their findings to the relevant law of evidence and procedure in the jurisdiction where the research has been conducted (see Konečni and Ebbesen, 1992).

Research into the reliability of witness testimony has the longest history in psychological research, its formal beginnings stretching back to the beginning of the century.[1] Interestingly enough, however, when McConkey and Roche (1989) administered a questionnaire to introductory psychology, advanced psychology, and advanced law students in Sydney, Australia, to assess their knowledge of eyewitness memory, it was found that they all had a relatively limited knowledge of the topic in question. Similar findings have been reported by American (Deffenbacher and Loftus, 1982; Sanders, 1986), Canadian (Yarmey and Tressillian Jones, 1982) and UK researchers (Bennett and Gibling, 1989; Noon and Hollin, 1987). Bennett and Gibling reported that police officers and members of the general public alike had rather poor knowledge of many important factors in eyewitness testimony (for example, the impact of violence, post-event contamination, witness confidence), indicating the need for improvement in police training. The voluminous growth of witness research is not surprising in view of the vast literature on human attention, perception, memory and narration processes involved in all testimony.

On both sides of the Atlantic experimental psychologists have been appearing in court more and more frequently as expert witnesses to tell the court and juries about the psychology of testimony in general and eyewitness testimony in particular (see Chapter 7). This is an interesting development in view of the myriads of cases, both criminal and civil, in which witness testimony plays an important part. While not suggesting that witness testimony is never reliable, the fact is that such testimony is often challenged in court and, as the empirical evidence in this and the next chapter shows rather convincingly, it is subject to error. This does not stop many lawyers, police personnel and the public at large from assuming that it is more reliable than other kinds of evidence. The available psycholegal research has not as yet eradicated the belief that human perception and memory operate like a tape-recorder or a video-camera, that witnesses see and hear correctly and so testify.

Of course, a witness may testify dishonestly or honestly but incorrectly, or may disappear, recant or die before the case comes on for trial (Greer, 1971). It is the honest, cooperative witness which is the concern of this chapter. As Lord Devlin (1976) put it: 'the highly respectable, absolutely sincere, perfectly coherent and apparently convincing witness may, as experience has quite often shown, be mistaken'. In most jurisdictions there is no shortage of cases of mistaken identity, including some unfortunate ones where the defendant was executed. More common are cases where people (see Hain, 1976) are arrested and prosecuted by the state on the basis of identification evidence that is subsequently discredited (Buckhout, 1974:23).

2 Characteristics of Human Attention, Perception and Memory

Everyday witnesses in criminal and civil cases all over the world are asked by police, lawyers and others in and out of court to recall details of events, to describe a face and so forth on the assumption that the human memory operates like a video-recorder. This misleading passive model of human attention, perception and memory has, in the last two decades or so, given way to the view that these are active processes, that perception and memory are also constructive processes, that a person's knowledge of the world around them is of paramount importance in understanding what and how he/she perceives events or other stimuli and what they remember about them (Clifford and Bull, 1978).

The available experimental evidence in cognitive psychology is evidence that goes back to Bartlett (1932) and his finding that perceptions are assimilated into organisation or *schemata*: that when we remember a story, for example, we try to 'make sense' of what we remember. Such evidence leaves no doubt that perception and memory are 'social systems' (Buckhout, 1974) with structural and functional limitations. Many aspects of eyewitness behaviour cannot be explained unless we consider what someone is, what they are trying to do and the ways their values, attitudes, expectations and motivations act not only at the time of attention and perception but also during the period of storage, and especially when they are being asked to remember. In other words, perception involves a contribution from the perceiver, human memory is both selective and constructive and 'we make sense of things and come to perceive them in terms of the sense we have made of them' (Lloyd-Bostock, 1988:5).

The mental processes by which we come to understand things is known as 'cognition' and is made possible by the combined work of attention, perception and memory. According to Davenport (1992), human attention can be thought of as a 'low capacity, single channel' operation which enables us to selectively attend to stimuli in our environment and within us (pp. 127–33). 'Perception' refers to those processes which take in, and make some sense of, all our sensations, that is, the input from our senses. Perception is an active process whereby we interpret what information we receive so that it is meaningful to us. How we interpret sensations is influenced by our age, cultural background, expectations, emotions, particular specialist knowledge and so forth (p. 135).

In a matter of a few years memory researchers have shifted from proposing a somewhat monolithic view of long-term memory to a view which differentiates different kinds of memory (Squire et al., 1993:485). The available research evidence points to an impressive degree of specialisation in how information is stored (p. 484). Finally, when psychologists distinguish between different kinds of memory, this is best understood 'as reflecting the different processes that can be used to access a common memory trace' (p. 482). While memory appears to be organised into separate stages or processes, the fact remains that its short-term storage lasts for less than 20 seconds, by which time new input will displace existing information, the memory can hold no more than seven items at one time unless information is passed into the long-term store for permanent storage, from where it can be retrieved (Davenport, 1992:153–4). Failure to retrieve information from our memory may reflect: failure to store information correctly; that information may have been displaced; the memory trace has simply faded away or decayed with the passage of time; or there may have been interference from later input which sounded similar and impacted negatively on the short-term memory or is semantically similar and interfered with information in the long-term memory (Davenport, 1992). In addition, many clinicians would argue that forgetting can be due to repression, that is, a process by which the mind pushes into the unconscious a memory of a traumatic experience. However, despite attempts to integrate the cognitive and the psychodynamic unconscious (see Epstein, 1994), as the discussion of the whole issue surrounding the subject of recovered memories of childhood sexual abuse shows (see below), the concept of repression is a rather controversial one (see Cohler, 1994; Loftus, 1993). Despite such controversies, there is general agreement that the human memory does not operate like a video-recorder and, therefore, there is an undisputed need that interviews of crime victims/witnesses by police and other investigators are informed by in-depth knowledge about the human memory and how it normally operates.

According to Davies (1993a:368), three representative theories of remembering which have impacted on the current controversy surrounding the processes involved when eyewitnesses recall are: (a) *schema theory* (Bartlett, 1932; Pitchert and Anderson, 1977); (b) *multiple-entry modular memory model,* or *memory monitoring* (Johnson, 1983); and (c) the '*headed records*' theory (Morton et al., 1985). While schema-based (constructionist) theories hold that memory is subject to post-event contamination through assimilation and distortion over time and one cannot, therefore, access the original memory because it no longer exists, monitoring memory and headed records posit that memory events leave records that cannot be altered and are accessible under the appropriate circumstances (see Davies, 1993a, for a critical evaluation of these three theories.

In considering the structure and functioning of human memory we must not forget such memory disorders as *amnesia, hypermnesia,* and *paramnesia* (see Kopelman, 1987; Yanagihara and Petersen, 1991). Amnesia (that is, some defect/s of the mental process/es responsible for registration, retention and retrieval of information) may be total or partial, temporary or permanent, and may be attributable to cerebral causes (for example, senile dementia, brain injury) or to inattention which, in turn, may be voluntary or involuntary. Someone charged with a crime such as murder may claim amnesia, but whether the amnesia is genuine or not would be a fact to be contested in court (see Gudjonsson, 1992a:96–9; Taylor and Kopelman, 1984, and the English case *R. v. Podola*, Court of Criminal Appeal, October 1959).[2] Hypermnesia refers to being able to retain and retrieve an incredible amount of detail (see Ham, 1996; Hunter, 1957, for descriptions of two such prodigies). Ham describes the case of Briton, Dominic O'Brien, who has won the World Memory Championships for three consecutive years and who in 1995 won by memorising 2080 playing cards – a total of 40 packs – in the exact sequence in which they were dealt (pp. 27–8). Paramnesia means false recollection, a clinical condition that can be attributed to 'a disorder of the mental processes responsible for the appreciation of feelings of familiarity' (Power, 1977:137). An everyday example of paramnesia is the occasional déjà vu experience familiar to most people. With increasing incidence, this experience becomes responsible for fabrications or 'illusions of memory'. The term 'confabulation' is used by clinicians to describe cases where people 'fill in' memory gaps with imagined experiences as when they suffer from Korsakoff's psychosis (Davison and Neale, 1974:416). Before turning our attention to the numerous factors that have been studied by witness memory researchers, one question that should perhaps be answered is: 'How good is witness memory'?

Early experimental psychological studies examining recognition rates for photographs (see Chance et al., 1975) reported accuracy of over 90 per cent even after a delay of up to 35 days. Such studies, however, lack ecological validity and their findings would not be of great interest to lawyers. In studies that have used a paradigm high on both experimental and mundane realism as well as ecological validity by staging an event rather than using a face photograph, accuracy turns out to be 12 to 13 per cent for identification (Buckhout, 1974; Dent, 1977) and between 25 per cent for recall details in civilians (Buckhout, 1974) and about 47.5 per cent for policemen in very simple, static but live, situations (Clifford and Richards, 1977).[3] Accuracy levels, however, need to be evaluated against the level of 'accuracy' one would expect on the basis of chance alone.

3 Eyewitness Testimony Research: Methodological Considerations

Psychological research into witness testimony enables psychologists to appear as expert witnesses in trials in the US (see Kassin et al., 1989, for a survey of such experts) where eyewitness testimony plays a crucial role more frequently (Loftus and Ketcham, 1991, see also Chapter 7) and has impacted on the rules governing the admissibility of children's evidence in England and Wales (Hedderman, 1987) where experimental cognitive psychologists (for example, Davies, 1986) have had an input into the specialist training given to police officers who produce composite pictures of suspects, and legal psychologists (for example, Dr Gudjonsson, Professors Bull, Clifford and Davies) have only relatively recently been allowed to testify as experts in court. At the same time, however, 'Nowhere are the problems of the generalizability and reliability of research findings more acute than in the study of witnessing' (Davies, 1992), and, 'Not surprisingly, the methodology and status of eyewitness research has been the subject of [considerable] debate and controversy' (p. 265).

The controversy has centred almost exclusively around the generalisability (external validity) of traditional, experimental laboratory research to forensic contexts. For some, such laboratory research is indispensable (for example, Cutler and Penrod, 1995a; Wells, 1993). For his part, Wells (1993:555) concludes that 'there is little or no evidence that the typical eyewitness experiment presents a distortion of what would be expected in actual cases in which the eyewitnesses experience real rather than simulated events'. For others, laboratory research is an anathema to the generalisability of such research findings to real life (Yuille, 1986) and it should be abandoned in favour of realistic field situations, while for others both research methods are so limited as to yield almost useless findings (McCloskey and Egeth, 1983). The strong concern expressed about controlled research, very often in a laboratory environment with psychology students as subjects who receive credit towards their studies for participating, is understandable given that such literature, without any justification being offered, generally treats the bystander eyewitness as the model for all witnesses. In fact, the unaffected eyewitness to a crime is a rather rare occurrence in forensic contexts when considering the number and type of witnesses interviewed by police as part of their criminal investigations (see Tollestrup et al., 1994). Furthermore, there is evidence from ecologically-valid research that people who participate in an event recall more details than do observers (Yuille et al., 1994). It is imperative that experimental psychologists validate their simulation studies by also carrying out real-world studies in the sociolegal context to which they wish to generalise their results (Konečni and Ebbesen, 1992:416). Bruck and Ceci (1995) discuss the issue of the external validity of laboratory studies in their amicus brief in the *Michaels* case regarding children's suggestibility (see Chapter 4). They conclude that, 'while we may never possess perfect knowledge about a phenomenon, we must base our inferences on the most scientifically rigorous evidence we have available' (pp. 308–9).

It would appear that the most defensible position for psycholegal researchers to adopt on this issue is best expressed by Yuille and Wells (1991:127), namely, that 'caution should be used in generalising from controlled research to real world contexts ... Whenever possible, a comparison of experimental research and the field contexts should be made and their apparent similarities and differences enunciated'. The fact is, of course, that: (a) more than two methodologies have been utilised in witness testimony research; and (b) 'no one research method can of itself provide a reliable data base for legislation or advocacy. Rather, problems need to be addressed from a number of perspectives ... Only by pooling the results of these different varieties of study is a reliable psychology of the eyewitness likely to emerge' (Davies, 1992:265). Such a view would seem to assume that some methodologies are not better for particular topics a priori. The discussion of five different research methods that follows draws heavily from Davies (1992, 1995).

3.1 Types of Research Methods Used

3.1.1 Slide Presentation

More than eighty-five years ago, Stern (1910), believing one method to be better a priori, strongly advocated the use of staged events as a more fruitful method of studying witness accounts than simply presenting them with static photographs. Showing slides depicting an event has been useful in researching subjects' face recognition (Young and Ellis, 1989). However, as Clifford (1978) pointed out, a series of slides shown to subjects ignores not only the dynamic nature of a criminal offence but also the richness of detail in an event, as well as the fact that in most cases witnesses are not given notice that a crime is about to take place and to focus their attention accordingly. In addition, in real life faces of suspects come with the rest of their bodies and, unlike in the psychological laboratory, it may be considerable time before a witness is asked to describe a crime suspect (Davies, 1992; MacLeod et al., 1994). Researchers have found a lower rate of misidentifications with slide presentations than with staged events (see Lindsay and Harvey, 1988) as well as lower recognition rates (Clifford and Bull, 1978).

3.1.2 Staging an Event

In a staged event that must have left an indelible memory on the minds of those present (jurists, psychologists and physicians attending a scholarly meeting), Münsterberg (1908) quite suddenly introduced a clown in colourful clothes followed by an African American with a revolver. To the surprise of those present, there took place shouts and other wild scenes. The whole episode was over in 20 seconds. Like a normal experimenter, Münsterberg asked his scholarly subjects to write down what they had witnessed. Only one of forty reports handed in contained less than 20 per cent of serious omissions while thirty-four of the witnesses made positively wrong statements. Finally, more than 10 per cent of the statements made were simply false in a quarter of the written testimonies. What made this early experiment the more noteworthy is that the witnesses were a scholarly bunch, supposedly astute observers and honest and decent citizens.

Research utilising staged events involving, for example, mock shootings (see Trankell, 1972)[4] has found that unsuspecting witnesses, unlike psychology student subjects in laboratory experiments who generally expect to be asked questions about what they have seen, are shocked and panic, experience shaking, dryness of the mouth, cold sweat and difficulty with breathing. Not surprisingly, perhaps, under such conditions their performance as witnesses is adversely affected. Such 'event tests' vary in complexity and the degree of violence involved. As already mentioned, some authors prefer this methodology (for example, Yuille, 1986). Davies (1992:226–7) points out a number of limitations of this particular method: for example, subjects watching a violent event may well dissociate themselves from it (Aronson, 1980); ethical considerations dictate that subjects consent to taking part in such a study – a factor that limits the data they will subsequently provide; and, finally, subjects used as offenders are almost always college students (Yuille and Cutshall, 1986). This context is a far cry from a bank-teller or service-station attendant whose life is being seriously threatened by a hardened, career offender committing an armed hold-up wearing a balaclava and brandishing a hand gun or sawn-off shotgun, for example (see Kapardis, 1989), or a teenage girl who, in tears, arrives at a police station to report that someone tried to abduct her on the way home from school or, finally, a pensioner who wakes up in the middle of the night and disturbs a burglar who proceeds to assault him/her. The shortcomings mentioned by Davies (1992) limit significantly the extent to which one can justifiably generalise findings about witness testimony from studies using such methodology. The desirability of research that allows a lot of control of the laboratory, while at the same time being forensically relevant, cannot be overemphasised (see Yuille et al., 1994, for an example of such research).

3.1.3 Field Studies

There are, of course, limits on the types of factors which can be examined by innocuously deceiving subjects involved in field studies and as they go about their daily routines. However, as already mentioned, there exists a strong argument for researchers attempting to replicate findings (first obtained in the laboratory with student subjects) in field studies. A finding obtained by using both methods is undoubtedly more convincing evidence (Konečni and Ebbesen, 1992:421). Admittedly, it is not possible to research the impact on witness accuracy of all variables that might be of interest to a researcher in a field because of both logistical and ethical constraints on such research. As Davies (1992:268) reminds us, in order to examine enough variables field studies need to be supplemented by archival research and case studies which paint a better picture of the reality of witnessing.

3.1.4 Archival Studies

Here the researcher examines, for example, police files to identify crucial variables. Illustrating with an example, Macleod (1987) examined 379 witness statements associated with 135 cases of assault. In support of earlier experimental findings (Clifford and Scott, 1978), it was found that, where injury occurred women gave fewer details of their assailant than did men. In addition, MacLeod (1987) also found that bystanders gave less information about both events and appearance than did victims – findings of some interest as laboratory studies have tended not to address the victim vs. bystander accuracy comparison. Davies (1992:269) also cites archival research which has confirmed the overwhelming saliency of a suspect's hair and upper facial features relative to lower ones, for example. The major limitation of archival studies of witness accuracy is the absence of information on the accuracy of the descriptions provided by witnesses to the police in cases where the perpetrator has not been apprehended or has been acquitted.

3.1.5 Single Case Studies

In view of the limitation of archival studies mentioned, Yuille and Cutshall (1986) and Yuille and Kim (1987) in Canada and Davies (1992) in England have examined the statements of a number of witnesses in a serious crime for which someone has been convicted. Yuille and Kim (1987) found that, contrary to what laboratory testimony researchers would have us believe, the testimony of witnesses to serious crime is reliable. Yuille and Kim, however, were only able to interview a self-selected minority of the witnesses to a gun-shop shooting in Burnaby, Vancouver, four to five months later, a limitation that casts doubt on the veracity of their findings. Davies' case study of an armed robbery in Birmingham in which shots were fired and which involved fourteen witnesses being summoned to the identification parades, concluded that his findings 'accord much more closely with the view of witnessing which emerges from laboratory research than that arising from [Yuille and Cutshall's, 1986] the Burnaby study' (p. 271). Davies (1992) concludes: 'Case studies, however crucial and illuminating, do not open the doors to some alternative reality which will overturn the findings of more traditional research' (p. 272). It becomes clear that no method for studying witnessing is 'the best' since different methods have different merits and defects. While the slide presentation is easy to carry out in the laboratory and lends itself to a good control of variables, staging an event in the laboratory is an easy way to attempt to simulate the dynamics of a crime but comes with poor control of variables involved. Staging events out in the field allows the researcher good control of variables while, finally, both case studies and archival studies are high on realism but poor on control of relevant variables. The dictum for psychological researchers is to ensure that their findings about the reliability of witness testimony are replicated across a range of paradigms, or to risk broad acceptance of their research results (Davies, 1992).

Ultimately, the findings of experimental research into eyewitness testimony must be generalisable to real-life situations. However, such psychological research has had a 'deserved credibility problem' because, according to Malpass and Devine (1981), notwithstanding a great deal of findings relevant to the operation of the criminal justice system, 'the empirical base of our contribution is derived from studies that appear to only remotely reflect the conditions experienced by witnesses to actual criminal events' (p. 348). The empirical eyewitness literature consists, in the main, of studies in which subjects are uninvolved, bystander, undergraduate student volunteers; memory for an event in such studies is commonly tested, at most, a few days later and, above all, there are no consequences for the 'witnesses' (Yuille (1992:207–9). As Yuille empha-sises, these conditions are in real contrast to what real-life witnesses experience – they are often victims of the crime they are asked to recall, crimes are often complex, fast-moving and 'absorbing' events and memory is tested months later (p. 208). Furthermore, often there exist long delays, ranging from months to years, between the event giving rise to a dispute and the trial. An extreme example is Longman's case (*Longman v. R.* (1989) 64 ALJR 73) where the delay was twenty-six years (Magner, 1995:25).

Unfortunately for the discipline of psychology and law, the great majority of eyewitness researchers do not seem to share the serious concern about the external validity of experimental simulation studies (Davies, 1992; Konečni and Ebbesen, 1992; King, 1986; Malpass and Devine, 1981; Yuille, 1992). In a climate of 'publish or perish', the majority of researchers will, understandably perhaps, continue to rely on experimental studies of often questionable ecological validity, journals will continue to depend largely on such studies for their continued existence, and eyewitness testimony 'experts' will continue basing their status (and fees) on having carried out and published such research and a minority will continue voicing their concerns about all this. This chapter emphasises the proposition that the discipline of psychology and law is better served by a combination of sound laboratory research and field as well as archival research. It does appear that the few psycholegal researchers who have expressed grave concern about the generalisability of a lot of experimental eyewitness research are researchers who have had first-hand experience of actual cases. The majority of those who apparently blindly adhere to experimental simulation as their only research method do not seem to consider familiarity with real cases important, or if they do, they choose not to invest time and resources to achieve it by spending time in the field, whether with operational police and/or practising lawyers and/or ex-jurors and/or crime witnesses. One partial solution might be for psychology students to be granted credit points towards their degree courses for exactly such involvement in the field. Rather than adopt entrenched positions, psychologists in both camps will go a longer way in bridging the remaining gap with lawyers if they take the middle ground rather than the high moral ground.

The 'credibility problem' referred to is less serious in the late 1990s than in the early 1980s, primarily because in recent years many eyewitness researchers have made use of the simulated crime methodology instead of presenting subjects with pictures depicting a crime scene or face photographs of suspects. Such simulations have involved, for example, subjects viewing a video of a staged 'crime' or subjects 'coming across' a 'crime' being committed, being asked questions about what they have seen/witnessed and, where applicable, also being debriefed. As a result, better-designed applied testimony research, despite the limitations mentioned above, is not as scarce as it used to be, especially as more researchers have come to focus on 'system' variables rather than continue to report findings pertaining solely to 'estimator' (witness) variables as showing that a human witness is a limited-capacity processor of information (see below).

4 Variables in the Study of Eyewitness Memory

Wells (1978) made an important distinction between '*system*' variables (that is, those factors the criminal justice system can do something about, procedures used to enhance the accuracy of eyewitness testimony) and '*estimator*' variables (that is, characteristics of the witness which influence witness accuracy that the criminal justice system cannot do anything about). While the distinction suggested by Wells is an important one when considering policy implications of research findings, it needs to be remembered that in the real world of crime victim and crime witnesses interviewed by police, the distinction between 'estimator' and 'system' variables is not always as clearcut as it appears. For example, the time when a witness is to be interviewed by particular police personnel is often the result of a little negotiation between the volunteer witness and police over the telephone to accommodate each other's preferences. Similarly, 'refreshing a witness' memory' is something which inevitably occurs as eyewitnesses discuss their experience with lawyers, friends, family members and others. However, it is also a common practice for the police officer who has the conduct of the case to 'refresh the memory' of a prosecution witness by ensuring the witness has reviewed the statement he/she made to the police at the first possible opportunity before going into the witness box (Magner, 1995:26). In the English case of *R. v. Da Sylva* ([1990] 1 WLR 3; 1989 90 Cr App R 233), after entering the witness box a witness was allowed to refresh his memory by reading the statement he had made to the police a year earlier. As Magner (1995:29) points out, psychologists have not addressed the question of the effect of refreshing memory from a document and the question whether such legal procedures 'exaggerate or mitigate the misleading information effect which might otherwise occur' (p. 33).

Drawing on a taxomony of variables first used by Clifford (1981:21), Hollin (1989) categorised eyewitness memory variables under the heading of 'social' (attitudes, conformity, stereotypes, prejudice, status of interrogator), 'situational' (complexity of event, duration of event, illumination, time delay, type of crime), 'individual' (age, cognitive style, personality, race, sex, training) and 'interrogational' (artists' sketches, computer systems, identification parades, mugshots, photofits). As Hollin pointed out, eyewitness researchers have been concerned with the effects of these variables at the stages of acquisition, retention, and retrieval. Other attempts to classify eyewitness testimony variables have included Ellis' (1975) distinction between 'stimulus' factors (for example, length of viewing time) and 'subject' factors (for example, sex of the witness) and Loftus' (1981) distinction between 'event' and 'witness' factors. Clifford (1979) suggested the additional category of 'interrogational'. In this context, it is worth noting that Wells' (1978) 'system' variables overlap with Ellis' (1975) 'stimulus' factors and Loftus' (1981) 'event' factors, while Wells' 'estimator' category overlaps with Ellis' 'subject' and Loftus' 'witness' category.

In reviewing studies of eyewitness testimony authors such as Goodman and Hahn (1987), Hollin (1989), Loftus (1981), and Penrod et al. (1982) have drawn upon the three memory stages of *acquisition, retention* and *retrieval.* These three stages have traditionally been identified in memory research and correspond to the stages involved in: (a) witnessing an event; (b) time taken before giving evidence; and (c) giving evidence. In reality, of course, these three stages are not distinct. For example, while waiting to give evidence, a witness may see a police artist's sketch of the suspect on television and/or may talk about the incident with other witnesses. As will be seen below, in the course of such exposure to information about the crime, a witness acquires information that becomes part of the memory to be retained for later recall. Furthermore, the terms 'event' and 'witness' variables are not always mutually exclusive. For example, 'type of event' and a witness' level of physiological arousal are closely related, while 'number of witnesses' can be both an 'event' and a 'witness' variable. Table 2.1 shows the variables considered in the literature reviews that follow below and in the next chapter under the categories of 'event', 'witness' and 'interrogational'.

In considering classifications of such factors it should also be remembered that memory errors are of two types: *errors of omission* and *errors of commission*. Errors of omission stem from inherent limitations of the way the human memory is structured and processes information.

Before reviewing available empirical evidence that a number of factors impact on the accuracy of eyewitness testimony, it should be noted that the empirical literature on witness testimony deals almost exclusively with the accuracy of identification rather than non-identification or misidentification (see Twining, 1983, on the issue of identification and misidentification in legal processes). A small number of researchers have examined the impact on mock juror verdicts of *non-identification*, that is, when the witness says: 'No, that's not the person I saw'. According to Wells and Lindsay (1980:776): 'Non-identifications generally are considered uninformative because of the belief that there are multiple plausible causes for non-identification (for example, memory failure)' and Williams et al. (1992:152) suggest that a non-identification

Table 2.1 Variables in the study of eyewitness testimony by category

Event	Frequency, time, duration, illumination, type of event, weapon.
Witness	Fatigue, physiological arousal, chronic anxiety, neuroticism, extroversion, reflection-impulsivity, need for approval/affiliation, morning–evening type, self-monitoring, field-dependence, breath of categorising, levelling-sharpening, mood, alcohol, age, race, gender, schemas/stereotypes, physical attractiveness, whether also victim of the crime, confidence, whether witness is a police officer, collaborative testimony.
Perpetrator	Gender, body size, height, ethnicity, gait.
Interrogational	Retention interval, type of recall, efforts made to recall, leading questions, memory retrieval therapy, cognitive interview.

may be construed as a 'non event' rather than as an important piece of evidence. Leippe (1985) reported that the probability of a defendant being found guilty by mock jurors in an experiment was reduced from 53 per cent to 14 per cent by a non-identifying witness even if it was in contrast to two witnesses who positively identified the defendant. It was also found that the impact of a non-identifying witness was completely negated if such a witness elected not to testify and the information was conveyed to the mock jurors by the lawyer. Finally, Bekerian (1993) has rightly argued against the notion of a typical eyewitness situation or typical eyewitness because psychologists 'might be asked to identify one in court' (p. 575).

5 Variables that Impact on Eyewitness' Testimony Accuracy

There already exist a number of works that provide excellent reviews of the eyewitness literature (Cutler and Penrod, 1995; Davies, 1993a; Thomson, 1995a; Williams et al., 1992). The aim of the discussion of the literature that follows is to reach conclusions about the importance of a number of 'event' factors in eyewitness' accuracy, considering the findings in a broader sociolegal context as much as possible, drawing on contemporary criminology and relevant law. A literature review of the categories of 'witness', 'perpetrator' and 'interrogational' variables is the subject of the next chapter.

5.1 Event Characteristics

Frequency: In some cases a bank-teller has spoken to the suspect of an armed robbery when he/she came into the bank to carry out sur- veillance and/or to do a 'dry run', or a suspect may have been seen at least once before in the vicinity of premises that have been broken into. Powel and Thomson (1994)[5] found that the greater the frequency of an event, the better people will remember it as having occurred and details about it. However, if people are asked to remember a specific occasion when a recurring event took place, the accuracy of recall decreases the more times it has occurred.

Time: Remembering accurately when an event actually took place would add to the credibility of an eyewitness' recall of event information including identification of a suspect alleged to have been involved in the event. According to Williams et al. (1992), in *Neil v. Biggers*, 1972, the US Supreme Court accepted the proposition that there is a strong correlation between a witness' memory accuracy and an opportunity for the witness to observe. In fact, the same court 'accepted this notion as a criterion for judging every witness' reliability' (p. 143). A witness' recall of an event or a description of an offender's face exists in a time framework. Despite the fact that 'Time is a richly elaborated concept, one that is resistant to analysis' (Friedman, 1993:44), there is a body of literature on memory for time. Both life memory studies and laboratory studies have reported the *forward telescoping* phenomenon. Forward telescoping refers to a 'tendency to give estimates that are too recent for events that are among the oldest in the range tested ... Respondents seem to import events that really took place before the cutoff in the question' (Friedman, 1993:51). It has also been found that judgements of time are more accurate when there is a more temporary structure to an interval than when peoples' activities are more homogeneous (Tzeng and Cotton, 1980); when two items belong to the same semantic category, such as 'sofa' and 'chair', and when two items are strongly associated, as in 'smoke' and 'tobacco' (Winograd and Soloway, 1985). A number of theories have been put forward to account for such findings (see Friedman, 1993, for a discussion). Friedman groups theories according to the type of information that each emphasises as the basis for memory of dates.

Duration: The time it takes to commit a particular crime can range from a few seconds to a few minutes or even longer. An assault may be over in a fraction of a second, an armed robbery of a bank or of a person in the street may well be over in less than a minute (Kapardis, 1989), while a brawl between two street gangs or an abduction or a rape could last for much longer. In the English case of *R. v. Turnbull* (1977) 65 Cr App R 242, Lord Widgery stated that a defining feature of 'good' quality witness identifications (as opposed to 'poor' ones) is that the witness had ample time to get a good look at the suspect. This common-sense belief is supported by the literature. A survey of 836 members of the public and 477 undergraduates in Kingston, Ontario, found that duration of crime was rated by potential jurors as the fourth most important determinant of eyewitness identification accuracy out of twenty-five variables (Lindsay, 1994a:372). In an experiment by Clifford and Richards (1977) policemen were asked to recall details of a person who had approached and conversed with them for either 15 or 30 seconds. They found better recall in the 30 seconds than in the 15 seconds exposure to the target person. In view of the existence of selective attention, however, greater exposure duration to an offence will not necessarily mean greater accuracy.

Illumination: Crimes take place round the clock and illumination, the amount of light available at the scene of the crime, is undoubtedly a relevant factor. Illumination was considered by the potential jurors in

Lindsay's (1994a) survey as the fifth most important determinant of eyewitness identification accuracy out of the twenty-five variables examined. Kuehn (1974) reported that witnesses could remember less about an incident that took place at twilight rather than during the day or at night and, similarly, Yarmey (1986b) found that accuracy of incident details and recognition of the people involved was better during daytime than at the end of twilight or during the hours of darkness. The fact that a crime occurred at night, of course, does not seem to discourage witnesses from having confidence in the accuracy of their testimony acquired under poor lighting conditions (see below). The ability to adapt to the dark can take up to 30 minutes depending on the intensity and duration of lighting conditions one was previously experiencing (Loftus et al., 1989:17). Consequently, eyewitnesses who experience abrupt changes from one lighting condition to another can also have trouble seeing what actually took place. As Buckhout (1974) reminded his readers, crimes very rarely take place under ideal light conditions, or in close proximity or last long enough or, finally, are free from other interference (p. 25). One can also add the important fact that actual witnesses may well be *fatigued* at the time of encoding, a factor that has been found to interfere with recall accuracy (Horne, 1992).

Wagenaar and van der Schrier (1994)[6] varied illumination and distance at which witnesses saw a person they were subsequently asked to identify. It was found that with moderately bright lighting in the evening, the identification of a person viewed at night in full moon at a distance of more than 3 metres is dubious. Experimental psychologists are well suited to test the accuracy of witnesses claiming to have seen the features of someone some distance away under poor light. Buckhout (1974) mentions a case in the US in which a policeman testified seeing the defendant, a black man, shoot a victim as the offender and the victim stood in a doorway 120 feet away. Checking light conditions at the scene of the crime for the defence, Buckhout found that the amount of light was less than a fifth of the light from a candle and it would have been impossible for someone to see a face that far away. Not surprisingly, perhaps, when the members of the jury went to the scene of the crime and asked one black person to stand in the doorway they were unable to make out his features and subsequently acquitted the defendant.

Type of Event: The range of offences witnessed in real life is much broader than that which has been studied by psychologists in simulated or field studies. Preliminary findings from a recent survey by the present author (in preparation) of police data on 1636 real crime victims/witnesses interviewed by specialist police personnel of the Criminal Identification Squad in Melbourne, Australia, for the purpose of constructing a composite colour computer image of the suspect during a nine-month period in 1994 indicate that such interviews mainly involved: burglary (19.8 per cent), theft (16.8 per cent), armed robbery (12.2 per cent), assault (11.1 per cent), wilful indecent exposure (9.4 per cent) and deception (4.6 per cent). It was also found that females were seven times more likely than males to have provided descriptions of suspects in rape and indecent assault and three times more likely to do so in abduction cases. Interestingly enough, 16 per cent of the witnesses were unable to remember enough details about the suspect's face for the police to construct a colour computer-face composite image to assist the investigators to apprehend the offenders (see also Chapter 10). Furthermore, failure in this context was not related to the type of crime involved.

Weapon: Firearms, especially hand guns, feature in crime in the US (Cook, 1983) to a much greater degree than they do in the UK, Australia or New Zealand (Cantor et al., 1991; Chappel et al., 1988). The use of a weapon to commit a crime is generally considered an aggravating factor when courts come to impose sentence on a convicted defendant (Thomas, 1979). Experimental psychologists have examined the effect of a weapon in the hands of an offender on witness testimony. A weapon, of course, does not have to be a loaded firearm or a knife – a broken bottle, a stone, a piece of wood, or a syringe and so forth are also defined as 'weapons' in many jurisdictions.

Physiological arousal: The presence of a weapon is undoubtedly stressful for both victims and bystanders, a factor that generally increases their level of physiological arousal. There is no doubt that subjects in simulation studies, whether laboratory or field ones, are unlikely to experience the varying degrees of emotional arousal, stress or the trauma experienced by real-life witnesses (whether as victims or bystanders) to such serious crimes as assault, rape, armed robbery, abduction and homicide. For example, researchers have found that witnesses to bank robberies are concerned about being taken hostages and/or receiving serious injury, even death (Christianson and Hubinette, 1993:372). Potential jurors in Canada have been found to consider stress and emotional arousal during the crime as the eleventh most important determinant of eyewitness identification accuracy out of twenty-five factors (Lindsay, 1994a:372). The resulting psychological trauma is recognised in law: a crime victim/witness can sue for damages in a civil suit; in various countries there exist schemes which aim, *inter alia*, to compensate the victim/witness for 'pain and suffering' and, finally, some organisations such as banks have a policy of giving time off work and providing psychological counselling to their employees who have been victims of or witnessed an armed hold-up at work (see Leeman-Conley and Crabtree, 1989).

Psychologists have long assumed that people's cognitive efficiency is related to their level of emotional tension arousal. More specifically, Yerkes and Dodson (1908) proposed an *inverted U-form relationship* between these two factors whereby cognitive efficiency is at its highest at a moderate level of arousal. Cognitive efficiency is said to decline if the arousal level increases beyond an optimal point. Easterbrooke's (1959) *cue-utilisation theory* has been used to account for what has come to be known in psychology as the 'Yerkes-Dodson law'. According to Easterbrook, as one's level of emotional arousal increases, the range of cues one can attend to and utilise decreases. A moderate level of arousal is conducive for attention and recall because one is in a position to attend to relevant cues and exclude irrelevant ones. However, as arousal increases beyond a certain point as a result of stress, the number of cues (including relevant ones) that can be attended to are reduced. Mandler (1975) extended Easterbrooke's argument by positing that the relationship between emotional arousal and cue utilisation is determined by our autonomic nervous system which allows for less attention and cognitive processing when one is highly aroused (Eysenck, 1982). Thus, a highly aroused (stressed) individual will focus on fewer cues in their environment for the simple reason that a lot of their energy will be expended on their anxiety. One serious limitation of such studies is a failure to take into account an individual's degree of neuroticism which appears to mediate on the alleged relationship between people's arousal and cognitive efficiency (see below).

Some psychologists have advocated a similar relationship between tension arousal and memory (Deffenbacher, 1983; Loftus, 1979; Loftus and Doyle, 1987). However, as will be seen below, this view has been seriously challenged. On the basis of a literature review, Christianson (1992:279) has challenged the unidimensional view of a simple relationship between emotion and memory, concluded that eyewitness memory for stressful emotional events 'should be understood in terms of complex interactions between type of events, ... type of detail information, ... time of test, ... and retrieval conditions ...' and questioned whether the Yerkes-Dodson law is a useful theory in eyewitness identification research (p. 303).

Violent/Traumatic event: The available literature on memory for violent or traumatic events has reported conflicting findings. On the one hand, experimental studies have reported that a high level of stress impacts adversely on memory (see Deffenbacher, 1983; Loftus, 1979). Interestingly, this also appears to be the view shared by the majority (79 per cent) of the US experts on eyewitness testimony surveyed by Kassin et al. (1989). Other researchers, however, utilising real criminal cases, have found that, contrary to what the experimental literature would predict, a high level of stress is good for memory (Yuille and Cutshall, 1986, 1989; Yuille and Tollestrup, 1992). Yuille and Cutshall (1986) reported a study of witnesses to a homicide which found that witnesses indicating the highest level of stress had a mean accuracy of 93 per cent when interviewed by police two days later and 88 per cent when interviewed by researchers four to five months later.

Yuille and Cutshall (1989) have argued that: (a) laboratory studies of the effect of stress on recall do not adequately simulate real traumatic experiences; (b) subjects in such experiments are not emotionally involved; (c) the memories reported by the two sets of studies are qualitatively different; and (d) the memory of traumatised witnesses is highly accurate and stands the test of time. For Yuille and his colleagues (see Yuille and Tollestrup, 1992) the difference between the two types of methodologies is that real-life traumatic events impact on the witness in such a way as to narrow their attention to details of core aspects of an incident which are stored and remembered for long afterwards. Consequently, laboratory studies cannot be said to have demonstrated that memory for traumatic events is unreliable. Indeed, experiments with the potential to test this hypothesis would probably be ruled out on ethical grounds.

In evaluating the findings from the real-life stressful events it needs to be remembered that, as Christianson and Hubinette (1993:366) point out, the Yuille and Cutshall study is limited by the mere fact that it only examined a single stressful event, and did not include an appropriate control event in support of their conclusion regarding the stress-memory relationship. In addition, unlike laboratory studies, Yuille and Cutshall ignored errors of omission when calculating their performance scores; witness recall of details about the personal appearance of the perpetrator of the crime, for example, was incomplete, as in laboratory studies and, finally, their figures may well have been inflated by the fact that only witnesses with complete or accurate memory volunteered to participate in their study (Christianson and Hubinette, 1993:366).

Christianson and Hubinette (1993) reported an interesting study of witnesses to twenty-two bank robberies. The witnesses comprised twenty bank-teller victims, twenty-five fellow employees, thirteen customers and eight who had an earlier experience of a bank robbery. In considering their findings it is worth remembering that bank robberies are significantly more likely to involve the use of firearms to intimidate the victim/s; can last for up to 3 minutes; often involve older, more experienced criminals; tellers are usually instructed to comply with the demands made by robbers and, consequently, victims are much less likely to sustain physical injuries than is the case with robberies of 'soft' targets, such as family-run corner shops in which the victim is more likely to resist the attack, for example (see Kapardis, 1989). Christianson and Hubinette (1993) found that teller-victims were no more emotionally aroused than bystanders and that, in general, information about such an emotional event is retained for a lengthy period of time (p. 375). Also, witnesses' recall of robbery details was consistent with what they had told the police, irrespective of whether they were victims or bystanders; recall was more accurate about such features of the crime as action, weapon and clothing but, contrary to what would have been predicted on the basis of the 'flashbulb' memory theory (see below), recall was less accurate as far as such specific details of robberies as date, time and other people are concerned. Finally, Christianson and Hubinette concluded that self-rated emotional stress did not appear to be strongly related with memory performance (p. 375).

One significant strength of the Christianson and Hubinette (1993) study is that it was based on a relatively large number of real-life violent events and numerous witnesses. By comparison, the Yuille and Cutshall (1986) study was based on one event and thirteen witnesses. Also, as Yuille and Tollestrup (1992) point out, robbery is a crime that takes place frequently in society, is often witnessed by many who have not seen the robber/s before and, also, it is a crime which traumatises both victims and bystanders. For these reasons robbery is a suitable event-type for testing the emotional arousal-memory hypothesis (Christianson and Hubinette, 1993:376). However, studies of such real traumatic events can be criticised for relying exclusively on retrospective self-reports of emotion and fear and for using a measure of memory which is not a measure of retention (Christianson and Hubinette, 1993:375). As the same authors point out, their own study would have been meth-odologically better if they had measured witnesses' memory of robbery details immediately after the crime was committed. The limitations of their study notwithstanding, the findings reported by Christianson and Hubinette contradict the view shared by a large number of eyewitness testimony experts in the Kassin et al. (1989) survey. The same findings also partly contradict claims by Yuille and Cutshall (1986) and Yuille and Tollestrup (1992) that detailed memories from traumatic events are generally accurate and withstand the test of time (Christianson and Hubinette, 1993:376).

The conflicting findings reported by studies in natural settings and laboratory studies are to some extent attributable to differences in methodology (see Christianson et al., 1992). Christianson and Hubinette

(1993:376) point out that some studies (Reisberg et al., 1988; Yuille and Cutshall, 1986, 1989) have focused on memory accuracy, while others (Neisser and Harsch, 1992) have been concerned with the decline of memory over time and inaccuracy in terms of errors of commission. Similarly, differences in emphasis also go some way towards explaining conflicting findings reported by laboratory studies. For example, Christianson (1984) and Heuer and Reisberg (1990) were concerned with the persistency of emotional memories, while others (Clifford and Hollin, 1981; Clifford and Scott, 1978; Loftus and Burns, 1982) measured errors of omission. Thus, 'the data in both real-life studies and laboratory studies show good and poor recall depending on how recall is tested' (Christianson and Hubinette, 1993:376).

Christianson (1992:302) concluded that there are no real grounds for a simple relationship between intense emotion and memory – 'the view that the more negative the emotion or stress, the poorer the memory is incorrect ...' – and that particular details of core aspects of a violent event and also information about circumstantial details are less susceptible to forgetting (p. 303). Yuille et al. (1994) had 120 trainee (probationer) constables at the Metropolitan Police Training Centre in Hendon, England, experience a stressful or non-stressful occupational simulation (a 'stop-and-search' scenario) as participants or observers and tested their recall after 1 or 12 weeks. It was found that stress decreased the amount recalled but improved both accuracy and resistance to decay over time. The arousal-memory relationship is, thus, best understood in terms of complex interactions between type of event, time of test, memory test and retrieval conditions. In conclusion, therefore, the Yerkes-Dodson (1908) law does not adequately describe the relationship between memory and arousal (p. 303).

Weapon Focus: As already mentioned above, the presence of a weapon in the context of a criminal offence is, without doubt, stressful for both victims and bystanders alike. On the basis of the empirical literature on the relationship between emotional arousal and memory, psychologists have tested the hypothesis that if witnesses are confronted with an obviously armed offender they will focus attention on the weapon for at least part of the duration of the event and, as a result, their ability to identify the face of the perpetrator will be reduced. Loftus et al. (1987a) examined the phenomenon of 'weapon focus' by presenting subject-witnesses with a series of slides depicting an event in a fast-food restaurant. Half of the subjects saw a customer point a gun at the cashier; the other half saw him hand the cashier a cheque. The researchers recorded the subjects' eye movements while viewing the slides. It was found that subjects made more eye fixations and for a longer duration on the weapon than on the cheque and that accuracy of recall was poorer in the weapon condition.

Maass and Köhnken (1989) simulated the 'weapon effect' in an experiment in which eighty-six non-psychology students were approached by an experimenter who was holding either a syringe or a pen and either did or did not threaten to administer an injection. They found that exposure to the syringe decreased line-up recognition while enhancing the accuracy of recall for hand cues to a statistically significant degree. The 'weapon effect' reported is explainable in terms of witnesses' level of physiological arousal narrowing their attention and resulting in poor memory of peripheral details of the event in question. Similar results were obtained by Kramer et al. (1990) who had witness-subjects (college undergraduates) confronted with the sight of a man carrying a weapon during an assault. In the scene viewed, the victim was approached by an assailant who broke a liquor bottle over his head. Kramer et al. manipulated the degree to which the weapon was visible and reported that fewer details of the incident were recalled in the highly visible weapon condition and, also, that self-reported arousal correlated negatively with memory accuracy. In a second series of experiments, Kramer et al. manipulated the 'time in view' of both the weapon and the victim's face using slides. They found that the weapon focus effect was present within a non-arousing, environmentally stark setting and was dependent on the percentage of time the weapon was visible.

According to Kramer et al. (1990:183), consistent with a number of modern theories of attention, a weapon can be seen as a salient object that demands a certain amount of attention from a witness. Kramer et al. concluded that the presence of a weapon reduces the accuracy of a witness' memory of the features of the person carrying the weapon. Some support for Kramer et al.'s conclusion is to be found in Steblay's (1992) meta-analytic review of twelve studies, permitting nineteen tests of the *weapon focus hypothesis*. Six of the tests yielded a significant difference, as would have been predicted between weapon-present and weapon-absent conditions. However, thirteen of the tests showed no significant difference. Steblay's analysis showed that as far as the identification accuracy in a line-up is concerned (a most important piece of evidence from the point of view of both the police investigation and the criminal trial), the weapon-focus effect was small (0.13). The weapon-focus effect was stronger (0.55) for accuracy of featural description. Steblay (1992:422) concluded that the weapon-focus effect is significant and 'a worthwhile focus for research. There is a need to more precisely identify the mechanics of the process in forensically relevant settings'. Contrary to what many confident-sounding witnesses would have magistrates, judges or juries believe (see below), their certainty that they will never forget the face of an armed bandit (Buckhout, 1974) may well be unjustified. The empirical evidence involving witnesses as bystanders or victims strongly indicates they are more likely to remember details of the weapon itself and perhaps the essence of the situation (Tooley et al., 1987; Kramer et al., 1990). As far as potential jurors' belief about the importance of this factor as a determinant of eyewitness identification accuracy is concerned, Lindsay (1994:372) found that it ranked thirteenth out of twenty-five variables.

Flashbulb Memory: Brown and Kulik (1977) put forward the notion of a 'flashbulb' memory to refer to cases when a most significant, unexpected event, such as the shooting of John F. Kennedy in 1963, results in rather vivid, detailed and accurate memory traces of all that was observed at the time (see Winograd and Neisser, 1992, for a discussion of 'flashbulb' memory research). According to Morse et al. (1993), psychologists have long been interested in 'flashbulb' memories. They cite an early study by Colgrove (1899) in which people were asked to recall when they heard of President Lincoln's death thirty-three years earlier. Colgrove found that the majority (71 per cent) reported they had vivid images of the moment at which they heard of that death.

Other researchers have reported that 'flashbulb' memories are not always accurate (Christianson, 1989; McCloskey et al., 1988; Neisser, 1982). They have been found to be vivid for John F. Kennedy's assassination but less vivid for Robert Kennedy's and Martin Luther-King's assassinations and even less vivid for the Senate Hearings for confirmation of Clarence Thomas to the Supreme Court of the US in October 1991 (Morse et al., 1993). Emotion was found to have no significant effect on memory in a study of people's recollection of the space shuttle Challenger explosion (Harsch and Neisser, 1989) and in a study by Christianson (1989) of people's recollection of the assassination of the Swedish Prime Minister, Olaf Palme. In other words, 'flashbulb' memory studies do not consistently support the view that there is a positive relationship between accuracy of recall and emotional stress.

Wright (1993) surveyed 247 students at three sessions (2 days (N=60), 1 month (N=76) and 5 months (N=111)) about the Hillsborough stadium disaster in England when, in the early stages of the Football Association semi-final between Liverpool and Nottingham Forest, an influx of people through the back of the Liverpool terraces resulted in ninety-five people at the front getting crushed to death. Subjects rated on a seven-point scale their emotional reaction, soccer enthusiasm, how important they felt the event was for them personally and for society (in the third session subjects were not asked about importance for society), their circumstances when they heard about the tragedy and of what it reminded them (Wright, 1993:131–2). Wright defined a 'flashbulb' memory in terms of whether subjects recalled either where they were, who they were with or what they were doing at the time. He found that most of his subjects had 'flashbulb' recollections of the event. It was also found that personal importance and emotional impact became more significant over time, supporting a reconstructionist explanation and Neisser's (1982, 1986) theory that memories of an important event are altered so as to accord with their symbolic status. Finally, Wright also reported that after five months subjects were more likely to be reminded of more general incidents. This indicates that, as Neisser's (1986, cited by Wright, 1993) theory holds, their memory of the Hillsborough tragedy had become 'integrated within the nested autobiographical memory ... becoming subordinate to more general event knowledge structures'. Wright concludes that his results support a reconstructionist explanation rather than Brown and Kulik's (1977) 'special mechanism' idea. Finally, in considering studies of 'flashbulb' memories it needs to be remembered that the defining feature of such memories is 'the undue confidence with which these memories are held' (Weaver, 1993:39).

It would appear that while a strong emotional experience enhances one's memory for salient details, no evidence has so far been reported that 'flashbulb' memories are unusually accurate. Also, it should be noted here that the accuracy of people's recall of such an important event as the assassination of a US president or a major soccer tragedy in the UK is impossible to determine because of the inevitable post-event interference (see below) by the substantial media coverage usually accorded such events. Independent of the stressful nature of a witnessed event, Loftus et al. (1989) point to chronic anxiety as an attribute that can cause a person's attention to be focused on such other concerns as to fail to adequately perceive event details, resulting in inaccurate testimony. Therefore, the next chapter, *inter alia*, considers the importance of a number of personality characteristics of the witness that are said to influence accuracy of identification.

6 Conclusions

Eyewitness testimony is of crucial importance in the investigation of a crime, the decision to prosecute a suspect and at the trial. Since the turn of the century there has been concern about the limitations of eyewitness testimony. More empirical studies have been reported in this than in any other area of psycholegal research. Interestingly, the general public, police officers, and university students of psychology and law have a rather poor knowledge of the topic. The available empirical literature on eyewitness testimony accuracy testifies both to limitations of the cognitive processes of attention, perception, and memory and to cognition being a dynamic mental process.

The empirical studies considered in this and the next chapter show that there are no simple, straightforward answers to a question by lawyers such as 'how good is visual memory'? Attempts to classify eyewitness testimony variables have been plagued by the difficulty that categories used are not necessarily mutually exclusive. Wells' (1978) classification into 'estimator' and 'system' variables is no longer adequate. The taxonomy provided in this chapter encompasses all the categories of variables shown to relate to eyewitness recall accuracy, namely 'event', 'eyewitness', 'perpetrator', and 'interrogational'.

Even though the quality of psychological studies of eyewitness identification accuracy has improved over the last ten years or so, dogmatism is unwarranted when it comes to deciding what particular methodology to use; the fact is that no single method is the 'best' and every effort should be made to replicate findings across a range of paradigms. Caution should thus be exercised in extrapolating findings from controlled studies to real-life situations. Also, the reader needs to be aware that, as the studies in this and the next chapter show, many psychologists have focused on the limitations of eyewitness memory. At the same time, a very small but widely publicised number of miscarriages of justice due to witness misidentification have helped to increase people's scepticism regarding the capacity of crime victims/witnesses for accurate recall. There is a danger of exaggerating that scepticism. To do eyewitnesses justice one needs to also bear in mind that, as Lindsay and Read (1994) put it: 'It is important not to exaggerate the fallibility of human memory. Memory is often wonderfully detailed and accurate' (p. 293). With this caveat in mind, the review of the literature on a number of 'event' characteristics, including frequency, type, duration, illumination, and the presence of a weapon, shows they impact significantly on witness' recall accuracy. However, laboratory and real-life studies of the effect of stress on recall have reported conflicting findings, highlighting the need for psycholegal researchers to combine different research methods.

Chapter 3

Eyewitnesses: The Perpetrator and Interviewing

- *Witness' personality, demographic and other characteristics.*
- *Perpetrator factors.*
- *Interrogational variables, interfering with the witness' memory.*
- *Repressed or false memory syndrome.*
- *Interviewing eyewitnesses effectively: the cognitive interview technique, forensic hypnosis.*

'At the end of the day, the clinician is in no different position from members of juries who must seek independent evidence to corroborate the authenticity of witnesses' evidence . . . The consequences of drawing premature conclusions, both for the client and significant others in the client's life, are likely to be far-reaching and irreversible.' (Thomson, 1995b:104)

Introduction

Psychologists have paid very little attention to the influence of individual differences in personality and their effects on identification (Hosch, 1994:328). Hosch attributes this lack of research to the facts that: (a) psycholegal researchers in the field have a background in social or cognitive psychology; and (b) many a psychologist's acceptance of Wells' (1978) argument and the focusing on system rather than on estimator variables in order to increase the practical usefulness of their work (p. 328). Let us, therefore, take a close look at the empirical literature on a number of witness' personality, demographic and other characteristics and their relationship with accuracy of eyewitness memory.

1 Witness' Characteristics

Neuroticism: As is so frequently the case in experimental psychology, when examining the nature of the relationship between two variables attention must be paid to possible intervening variables. One variable that has been shown to be important in investigating the relationship between accuracy of witness testimony and the witness' level of physiological arousal is a person's degree of neuroticism as a personality attribute. Neuroticism, like extroversion, is a personality trait that features in psychological explanations of criminal behaviour (see Blackburn, 1993:124–7; Eysenck, 1977). Bothwell et al. (1987a) found that as arousal level increased from low to moderate to high levels, the identification accuracy of witnesses classified as low on neuroticism increased. The reverse was found for witnesses high on neuroticism. It would appear, therefore, that failure to control the subject's neuroticism will compound any relationship between arousal and witness recall accuracy.

Extroversion: In addition to neuroticism, individual differences in eyewitness performance have been found to relate to a person's level of basal arousal as exemplified, for example, in their degree of extroversion (see Eysenck, 1982). In examining the importance of one's extroversion, researchers must take into account the following facts: (a) *time of day* is important because introverts reach their arousal peak sooner than extroverts; and (b) people's memory performance varies depending on the time of the day and the type of memory called for. Thus, if immediate or short-term memory, or verbatim and ordered memory, if shallow processing of material is required, the morning is better. If what is called for is delayed memory, prose memory and semantic or deep processing, then the evening is better (Diges et al., 1992:317).

Reflection-Impulsivity: Another personal characteristic that appears to be related to eyewitness accuracy is reflection-impulsivity (see Kagan et al., 1964).[1] A reflective individual is someone who has a strong tendency to consider a number of possible answers to a question before responding. Thus, in being asked to decide whether the culprit is in a line-up, an impulsive individual will take less time to decide than a reflective one. Indeed, such a finding was reported by Sporer (1989) and Stern and Dunning (1994) who also found that correct line-up identification correlated with speed of identification (see Chapter 10 in this volume).

Need for Approval/Affiliation: Human beings vary in the extent to which their everyday lives are characterised by grouping. This process of grouping is also known as 'affiliation'. Affiliation refers to 'forming associations involving cooperation, friendship and love' (Davenport, 1992:123). Schill (1966) reported that persons high in need for affiliation (n-Aff) showed greater perceptual sensitivity to face-related stimuli than those low on n-Aff (Atkinson and Walker, 1955) and, similarly, persons high in need for approval (n-App) performed better in a memory task for faces than those low in n-App.

Morning–Evening Type: Different people prefer different schedules in their daily lives. More specifically, morning-type of individuals (known as 'larks') are said to reach their arousal peak 3 hours before the evening-type ones – known as 'owls' (Kerkoff, 1985). In fact, in free recall, 'larks' perform better in the morning and the 'owls' perform better in the evening (Lecont, 1988).[2] Where a person is located in the 'morningness–eveningness' dimension can be measured by Horne and Ostberg's (1976) questionnaire.

In an interesting experiment Diges et al. (1992) showed morning- and evening-type subjects a very brief film of a traffic accident at 10 a.m. or 8 p.m. Utilising two measures of arousal from McNair et al.'s (1971) *Profile of Mood States*, they found that the main factor affecting witness testimony is time; in other words, accuracy of recall is significantly better when people are more aroused. Diges et al. also found, however, that there was a systematic superiority of the 10 a.m. (testing time) as compared with the evening test at 8 p.m. Finally, evening-type subjects in the morning test failed to discriminate as much accurate from irrelevant information. The authors explained the last finding in terms of evening-type individuals' tendency to be extroverts (Kerkhoff, 1985). The owls' low basal level of arousal in the morning, Diges et al. argue, is related to 'scarce cognitive resources' that permit them to 'catch' a lot of accurate details of the event but they do not guarantee that the details will be properly integrated in a factual way. Being extroverts, more assertive and self-confident, the same authors suggest, explains why 'owls' differ in the way they face their task as witnesses: 'owls' seem to have a lower decision criterion when they recall details of an event. Consequently, they were found to write longer reports, to perform hurriedly and make mistakes when trying to integrate the information (p. 320). It is obvious that researchers are a long way from closing the chapter on individual differences in arousal and witness accuracy.

Self-Monitoring: Snyder (1979, 1987) has distinguished between persons who are high self-monitors (HSMs) and low self-monitors (LSMs). This attribute refers to 'the extent to which people observe, regulate and control their public presentation of self in social situations and in their interpersonal relationships' (Hosch, 1994:329–30). Thus, HSMs care about social situations within which they interact and put considerable effort into monitoring and controlling the way in which they present themselves and the images they project (p. 330). In a number of studies Hosch and his co-workers have examined differences in eyewitness identification as a function of differences in one's degree of self-monitoring ability (see Hosch and Cooper, 1982; Hosch and Platz, 1984; Hosch et al., 1984). Hosch (1994) concludes that while HSMs appear to be more accurate as eyewitnesses on identification tasks, the relationship between witness accuracy and degree of self-monitoring ability 'is not necessarily a simple one' (p. 332). HSMs have been found to be more accurate (but no more confident) witnesses when they are the 'victims' of a staged crime instead of bystanders (p. 332). Snyder (1987) has argued that individual differences in self-monitoring are biologically based. In support of this view, Pannell et al. (1992)[3] found significant differences in evoked potentials between HSMs and LSMs in a facial recognition task, suggesting important differences in the way the two types of individuals search their memory and decide such a task.

Cognitive Style: Kogan (1971) defined 'cognitive style' as a characteristic way of perceiving, storing, transforming and utilising information. A widely cited example of cognitive style in psychology is *field dependence/field independence.* This construct describes one's ability to discriminate parts from the whole in which they are embedded. The same construct is referred to as *articulated* vs. *global psychological differentiation* (Hosch, 1994:341). Field independence has been theoretically linked with facial identification accuracy. Witkin et al. (1962, cited by Hosch, 1994:342) maintained that field-dependent persons should be better at recognising faces than field-independent ones because they are generally more attentive to faces. Studies that have tested this hypothesis have reported conflicting findings (see Hosch, 1994:341–3, for reviews). Durso et al. (1985) reported that field-dependent persons are more likely than field-independent ones to confuse memories of actual and illusory events. This finding lends support to the view that field-dependent individuals differentiate self less sharply from non-self compared to field-independent ones.

Breadth of categorising is another cognitive characteristic which has been considered in eyewitness identification accuracy (Kogan and Wallach, 1967)[4] and 'refers to a preference for being inclusive, when establishing an acceptable range for specified categories' (Hosch, 1994:338). Thus, if a witness is over-inclusive, then he/she would be more likely to pick a foil in a line-up. Hosch (p. 339) cites empirical evidence that breath of categorising is positively related to facial recognition accuracy (Messick and Damarin, 1964) and is predictive of eyewitness accuracy (Hosch et al., 1990; Hosch et al., 1991).

Levelling-Sharpening: Hosch (1994:343–4) has also suggested that a witness' position on this dimension could be related to suggestibility to unconscious interference (see Ross et al., 1994) and the misinformation effect (see Lindsay, 1994b; Weingardt et al., 1994, and below in this chapter). 'Levelling-sharpening' refers to reliable individual variations in assimilation in memory (Gardner et al., 1959).[5] Levellers have been described as tending to blur similar memories and to merge perceived objects or events with similar but not identical events recalled from previous experience (Hosch, 1994:343).

Mood: It has long been known in cognitive psychology that people find it easier to recognise something than to recall and describe it. In accounting for difference between recall and recognition, *context* is of paramount importance (Geiselman et al., 1986; Gudjonsson, 1992a; Lloyd-Bostock, 1988). Cues to recognition may be present within the witness when reliving the original incident and feeling the same way they did at the time (see Haaga, 1989; Schare et al., 1984) and/or in the external environment (Davies, 1986; McGeoch, 1932). McGeoch (1932)[6] termed the first context 'intra-organic condition' of the learner and the second 'stimulus properties of the external environment'.

The 1980s saw a burgeoning of research on the relation between emotional states and cognitive processes (Ellis and Ashbrook, 1991:1). Researchers have examined the hypothesis that a person's mood at encoding will subsequently serve as a retrieval cue for the learned information during recall. This is known as *state-dependent effect* (Mayer and Bower, 1986). On the basis of their discussion of relevant empirical studies, Ellis and Ashbrook (1991:14) concluded that state-dependent effects seem to occur seldom and the results are often impossible to replicate. The same authors reported stronger support for the '*mood-congruency effect*', that is, the view that individuals retrieve more easily material which is congruent with the mood state prevailing at the time of encoding. According to Ellis and Ashbrook, this phenomenon is quite robust across a broad range of experimental conditions. Support for both state-dependent and mood-congruency effects has been reported by clinical studies (see Weingartner et al., 1977; Ingram and Reed, 1986; Blaney, 1986).[7] However, studies of the effects of emotional states on the retrieval of personal experiences in one's childhood or more recently have reported contradictory findings (see Ellis and

Ashbrook, 1991:16). *Network theory* (Bower, 1981, see below) and the *resource allocation* or *capacity model* (see Ellis and Ashbrook, 1988) have been applied to the literature on mood and memory. Ellis and Ashbrook (1991) do not consider these two theoretical approaches as competing but rather as complementary.

According to Gudjonsson (1992a), the basic idea is that people find it easier to remember an event if they are in a similar mood (Haaga, 1989) or under the influence of a particular drug (Overton, 1964) or alcohol (Lisman, 1974) as when they witnessed the event. As far as the facilitating effect of cues in the external environment is concerned, the important finding is that reinstating the witness in the original context (for example, returning the witness to the scene of the crime, showing the witness photographs of the scene of the crime or asking him/her to form an image of the crime scene) enhances recall by maximising retrieval cues (Gudjonsson, 1992a:90; see also 'cognitive interview' below). Cutler and Penrod (1988) found, for example, that identification accuracy can be increased if police reinstate strong physical context cues associated with the offender, such as his/her voice, posture and gait.

The effect of context on memory can be explained by Bower's (1981) '*associative network theory*' which holds that one's emotions serve memory units and are linked to what has been seen and experienced. In other words, one maximises retrieval cues by reliving the original context (Gudjonsson, 1992a:90). Reinstating the context is a crucial component of one particular technique for enhancing witness memory, namely, the 'cognitive interview technique' (see below).

Alcohol: Alcohol abuse afflicts many a society (see De Luca, 1981; Saunders, 1984) and very few would doubt that, in addition to its astronomical social cost, alcohol also impairs many sensory motor and cognitive functions. Generally, the more the alcohol consumed the greater the impairment, but this relationship is 'subject to a host of task, instructional, cognitive process and individual variables' (Read et al., 1992:427). Alcohol, of course, features frequently in the commission of a large volume of such criminal offences as homicide, rape, serious assault, robbery and culpable driving (Feldman, 1993:276–7; Kapardis, 1989; Kapardis and Cole, 1988; National Committee on Violence, 1990). It is often a requirement for judges in jury trials in common law countries to direct the jury that intoxication could render a witness' recollections inaccurate.[8]

Empirical studies of the impact of alcohol on memory performance have reported conflicting findings. On the one hand, Steele and Josephs (1990) and Yuille and Tollestrup (1990) found that alcohol interferes with the acquisition and encoding of information and Read et al. (1992) reported that it significantly impairs subjects' recall of peripheral information. On the other hand, Parker et al. (1980) found that consuming alcohol during the retention interval correlated with better recognition and recall performance than when subjects did not. More research is needed before the alcohol-memory performance relationship is elucidated. Lindsay's (1994a:372) survey found that the level of witness intoxication during the crime was ranked tenth by potential jurors in importance as a determinant of eyewitness identification accuracy out of twenty-five variables. Alcohol is one kind of *drug*. A commonly taken drug that is illegal in many countries is *cannabis*. It has been found that being high on cannabis interferes seriously with one's recall accuracy of recent events (Thomson, 1995a:127). On the basis of what is known in psychological pharmacology, such illicit drugs as heroin, cocaine, and amphetamines can only be expected to influence adversely both a witness' initial perception of an event and his/her memory of it (Spiegel, 1989). Also, given the large number of people in society who are on such prescribed drugs as antidepressants and barbiturates and so forth, there is a need for research into how such individuals' performance as eyewitnesses is affected by their medication.

Age: In view of the increasing concern in recent years about abuse of children in general and their sexual abuse in particular, a lot of empirical literature on the relationship between the age of a witness and accuracy of recall has focused on child evidence (see Chapter 4). At the same time, largely due to improvements in medical care, an increasing proportion of the general population, especially of western countries, comprises elderly people. The last few years have also witnessed an increasing concern about the abuse of elderly people in the home, in institutions, and as vulnerable victims of crime (Groth, 1979), who often live in fear of crime even though they are the least likely to be victimised by strangers (Kapardis, 1993; Kennedy and Silverman, 1990; Parker and Ray, 1990). In criminal law, the fact that a victim of an offence is of advanced age is regarded as an aggravating factor at the sentencing stage (Kapardis, 1985:103–5; Thomas, 1979).

According to Light (1991): 'Older adults complain more about memory than younger adults' (p. 333). Laboratory studies of memory[9] have found that persons over the age of 60 perform less well than persons in their twenties on free recall, recognition of lists of words or sentences. Light also reported that older adults on forensically relevant tasks remember less of buildings along the main roads in towns they have lived in for a long time, about what coins and telephones look like, activities they have participated in, names and faces of people and, finally, they have poorer memory for prose (p. 334). There is also ample evidence pointing to 'cognitive slowing' with aging, that is, that as one gets older one gets slower as far as the rate of rehearsal during a memory task, scanning in memory search tasks, or responding in primary and secondary memory tasks is concerned (Light, 1991:361). Apparently, also, older people are disadvantaged if their recall accuracy is tested by means of multiple-choice questions instead of 'yes' 'no' answers (List, 1986; Yarmey and Kent, 1980).

There is disagreement among researchers as to whether there is a peak age beyond which memory does not improve and may decrease. Diamond and Carey (1977) claimed to have found that memory peaks at 10 while Carey (1981) and Chance et al. (1982) reported that adult-like levels of face recognition on performance may not, in fact, be achieved until about 16 years of age.[10] There is agreement, however, that elderly people of 70 years or older have poorer perceptual and memorial faculties (Wallace, 1956). A common loss suffered is in short-term memory retention (Craik, 1977) and in visual acuity for both near and distant objects, as well as the ability to discriminate colours adequately. Elderly people have also been shown to have a strong tendency to emphasise the accuracy of what they say at the expense of speed of saying it (Botwinick and Shock, 1972); are less able than younger subjects to pay attention to stimuli on the periphery when driving (Manstead and Lee, 1979); have less confidence in their testimony and may well approach memory tasks differently (Yarmey and Kent, 1980).

The available literature also indicates that the elderly are also more prone to recognition errors for faces seen only once before (Bartlett and Leslie, 1986; Smith and Winograd, 1978). However, this age-related deficit disappears if a face has been seen from a number of viewpoints (Bartlett and Leslie, 1986; Yarmey and Kent, 1980). Bartlett and Leslie (1986) reported that there may be an age-related deficit where the suspect is young and/or is seen only at a glance. Another defect which the elderly suffer is in verbal free recall of events they have witnessed (List, 1986). Finally, it should be noted that studies reporting no significant differences between elderly and young subjects (Tickner and Poulton, 1975) defined 'elderly' to mean an average age of 50 years while others reporting differences (Yarmey and Kent, 1980) used 'elderly' to refer to subjects aged 65 to 90 years. For American potential jurors, however, the age of the witness is not considered an important determinant of eyewitness identification accuracy. Lindsay (1994a:372) reported that it was ranked eighteenth in importance out of the twenty-five factors considered. Ross et al. (1990) carried out three experiments on mock-jurors' perception of the average 74-year old's credibility as a witness compared to an average 24-year old and reported inconsistent results. There was general agreement, however, that elderly witnesses are honest.

In her review of the literature on memory and aging Light (1991) discussed four classes of explanation for age-related decrements in memory, namely: (a) *metamemory* (in terms of deficient knowledge about memory; deficient strategy use; memory monitoring); (b) *semantic deficit* (for example, in terms of richness, extensiveness and depth of encoding; encoding inferences); (c) *impairment* of deliberate recollection; and (d) *reduced processing resources*. Light concluded that, whether separately or combined, these hypotheses do not account adequately for what is known about the memory performance of elderly people (p. 366). In other words: 'Memory impairment in older adults does not seem to be accounted for by deficiencies in strategies used, or by problems in language comprehension' (p. 366). Future research into memory and aging needs, for example, to clarify the concepts of 'attention' and 'effort' in evaluating the attention capacity hypothesis (Light, 1991:363). Such research would also need to investigate further whether the same mechanisms underlie problems in recalling recent events and in remembering old information. At the same time, the need for such research in forensic contexts cannot be overemphasised. On the basis of his literature review, Bornstein (1995) suggests the following means of improving elderly eyewitnesses' memory: use recognition; ask precise questions; avoid leading questions; emphasise that a high degree of certainty is needed before deciding to select someone out of a line-up; present a line-up sequentially and, finally, make use of the cognitive interview technique (see below).

Race: As criminologists are not tired of reminding us, 'blacks [in the US] are vastly over-represented in prison populations, in the official statistics of arrest and in victim reports of robbery and assault' (Feldman, 1993:69). Aborigines in Australia are also over-represented in official criminal statistics (National Committee on Violence, 1990: 36–8; Walker and McDonald, 1995) as are West Indians in Britain (Ouston, 1984). A substantial body of research spanning more than two decades has been reported that focuses on *racial* and *cross-racial identification*. The general conclusion is that cross-racial identifications are more difficult, less accurate and thus less reliable than within-race identifications by adult witnesses.[11] A meta-analysis by Bothwell et al. (1989) on cross-racial identifications found that the own-race bias is consistent for both white and black subjects. In other words, testimony will be of doubtful validity when the race of the witness and the suspect is not the same. Cross-racial identification is also characterised by a higher rate of false identifications (Thomson, 1995a:136). Interestingly, race of the witness and the criminal was rated as one of the least important factors (twentieth out of twenty-five) in eyewitness identification accuracy in the Lindsay (1994a:372) study. The issue of the cross-race effect is discussed further in the context of line-ups (see Chapter 10).

Gender: According to Wootton (1959): 'If men behaved like women, the courts would be idle and the prisons empty' (cited by Feldman 1993:66). The gender gap in criminal offending has been known in criminology for a long time and victimisation surveys confirm it (Feldman, 1993:66; Blackburn, 1993:50–2). A number of studies have focused on gender as an influencing variable in eyewitness identification/facial recognition. Levine and Tapp (1971)[12] interviewed informally members of a large police force in the US and found they seemed to prefer female to male witnesses. But how important is gender in witness testimony? (See Loftus et al., 1987c, for a review.) It is established that, generally, people tend to overestimate the duration of an event but it appears that females exhibit the tendency more than males (Loftus et al., 1987c). Males, on the other hand, are significantly more likely to suffer colour deficiency (Hurvich, 1981) and hearing loss (Corso, 1981), deficiencies which inevitably have a detrimental effect on their accuracy as witnesses. In addition, a witness' gender has been found to influence the types of details that are remembered from an incident. Powers et al. (1979) reported that females are more accurate in their memory recall than males for 'female-oriented' details and vice versa, suggesting that a witness' interest (see below) may well be another important factor in testimony. Lindsay (1994a:372), however, found (without taking type of crime into account) that the potential jurors in his study considered the gender of the witness to be rated the least important variable in eyewitness identification accuracy of all the twenty-five examined.

A series of other studies of the importance of gender have yielded inconsistent findings. While some (Cunningham and Brigham,1986; Lindsay, 1986) found no gender differences in identification/facial recognition accuracy, others reported that females have higher accuracy of recall and are better than males in identifying a bystander (Howels, 1983; Lipton, 1977; Shapiro and Penrod, 1986; Yarmey and Kent, 1980). There is also some evidence (contradicted by Cross et al., 1971) that accuracy is greater for same-gender than cross-gender targets (Jalbert and Getting, 1992; Shapiro and Penrod, 1986).

As far as violent incidents and the effects of arousal are concerned, Clifford and Scott (1978) found that female subjects were less accurate than male subjects about event details but were equally accurate as male subjects after viewing a non-violent incident. MacLeod and Shepherd (1986) compared 379 witness reports for assaults that involved either physical injury or no physical injury to the victim. They found no differences in the kinds and amount of details reported by male and female witnesses when the victim was not physically injured. However, when the victim sustained physical injury, female witnesses reported significantly fewer details about the perpetrator's appearance than did male witnesses. Finally, Jalbert and Getting (1992) reported a tendency by male subjects to make more false identifications than females, irrespective of the race of the suspect. In considering contradictory findings on gender and person identification we should note that different studies have used different events: rape (Yarmey, 1986b; Yarmey and Jones, 1983), a robbery (Loftus et al., 1987a) or a non-criminal event or a snatch-theft of a satchel (Sanders and Warnick, 1981). Also, as Foster et al. (1994:110) point out, none of the studies just mentioned examined consequentiality or type of line-up instructions. We can see that while gender does appear to be an important factor in the reliability of eyewitness testimony, for the most part the often contradictory findings reported do not allow any definitive conclusions to be drawn other that the weight of the evidence points to a same-gender bias.

Schemas/Stereotypes: Social psychologists are particularly interested in social perception/cognition. For a number of years now, it has been known that in some circumstances (for example, of ambiguity, as when one has got a glimpse of a robbery being committed in a matter of seconds) people tend to report seeing what they expect to see, or desire or need to see (Whipple, 1918). As Buckhout (1974:26) put it: 'Expectancy is seen in its least attractive form in the case of biases or prejudices'. Very relevant to the impact of people's expectations on their testimony is their social schemas, that is, mental representations of social categories. Schemas can refer to persons, social events, and social roles (see Lilli, 1989; Wippich, 1989). They include some knowledge about a particular object or person, some information about the relationships among the various thoughts concerning that object or person as well as some specific examples (Taylor and Crocker, 1980). Our social schemas often influence the impressions we have of others. Once we have decided that a person fits a particular category then our mental representations about that group of people may influence our expectations, how we subsequently remember and what inferences we make about that person as well as how we judge them (Goodman and Gareis, 1993). Similarly, there is also evidence that when we observe an ambiguous social event we may well perceive causal relations that are not actually present because two acts happen at the same time (Dahmen-Zimmer and Kraus, 1992). In other words, when the picture we have of a social event is incomplete, as witnesses we show *phenomenal causality*.

Unlike Sheldon (1942), most contemporary criminologists would not accept that there is a relationship between criminal behaviour and certain body types. As most people are aware, however, film-makers, fiction writers and television producers have traditionally portrayed criminals as dark and swarthy while the heroes have tended to be blond. Such stereotypes would seem to reflect popular stereotypes about the appearance of criminals (Bull, 1979; Bull and Green, 1980; Shoemaker et al., 1973). Yarmey (1994) has reported that stereotypes also impact on earwitnesses (see Chapter 10), that is, that listeners attribute personality characteristics to individuals on the basis of speech characteristics (p. 107) while MacLeod et al. (1994) have emphasised the importance of stereotypes when it comes to qualities people associate with certain body types. We are not concerned here with whether such stereotypic notions are valid – in fact, the question of validity is irrelevant – but with their influence in how people perceive and subsequently remember and describe others (Liggert, 1974).

A stereotype is a set of beliefs about the personal attributes shared by a group of people. Stereotypes are a type of schema and, therefore, they distort reality (as do all such concepts) and oversimplify it to a certain degree. A study by Quattrone and Jones (1980) reported evidence for distortion and oversimplification attributable to the operation of stereotypes. They found that people have a tendency to see out-group members as relatively homogeneous in opinions and behaviour, whilst they perceive their own group as more heterogeneous. An early experiment by Allport and Postman (1947) as part of a 'rumour-chain' illustrates the importance of stereotypes. Allport had subjects hear about a drawing of seven people on a subway train that included a seated woman holding a baby in her arms, a black man in jacket and tie standing up and a white man with sleeves rolled up standing near him holding an open cut-throat razor in his left hand. The white man seemed to be saying something to the black man, waving his finger at him at the same time. When later asked to describe what they had seen half of the subjects reported that the open razor had been in the hand of the black man. Buckhout (1974:26) maintains that 'most people file away some stereotypes on the basis of which they make perceptual judgements; such stereotypes not only fit in with prejudices but they are also tools for making decisions more efficiently'. However, the empirical evidence regarding the importance of ethnic stereotypes in the weapon-transfer phenomenon is equivocal.

Testing both recall and recognition, Boon and Davies (1987) showed subjects slides. For half the subjects the slides showed a white man holding a knife and talking to another man who was black, for the other half of the subjects the white man with the knife was talking to another white. The weapon-transfer phenomenon when the other man was black was observed when subjects went through a recognition test first before recall. Treadway and McCloskey (1989) failed to replicate the weapon-transfer phenomenon. It is not clear, however, whether Treadway and McCloskey's negative finding is evidence against the importance of ethnic stereotyping or an artifact of their methodology. In view of the limitations of slide presentation as a research method discussed above, there is undoubtedly a need to investigate racial stereotypes in eye-witness recall/recognition accuracy utilising a combination of different research methods.

Social psychologists have long established that if people know some key features of a person (for example, that they are 'warm-hearted' and 'honest' or 'ruthless and brutal') they tend to infer other physical and personality characteristics consistent with the limited original description (Hurwitz et al., 1975). Loftus (1979) identified four different types of expectations that can influence how we perceive and act: cultural expectations or stereotypes, expectations from past experience, personal prejudices and temporary expectations. Such expectations, of course, will impact more on people's perception and memory when they have got but a glimpse of a brief and complex incident or a face, and/or when the memory has become rather vague and there is perceived pressure to recall a complete image.

Physical Attractiveness: A good example of a popular stereotype is the general belief that 'what is beautiful is good'. Indeed, the available psychological literature shows that it does pay to be tall (Jackson and Ervin, 1992) and to be good-looking, when being judged by a stranger who does not know much about you (Felson, 1981). Researchers have reported that the more attractive someone's face is, the less severe the sentence given by mock jurors (Efran, 1974; Landy and Aronson, 1969; Sigall and Ostrove, 1975). But what is the impact of a person's physical attractiveness on witnesses' testimony? Attractive faces are better recognised than unattractive ones (Cross et al., 1971); male witnesses better remember details of a female's clothing if they have seen her wearing make-up than without (Kleck and Rubinstein, 1975); and, finally, subjects are more likely to remember later on details of a conversation they had with someone over the phone if that person has been described to them as attractive rather than unattractive. The apparent significance of physical appearance is not reflected in potential jurors' beliefs about what is an important determinant in eyewitness identification accuracy. Lindsay (1994a:372) reported that the accused's appearance was ranked as one of the least important variables – twenty-second out of twenty-five variables by potential jurors.

Whether the Witness is Also a Victim of the Crime: One of the very few roles in which crime victims are seen in a public place is as a witness to a crime in criminal trials (Rock, 1991). In his study of the treatment of victims and use of space in the Wood Green Crown Court in North London, Rock (1991) describes crime victim witnesses as 'an admixture of pariah and saint' (p. 278). Rock also found that a victim-witness' cross-examination often comes after lengthy and lonely periods of waiting around the courtroom precinct. Unlike the psychological laboratory, in real life a frequent key witness to a crime is the victim him/herself. If he/she happens to be a victim of a violent crime such as a robbery or rape or assault (see North et al., 1989, regarding short-term psycho-pathology of mass murder eyewitnesses) it is possible they will experience difficulty in accessing details of the incident because of their psychological state when being asked to describe or identify the suspect soon after the crime. On the other hand, however, it is also possible that a victim of crime is more motivated to focus on the criminal's face and to remember it well. While it has been found that recall for such witnesses becomes better with time (Bradley and Baddley, 1990), as far as the accuracy of victim-witnesses vs. witnesses-only is concerned, studies have reported conflicting findings. MacLeod's (1987) study of real-life witnesses found that bystanders gave less information about both events and appearance than did victims. One possible interpretation of MacLeod's results is that victims of crime get asked a lot more questions by police than is the case with bystanders, on the assumption that victims are in a better position to 'assist police with their enquiries'. However, it has been found that in the context of theft their respective levels of accuracy are not different (Hosch and Cooper, 1982; Hosch et al., 1984). Similar findings were reported by Farrington and Lambert (1993) in their study of burglary and violent offenders in Nottingham, England. Table 3.1 shows the highest degree of agreement between offender characteristics, as recorded by police when offenders were apprehended, and victim and witness descriptions.

Farrington and Lambert (1993) concluded that: 'it seems clear that reports by victims and witnesses about sex, ethnicity, age, height, build, hair colour, hair length and facial hair of offenders (at least) might usefully be included in an offender profiling system'. As Farrington and Lambert point out, when comparing the accuracy of victim and victim-witness descriptions of criminal suspects' characteristics it should be remembered that such comparisons are not possible for some types of crimes. For example, most burglaries take place when the victim is not

Table 3.1 Offender characteristics recalled by victims and witnesses

	Victim's Description (%)	Witness' Description (%)
Burglary		
Sex	98.0	99.0
Ethnicity	85.3	82.6
Age	31.3	22.8
Height	–	18.3
Build	–	33.3
Hair colour	–	34.9
Hair length	–	83.1
Violence		
Sex	90.2	88.3
Ethnicity	82.5	82.0
Age	14.3	14.8
Height	18.3	20.9
Build	22.1	23.0
Hair colour	29.4	30.5
Hair length	57.0	59.3
Facial hair	31.9	32.2
Accent	45.5	–
Facial feature	94.0	94.3

at home and some crimes are committed under circumstances where the only witness is the victim. Finally, whether the witness is a victim or a bystander is considered an important determinant (ranked seventh out of twenty-five) of eyewitness identification accuracy (Lindsay 1994a:372).

Confidence: According to McGuire (1985),[13] there are two components to credibility: trustworthiness and expertise. In addition to consistency in a witness' account (Stone, 1991), a witness' appearance and demeanour (for example, confidence) may influence the assessment of his/her credibility, the defendant's guilt and the severity of the sentence imposed (Efran, 1974; Kapardis, 1985). When it comes to ascribing credibility to an eyewitness his/her confidence 'is the most powerful single determinant' (Wells, 1985:58).

Regarding the relationship between witness confidence and accuracy, one would expect that a normal person who is more confident in the accuracy of what they are describing would, on average, be more accurate. As Williams et al. (1992:152) put it, people believe those who seem credible. In fact, available evidence suggests that mock/potential jurors rely heavily on eyewitness confidence to infer witness accuracy (see Cutler et al., 1988; Wells, 1984). As Leippe (1994:385) reminds us, many a jury has been persuaded by a confident eyewitness testifying before it. Furthermore, the US Supreme Court, rather amazingly, in *Neil v. Biggers* (1972) and *Manson v. Brethwaite* (432 US 98 (1976))[14] stated that eyewitness confidence is a significant indicator of witness accuracy. The claim by the US Supreme Court is of interest in view of conflicting findings reported regarding the relationship between witness' confidence and accuracy.[15] Eyewitness confidence accounted for less than 10 per cent of the variance in eyewitness identification accuracy in Wells and Murray's (1984) study. This is not surprising, perhaps, when we remember that it is decisions by police officers, magistrates, jurors, judges and other fact-finders about eyewitness testimony rather than testimony itself that can lead to wrongful convictions. Thus, a fact-finder ends up believing an inaccurate witness or doubts an accurate one (Leippe, 1994:385).

A number of reviews have concluded (but see Sporer et al., 1995, below) that, contrary to what some fact-finders would expect, there is no significant relationship between witness confidence and identification accuracy (Bothwell et al., 1987b; Leippe, 1980, 1994; Luus and Wells, 1994a, 1994b; Wells and Murray, 1984). Different explanations have been offered for this finding. Leippe (1980) suggested that the accuracy and confidence of witnesses could be controlled by different mechanisms; Bothwell et al. expressed the view that the better the encoding conditions the better the relationship between confidence and accuracy, while Wells and Murray (1984) attributed differences in the findings reported to differences in the methodologies used by the different researchers. More recently, Leippe (1994) has suggested that fact-finders' perceptions of witness credibility can be understood by utilising a witness communication-persuasion model. For Leippe, 'the witness, in essence, is an influence agent delivering what we might call a "memory message"' (p. 386) in an interactive context (p. 387). Thus, according to Leippe, how a fact-finder judges a memory message is influenced by: (a) the content and delivery of what the witness says; and (b) the fact-finder's own beliefs and preconceptions about eyewitnesses. Furthermore, the content and delivery style of the witness are, themselves, influenced by witnessing conditions, questioning factors and such attributes of the witness, such as his/her age. Williams et al. (1992) draw on 'cognitive dissonance' (that is, the social psychological explanation for a person wanting to maintain consistency with a view they have expressed publicly) to explain the role played by a witness' confidence in testimony. Williams et al. state that a witness' confidence in the accuracy of their recall increases as they repeat and repeat the same account to others; in other words: 'Confidence in memory is a social phenomenon, as well as a social issue, and as such, is subject to social influence' (p. 152). Pressure to be consistent would also be a strong factor operating in this context resulting, perhaps, in what Smith et al. (1989) refer to as the 'I was there so I should know' situation. Alas for magistrates, judges and juries, Brown et al. (1977) found that, with time, people who are confident of accurate memories are also confident of inaccurate memories. Furthermore, like mock jurors (Brigham and Bothwell, 1983), police officers, too, and lawyers (especially prosecution ones) have been found to share the belief that confidence and accuracy go hand in hand (Brigham and Wolfskiel, 1983). It would also appear that a witness who is confident in their testimony will insist on the accuracy of even specific details in his/her testimony – a factor that helps to convince jurors further (Bell and Loftus, 1988). In this context, Freedman et al. (1996) have reported that a more detailed statement by a witness has a significantly greater impact on judgements of guilt when the honesty of the witness is not an issue; if a witness' honesty is an issue the finding obtained only applies if the amount of detail in the statement is at an intermediate level.

Recently, a meta-analytic review by Sporer et al. (1995) of thirty studies using staged-event methods that included target-present and target-absent line-ups has cast serious doubt on the findings of earlier reviews that the confidence-accuracy relationship in eyewitness research is a weak one. Sporer et al. included choice as a moderator variable and found that: (a) in every study reviewed, the mean confidence level was higher for correct choosers (that is, witnesses making positive identifications) than for incorrect ones; and (b) that the confidence-accuracy relationship was reliably and consistently higher for choosers but was not so for non-choosers. On the basis of their literature review, Sporer et al. suggest that 'it might be advisable to video-tape the witness' statement and introduce the video-tape into evidence' (p. 324) in order to preserve it for juries and also allow the confidence expressed by a witness at the time of the identification decision to be scrutinised in cross-examination. Regarding the role of the expert witness in this context, the same authors suggest that 'the expert might emphasise that witness confidence should, in any event, be considered together with a number of other variables that can influence eyewitness performance' (p. 324).

Attempts to identify the conditions that impede or enhance the confidence-accuracy relationship have highlighted the importance of exposure time (Bothwell et al., 1987b) and the distinctiveness and unattractiveness of the target's face (Brigham, 1990) at the encoding stage 'as well as the witness' willingness to choose someone from the line-up they viewed'. Also, Kassin (1985) found that allowing witnesses to gain 'retrospective self-awareness' (that is, to view video-tapes of themselves identifying a suspect from a photospread before being asked to rate their confidence in their identifications) could improve the confidence-accuracy relationship. Luus and Wells (1994a, 1994b) have shown that not only is eyewitness confidence malleable but it is bidirectional. In their study witnesses observed a staged theft, made a photo-line-up identification and received different types of information regarding the alleged identification decision of their co-witnesses. It was found that witness confidence was inflated or deflated depending on whether they were informed their co-witness had identified the same person as themselves or not. Luus and Wells (1994a:355) have suggested that knowledge about the witness variable moderators relevant to the confidence-accuracy relationship could be conveyed in expert testimony and communicated to jurors, while findings pertinent to system variable moderators could be used to improve police procedures.

Given that fact-finders indeed believe in a witness confidence-accuracy relationship, it is important to identify the types of variables that are perceived as determinants of eyewitness accuracy. Lindsay (1994a:373) reported that the most important variables were related to the crime itself (illumination, duration); witness characteristics that would impact on encoding (whether the witness was a victim of the offence, stress, alcohol, whether he/she had paid attention to the crime or the offender; prior acquaintance with the offender); and, finally, variables that would influence the retrieval process (whether the offender had changed his/her appearance since the offence, time interval for identification). Lindsay also found that witness' confidence was rated as less important by respondents than illumination, exposure time, alcohol and stress but more important than the age, race and gender of the witness and the suspect. Lindsay then proceeded to test the importance of the variables identified as important determinants of eyewitness accuracy in a series of experiments with mock jurors in line-up identifications (see Chapter 10).

Konečni and Ebbesen (1992:419) have strongly criticised experimental simulation studies of the relationship between witness confidence and testimony accuracy. They maintain that such researchers 'have failed to design the experiments and analyse the results in a manner that takes into account the everyday function of the legal system'. Evidently, a simple fact ignored by such research is that the prosecution relies on witnesses who show high confidence that they can positively identify the perpetrator/s. Konečni and Ebbesen go further and argue that published claims by such researchers and the 'experts' litanies in court have potentially tilted the scale of justice toward unjustified acquittals by lowering the jurors' quite justified reliance on witness confidence' (p. 419). Konečni and Ebbesen's conclusion should be taken very seriously by psycholegal researchers who should reflect on what they research, how they research it, and what they do with their findings. Confidence is a complex construct that warrants a more sophisticated analysis than has been the case in a lot of the eyewitness research. Witness testimony confidence, of course, is but one factor that will contribute to the magistrate or jury or judge coming to regard a witness as credible. Other factors are: internal consistency of the testimony, its improbability, whether it is consistent with other facts already established and with circumstantial evidence.[16]

One of the aims of cross-examination for most lawyers is to discredit a key witness of the other party. One strategy that is routinely used is to try to show during cross-examination that a witness is *inconsistent* in what he/she remembers and the fact-finder should infer that the testimony is unreliable. Practising attorneys are probably not surprised to be told that experimental evidence confirms the effectiveness of this cross-examination strategy (Berman and Cutler, 1996; Berman et al., 1995). In some jurisdictions, in fact, a judge is required to make directions to the jury concerning a witness' prior inconsistent statements (*Davies v. R.* (1995) Supreme Court, South Australia, Crt Crim App, 8 September). Interestingly enough, however, Loftus (1974) reported that mock jurors were still influenced by the testimony of a '*discredited witness*' even when they were informed that the witness normally wore glasses and was not wearing them at the time of the incident. Later studies found that the impact of a discredited witness' testimony can be removed if, for example, the witness admits to poor eyesight and apologises for the testimony (Elliott et al., 1988; Havatny and Strack, 1980) and, finally, that the status of the discreditor is a relevant factor (Weinberg and Baron, 1982).

Whether the Eyewitness is a Police Officer: The well-known pioneer forensic psychologist, Münsterberg, himself a careful observer, testified under oath following a burglary at his house only to find his sworn detailed statements proven wrong by the police investigation! One of the skills which basic training at police academies and specialist training at detective training schools all over the world aims to develop is a sharp ability to observe and a good memory for details. Furthermore, many people will go along with the belief that because of their training and experience police are more accurate witnesses than civilians (Yarmey, 1986a). First of all, as far as memory capacity is concerned, police have been found to be similar to civilians in the amount of information they retain from their daily briefings, irrespective of whether the information is presented face-to-face or not (Bull and Reid, 1975). Bull and Reid also found some evidence that better recall of information was associated with greater length of service in the police. However, different findings were reported by Ainsworth (1981). In Ainsworth's study the subjects comprised: (a) police officers with an average of nine years' experience; (b) new police officers (averaging less than a year); and (c) a control group of members of the public. Subjects were shown a film in which a staged event took place including, for example, a car theft, a man loitering suspiciously outside a bank and traffic offences. No significant differences were found between the three groups of subjects regarding the number of offences detected and, with the exception of the traffic offences, the inexperienced officers exhibited the highest reporting and the experienced ones the lowest. Given the small and very likely unrepresentative groups of subjects in Ainsworth's study, his findings should be treated with caution. His findings, nevertheless, do not support the popular belief that police officers, because of their special training, are more vigilant in perceiving offences and suspicious circumstances (p. 235). The finding that young police officers focused on traffic offences at the expense of other offences could possibly be due to the fact that a lot of attention is paid to traffic offences early in police training in Britain and elsewhere and/or a wish on the part of the young constables to maximise their performance by focusing on an offence they perceive as easier to detect (p. 236). Finally, another interpretation of Ainsworth's (1981) findings could be in terms of police officers having been taught to exercise caution before recording a piece of behaviour as an offence. The need for further research in this area cannot be overemphasised.

It turns out that precisely because of their very training and experience police also develop a *mental* 'set' and are thus more predisposed to selectively perceive and interpret information about an event in such a way as to even impute and remember details of a criminal nature which, in fact, never existed. Verinis and Walker (1970) used ten black and white photographs, some of which depicted criminal details, such as a car parked in a back alley with a bent-up licence plate, or a parked car with a bag of tools on the back seat or a man walking around the corner of a building carrying a can of petrol. They showed the photographs to ten policemen and ten teachers. No significant differences were found between the two groups as far as immediate recall of details of the 'criminal' scenes was concerned. Marshall and Hinsen (1974)[17] showed police and civilian subjects a 42-second film in which a man approached a pram, pulled down its protective net and then walked off. As he was walking away, a woman appeared out of a house. It was found that while police remembered more details about the persons depicted, they also remembered twice as many incorrect facts (that is, non-existent details) than did the civilian subjects. A similar finding was reported by Tickner and Poulton (1975) who showed twenty-four police and 156 civilians a film lasting for 1, 2 or 4 hours. The film depicted several different events including 'criminal' ones. No significant differences were found between the two groups regarding recall of details about people and actions.

In an interesting study by Clifford and Richards (1977) police and civilians were asked to describe the appearance of a target who had walked up to them to ask the time (short duration, 15 seconds) or to ask for directions (long duration, 30 seconds). Using data from stationary police and civilians and from the subjects who really looked at the target, it was found that at short exposure there was no difference in the amount of target detail recalled by the two groups but the police recalled more such detail in the long exposure condition. On the basis of those findings Clifford and Bull (1978:191) stated that 'providing an irreducible minimum time for viewing was not prevented, police had processing skills which could be employed and which eventuated in better recall'.

A Canadian study by Thomassin and Michael (1990) had subjects view a staged non-violent event in a classroom. It was found that while police science students provided more physical and clothing descriptions than medical biology students they were not more accurate. Also, the former group made more mistakes in the visual identification and were more certain of their selections than the civilians. These results support Ainsworth's (1981) conclusion that: 'The claim that police officers are specially trained in the perception of offences and suspicious circumstances was not supported by the data ...' (p. 235). As far as race recognition is concerned, the study by Billig and Milner (1976) concluded that police officers are no exception to the finding that such recognition is poor, irrespective of whether they have worked in black neighbourhoods or not. Finally, researchers (see Verinis and Walker, 1970; Tickner and Poulton, 1975) have found that because of their training and experience police officers view events in predictably different ways from civilians. More specifically, they are prone to construe an event as criminal, as involving the commission of an offence, and thus to remember events and details that never existed.

Logie et al. (1992) compared the recognition accuracy of: (a) ten residential burglars in a remand centre with an average age of 16.1 years; (b) fourteen male police detectives (twelve constables, one sergeant and one inspector); and (c) ten highly educated law-abiding members of the public with a mean age of 39 years. They used photographs of houses, and subjects were given a surprise recognition test where, in some photographs, physical features had been changed. It was found that recognition memory was better for the group of burglars than for the police officers who, in turn, were better than the law-abiding members of the public. In a second experiment, Logie et al. compared nineteen male juvenile burglars with a mean age of 15 years 2 months with a control group of ten boys whose mean age was 14 years and who had been charged with a non-burglary offence. Both groups of boys were in a British, residential and day school for children with special educational needs. It was found that the juvenile burglars' recognition memory performance was significantly better than that of the other offenders. The Logie et al. findings point to burglary offenders possessing a level of expertise which is associated with their experience of offending. In view of the fact that police officers, like civilians, have poor knowledge of many important factors in eyewitness testimony (see Bennett and Gibling, 1989), the need for improvement in police training to address this important aspect of the work cannot be overemphasised.

In an interesting study by Stephenson et al. (1989) the recall performance of uniform police members, mainly constables, with at least three years' experience was compared with that of students. Stephenson et al. had subjects listen to a tape-recording of a script featuring a fictional interrogation by two police officers, one male and one female, of a woman who alleged she had been raped. Under free recall, individual police officers performed consistently worse than students. Police recall was much better than that of students when they were working in dyads or four-member groups (see also below) but they also produced more errors than did the students.

On the basis of the studies mentioned, the weight of the evidence indicates that police are: no more vigilant unless an event of short duration is involved; their recall is no more accurate than that of civilians and, in fact, they may make more errors of commission and feel very confident in their testimony nevertheless; their cross-race recognition accuracy is as poor as that of civilians, even when police officers have worked in black neighbourhoods; generally, their reliability as witnesses does not seem to improve with length of service and, finally, they are prone to put a criminal construction on events they witness and to even report events and details that never existed. Contrary to how the police are usually portrayed, their testimony is no more reliable than that of members of the public. Consequently, their credibility is unwarranted and they should not be regarded as 'experts' when testifying as witnesses in court. To make things worse for police officers, available evidence shows that, with the exception, perhaps, of recognition of faces of a different race, it is impossible to train adults to improve their face

recognition accuracy (Williams et al., 1992:147). This somewhat pessimistic picture for police eyewitnesses may, however, change in view of
the increasing involvement of psychologists in police training programs
and further field studies.

Number of Witnesses: Despite the fact that people witness a crime in a
social context, and often enough there is more than one witness who
is likely to talk about it with other witnesses, and/or talk to others about
it as well as answer questions by police personnel, very few studies
have concerned themselves with *collaborative testimony.* According to
Stephenson et al. (1989), in the UK: 'There're no legal rules forbidding
collaboration by police officers or anyone else ... The only rule is that if
you do collaborate, you should say so ... Collaborative testimony itself is
admissible, and indeed, one officer may give evidence on behalf of a
group of officers ...' (p. 324). Furthermore, 'There are important legal
issues raised by this practice' (p. 255). Stephenson et al. (1982) asked
dyads of subjects in Austria who listened to a story to recall details by
themselves or in dyads. The dyads were encouraged to discuss the story
and to agree on a single version. It was found that dyads produced more
correct answers than individuals, both immediately and one week later.
As far as errors are concerned, dyads had a strong tendency to produce
more implicational errors (that is, to go beyond the original but not to
contradict it) than did individuals (p. 257). Using a tape-recording of a
script of a police interrogation, Clark et al. (1986) replicated the finding
that dyads gave more correct answers than did individuals. Four-
member groups were found to have twice as many correct answers than
did individuals. In other words, a relationship was found between group
size and number of correct answers. However, Clark et al. also found
that groups of four subjects 'were virtually certain of the correctness of
their wrong answers' (p. 258).
    Stephenson et al. (1989) examined differences between police offi-
cers and students as a function of group size (individual, two-person,
four-person) and reported the following: in responding to a questionnaire, individual policemen, police in dyads and four-person groups
answered more questions correctly than did students; policemen in
dyads and four-person groups did better than students under free
recall and, finally, police dyads were almost twice as productive as
individual policemen (p. 261). Stephenson et al. interpreted their
findings as indicating that police respond more to the stimulus of the
group (p. 262). It is interesting to also note in this context that
Stephenson et al. (1989) also found confidence (for the wrong reasons)
increased with group size, while in an earlier study (Stephenson et al.,
1986a) it was reported that when there is disagreement between

individuals, the more confident member of a dyad normally prevails. Stephenson et (1989:265) suggested, therefore, that there may be some merit in individuals attempting to recall tasks prior to discussion and decision.

In the light of their findings, Stephenson et al. (1989:268) concluded the following about the practice of admitting collaborative evidence: (a) potentially useful information is excluded by groups; (b) group remembering is selective remembering; and (c) the practice of permitting one police officer to represent a group is a dubious one.

In the same vein, Stephenson et al. (1991) also warn that a group of individuals who have a vested interested in what they remember (for example, two police officers remembering details of an assault in which they themselves were the victims) may be motivated to fill any gaps in their recall by inferring some of the details and, also, to testify falsely about the incident, appearing very confident in court. These concerns take on greater significance when we remember that there is no precedent for the cross-examination of a group (p. 269). Other studies, however, have yielded results that are different to those reported by Stephenson and his co-workers.

On the basis of their evaluation of the existing literature dealing with the question of whether 'two heads are better than one' (that is, the social facilitation of memory hypothesis, see Edwards and Middleton, 1986), Meudel et al. (1992) maintain that those studies that have taken information-pooling into account (Hinsz, 1990; Stephenson et al., 1986a, 1986b) have found that group recall is either at or below the level that such pooling would predict; in other words, that groups do not outperform the pooled contributions of their constituent members (p. 526). Meudel et al. could find no evidence whatsoever that dyads of subjects generate new information that was not available to either member of the pair, that is, they could find no support for the social facilitation of the memory hypothesis.

Underwood and Milton (1993) showed student subjects a video of a two-car collision at an intersection. They used a questionnaire to test subjects' recall individually or in groups of three after 1 hour. Groups of subjects were encouraged to talk to each other during the showing of the film and in the period immediately after the accident before being questioned. They found no overall differences between the recall accuracy of individual and group witnesses. However, when expecting to see a collision, the group witnesses were more accurate than the individuals. Thus, Underwood and Milton's study provides partial support for the social facilitation of memory. However, unlike Meudel et al. (1992), Underwood and Milton did not compare the recall of individuals and groups taking information-pooling into account – an omission that detracts from their findings. In view of differences in the subjects, materials and measures used in Stephenson et al. (1989), in Underwood and Milton (1993) and Meudel et al. (1992) studies, the jury is still out on whether two heads are better than one in eyewitness testimony. Collaborative testimony does, of course, warrant more attention than it has enjoyed by psycholegal researchers.

2 Perpetrator Variables

Despite the fact that we often make judgements about other people not just on the basis of what their faces look like (Lerner and Korn, 1972), very limited attention has been given to 'the role of non-facial information such as body shape, dimension and movement in person perception and recognition' (MacLeod et al., 1994:125). In demonstrating the relevance of whole body information to eyewitnesses MacLeod et al. cite a study by Barclay et al. (1978) which found that subjects can accurately identify the *gender* of targets just by means of a moving light on each ankle. MacLeod et al. reported that when they asked subjects whether two people in a film were of similar or different *body size* subjects were significantly more likely to perceive an ambiguous shove by the perpetrator as aggressive or violent if the perpetrator was perceived to have been large and the victim small (p. 128). It is worth noting in this context that witnesses' estimates of an offender's size can be influenced by post-event information. Christiansen et al. (1983)[18] showed that telling subjects that a male person they had encountered earlier on was a truck driver gave heavier weight estimates than when he was described as a dancer.

As far as the *height* of perpetrators is concerned, Flin and Shepherd (1986) identified a tendency by members of the public to underestimate the height of a male person who had earlier on asked them for directions in a busy city centre. Furthermore, it was also found that the subjects' degree of inaccuracy in estimating height was related to their own height, with shorter ones being the more likely to underestimate. The *ethnicity* of both the witness and the perpetrator has been shown to be an important factor in estimating someone's height. Chen and Geiselman (1993) reported that Caucasian and Asian subjects recalled an Asian perpetrator as being shorter than a Caucasian one, despite the fact they were both of exactly the same height. Caucasian, Hispanic and Asian subjects in Lee and Geiselman's (1994) study first saw a photo of an Hispanic, Caucasian or Asian male (all of the same height, 1.71 m) and then watched a 40-second video-tape of a robbery featuring the same male as the perpetrator. Subjects were tested in groups of one to five immediately after viewing the video-tape. It was found that the

Caucasian, who was shorter than the normative height for Caucasians (1.73 m), was recalled as being taller than his actual height. Pooling the results from Chen and Geiselman (1993) and Lee and Geiselman (1994), it appeared that perpetrators from different ethnic groups who differ from their own ethnic height are likely to be remembered by witnesses as being more consistent with their normative ethnic height than their actual height.

It is sometimes the case that a witness sees a perpetrator's back and *gait* as he/she is leaving the scene of a crime. There is some limited evidence that people can accurately: (a) distinguish the two genders; and (b) identify individuals known to them on the basis of gait (Cutting and Proffitt, 1981). Alas, as far as it has been possible to ascertain, there has been no research into the accuracy of identifying strangers viewed by their gait. According to MacLeod et al. (1994), 'one's own physical characteristics can affect judgements about the height and weight of other individuals' and people use their own body measurements 'as norms, or anchors, against which relative judgements are made' (p. 129). On the basis of their work on descriptors, scales people use to describe body features of static (for example, height, build/weight, and torso) and moving individuals (for example, smoothness of gait, pace and length of stride), MacLeod et al. advocate utilising whole body information in computer searches for suspects during criminal investigations. There is no doubt that psychologists should pay more attention to witness identification accuracy for perpetrator appearance in general, rather than just for facial features. Furthermore, such research should aim to identify interaction effects between characteristics of the event, the eyewitness, the perpetrator and the questioning by police. Only then will psychologists be able to provide a holistic picture of eyewitness testimony from the forensic point of view.

3 Interrogational Variables

Being unable to access and retrieve information stored in our memory is a common experience and underpins a lot of forgetting (Tulving, 1974, 1983). We have seen already that recall accuracy of an event or a face is associated with a number of event, witness and perpetrator factors. The report of a witness' memory can be modified during the retrieval stage by such factors as mode of recall, the context in which retrieval takes place, how questions are worded and pressure on the witness to remember. In other words, inaccuracy can be introduced into eyewitness evidence by police and court procedures used to elicit such testimony.

Retention Interval: Memory issues arise in the law in a variety of contexts. In fact, the law's assumptions about memory impact, for example, on statutes of limitations, are implicit in the procedures governing the jury's function (Johnson, 1993:604–5). Thus, in the case of civil actions for childhood sexual abuse in the US: 'Many courts and state legislatures have recently recognised an exception to the traditional statute of limitations ...' (p. 604; see Hagen, 1991; Kanovitz, 1992). In most cases, witnesses to a crime will be asked to describe what they saw happen some time after an incident. This is known as retention interval. In real life this delay can range from a few minutes to a few months and even years. To illustrate, in the late 1980s a Jerusalem court tried, convicted and sentenced to death as a Nazi war criminal John Denmjanjuk, then an American citizen who had been deported to Israel to face trial as 'Ivan the Terrible', the camp guard at Treblinka concentration camp, who was responsible for the extermination of 850 000 Jews there in the second world war. The defendant protested his innocence but to no avail. To the embarrassment of both the Israeli and US governments he was released when access to wartime archives following the collapse of the Soviet government established the true identity of the real 'Ivan the Terrible'. The court believed nine elderly witnesses, not the expert testimony for the defence by Professor Willem Wagenaar of Leiden University in the Netherlands (see Wagenaar, 1988; Cutler and Fisher, 1993). It is comfortable to know, therefore, that the time interval (delay) between crime and identification was considered by the potential jurors in Lindsay's (1994a:372) questionnaire survey to be the most important determinant of eyewitness identification accuracy.

In a recent study (in preparation) by the present author of a large number of actual victims/witnesses interviewed by specialist police personnel in Melbourne, it was found that over half (52 per cent) of the witnesses were interviewed more than three days after the offence had been committed; in fact, 37 per cent of them were not interviewed until five to six days after the commission of the crime. During the intervening period their memory of the event would generally deteriorate as a result of inevitable, normal forgetting as well as interference (see below). It is well established in psychology that recall and recognition accuracy declines through function of time (Hunter, 1968; Thomson, 1984; Shapiro and Penrod, 1986). Recall and recognition is at its best immediately after encoding information, but both decline, rapidly at first and then gradually. This means that often the original statements of witnesses are a great deal more accurate than what they remember months, or sometimes even years, later at the trial. Face recognition and person identification, however, in an identification parade (see below) has been found to be more resistant to the adverse effects of delay in recall (Deffenbacher, 1989; Ellis, 1984; Loftus, 1979; Shepherd et al., 1982). This does not mean, however, that long delays in recall are justified because long delays significantly increase the likelihood of post-event memory interference (see below) as well as distortion and mis-identification. Therefore, in order to enhance witnesses' accuracy, police would be well advised to obtain a witness' description of a suspect's unfamiliar face as soon as possible.

As the criminal law stands in common law countries, the basic evidence is what witnesses tell the magistrate, judge or jury during the trial months, or even years later in some cases. If a witness' present testimony is inconsistent with statements he/she made to the police earlier the lawyer for the other side will refer to these inconsistencies in cross-examination in order to discredit the witness. Despite the fact that 'The alteration of recollection appears to be a fact of life' (Williams et al., 1992:149), the basic legal position and practice seriously under-mines the credibility of the processes by which relevant facts that are in dispute in a trial are established. Stuesser (1992) has advocated reform-ing the law (in Canada) so as to leave a discretion with the trial judge to admit prior inconsistent statements for their truth, where the statements are seen to be both reliable and necessary. The main reason for allowing prior inconsistent statements to go in for their truth is that the person who has made the statements is in court and can be examined. Adopting a practice of admitting the original statement as the primary evidence has also been advocated by Thomson (1984:111) in Australia on the grounds that evidence can only be useful if it is accurate and by admitting the original account as the primary evidence will also prevent a dishonest witness from making up a story.

Type of Recall: A witness may be asked to tell everything they saw hap-pening during an incident in their own words and at their own pace. This is known as 'free recall' and it would be normal police practice to follow it with cued, 'interrogative' recall. According to Hollin (1989) the distinction between '*free*' and '*interrogative*' recall was made by Binet (1900). Experiencing difficulty in remembering a witness may well hesitate. Rather unwisely, police investigators may encourage a hesitant witness to 'have a guess' in furnishing a physical description of the suspect, for example, or in picking him/her out from a photospread, an identification parade or in a 'show-up' (see Chapter 10). Such encouragement has been shown to have an adverse effect on accuracy later on.

Psychologists have known for a long time that, generally speaking, an interrogative recall produces a greater range of information (that is, it is more complete) than free recall, but it is less accurate. In contrast to what early researchers (for example, Binet, 1900; Gardner, 1933; Stern, 1939; Whipple, 1909) reported, the picture for the effect of mode of recall on testimony is more complex; interrogative, structured questions can lead to more complete recall but also produce more inaccuracy when asking a witness about difficult items of information (see Clifford and Scott, 1978). In other words, from the point of view of law-enforcement personnel, testimony accuracy and completeness are directly related to how specific a question is as well as how difficult is the information being asked of the witness. Police investigators, therefore, need to be aware of the trade-off here.

Number of Efforts Made to Recall: First-hand knowledge of how crime victims/witnesses are processed by police personnel leaves no doubt that it would be most unusual for a witness to be asked only once to recall details of the offender's face or of an incident. Repeatedly recalling stories was an issue that attracted the attention of Bartlett (1932), and its significance was noted by Penrod et al. (1982), for example, but the number of studies devoted to it are few in number (for example, Dunning and Stern, 1992; Jobe et al., 1993; Scrivner and Safer, 1988). Both laboratory and survey studies have found that amount of cognitive effort influences the quality of recall (Jobe et al., 1993:573). Hypermnesia, first observed by Ballard (1913),[19] is a phenomenon of improved memory performance with repeated testing. In fact, one of the recommendations of the architects of the cognitive interview technique (see Fisher and Geiselman, 1992) that enhances eyewitness accuracy is to solicit multiple recalls from witnesses in order to increase the amount of information provided (see below). Payne (1987) suggested that 'hypermnesia' be used to refer to increases in net recall in successive trials and 'reminiscence' as referring to gains in gross recall.

As would have been expected on the basis of the literature on the usefulness of the cognitive interview, in a series of experiments Turtle and Yuille (1994) obtained evidence supporting the reminiscence notion, that 'multiple eyewitness recalls can be beneficial in terms of overall recall without a severe increase in errors' (p. 268). As for how hypermnesia and reminiscence occur, Turtle and Yuille (1994:261) accept a process, put forward by Estes (1955), as stimulus sampling, that is, as witnesses repeatedly attempt to access their memory they obtain different samples from a population of potential information about the trace in question. Like Turtle and Yuille (1994), Otani and Hodge (1991) found no support for hypermnesia in two forced-choice recognition experiments. Otani and Hodge, however, found support for hypermnesia in two cued recall experiments and explain their findings in terms of relational processing that increases the availability of retrieval cues and thus aids recall of target words (see Hunt and Einstein, 1981). Turtle and Yuille (1994) remind us that while repeated recall may well produce more accurate information for the police investigation, any inconsistencies between successive accounts by the witness will be useful ammunition for the lawyers in court to discredit such a witness. This concern, they point out, will be counterbalanced by the fact that repeated recall will yield more facts about the case and, also, that 'a unified position on how it is affected by multiple-retrieval attempts should make people aware that gaining and losing details on successive recall is typical of how memory works' (p. 269).

Post-Event Interference: It is common police practice to ask witnesses to a crime for a verbal description of the suspect/s, to assist in making a photofit or an artist's impression with or without the aid of a computer, and to also ask witnesses to take a look at photographs of known offenders and try and identify the suspect they have seen. In addition, police may later ask a witness to identify the suspect in an identification parade/line-up (see Chapter 10). It is interesting to note in this context that the Devlin Committee (1976) examined all line-ups in England and Wales in 1973 and they found that 347 cases were prosecuted when the only evidence was identification by one or more eyewitnesses. Three-quarters of the accused were convicted. The significant impact of eyewitness testimony on findings of guilt is also documented by experimental studies (see Loftus, 1974; Wells et al., 1979). In asking witnesses questions the police may inadvertently contaminate their memory.

A very popular paradigm for eyewitness testimony researchers during the last two decades has been the use of the 'misinformation' paradigm to study how and when information encountered after an event contaminates a witness' memory and makes it unreliable. The considerable interest in the misinformation effect is evident by studies[20] in the US (for example, Belli, 1989; Metcalfe, 1990), in Australia (Sheehan, 1989), in Germany (Köhnken and Brockman, 1987) and in Holland (Wegener and Boer, 1987). In such studies, planting misinformation on subjects has been found to lead to misrecall, a witness remembering a car as being of a different colour, a 'give-way' sign as a 'stop' sign, seeing broken glass and even a barn never seen (Williams et al., 1992:149). Similarly, as a result of misinformation, a man with a moustache, straight hair, a can of Coca-Cola and breakfast cereal were recalled as clean shaven, curly hair, a can of peanuts and eggs respectively (Hoffman et al., 1992:293). There is disagreement amongst cognitive psychologists whether the later information causes an irrevocable alteration of the original memory, or whether the original memory is retrievable under appropriate circumstances (see below). There is, however, consensus among researchers that memory can be contaminated by means of leading questions.

Leading Questions: During a trial a lawyer is generally not allowed to ask leading questions either in examination-in-chief or in cross-examination, that is, questions suggesting how a lawyer wishes a witness to answer them (Waight and Williams, 1995:251). Practising lawyers might be interested to know that, from a psychologist's point of view, asking a witness a question is analogous to an experimental treatment situation and the type of question and manner of asking it impacts on the answer given (Lilli, 1989:223–4).

A very common method of contaminating someone's memory of an event (that is, introducing errors) is to ask them a leading question containing an item of information that never existed in the original incident. In a study by Loftus and Palmer (1974) subjects viewed a film of a car accident and were asked to estimate the speed of the car at the moment of impact. It was found that estimates of speed varied as a function of the verb used to describe the accident. Asking subjects how fast the cars were travelling when they 'contacted' one another as opposed to when they 'smashed' into each other yielded speed estimates of 31.8 mph and 40.8 mph respectively. Furthermore, when subjects were later asked to describe the accident it was found that those exposed to the 'smash' condition were more likely to report having seen broken glass at the scene of the accident when, in fact, none existed. It is now well established that subjects exposed to misleading post-event information are likely to report such information on subsequent memory tasks and to do so confidently (see Holst and Pozdek, 1991; Lindsay, 1994b; Loftus et al., 1978; Loftus et al., 1989; Weingardt et al., 1994). Loftus et al. (1978) found that greatest post-event contamination/misinformation effect occurs when the misleading information is introduced following a long delay after acquisition and before recall. Dristas and Hamilton (1977)[21] reported that post-event information interferes more easily with peripheral, rather than central, features of one's memory of an incident. The available literature leaves no doubt that asking a witness questions can influence their memory of an event. Loftus and Zanni (1975) reported that the presence of the indefinite article ('a') instead of the definite article ('the') gives rise to different expectations about the existence of an object. Using 'the' significantly increases the percentage of subjects who say they saw something that was not present in a film.

The literature on post-event misinformation has given rise to an ongoing controversy regarding whether the new information changes the original memory – the '*integration*' view (see Loftus and Ketcham, 1983) – or whether the effects found by Loftus are attributable to the processes used rather than to permanent changes in memory (see McCloskey and Zaragoza, 1985; Zaragoza and Koshmider, 1989: Zaragoza et al., 1987). Zaragoza and Koshmider (1989) have argued that misinformation-based responses do not necessarily mean that the witnesses actually believe the details concerned happened in the original event; that subjects' responses are indicative of 'demand characteristics'. McCloskey and Zaragoza (1985), in fact, believe that memory for an original incident is not impaired by post-event contamination and advocate the 'coexistence' theory, that is, that the original memory could become accessible under appropriate circumstances at retrieval.

Bonto and Payne (1991) examined the effect of varying the context of presentation of the original event and the post-event information and found it did not have an effect on subjects' performance. The robustness of the misinformation effect has been further reinforced by Weingardt et al.'s (1994) study which found that even when subjects were instructed to exclude suggested items from their recall lists they continued to include them. This finding led them to conclude that 'Witnesses can exhibit strong beliefs in their memories, even when those memories are verifiably false' (p. 25). Lindsay and Johnson's (1987) own work in this area has produced results that are consistent with Loftus and her associates. Lindsay and Johnson (1987) and Lindsay, D. S. (1994), however, proposed that a satisfactory explanation for the misinformation effect lies in what they term '*source misattribution*' by witnesses in terms of their source monitoring processes, that is, that although the original event and the post-event information may exist in the memory, misled subjects may experience confusion as far as sources of the two types of information is concerned.

Watkins (1990) has suggested that cognitive psychology may not be able to resolve the question of whether misleading post-event information does, in fact, alter memory traces or simply makes them less likely to be retrieved. It is unlikely this fierce debate between the '*integration*' and '*coexistence*' view of post-event influences on memory will be resolved in the very near future. It is, therefore, worth remembering that both sides to the dispute are in agreement that post-event misleading information can have a significant effect on what a witness remembers and the accuracy of his/her testimony. Finally, available research indicates that post-event contamination by interviewing police officers is more likely when a witness believes the police know exactly what happened (Smith and Ellsworth, 1987). This finding is of particular importance when it is remembered that both developmentally handicapped and mentally disordered witnesses are particularly vulnerable to the misinformation effect (Gudjonsson, 1995; Perlman et al., 1994).

4 Repressed or False-Memory Syndrome?

Until the early 1980s reports of abuse, especially sexual abuse, said to have taken place many years earlier in childhood and not reported for years were rare indeed. Since then, however, such reports have become increasingly more common. Therapists use a diversity of alternatives to 'assist' their clients to 'recover' their allegedly repressed memories including: Eye Movement Desensitisation and Reprocessing (EMDR), age regression, psychodrama, visualisation, guided imagery, body work, art therapy, group therapy, dream interpretation, having the client read popular books on the subject, and various drugs.

The following case from Western Australia, cited by Freckelton (1996), illustrates the use of a series of psychotherapeutic interventions in repressed memory syndrome. In the *Bunbury case* (*R. v. Jumeaux* (unreported, Supreme Court, WA, 23 September 1994)), claiming their memories had been repressed, two daughters made sixty-five allegations of sexual abuse against their father. Daughter A underwent psychotherapy after her depression had not responded to antidepressants. Earlier on she had described uncomfortable feelings after recovering from an anaesthetic. During psychotherapy she experienced 'abreaction', that is, a free expression or release of an emotion that has been repressed. She also later had flashbacks of abuse, both in and outside therapy. While daughter A was undergoing psychotherapy, her sister sought the help of a medical doctor out of concern that her own memories of sexual abuse might have been repressed. She came to 'recover' memories of such abuse after being hypnotised a number of times and seeing two medical practitioners. At the trial a number of experts testified on the topic of repressed memory syndrome. Justice Seaman stated that, 'evidence based upon memories by various forms of counselling and psychotherapy have similar inherent dangers; namely, the production of false evidence by means of suggestion' (cited in this context by Abadee J. in *Tillott v. The Queen* (unreported, Crt Crim App, NSW, 1 September 1995, cited by Freckelton, 1996)).

Given cognitive psychologists' belief in the malleability and suggestibility of memory, it comes as no surprise to be told they have been at loggerheads with psychotherapists over the issue of *recovered memories of childhood sexual abuse* (see Thomson, 1995b, and Freckelton, 1996, for a discussion of the false memory syndrome). Whilst not disputing that child sexual abuse exists and is serious, Read and Lindsay (1994:430) have argued that 'memory recovery therapy, like ECT in the 1940s, is being used too often, too indiscriminately, with overly large "doses", and with insufficient safeguards for the well-being of clients, and that it has consequently harmed some of the people it was intended to help'. The concern expressed by some cognitive psychologists is that memory recovery therapies may lead clients of psychotherapy to, in fact, create illusory memories and that there exists a high rate of false diagnosis of child sexual abuse (Ceci and Loftus, 1994; Loftus, 1993; Lindsay and Read, 1994; Read and Lindsay, 1994; Slovenko, 1993). As already mentioned, concern about recovered memories of abuse has been expressed by the judiciary in Australia (see, also, *R. v. Thorne* (unreported, Crt Crim App, Victoria, 19 June 1995)). According to Freckelton (1996), the same concern has also been voiced in judicial judgements in the US (see *New Hampshire v. Hungerford and Morahan* (unreported, Superior Court, New Hampshire, Hillsborough County, 23 May 1995) and in Canada (see *R. v. Norman* (1993) 87 CCC (3d) at 168–9). At the time of writing, however: 'The admissibility of expert evidence about repressed memory syndrome and false memory syndrome remains to be authoritatively determined throughout common law jurisdictions' (Freckelton, 1996:122), and 'Repressed memory syndrome could not at this stage qualify as reliable under the [US] *Daubert* test of falsifiability, the test that governs the admissibility of scientific evidence generally under the United States Federal Rules of Evidence' (p. 29). Rather concerned that false memories of childhood sexual abuse may be falsely implanted or encouraged by mental health professionals without regard for their accuracy, Slovenko (1993) has argued the need for corroborating evidence of abuse in order to justify the application of the discovery rule in such cases in the US. For its part, the Australian Psychological Society (1995) in its *Guidelines Relating to the Reporting of Recovered Memories* exhorts psychologists to exercise 'special care' in dealing with allegations of past abuse (see also American Psychiatric Association, 1993, *Statement on Memories of Sexual Abuse*). As shown in the next chapter, it is well established in the empirical psychological literature that memory for early childhood events is poor. Furthermore, as Thomson (1995b:200) reminds us, 'There is an inherent difficulty in any study that attempts to examine childhood memories'.

Lindsay and Read (1994:294–8) and Loftus (1993:525–6) attribute the alleged high rate of false diagnosis to both popular publications on child sexual abuse (for example, *The Courage to Heal* by Bass and Davis, 1988) and poorly trained therapists who unintentionally, perhaps, suggest to their clients that they must have been sexually abused as children on the basis of insufficient evidence, leading: (a) to numerous legal cases on both sides of the Atlantic involving allegations of child sexual abuse (in the main, incest) by men and women in the wake of memory recovery therapy (see Bulkley and Horowitz, 1994; Wakefield and Underwager, 1992); and (b) to legal reforms permitting plaintiffs to sue for recovery of damages for injury suffered as a result of child sexual abuse within a period (up to three years in Washington, for example) of the time they remembered the abuse (see Sales et al., 1994, regarding the admissibility of child sexual abuse memories in the US) and to even bring criminal charges against their alleged abusers many years later (see Loftus, 1993:520–1). Such critics of memory recovery therapies point to the evidence for suggestibility of memory, and suggest that not only is repression a rare phenomenon (Read and Lindsay, 1994:418) but it also lacks scientific support (Loftus, 1993:519) and is therefore problematical as an explanation for recovered memories (Thomson, 1995b:101). It has also been argued that there is no conspicuous syndrome of child sexual abuse (Ceci and Loftus, 1994:354) and that memory recovery therapists make very questionable assumptions about the human memory (for example, that people can remember events in their childhood that took place before the age of 5, despite the evidence for 'infantile amnesia' – see Fivush and Hamond, 1990) that are not consistent with the weight of the empirical evidence provided by cognitive psychologists (Lindsay and Read, 1994:284, 286). In the light of the various arguments against repression as an explanation for recovered memories of abuse, Thomson (1995b) has argued that an explanation of such memories in terms of 'suppression' (that is, when someone chooses not to report a particular event they are aware of and remember it for one reason or another) is more convincing than repression (p. 202).

Undoubtedly, a major criticism that has been levelled against memory recovery therapists is that they are subject to 'confirmatory bias' (that is, that they tend to search for evidence that confirms rather than disconfirms their own hunches) and, thus, lead their client's memory with suggestions about childhood sexual abuse (Loftus, 1993:530). Research in Australia by Thomson (1995b) has also found that such therapists' own expectations of what may have happened affects the types of questions they ask which, in turn, influence what the interviewee reports of the original event. In other words, 'people's memory of a particular event can be shaped in more subtle ways via direct suggestions' (p. 104). Finally, Thomson (1995b) found there is no scientific evidence that memory recovery therapy is effective. Accepting these arguments casts serious doubt on a range of legal changes introduced, perhaps prematurely, to facilitate criminal and civil action against the alleged abusers (Wakefield and Underwager, 1992).

A number of authors, however, have defended memory recovery therapists against the onslaught by the cognitive psychologists. Berliner and Williams (1994) point out that the polarised debate is really a dispute between academic researchers and clinicians, with each group pursuing their different goals (pp. 384–5), and argue that Lindsay and Read (1994) exaggerate the significance of a few studies, claiming to have produced false reports (p. 380), charge them with selective use and evaluation of studies (p. 381) and maintain that: 'While there is evidence based on laboratory studies for the fallibility of memory, suggestibility and inaccuracy, it has not been proven that full-blown memories for traumatic childhood experiences can be created from nothing' (p. 385). Berliner and Williams suggest that if cognitive psychologists spent more time investigating the effects of trauma on memory as well as alerting us to the dangers of some clinical practices, the debate would be less polarised (pp. 385–6). Redzek (1994), in her comment on the Lindsay and Read (1994) article, in the same special issue of *Applied Cognitive Psychology*, also disputes some of their claims and, in an attempt 'to generate more light than heat', proposes recasting the real vs. illusory memory debate by replacing the 'all true vs. all false' approach with a Signal Detection Model that distinguishes the signal (true memory) from the noise (illusory memory). In their rejoinder to the commentaries by Berliner and Williams (1994) and Redzek (1994), Read and Lindsay (1994) defend the claims they make about memory recovery therapists, make the point that a minority of such therapists (who use highly suggestive techniques and are in need of some retraining and education by cognitive psychologists) contribute a disproportionate number of 'tragic false alarms' but concede that 'some cases of inaccurate delayed accusations might be better characterised as involving false beliefs rather than illusory memories. The reason this is important is that it is probably much easier to induce false beliefs than it is to induce full blown illusory memories' (p. 429). On the basis of there being 250 000 therapists in the US, 10 per cent of whom, with caseloads of twenty clients per year, use highly suggestive techniques that are applied to non-abused patients 10 per cent of the time and create illusory beliefs and memories of child abuse in only 10 per cent of such cases, Read and Lindsay (1994:416) estimate 5000 cases of false alarms a year, that is, a rate of one per 100 recovery therapy clients 'treated' by such memory recovery therapists.

At the basis of the controversy surrounding recovered memories of child sexual abuse are two contrasting schools of thought. On the one hand, there are those who are prepared to rely on assumptions, to infer internal psychological states and mental processes even though they lack scientific support. The psychotherapists who identify with this school of thought tend to accept without question what clients tell them and/or to encourage such 'revelations' by means of suggestive questioning (Wakefield and Underwager, 1992:503). On the other hand, there are those cognitive psychologists who are concerned about the claims being made by therapists regarding recovered memories of child sexual abuse because they espouse a constructive model of human memory, in the Bartlett (1932) tradition. The fact is, of course, that, as seen earlier in this chapter, there are competing models of memory and the constructionist cognitive psychologists' case is not as convincing as is presented (see Davies, 1993a). The constructionist camp, however, can point to some hard evidence supporting their model of memory and thus justify their concern to some extent and the ringing of alarm bells in the first place about the innocent individuals whose lives are destroyed as a result of accepting what therapists claim. The legal system has been shown to be an ineffective answer to a broad range of societal problems, ranging from alcohol abuse, violence (both domestic and public) and criminal behaviour in general. Finally, there is a crucial sociolegal question about the whole issue: how valid is the assumption that adults claiming to have recovered memories of childhood abuse stand to benefit more by taking legal action, civil and/or criminal instead of resolving their psychological harms in therapy? Bulkley and Horowitz (1994) pose this very question and, after a lot of serious discussion of the arguments for and against, conclude the answer is a cautious negative one.

Following the excessive claims made for memory recovery therapy in the 1980s, Read and Lindsay (1994) provided a well-argued, well-intended and timely reminder to psychotherapists to at least be careful with their use of techniques to help their clients recover suspected memories of childhood sexual abuse (pp. 430–1). As a step in the right direction, Ceci and Loftus (1994) suggest that in attending to the needs of true abuse survivors, therapists need to be very conscious of the dangers of suggestive questioning and that failure to do so results in false alarms that cast doubt on the therapists themselves and undermine sympathy for the unfortunate victims of childhood abuse (p. 362). Meanwhile, 'Because there is no clear way of discriminating between authentic and fabricated memories' (Thomson, 1995b:104), there is an urgent need to subject the various techniques used by proponents of recover memory therapy to procedural safeguards or guidelines as have been adopted, for example, for the use of hypnosis in the *Evidence Code of California* (Freckelton, 1996). In addition, the need for research into how best to discriminate between accurate and illusory memories cannot be overemphasised (Raskin and Esplin, 1991). For therapists, it may be a consolation to know that they can pay and attend workshops advertised as providing adequate knowledge and skills in how best to handle memories-of-abuse cases and so minimise their risk of legal liability, against the backdrop of guidelines issued by their psychological society, for example. Finally, in some jurisdictions like Victoria, Australia, those victims, whose allegations were believed by juries not warned of the difficulty faced by the accused in proving innocence on uncorroborated dated sexual abuse charges based on 'recovered' memories of sexual abuse, can keep the money awarded them as compensation for their injuries despite the fact that the accused is subsequently acquitted (Arndt, 1995).

Meanwhile, the optimistic student of legal psychology can take comfort in the fact that in psychology, as in other disciplines, often knowledge is advanced through three stages (Watkins, 1993:309): (a) *thesis* (that is, when a finding such as recovered memories of childhood sexual abuse is made in the context of therapy – and there is a spate of studies reported, books published, etc. supporting the basic finding); (b) *antithesis* (that is, when the earlier reports are challenged by methodologically more robust studies of suggestive questioning); and (c) *synthesis*, when researchers proceed to resolve the issue by somehow integrating valuable knowledge generated during the thesis and antithesis stages. The synthesis stage in dealing with recovered memories of childhood sexual abuse will involve researchers finding 'ways of distinguishing verifiable from fantasized or contaminated memories' (Watkins, 1993:310), undoubtedly a tall order indeed.

5 Interviewing Eyewitnesses Effectively

Interviewing crime victims/witnesses is a crucial part of evidence gathering in law enforcement investigations. It is essential, therefore, that when various professionals interview witnesses they obtain the maximum accurate recall but without contaminating the recollection of the witness. Both the *Cognitive Interview* technique and *forensic hypnosis* are two aids to recall that have attracted a lot of researchers' attention.

5.1 Cognitive Interview

Until recently, however, a police officer was expected to learn interviewing skills 'on the job'. The availability, therefore, of an effective technique for interviewing witnesses can only assist police and other investigators. Such a procedure now exists, is known as the *Cognitive Interview* (CI) technique, and has been adopted by police forces on both sides of the Atlantic, on continental Europe and in Australia, as well by other professionals whose work brings them into contact with children, like social workers. The CI has been largely the work of American psychology professors Fisher and Geiselman (see Fisher and Geiselman, 1992; Geiselman et al., 1984). They have utilised four principles derived from the empirical literature on information retrieval (Bower, 1967; Tulving, 1974) which increase recall accuracy without increasing the amount of inaccurate information remembered. According to Geiselman et al. (1984), the four principles (mnemonic aids) are: (a) *reinstate the context*, that is, the conditions under which the event in question was encoded; (b) *report everything*, however trivial it may seem; (c) recount the event in *different orders*; and (d) recount the event from *different perspectives*.

Geiselman et al. (1984) compared the CI with the hypnotic interview along the lines suggested by Orne et al. (1984) and a 'standard police interview' in a study in which student subjects saw a video showing an armed robbery. The hypnotic interview and the CI were found to yield 35 per cent more accurate information than did the standard police interview without an increase in inaccurate and fabricated information. The CI has also been shown to significantly reduce the impact of misleading questions on witness accuracy (Geiselman et al., 1986). In the light of studies with serving police officers, the original CI was revised by Fisher et al. (1987). The revised version places less importance on asking the witness to recall, using different perspectives and in different order and stresses the importance of *repeated recall* and *listening skills*. Fisher et al. (1987) found the revised version produced significantly more (45 per cent) accurate information in police detectives' interviews of crime witnesses without increasing inaccurate recall. Subsequent laboratory and field studies with both children and adult eyewitnesses and a meta-analysis by Köhnken (1992) have reported findings in support of the CI as a superior interview technique with crime witnesses (Fisher and Geiselman, 1992; Memon and Bull, 1991). More recently, British researchers Clifford and George (1995) reported a field study with twenty-eight experienced policemen and policewomen interviewing real crime victims/witnesses which compared three methods of investigative interviewing: CI, conversation management (CM) and a combination of both (CI and CM). Their findings provide strong support regarding the ecological validity of the CI as a superior investigative interviewing technique.

However, a number of ecologically-valid studies have failed to find support for the CI as a superior interviewing technique and point to difficulties in training experienced police investigators to use the technique (Memon et al., 1995). Some researchers have also failed to find evidence that all four techniques used in the CI increase witness accuracy significantly. Boon and Noon (1994) reported that the changing perspectives mnemonic did not facilitate recall of accurate information by student subjects. Finally, Milne et al. (1995) have examined the degree to which the CI helps children to resist the impact of misleading questions. It was found that whilst the CI enhanced children's recall of person and action details, it increased their person errors and confabulations; children were significantly more likely to resist script-inconsistent than script-consistent misleading questions and, finally, the CI enhanced children's resistance to misleading questions only when the questions were presented after the CI. The CI is a very good example of the application of psychological theory from the laboratory to the field. The available empirical evidence shows that while it enjoys a number of merits, it also has to overcome a number of apparent defects, especially when used with child witnesses, before being unreservedly recommended for adoption by law-enforcement investigators and other categories of investigators whose work includes interviewing witnesses. The need for additional ecologically-valid studies to maximise the effectiveness of the CI becomes the more important when we remember that the usefulness of such aids to recall as the Identi-Kit, E-Fit, and FACE, all of which have been found to be of limited use in apprehending offenders (Clifford and Davies, 1989; Davies, 1983; Kapardis, in preparation).

5.2 Forensic Hypnosis

Haward (1990) defined forensic hypnosis as 'Hypnotic techniques applied to information-gathering for evidential purposes' (p. 60). Reiser (1989) is a strong advocate of the view that hypnosis could be used to enhance witness memory accuracy. Orne (1979), however, sees hypnotic techniques to be most appropriately utilised in the investigative context. Hypnosis itself, of course, has a long and impressive history as a therapeutic tool in psychiatry and clinical psychology. In the early days of hypnosis in the first half of the 19th century the law's interest was in controlling its use but since the second half of the 19th century the law's interest has been in the field of forensic hypnosis (Evans, 1994). In the late 1990s, an unsatisfactory state of affairs still characterises the relationship between hypnosis and the law.

Hypnosis interviews by police to assist witnesses to remember were first used in the US in the early 1950s and by 1975 experienced detectives were being trained in hypnosis. Within one year such Los Angeles detectives handled seventy major crime cases and the practice spread to other police departments (Reiser, 1989). In the UK (see Gudjonsson, 1992a) and in Australia (see McConkey and Sheehan, 1988; Judd et al., 1994) hypnosis is usually conducted by psychiatrists

and qualified psychologists and, in stark contrast to the US, never by
police officers.

Reiser (1989:151) describes a few cases to illustrate the usefulness of
investigative hypnosis. In one such case in California, a 15-year old
female hitch-hiker accepted a lift from a man driving a van. The driver
tied her up, raped her, cut off her forearms with an axe and forced her
into a highway drainage tunnel. When he left, the victim managed to
crawl out, stopped a passing car and was taken to the hospital. Because
of her extremely traumatic experience her memory of the suspect and
of the events was rather limited. When interviewed under hypnosis,
however, she was able to recall the suspect's name, his occupation,
described the van and helped a police artist construct a composite
drawing of the suspect. The offender was arrested and convicted.

Haward (1981b:110) points out a number of constraints on the
use of hypnosis: admissibility of hypnotic evidence and the reimposition
of amnesia; not all victims are willing to be hypnotised; some people are
poor hypnotic subjects; age-regression requires considerable time;
parents may not consent to their children, especially if female, who have
been victims of crime being hypnotised and, finally, hypnosis is powerless to obtain recall if the memory of a particular fact simply no longer
exists. Sheehan (1994:66–7) has also drawn attention to another major
issue in forensic hypnosis, namely, the civil rights of the person who is
hypnotised, especially when the individual is under suspicion of a crime.
One concern is, for example, that such a person may report incriminating evidence under hypnosis which comes to the attention of the
police (p. 67). On the question of whether hypnosis could interfere with
a witness' memory of an event, Gudjonsson (1992a:170) points out
three risks: witness' vulnerability to confabulation, to suggestibility and
to overconfidence. Gudjonsson adds, however, that the experimental
evidence on confabulation, susceptibility to leading questions and overconfidence as a result of hypnosis is not unequivocal (p. 171).

Regarding the extent to which the hypnosis interview increases the
accuracy of witness recall, McConkey (1995) concludes his assessment
of the laboratory evidence on hypnotic hypermnesia and hypnotic
pseudomemory stating that:

> there is no guarantee that any benefits (such as increased accurate recall) will
> occur, and there is a likelihood that some costs (such as inaccurate recall, and
> inappropriate confidence) may be incurred when hypnosis is used to
> enhance memory ... [and] ... A similar conclusion comes from using
> hypnosis in the forensic setting. (p. 2)

Taking hypnotised subjects back to the scene of the crime and
methodically questioning them about various aspects of the event may

indeed help some witnesses to remember more details. This is not surprising because the technique involved is similar to the cognitive interview technique. However, when there is no external corroborative evidence there is the difficulty of not knowing in such a situation what is accurate and what is not (Haward, 1981b). It is, therefore, not possible to decide whether forensic hypnosis solves more problems than it creates. It is, of course, a must that the hypnosis be carried out by a properly qualified professional such as a psychiatrist, a psychologist or medical practitioner who is trained in witness interviewing techniques and who is not involved in the case, preferably with the whole session being video-taped continuously.

Despite its popularity among police investigators, especially in the US, the use of forensic hypnosis has had a mixed treatment in psychology (see McConkey, 1995). Some authors (for example, Haward, 1981b) have attacked the practice of training police investigators on a brief course to use hypnosis. Two of the concerns expressed in this context include: protection of the mental health of the witness, as well as the possibility of inadvertently planting items of information, pseudo-memories, which become part of what a hypnotised witness will remember later (Haward, 1981b). Lloyd-Bostock (1988:19) concluded that:

> Hypnosis is not . . . the wonder tool it has been held to be. There is no video-recording faithfully stored in the brain awaiting to be uncovered and played back at the convenience of the forensic hypnotist: the appearance of full and clear recall under hypnosis can be spurious despite the best intentions of witnesses and hypnotist.

In view of strong arguments against the admissibility of hypnotically enhanced testimony, one could argue that it should not be allowed to be used as a method for 'creating' an eyewitness whose memory has been reconstructed by hypnosis and, furthermore, that such a witness should not be allowed to testify to this new memory in the court. It is possible, of course, for one to agree to hypnosis being used selectively and under safeguards to assist during the investigation process but not to its being admitted as evidence by the courts.

For over two decades now, many law-enforcement officers have embraced hypnosis as a panacea for the frailties of human memory, a tool that would greatly assist them to clear up more serious crime. However, the enthusiasm by law-enforcement agencies, some forensic psychologists and the public at large about forensic hypnosis seems to be unwarranted in the light of both the experience with crime detection and hard facts from within psycholegal research. On the basis of the existing literature it can be safely stated in conclusion that: 'Properly controlled hypnosis may be very useful in appropriate cases [with witness victims in cases where memory recall is inhibited by emotional trauma], but indiscriminate use and a false impression of its power can do a great deal of harm' (Lloyd-Bostock, 1988:21). Evidence obtained by forensic hypnosis should, therefore, be viewed with a great deal of caution. Finally, forensic hypnosis should only be allowed to be used under strict guidelines (including the video-taping of such hypnotic interviews), like those provided in the Californian legislation regulating the admissibility of post-hypnotic evidence and approved in New Zealand in *R. v. Felin* [1985] 2NZLR 750 at 753 (Freckelton, 1996).

6 Conclusions

At best, what can be confidently stated is that psychologists have identified a number of important correlates of eyewitness identification inaccuracy to do with the witness, the perpetrator, and how witnesses are interviewed by law-enforcement personnel. Admittedly, the empirical evidence is more convincing for some variables than for others. Unfortunately, in the late 1990s psychologists have not yet tackled the question of how different crimes or different aspects of a crime are remembered by different eyewitnesses, or how, for example, disguises worn by armed robbers affect witness accuracy, as has been suggested by Clifford (1981). Research, especially of a non-laboratory nature, is badly needed to examine whether and how different variables that have been identified as important indicators of witness identification accuracy interact to impact on eyewitnesses.

McCloskey and Egeth's (1983) article in the *American Psychologist* entitled 'Eyewitness identification: What can a psychologist tell a jury?' concluded 'not much'. Ten years later, in the same journal, in answering the question 'What do we know about eyewitness identification?', Wells (1993) focused on system variables and concluded that in line-up and photospread identification: 'Scientific research methods used by psychologists in conjunction with bodies of knowledge in memory, cognition, social perception, and social influence provide powerful methods and theories that make research psychologists uniquely well suited to contribute to the eyewitness identification problem' (p. 568). Egeth's (1993) article, in the same journal, on 'What do we not know about eyewitness identification?' was concerned with both estimator and system variables and concluded that both the quantity and quality of psychological research into eyewitness testimony has increased in the intervening years, to the extent where psychologists appearing as expert witnesses may not have much to enlighten jurors about but may have something valuable to communicate to the police (p. 579).

The psychological literature discussed permits the following conclusions:

1 A range of witness characteristics, namely, personality, cognitive style, age, gender, race, stereotypes, whether the witness is also a victim of the crime and number of witnesses have also been shown to be important indicators for psychologists who testify as experts in the courtroom.

2 Factors relating to the perpetrator have been neglected by psycholegal researchers. What limited evidence there is indicates that physical attractiveness, gender, body size and height are related to how an eyewitness will perceive and remember a crime suspect.

3 The police would do well to remember that the length of the delay between the commission of an offence and when they interview eyewitnesses impacts on witnesses' accuracy as does the number of efforts made to recall. Also, being a police officer does not confer superior perceptual or memory capabilities but comes with a 'mental' set to selectively perceive and interpret an event as to even impute and remember 'criminal' details that, in fact, never existed. The practice of permitting one police officer to represent a group of police eyewitnesses is a dubious one. When they ask witnesses leading, suggestive questions, police may well construct the answers they will get. The police also need to take note of evidence from studies of actual police interviews of witnesses that they use directive questioning, a significant part of which is often characterised by inappropriate, counter-productive questioning, such interviews treating witnesses worse than criminal suspects (McLean, 1995).

4 As far as the whole debate about recovered memories of childhood sexual abuse is concerned, therapists, like the police, need to be sensitive to, and guard against, the potential problem that is endemic in suggestive questioning.

5 The effectiveness of the CI technique in enhancing the accuracy of eyewitness recall provides further support for the view that experimental psychologists have a great deal to contribute to law enforcement in general and crime suspect identification in particular.

   While not denying that forensic hypnosis can be crucial in obtaining crucial evidence from eyewitnesses in appropriate cases, in view of the fact that hypnosis has been shown to have a number of limitations its use needs to be strictly regulated by statute.

6 Finally, a major challenge for psycholegal researchers is to determine whether and how particular combinations of event, witness, perpetrator and interrogational factors impact on the accuracy of identification accuracy.

The psychological knowledge presented should also serve to dispel myths adhered to by the legal profession, law-enforcement personnel and the public alike that human perception and memory behave like a video-recorder. Notwithstanding the fact that the work of psychologists contributes to reducing the risk of false identifications (which, as Wells (1993:568) points out, cause double injustice because they penalise the innocent, their friends and relatives but also mean the real culprit remains free), the same knowledge should also help to remind psychological researchers that not all eyewitness evidence is unreliable.

Psychologists in the US (for example, Loftus, Buckhout), in the UK (for example, Bull, Clifford, Davies, Gudjonsson) and in Australia (for example, Byrne) have advised as expert witnesses in cases involving witness testimony. Unlike in the US, in the UK and Australia the evidence of psychologists as experts on eyewitness testimony does not enjoy the same degree of recognition by the courts, but psychologists can still advise defence lawyers or the police on factors relevant to witness reliability. Recently, the British Academy of Forensic Sciences organised a seminar in London on eyewitness testimony for judges, lawyers and other professionals involved in the criminal justice field. The seminar was chaired by the chairman of the Criminal Committee of the Judicial Studies Board (see Heaton-Armstrong, 1995a). The question of whether psychologists are justified in testifying as experts in courts of law is discussed in Chapter 7. Suffice it here to emphasise that the very best psychologists can do is draw the attention of magistrates, judges and jurors to the kinds of factors that contribute to the unreliability of eyewitness identification accuracy. Understandably, some expert witnesses may find this conclusion rather difficult to accept but the empirical evidence presented in this chapter does not justify their doing more than sounding general warnings. Also, psychologists would do well to remember that, while different category variables are important in eyewitness evidence (Cutler et al., 1987), defence lawyers are more likely to accept findings pertaining to system variables.

On the basis of the empirical evidence on mistaken identification and a small number of known miscarriages of justice due to such misidentification, Davies (in press) believes it is now time to reconsider Lord Devlin's (1976) recommendation that a positive identification should stop being the primary or principal premise on which someone can be prosecuted. Also, Davies argues for the adoption in England and Wales of the Scottish legal position whereby all identifications must be independently corroborated. Davies' suggestion warrants serious consideration by the legal fraternity, researchers and the public alike.

Chapter 4

Children As Witnesses

• *Legal aspects of child witnesses.*
• *Legal reforms to protect child witnesses.*
• *Evaluations of the 'live link'.*
• *Popular beliefs about child witnesses.*
• *Children's remembering ability.*
• *Factors impacting on children's testimony.*
• *Children vs. adults.*
• *Enhancing children's testimony: the Cognitive Interview.*
• *Interviewing children in sexual abuse cases.*
• *The use of anatomical dolls.*

'*Children have a right to justice and their evidence is essential if society is to protect their interests and deal effectively with those who would harm them.*' *(Jack and Yeo, 1992)*

'*To permit adult witnesses to relate children's unrecorded hearsay from investigative interviews is to tolerate listener distortion, foster professional ineptitude, and again to frustrate justice.*' *(McGough, 1995:385)*

'*The demonstrable fact that investigative interviews with young children can be rendered worthless by inept practice should not blind us to the substantial literature demonstrating that reliable information can be elicited from young children who are competently interviewed, however.*' *(Lamb et al., 1995:446)*

Introduction

Psycholegal research into children as witnesses has a history going back to the beginning of the century (Binet, 1900). Since the 1970s there has been an increasing interest in western countries in victims of crime, especially sexual abuse. The last decade or so has witnessed a great deal of research into the accuracy of young children's memories and how reports of sexual abuse can be interfered with by the interviewer. Allegations of sexual abuse are also made in the context of divorce and custody disputes (Byrne and Maloney, 1991; Wakefield and Underwager, 1991). Contrary to popular belief, however, McIntosh and Prinz (1993) in the US found that a survey of 603 family court files pertaining to divorces involving children revealed that in only 2 per cent of cases in which custody or access were contested were sexual abuse allegations made. The focus on, and the concern with, child victims and child witnesses since the 1980s by the media and researchers alike has been instrumental in the legislatures in various countries responding to demands that the law of evidence and procedure become more sensitive to the needs of victims in general, and female and child victims in particular.[1] However, despite all the attention paid by a broad range of professionals to the topic of the child witness for over fifteen years now, and the enactment in many countries of mandatory reporting laws for child abuse, there is still a noticeable lack of adequate training for child protection services workers (Doris et al., 1995).

The empirical evidence discussed in this chapter leads to the inescapable conclusion that children as young as 3 to 4 years old can provide us with reports about an alleged incident that are of significant potential forensic usefulness but, like adults, their performance is also influenced by situational demands. We know a great deal about child witnesses, and significant progress has been made in the law's treatment of child witnesses in western common law countries, but a lot remains to be done.

1 Legal Aspects of Children as Witnesses

Police Standing Orders and statutory provisions in various jurisdictions[2] require that where a child is questioned, a parent, guardian, relative or in special circumstances a responsible adult be present, except where it is impracticable or for other sufficient reasons. Not surprisingly, too, the courts have routinely scrutinised confessional evidence of young persons with particular care. Traditionally, the law in the UK (see Flin, 1995; Spencer and Flin, 1990, 1993), in the US (Myers, 1993) and in Australia (see Byrne, 1991; Waight and Williams, 1995) 'has taken a very restrictive use of child witnesses, regarding them as inherently unreliable. When children have been permitted to testify they have done so on adults' terms' (Naylor, 1989:82). These suspicions about the reliability of child witnesses are seen in the competency requirement and the requirement for corroboration still in existence in various jurisdictions. In fact, it would not be an exaggeration to say that until very recently 'children were treated as second-class citizens in the eyes of the law' and, not surprisingly, only a small proportion of offenders who have sexually abused children have been successfully prosecuted (Davies, 1991:178–9). Many countries, including the US and Canada, still make use of competency examinations for children under the age of 14 years. In such examinations, a child's competency will be decided following a *voir dire* (interview).

The field of children's evidence has been in turmoil during the last two decades or so. This is seen, for example, in the plethora of publications in the UK,[3] in the US[4] and in Australia.[5] The turmoil has also been reflected in a number of legal reforms largely intended to relax the rules pertaining to children's competency. Examples of such reforms are recent amendments to the Criminal Code of Canada Evidence Act to allow children under 14 years to provide either sworn or unsworn testimony (Ruck, 1996). In the US, various grounds of witness incompetence, including age, have been eliminated by Rule 601 of the Federal Rule of Evidence, the consequence of which is that child witnesses are treated by the courts like witnesses generally as far as competency is concerned. In other words, the basic test is: does the witness understand the difference between lying and telling the truth in court and does the witness, whether on oath or in affirmation, also understand the duty of telling the truth? Similar reforms to children's testimony requirements have included the abolition of the corroboration requirement in New South Wales, Australia, in 1985; the abolition in the Criminal Justice Act 1988 in England and Wales of the rule that there could be no conviction on the unsworn evidence of children, and the Criminal Justice Act 1991 which allows for a video-recorded interview with a child witness to be shown in court as the child's evidence-in-chief. Courts in England and Wales, however, have the power not to show part or all of a video-recording if the interview has not been carried out in compliance with relevant legislation.

Despite the importance of children's own understanding of providing testimony in legal contexts, there has been very little research 'pertaining to those situations where the child may be motivated or influenced to withhold the truth' (Ruck, 1996:104). In order to examine the development of children's understanding of telling the truth in court Ruck presented short story vignettes to children aged 7, 9, 11 and 13 years. The main character in the vignettes was a child who had either witnessed, been involved with, or committed a crime, and who was required to testify in court and faced the dilemma of whether to tell the truth or to lie. It was found that younger children (aged 7 to 9) were more likely to perceive telling the truth when giving testimony in court as a way of avoiding punitive consequences while older children (aged 11 to 13) were more concerned with upholding the laws and rules of society. More knowledge about why children decide to tell the truth in court could suggest ways of assessing children's reasoning and competence in both civil and criminal proceedings, especially since 'the *voir dire* (interview) is an imperfect metric of a child's understanding of telling the truth in court' (Ruck, 1996:115).

The 1988 English Criminal Justice Act also abolished the mandatory caution from judges in dealing with children's evidence in their summing up, and introduced the principle of the live video-link as a means by which children could simultaneously communicate with the courtroom without having to confront the accused (see Davies and Noon, 1991, 1993; Flin, 1992). According to Davies and Noon (1993:22), the 'Live Link', as it is known, is available to children under the age of 14 in cases involving violence and to those under 17 in cases involving sexual assault. In England and Wales the link enables a child to give evidence from a smaller room adjacent to the courtroom, in the company of a court-approved supporter. A child witness can see the particular person speaking to them and those in the court can see the child giving evidence. The same piece of legislation raised the age limit for the video-link from 14 to 17 years.[6] Closed-circuit television is also available in most jurisdictions in Australia (Cashmore, 1991; Waight and Williams, 1995:46).[7]

However, it was the US that pioneered the use of closed-circuit television for child witnesses in criminal cases in 1983. The Supreme Court in *Maryland v. Craig* 497 US 836 (1990) upheld the use of one-way closed-circuit television procedure to question child witnesses. In a majority decision in that case it was held that the Sixth Amendment does not guarantee a defendant's absolute right to meet with the witnesses against him/her face-to-face except 'Where an important public policy is furthered and where the reliability of testimony is otherwise assured' (Small and Melton, 1994:229). The Supreme Court outlined three criteria that must be satisfied for the state to show 'necessity', a finding that is required to allow a child to testify via a video-link. According to Small and Melton (1994:228), by 1990 thirty-seven States allowed the use of video-taped testimony of alleged sexually abused children, twenty-seven States authorised the use of one-way television testimony in such cases, and eight States permitted the use of a two-way video-link. It should be noted in this context, however, that despite a number of important legal reforms on both sides of the Atlantic, in Australia, New Zealand and Canada (see O'Neil, 1992), 'The most important class of legally incompetent witnesses that remains is little children' (Spencer and Flin, 1990:38).

While a minority of children prefer facing the accused in court (Cashmore, 1992; Davies et al., 1995), and some have argued that children should have the choice of testifying on closed-circuit television or in open court, available evidence shows that what children witnesses testifying in court fear most is being watched by the accused (American Psychological Association, 1990; Flin et al., 1988). Despite such evidence, Montaya (1995), a strong critic of the ruling in *Craig*, has argued that shielding child witnesses: does not invariably produce 'better evidence', it 'may impair a defendant's right to represent a defense' and, finally, recommends that 'the judge should personally interview child witnesses before determining the need for shielding' (pp. 366–7). The introduction of closed-circuit television for child witnesses in a number of different jurisdictions has been done to avoid a situation where the victim has to confront the defendant in court, as well as to save the child the traumatic experience of testifying in the formal and anxiety-provoking atmosphere of the courtroom (Goodman et al., 1992). As application must be made to the court for some means of separation such as closed-circuit television to ensure that a child does not meet a criminal defendant face-to-face in the courtroom, there is scope for psychologists to conduct psychological evaluations regarding the potential trauma a child may experience in confronting the accused in a criminal trial (see Small and Melton, 1994). But how effective are such video-links in protecting child witnesses?

2 Evaluations of the 'Live Link'

One such evaluation study was carried out for the British Home Office by Davies and Noon (1991, 1993). The researchers monitored the scheme during its first twenty-three months during which time they surveyed courtroom personnel (judges, prosecutors and barristers) as well as a smaller number of police officers and social workers. Observational data were collected from 100 trials involving 154 children (100 girls and 54 boys) testifying via the link. The performance of children in court was assessed using rating scales provided by Gail Goodman. The average age of the witnesses was 10 years and 1 month and the great majority (89 per cent) were alleged victims (96 per cent) of sexual abuse rather than bystanders. It was found that the majority of the courtroom personnel thought favourably of the link, 74 per cent of the children were rated as happy when testifying and most were rated as giving their evidence effectively. Davies and Noon (1993:24) concluded that their data 'present a consistent picture of the advantages accruing to children testifying via closed-circuit television and clearly justify the extension of the scheme currently under way'. The question of the scheme's effectiveness, however, needs to be answered against the knowledge that only eight out of the 154 children studied had met their counsel prior to being examined on the link; children waited an average of 10 months for their case to come to trial; despite arriving at the start of court business, they had to wait an average of 2 hours 28 minutes before giving evidence and, finally, no measures were taken to ensure that a child could not come into contact with the accused or their supporters during recess in the corridors of the court or in the canteen (Davies and Noon, 1993:24–5). It can be seen that schemes such as the 'Live Link' on their own can only provide a partial solution to the child witnesses' problem of having to confront the accused when they are testifying in court.

Video-taped interviews in England and Wales (which save a child aged under 14 years in the cases of physical violence or under 17 years in cases of sexual assault from giving their evidence-in-chief at trial) must be conducted by a police officer or a social worker. Such interviews are governed by the *Memorandum of Good Practice* jointly issued by the Home Office and the Department of Health in 1992 (see below). A recent evaluation of video-taped interviews with child witnesses for the British Home Office by Davies et al. (1995) from Leicester University reported the following: of the 1199 trials, predominantly indecent assault cases, that took place in England and Wales during the twenty-one-month period (October 1992 to June 1994 inclusive) involving child witnesses, 640 (53 per cent) included an application to show a video-taped interview, 73 per cent of those applications were granted and in 43 per cent of those cases the tape was, in fact, played in court; in other words, a tape-recorded interview was played in court in 17 per cent of the total number of trials during the period in question. It was also reported that judges were significantly more positive in their evaluation of video-taped interviews than were barristers, while 98 per cent of police officers and all social workers surveyed believed the main advantage was a significant reduction in stress for the child. Examination of forty video-taped interviews, most of which had been conducted by female police officers, revealed that generally the interviews were conducted in accordance with the guidelines provided in the *Memorandum of Good Practice* (1992) but in enough cases children were not allowed enough opportunity to describe the incident in their own words; the evidential quality of the majority of the tapes (75 per cent) was judged to be satisfactory (that is, gave a clear account of the incident). Finally, those interviewing a child on tape (mainly female police officers) were generally more supportive and more likely to adjust their questioning to the child's linguistic style and, in such cases, the child was rated as less anxious than in interviews conducted during the trial by lawyers.

Mock-juror research by Ross et al. (1994) in the US has reported that subjects (psychology students) who observed a 2-hour video based on a real trial and showing a 10-year-old girl give evidence in open court (as opposed to doing so behind a screen or video-link) against her father accused of sexual and physical abuse and who never got to give evidence himself, were more likely to convict the defendant. Ross et al. concluded that the use of protective shields and video-link, devices aimed at protecting children from trauma in the courtroom, do not impact adversely on the interests of defendants. Davies et al. (1995) found no significant differences between video-taped evidence and live examination-in-chief as far as actual jury verdicts in England and Wales were concerned. Davies et al. also reported that children waited an average of 5 months for their case to go to trial; waited 2 hours and 20 minutes inside the courtroom to testify; most of them were given a tour of the courtroom before testifying and a minority were introduced to the live link, but 30 per cent received no such preparation. Finally, most children would have preferred not to have given their evidence at trial. On the basis of their findings, Davies et al., *inter alia*, recommend improving interviewer training so that a greater percentage of such interviews will comply with the guidelines provided in the *Memorandum of Good Practice*; fast-tracking cases involving children as witnesses to avoid delays and, finally, encouraging judges to be more effective in protecting children from inappropriate or intimidating tactics by counsel (see also Davies, 1994; Walker, 1993; Westcott, 1995).

3 Child Witnesses and Popular Beliefs About Them

Children, of course, appear as witnesses in both criminal and civil cases. It should also be noted in this context that official figures for child molestation, for example, grossly underestimate the sexual abuse of children (Feldman, 1993:13). But what is generally known about children who are likely to end up as a witness in a criminal trial? Lipovsky et al. (1992) examined the characteristics of 316 criminal cases which involved children as potential witnesses in nine judicial circuits in three States in the US that were adjudicated through a guilty plea, acquittal or conviction. Most of the cases involved sex crimes against children. It was found that only 16.8 per cent of the cases went to trial as most were resolved by a guilty plea. It was also found that the average child involved in the criminal justice system was a 10-year old, white female who had been victimised by a parent or an acquaintance.

According to Davies (1991:179) and Gudjonsson (1992a:93), a number of views have underpinned the law's traditional treatment of children as second-class witnesses, namely that: they are not as good as adults as far as observing and reporting events is concerned; they are prone to fantasise about sexual matters (Freud, 1940); they are highly suggestible (Binet, 1900); they are relatively unable to distinguish reality from fantasy (Piaget, 1972); and they are prone to confabulate (Saywitz, 1987).

Let us next examine the validity of these myths by taking a close look at empirical studies reporting on children as witnesses.

4 Children's Remembering Ability

As Fivush (1993) rightly points out, examination of the literature on children as witnesses reveals an imbalance: whilst there now exists a large volume of published studies on the accuracy and suggestibility of children's memory, very few researchers have concerned themselves with children's memory performance from a developmental psychology perspective (see Bauer, 1996; Fivush and Shukat, 1995; Wilson, 1995). In this context two crucial questions are: (a) what differences in memory accuracy exist between children of different ages?; and (b) how do children of different ages compare with adults in terms of accuracy of their reports? As far as the meaning of 'accuracy' is concerned, writing about research into autobiographical recall Fivush (1993) has offered an operational definition in terms of the 'agreement between the individual's recall and either an objective record of the event or social consensus from other participants of the event as to what occurred' (p. 2).

Regarding the relationship between children's memory accuracy and age, as early as 1902, on the basis of his memory experiments with subjects aged 7 to 18 years, Stern reported that the amount of information free-recalled increased steadily with an age. Stern (1902, cited by Davies, 1991:179–80) also found that the older the subject, the more accurate the answers elicited by direct questioning, especially by means of accurate leading questions, but at the expense of a higher proportion of error. Goodman et al. (1987) also confirmed Stern's finding that whilst 6-year-old children generally remember less information than adults, they are able to give accurate descriptions if asked to free recall, but 3-year-old children are less accurate than older children. Clifford (1993) reported experimental comparisons of children aged 4/5 vs. 9/10 under immediate recall or one week's delay and children aged 7/8 vs. 11/12 recalling what they saw on a video after one or five days. Clifford found that memory increases with age. Pillemer and White's

(1989) comparison of a 3-year-old's vs. a 5-year-old's recall of a fire-drill found that the younger children confused what had occurred first – the fire alarm or leaving the building. Leippe et al. (1991) reported that, with a 5-minute delay, 5- to 6-year olds recalled less information about being touched than did 9- to 10-year-olds. Regarding the importance of a child's age at the time of encoding and the length of a retention interval, Hamond and Fivush (1991) interviewed children who had been to Disneyworld at, approximately, the ages of two-and-a-half or four-and-a-half after an interval of 6 or 18 months and found that the older children's recall was more spontaneous and more detailed. Finally, Brigham, Van Verst and Bothwell (1986) found that fourth-grade children did significantly worse in a photo line-up identification task of a familiar person than did eighth- and eleventh-grade children.

The literature review by Fivush (1993) of the amount and accuracy of children's autobiographical recall concludes that the empirical evidence shows even young preschoolers to be rather accurate and to retain over considerable time information about events they experienced themselves (p. 8). The same studies,[8] however, show that preschoolers' recall is not as detailed or as exhaustive as older children's recall; preschool children recall better with the assistance of cues, prompts and so forth and they do not recall as much information spontaneously irrespective of the length of the retention interval (Fivush, 1993:9); and, finally, unlike older children or adults, preschoolers focus on and remember different aspects of an event (p. 17).

Of course, as Fivush reminds us, if a child requires numerous specific questions to remember an event in the courtroom the less credible such testimony will be seen, a factor that no doubt will be exploited in cross-examination. Furthermore, if a child is asked cued questions, they may well be objected to as being 'leading questions' or even misleading, while if the child's recall is in response to open-ended questions only then is his/her testimony likely to be incomplete and to be perceived as inaccurate. It is in such a context – having to strike a balance between the two types of questioning with their respective dangers – that a technique like the 'cognitive interview' is useful (see Chapter 3 and below).

Another factor that may very well impact on a magistrate's, judge's or juror's perception of a child's testimony accuracy is *degree of consistency* (that is, stability over time) that characterises a child's recall of the same event on different occasions.[9] Such inconsistencies seem attributable to the fact that young preschoolers have limited general knowledge, limited retrieval structures and focus on routine and general information (Hudson, 1986; Nelson, 1986, cited by Fivush, 1993:12). Consequently, even though they encode a great deal of information, they have difficulty retrieving it when interviewed and are thus vulnerable to the effects of multiple interviews. The fact is that young children (for example, aged 3 to 6) can be accurate if asked specific questions. However, if such children are asked different questions about the same event in different interviews, they are likely to yield inconsistent responses (Fivush et al., 1991), even though they are not likely to incorporate much of the information supplied them by an adult during questioning into their subsequent recall of the event (Fivush, 1993:15).

5 Factors that Impact on Children's Testimony

Researchers have established that a child's mind interacts with his/her physical and inter-personal environment (Fischer and Bullock, 1984). Therefore, it makes sense to conceptualise a child's accuracy or suggestibility as a witness not as something which the child is not capable of because of his/her level of cognitive development but as reflecting a particular context (Batterman-Faune and Goodman, 1993:303). In other words, the extent to which a child is familiar with a particular environment and what his/her expectations are about a particular context will impact on how a child will perceive and later remember a situation. It follows that a child's age is but one important factor in evaluating children as witnesses.[10]

Presence of the Perpetrator: Researchers have paid very little attention to the importance of sociocognitive factors, such as a witness' motivation, expectation in children's eyewitnessing, concentrating instead on whether children are reliable witnesses (Bussey, Lee and Grimbeck, 1993:148). Social cognitive theory emphasises the significance of a witness' anticipated outcome of disclosing an event (Bandura, 1986). Such outcome could be whether one would be believed, supported, embarrassed, shamed or punished as a result of reporting an event, especially if a witness has promised not to do so or has been warned against doing so and threatened with adverse consequences. Such concerns by children could well underpin false allegations and false denials by children. It has been found, for example, that the presence of the perpetrator makes it less likely that children aged 3, 5 and 9 years will report the perpetrator's misdeed (Bussey et al., 1991, cited by Bussey et al., 1993). Furthermore, the intimidating presence of the perpetrator can influence a child's testimony itself. In a study by Peters (1991) children witnessed a staged robbery and were then interviewed alone or with the robber present. In the robber-present condition the amount and accuracy of what the children reported was significantly affected, resulting in five times fewer children reporting what they had seen. Findings like this provide experimental simulation support for the US Supreme Court's decision in *Maryland v. Craig*, allowing children not to have to confront their defendant. Not paying attention to motivational factors is indeed a major omission by researchers when we remember that, contrary to popular belief, children as young as 5 (Peterson et al., 1983) and even 4 years (Haugaard and Crosby, 1989, cited by Bussey et al., 1993) can correctly identify lies and can themselves intentionally lie or tell the truth.

Children can, and are, routinely interviewed about an alleged event in a great variety of contexts. Tulving's (1983) principle of encoding specificity emphasises the importance of reinstating the environmental context at the coding stage when asking subjects to recall an event. Providing cues specific to the context of the event in question is especially likely to facilitate children's recall (Dietze and Thomson, 1993). This finding has implications for interviews of children in legal contexts and points to the importance of social workers, police, lawyers, judicial officers and other professionals who interview children about allegations of sexual abuse, for example, being familiar with such psychological literature.

Stressful Events: Like adults, children get exposed to a lot of violence in society in one way or another. As already mentioned, testifying in a courtroom is, in itself, a source of significant stress for most children and often impacts negatively on their testimony in terms of both the quantity and accuracy of their reports (Hill and Hill, 1987). In fact, a child may be too frightened to attend court to give evidence in a trial (*Neil v. North Antrim Magistrates' Court and another* [1992] 4 All ER 846). This fact should be of great concern to all who are interested in the welfare and rights of children. While it is important to balance the rights of child witnesses with the rights of defendants, it should be remembered that children are called to testify as victims and/or witnesses to such traumatic events as sexual abuse, domestic violence, shootings, stabbings, robberies, murder,[11] even the killing of one parent by another (see Burman and Allen-Meaves, 1994), and serial murder and are psychologically affected[12] (Herkov et al., 1994). It is therefore of crucial importance to know how well children remember and testify about such experiences.

It has been reported that children's memories for very traumatic incidents, such as kidnappings, killings of loved ones and a sniper firing on a school, contain both accuracies and inaccuracies (see Pynoos and Eth, 1984; Terr, 1991). Warren and Swartwood (1992) found that children who were more upset by the space shuttle Challenger tragedy remembered more details of the event than did children who were less upset. Similarly, a study by Steward (1992)[13] reported that children who were more upset by a painful medical procedure remembered more details and were more accurate than children who were less upset. These findings are consistent with results reported by Goodman et al. (1991). However, the relationship between anxiety and memory in the context of testifying about a stressful event is more complex than some authors (for example, Peters, 1987) have suggested. In contrast to Goodman, Hirschman, Hepps and Rudy (1991) and Peters (1987), Vandermaas et al. (1993) reported a negative impact of anxiety on 3- to 8-year-olds' identification accuracy of target persons associated with a dental visit. Vandermaas et al. (1993) had children aged 4 to 5 and 7 to 8 years visit for a teeth-cleaning check-up or an operative procedure. They found that: high anxiety had a detrimental effect on the reports of the older but not the younger children; while experience with the dental event was found to mediate the influence of age and anxiety on memory, older children did not offer incorrect information spontaneously, and that young children infrequently made errors of this type; asking younger children specific questions was what caused them to give incorrect information; all children gave incorrect information in response to specific questions regarding peripheral details about a routine event (Vandermaas et al., 1993:123); and, finally, there was no difference in recall of central vs. peripheral information due to anxiety level as would have been predicted on the basis of Easterbrook's (1959) hypothesis (see Chapter 2). Differences between studies in this area would seem to reflect differences in the types of events involved and children's degree of familiarity with them as well as differences in how soon subjects are asked to recall (for example, immediately or weeks later), the level of anxiety involved and how it is measured. On the basis of the existing literature no definitive conclusions can be drawn about the effects of stress on children's testimony.

Leading Questions: Children can be asked to free recall an event, can be asked specific questions about it or leading and even misleading questions. One primary concern about children's testimony has been that they are susceptible to the effect of suggestive questioning, that is, that they are suggestible (Bruck and Ceci, 1995; Ceci and Bruck, 1993; Spencer and Flin, 1990). Widely publicised child abuse cases like the *McMartin* case in California (*People v. Buckey*, No. 750900 (Cal.Cr.Dt.Ct 1984)), portrayed in the film 'The Indictment' and *Michaels* in New Jersey (*State of New Jersey v. Margaret Kelly Michaels* 625 A.2d 489 NJ Super.Ct.App.Div. 1991 – see Rosenthal, 1995, for an account) and the Report into child abuse in Cleveland in the UK illustrate rather convincingly the dangers that are inherent in suggestive questioning and how zealous and unethical therapists and investigators can use such interview procedures to elicit the answers they need from child witnesses, rather than the facts of the case, in order to safeguard their own vested interest and in the process also construct the case for the prosecution. Grave concern about children's suggestibility and vulnerability to suggestive questioning underpinned the *amicus* brief filed in the *Michaels* case (see Bruck and Ceci, 1995) and co-signed by social scientists, psychological researchers and scholars. In the *McMartin* case, members of a family, including an elderly grandmother, who were running a child-care centre, were charged, on the basis of a great deal of rather questionable evidence obtained by means of suggestive questioning, with numerous counts of child sexual abuse against many of the children at the centre. After 2489 days of the court's time and $15 million costs the case ended up with a hung jury at the retrial. Dubious procedures by one particular therapist and district attorney investigators combined with the effects of sensationalist wide coverage by the media ensured that the principle of the innocence of those accused until proven guilty went out of the window, forever marring the lives of the children themselves and their families as well as the innocent individuals falsely accused and kept in custody for years. During the last ten years or so experimental psychologists have amassed a lot of knowledge about various potential sources of children's suggestibility. The psychological insights gained can be used to identify poor interview procedures with child witnesses that corrupt the reliability of the prosecution's evidence and provide guidance on how to guard against suggestive interviewing, useful in the training of various professionals.

Bruck and Ceci's (1995) *amicus* brief in *Michaels* provides an excellent summary of research findings regarding children's suggestibility. They identify the following nine potential sources of suggestibility for children which they document with references to empirical studies:

5.2.1 Interviewer Bias

If an interviewer believes that a child has been sexually abused and that is the only hypothesis he/she is interested in confirming, he/she may very well bias the interview outcome by utilising one or more of the ways mentioned next in order to obtain from the child a report that is consistent with his/her blinkered view of the allegations made (pp. 273–9).

5.2.2 Repeating Questions

Doing so in the course of the same interview or across different interviews may lead preschoolers to change their original answers (p. 279).

5.2.3 Repeating Misinformation Across Interviews

As a result of this, children may well come to incorporate the misleading information in their subsequent reports and/or to distort the misinformation itself (p. 280).

5.2.4 The Interviewer's Emotional Tone

Children may be led to fabricate information if they are asked in an accusatory tone: 'Are you afraid to tell?', or are likewise told that: 'You'll feel better if you tell' (p. 281).

5.2.5 Peer Pressure or Interaction

Telling children in an interview that their peers have already answered a particular question and/or that another child victim has already named them as having been abused makes them want to change their answers so as to be consistent their peers (pp. 283, 285). A child can also be pressured into providing the answers an interviewer wants to hear if threatened with exposure to his/her peers for being uncooperative (p. 283).

5.2.6 Being Interviewed by Adults in Authority/of High Status

A child being interviewed by a police officer or a Youth and Family Services investigator or a sexual abuse consultant is likely to want to please such an adult figure by providing answers the child believes the authority figure would like to hear and to also accept such an adult's account of an alleged event (p. 285).

5.2.7 The Induction of Stereotypes

Suggestive interviewing may take the form of the interviewer telling a child that a particular person 'does bad things'. Such information may then be incorporated by the child into a subsequent report about his/her interaction with that individual (p. 287).

5.2.8 The Use of Anatomically Detailed Dolls (see also below)

Three-year-old children interviewed with the aid of such a doll are likely to inaccurately report being touched and/or to insert their fingers into the anal or genital cavities in the doll even though nobody has done so to them (pp. 289–91).

5.2.9 Source Attribution Errors

Young children (6-year-olds) are vulnerable to confusing what they have seen with what has been suggested to them and, consequently, to make false reports (pp. 294–6).

Bruck and Ceci (1995) go on to add that children who have been subjected to suggestive interviewing often appear highly credible and can fool even well-trained professionals (p. 301) and, furthermore, the effect of such interviewing 'may be long lasting' (p. 303). Finally, they also conclude that the interrelationships of the factors affecting children's suggestibility are complex and 'Even though suggestibility effects may be robust, the effects are not universal. Results vary between studies and children's behavior varies within studies' (p. 310). Bruck and Ceci also emphasise that 'poor interviewing procedures make it difficult to detect real abuse' (p. 310).[14]

Adults, too, have been shown to be suggestible (Gudjonsson, 1992a:143). In contrast to the popular belief that suggestibility is age-related and a personality trait, in Gudjonsson and Clark's (1986) social psychological model suggestibility is conceived of as the outcome of a complex and dynamic interaction between an individual, the environment and other important persons in that environment. Gudjonsson and Clark believe there are three factors that predispose someone to be susceptible to leading questions: uncertainty, interpersonal trust and expectations. However, even if these factors are present in an interview, a witness is likely to resist the effect of suggestive questioning if he/she is suspicious of the interviewer (Gudjonsson and Clark, 1986; Siegal and Peterson, 1995; Warren et al., 1991). Four potential sources of suggestibility for children are: (a) demand characteristics; (b) the credibility of the misleading information; (c) repeated interviews; and (d) the linguistic form of the question (Gudjonsson, 1992a:94–5; Moston, 1990).

While some authors point to the increased suggestibility of especially preschool children (Ceci and Leichtman, 1992),[15] others emphasise children's ability to resist the influence of leading questions (Siegal and Peterson, 1995),[16] while others have found 6-year-olds more suggestible than 8-year-olds to negative- (that is, suggesting incorrect 'facts') but not to positive-leading questions (Cassell and Bjorklund, 1995). Goodman, Rudy, Bottoms and Aman (1990) reported that children as young as 3 to 4 years can resist suggestive questioning of the type used in sexual abuse investigations for up to a year after the incident. A child's ability to resist the effect of suggestive questioning appears to be a function of a witness being suspicious of the interviewer (Gudjonsson and Clark, 1986; Siegal and Peterson, 1995; Warren, Hulse-Trotter and Tubbs,

1991). The Australian study by Siegal and Peterson examined resistance to suggestibility among 4- and 5-year-olds, utilising a story about a little girl who has a stomach-ache from eating toast too fast before her first day at preschool. It was found that presenting children with a rationale to cancel the implication conveyed in biased information that the original details were irrelevant to producing an accurate report of the story reduced the preschoolers' suggestibility. Siegal and Peterson concluded that: 'children are not inevitably vulnerable to suggestion in simple salient situations where they have a strong knowledge base' (p. 40). Support for this view was provided by the Saywitz, Moan and Lamphear's (1991)[17] study which found that exposing children to an alternative set of expectations and beliefs about answering questions resulted in a 26 per cent decline in error when responding to misleading questions in comparison to a control group.

Davies (1993b) provides an excellent discussion of the empirical literature on children's identification. On the basis of his review he concludes that, even though the testimony of young children (4 to 8 years) is not likely to be as accurate and complete as that of older children, children can provide identity information of significant potential forensic usefulness, but such information must be elicited by skilled interviewers and appropriate questioning (p. 243). More specifically, children are least likely to show age differences in identification tasks but most likely to do so if asked to estimate a suspect's height or weight or to furnish a description of a suspect's face for police to construct a face-composite image (pp. 252–3). Finally, like adults, children's performance as eyewitnesses is influenced by situational demands. In other words, both their cognitive development and how they are approached as witnesses play a significant role in their accuracy as eyewitnesses. It should be remembered, however, that the findings reported by empirical studies of child witnesses are based on group accuracy data. This should not be allowed to detract from the potential usefulness of the individual child of rather young age who has every right to be heard and evaluated as a witness in open court like everybody else (Davies, 1993b:253).

6 Children vs. Adults

Children as young as 4 years have been found to be as good at colour memory as adults (Ling and Blades, 1995). Generally, however, research into children's memory vs. adults' has yielded inconsistent results (Leippe, Manion and Romanczyk, 1993:170). To illustrate, in a highly cued memory task Sheingold and Tenney (1982) found that school-age children could recall accurately as much as adults about the birth of a sibling when the subjects were 4 years old. However, in another study involving cued recall of being touched, Leippe, Romanczyk and Manion (1991) compared 5/6-year-olds, 9/10-year-olds and adults. They reported that 5/6-year-olds performed more poorly than did the adults in free recall and when asked objective questions, but both groups of children performed significantly more poorly than did adult subjects in a line-up identification task (both in correctly identifying the person who had touched them as well as correctly rejecting a target-absent line-up – see also Chapter 10).

Clifford (1993) has drawn attention to the fact that if one reads five pre-1984 textbooks on eyewitness testimony one finds they state that children are poorer witnesses than adults, presumably on the basis that they have poorer memory capabilities. This is in contrast to post-1984 literature which portrays children as being much better witnesses than was thought earlier on and in some ways as being not significantly different, if not better, than adults (p. 15).

Clifford (1993) reported an impressive series of six experiments concerned with comparing adults and children as eyewitnesses. The experiments involved the following:

• Experiment 1: 7- to 8-, 11- to 12- and 20- to 32-year olds, a 15-minute video-taped television program ('The Wonder Years'), immediate recall in response to twenty multiple-choice questions;

• Experiment 2: two videos (one a dummy filler), 4- to 5-, 9- to 10- and 18- to 35-year-olds, fourteen objective and six misleading questions, recall immediately or after one week;

• Experiment 3: 7- to 8-, 11- to 12- and 15- to 18-year-olds, an 8-minute video-clip from 'Dempsey and Makepeace', recall of actions, descriptions and verbalisations by means of a twenty-item questionnaire and recognition and identification from blank and filled video parades, testing after one or five days;

• Experiment 4: 7- to 8- and 18- to 39-year-olds, two videos depicting people engaging in different activities for about one and a half minutes each, testing after two days with questionnaire which did or did not include misleading questions, testing after four days for recall with yes/no questions, as well as matching actors to activities and sequencing the activities seen previously;

• Experiment 5: 12-year-olds and adults, a 2-minute interaction with an Asian confederate of the researcher in a McDonald's restaurant, recall tested by objective and misleading questions, identification of confederate from filled or blank photographic line-ups;

• Experiment 6: 5-year-olds and adults (mean age 27.8 years), interact with a confederate for three and a half minutes (including physical contact), free recall of event details tested a week later as well as identification of blank or filled photospread.

On the basis of his findings Clifford concluded that: whether one considers studies using children as actively involved witnesses or as mere bystanders, there is no strong evidence that young children's recall or identification performance is not significantly different from that of adults. In fact, if one focuses on the more forensically relevant studies, children emerge as inferior eyewitnesses to adults; the term 'young' as used in the literature is ambiguous and needs scrutiny; 11- to 12-year-olds are comparable to adults as witnesses; and, finally, one needs to turn to the sociology of knowledge for an answer to why the question of whether children are comparable to adults as eyewitnesses was answered by numerous researchers in the negative until the mid 1980s but in the positive since then (p. 20).

In support of Clifford (1993), Loftus et al. (1989) reported that the amount of information free-recalled by children aged 12 or older is as good as that provided by adults and, furthermore, they are no more susceptible to the effect of leading questions. We now know (see Goodman et al., 1987) that when children's recall is influenced by leading questions, it is not with reference to central detail but rather peripheral. There are, of course, situations when children can be vulnerable. Children seem more prone than adults to make false identification in a line-up of strangers they have seen briefly (Parker and Carranza, 1989). Davies et al. (1988) asked children aged 7 to 8, 8 to 9 and 10 to 11 years, who had helped a stranger at their school set up a film show, to try and identify him from twelve photographs. It was found that all age groups selected him 65 per cent of the time when his photograph was present in the array. However, when his photograph was absent, 87 per cent of the 7- to 8-year-olds selected a photograph compared to 50 per cent of the two older age groups; in other words, the 7- to 8-year-olds had an apparent 'urge to please' (Davies, 1991:182).

When considering the importance of a child's or a young person's testimony, it is also important to remember that a witness' age appears to be related to how credible he/she is perceived and, consequently, to the likelihood of the defendant being convicted. Nightingale (1993) reported that the number of guilty verdicts and the witness' credibility in a sexual abuse case decreased as the age of the child in the experiment was increased from 6 to 14. Nightingale also found that mock jurors blamed the older victim more.

Davies (1991:182) concluded that the completeness and accuracy of children's testimony parallels their general cognitive development with increased age. However, it is not possible to identify a particular age before which children are 'bad' witnesses. Quality of recall is largely context dependent, that is, 'the same child may be a good witness in one situation and poor in another ... Children can be convinced that one set of photographs must be of a man they have seen before but not [that] the same stranger who sexually assaulted them' (p. 182). While children with mild learning disabilities are vulnerable to suggestion, even when interviewed utilising the Cognitive Interview (Milne and Bull, 1995), Davies' conclusion that *suggestibility* is not some kind of universal trait with which all children are invested is supported by Gudjonsson (1992a:94–5) and Ceci and Bruck's (1993) comprehensive review of the concept.

We can conclude that the available psycholegal research shows that, as Naylor (1989) put it, 'children can be good witnesses when their special needs are understood' – a conclusion that has clear legal implications (p. 82). The importance of social support for children in order to reduce stress during interviewing, an area neglected by researchers (see Moston and Engelberg, 1991), cannot be over-emphasised. Meanwhile, legal psychologists should be cognisant of the importance of the 'sociology of knowledge' for the type of research they carry out and what they decide to report. By 'sociology of knowledge' in operation Clifford (1993:15) means that knowledge (that is, research and the reporting of research) does not take place in a social vacuum; on the contrary, researchers produce what society demands and/or what it accepts as valid. Clifford has argued that the cause of children is better served by an acceptance of the evidence that children and adults differ as far as their memory capacities are concerned. Such an acceptance would lead the legal system to be more sensitive to children's needs when 'placed in situations that are inherently difficult for them' (p. 20).

7 Enhancing Children's Testimony

We have already seen that providing contextual cues improves children's recall by aiding the retrieval process, as would be predicted on the basis of Tulving's (1983) 'encoding specificity' hypothesis. Given that children's recall of events is likely to be accurate but incomplete, findings from memory training studies can be useful to assist their recall (Saywitz and Snyder, 1993:125). In a study by Saywitz, Snyder and Lamphear (1990) children aged between 7 and 11 years were trained to use external visual cues, drawn on cards, to remind them to report a specified level of detail from categories of information (setting, participants, conversations, effective states, actions and consequences)[18] that would be useful in a criminal investigation two weeks after participating in a video-taped classroom event. It was found that the training resulted in better and more accurate free and cued recall without increases in inaccuracies (Saywitz and Snyder, 1993:128). Interestingly, it was also found that merely instructing the same children to be more complete was not effective. This study shows that, without infringing on the rights of the accused, children can be assisted with providing more complete recall before they are interviewed by police or testify in a courtroom.

Saywitz and Snyder (1991) trained children to be better at monitoring how far they understood what was being communicated to them and found that, unlike a control group, when confronted with difficult-to-comprehend questions about easily recalled information, they were more likely to communicate that they did not understand a question and to request that it be rephrased (p. 137). As Saywitz and Snyder point out, a great deal of additional research is required before these methods can be used in actual forensic contexts (p. 138). On the basis of existing psychological knowledge, however, the potential exists for social workers, police personnel, lawyers and judicial officers to reduce significantly the negative influence on children's testimony of their limited communication skills.

7.1 Using the Cognitive Interview Technique

The Cognitive Interview (CI) technique (described in Chapter 3) which has proved to be useful with adult witnesses (Geiselman, Fisher, MacKinnon and Holland, 1985) has also been used to enhance the amount and accuracy of children's recall.[19] Geiselman and Padilla (1988) interviewed children aged 7 and 12 years three days after showing them a video of a simulated liquor-store robbery. The interviews were carried out by research assistants trained in how to use the CI. It was found that, without increasing errors and confabulations, the CI produced 21 per cent more correct 'items' of information than did the standard interview where the interviewer only asked about the facts.

The study by Geiselman, Saywitz and Bornstein (1990) used a 'Simon says' touching game that involved an unfamiliar adult, one child 'victim' and one child witness. Again, it was found that significantly more facts were elicited using the CI than the standard interviewing technique with 7- to 8- and 10- to 11-year-olds. Geiselman et al. also reported, however, that: (a) there were differences between the interviewers regarding the extent to which they use the CI techniques; and (b) the interviewees differed in the ease with which they used different CI techniques, more specifically, the 7-year-olds especially had difficulty understanding what was meant when the interviewer instructed him/her to 'change perspective'. Geiselman, Saywitz and Bornstein (1993) used a slide presentation and also staged two live events in front of groups of three or four third-graders aged 8 and 9 years and 11 and 12 years. Children were randomly assigned to a 2 by 3 matrix, that is, two grade levels and three types of interview (CI with practice, CI without practice and standard interview). Psychology majors interviewed the children about the live event and police detectives carried out the interviews about the slide presentation. It was found that CIs elicited more correct facts and that giving children 'practice' with the CI techniques increased their recall performance even more. Like Memon et al. (1993) (see below), Geiselman et al. (1993) also found that there were differences between the interviewers regarding the frequency with which they used various CI techniques. Geiselman et al. (1993) concluded that CI techniques can improve the completeness of children's recall, that children benefit from having prior practice with CI techniques before receiving a CI and, finally, that giving children practice with the CI about an unrelated event is a good investment because it produces a more complete report from child witnesses and reduces the likelihood of children having to retell and relive details of traumatic experiences (pp. 88–9).

Problems in using the CI technique with children have been reported by Köhnken et al. (1991)[20] who found that the CI increased confabulation. A British study by Memon et al. used a 2 (interview type: CI, standard) by 2 (test phase: 2 days, 6 weeks) with 6- to 7-year-olds who were video-taped while having their vision tested. The cameraman was a stranger who was introduced to them by name as the children arrived for their eye test. Children were asked to recall details of the event and the appearance of the cameraman. Memon et al. found that there was no difference in the relative effectiveness of the CI when used with children as compared with the standard interview, irrespective of the measure used to assess effectiveness. The one exception to this finding was that the CI elicited significantly more information about locations of objects and people (p. 7). One weakness of the Memon et al. study, which the authors acknowledge, is that their subjects may have reinstated context when they were instructed not to do so by virtue of the fact that subjects' recall was tested in a familiar setting (p. 8).

Differences between Memon et al. (1993) and other CI studies (for example, Fisher, McCauley and Geiselman, 1992; Geiselman, Saywitz and Bornstein, 1993) concerning the effectiveness of the CI vs. the standard interview reflect differences in how 'effectiveness' is measured. As Memon et al. (1993:7) point out, Geiselman and Fisher have always used total correct information as their measure of effectiveness when reporting the CI as more effective; however, when the 'proportion correct' measure is used, no significant differences between the effectiveness of the CI and the standard interview have been reported. In the absence of a standard scoring system for studies of this kind, inconsistent findings are inevitable and evaluations of the CI technique remain inconclusive.

More recently, British research by Milne et al. (1994) examined the effectiveness of their revised version of the cognitive interview (CI) for children aged 8 to 10 years. They found that as far as person details are concerned, CI children showed more incorrect recall and confabulations; in questioning subsequent to an initial free recall, the CI children yielded 20 per cent more accurate information than structured interview (SI) children. It was also reported that interviewing children with the CI reduced the impact of subsequent suggestive questioning. Another study by Wark et al. (1994) used the revised version of the CI as was used in the Milne et al. (1994) study with 8- and 9-year-old children and reported rather similar findings. Wark et al. also found, however, that there were no significant differences between CI and SI children when recall was tested eleven days after the event – the CI produced more correct information than the SI two days after the event recall only. On the basis of the studies cited, it can be concluded that the empirical evidence supporting the usefulness of the CI with children is not unequivocal.

8 Interviewing Children in Sexual Abuse Cases

In view of the need to minimise both false allegations and false denials of child sexual abuse, the importance of conducting adequate interviews of children cannot be overemphasised (see Bull, 1995a, 1995b; Lamb et al., 1995). It is imperative that the interviewers in such cases have adequate knowledge of sexual development, the numerous ways in which children can be sexually abused, 'as well as specialist knowledge to interact appropriately and sensitively with them' (Yuille, Hunter, Joffe, and Zaparniuk, 1993:98). Yuille et al. recommend that, if an interviewer has concerns about the suggestibility of a child, he/she should ask a few questions about irrelevant issues before concluding the interview in order to decide whether the interviewee's answers can be relied upon.

In their *amicus* brief in the *Michaels* case Bruck and Ceci (1995:309) conclude that the following reduce the risks of suggestibility effects:

- A child's report after one interview than after multiple interviews.
- Asking a child non-leading questions.
- The interviewer not having a confirmatory bias, that is, blindly following only one hypothesis.
- Not repeating close-ended yes/no questions during the same or different interviews with a child.

- If the interviewer is patient, non-judgemental and does not try to create demand characteristics, that is, does not in any way, subtle or otherwise, bias a child to answer a question in a particular way.

Yuille et al. (1993:99–100) advocate using their method known as the 'Step-Wise Interview'. It is a non-suggestive method of interviewing, it comprises a series of nine steps during the interview, and is meant to maximise recall while minimising contamination. The nine steps are:

1 Rapport building.
2 Requesting recall of two specific events.
3 Telling the truth.
4 Introducing the topic of concern.
5 Free narrative.
6 General questions.
7 Specific questions (if necessary).
8 Interview aids (if necessary).
9 Concluding the interview (from Yuille et al. (1993) Table 5.1, p. 99).

Yuille et al. also list four major goals of an investigative interview, namely:

1 Trauma-minimisation of the investigation for the child.
2 Obtaining maximum information from the child about the alleged event/s.
3 Minimising the interview contamination effects on the child's memory for the event/s in question.
4 Maintaining the integrity of the investigative process (p. 100).

They suggest combining the 'Step-Wise' method with 'Statement Validity Analysis' (see Steller and Köhnken, 1989 in Chapter 9). According to Marxsen et al. (1995): 'The step-wise protocol has been officially adopted by both police and child protection workers in many parts of Canada, the United Kingdom, and the United States' (p. 454). The Pigot (1989) report in the UK into issues concerning children's evidence had, in fact, recommended the adoption of the 'Step-Wise Interview' method as a national standard.

Another systematic approach to gathering evidence in cases involving children in general and alleged sexual abuse in particular has been developed at Liverpool University in England. This particular model is known as the 'Systematic Approach to Gathering Evidence' (SAGE) and has been developed in response to such events in the UK as the

Cleveland Inquiry and reforms regarding children's evidence introduced by the Criminal Justice Act (1991). SAGE has been tested within
family courts (Roberts and Glasgow, 1993:10). SAGE has the following
six aims:

1 To make decision-making explicit and to encourage investigators to
  'opt in' to particular actions and behaviours.
2 To provide the investigation with a structure and to make clear to
  investigators the relevant information they need to collect.
3 To encourage communication about the child's world – experiences,
  significant other influences and abilities – not only about allegation
  of abuse.
4 To provide testing of the child's competence and to encourage
  accuracy within the process of the investigation.
5 To facilitate professional 'working together', providing practical ways
  of expediting this process and to provide a context of training.
6 To investigate alleged experience of child sexual abuse within a
  single-case methodology framework (p. 10).

SAGE aims to compare and contrast the child's response to stimuli
presented in a series of planned and controlled brief sessions. As
Roberts and Glasgow (1993) acknowledge themselves, however, 'the
most common criticism of SAGE is that it takes longer [several brief
sessions, often no longer than 30 minutes each] than the "one or at
most two" interviews recommended in the Cleveland Report'. There is
undoubtedly a need for evaluation studies of the comparative strengths
and weaknesses of interview methods such as 'Step-Wise' and SAGE in
forensically relevant contexts.

Finally, Bull and Davies (in press) describe a procedure for assist-
ing children to understand what is being asked of them in investigative
interviews, known as 'felt board' and devised by Poole (1992). It entails
drawing on the 'felt board' the outline of an adult's head and a child's
head, the child's head containing a fair number of felt triangles of
a different colour from the 'felt board'. The interviewer explains to
the child that the triangles in his/her head stand for all that the child
knows about the matter at hand. As the interview proceeds and the
child passes on information about the incident, triangles are moved
from the outline of the child's head to the interviewer's sketched
head. Poole (1992) and Sattar and Bull (1994) found this procedure to
result in children giving longer (but no more accurate) responses. In
addition, Poole (1992) also found that a child's recall is facilitated if
an audio-tape of a child's first attempt at remembering is played back
to him/her.

9 Anatomical Dolls and Interviewing Children

During the last fifteen years or so the practice of using anatomically detailed dolls (AD dolls) when interviewing children in cases of alleged sexual abuse has become very widespread (see Koocher et al., 1995, for a literature review). Morgan (1995) points out that anatomical dolls are being used in interviews in all fifty of the States in the US and in many other countries. Utilising data in trial court transcripts, Mason (1991) examined 122 appellate court decisions in the US in which expert testimony on the characteristics of sexually abused children was challenged. It was found that in seven out of nine cases that involved testimony based on interviews using anatomical dolls, expert testimony was not admitted on the basis that the use of AD dolls was not scientifically accepted (pp. 195–7). Given the controversy surrounding this practice, what can be said about it on the basis of the existing literature? The general consensus of opinion is that first of all professionals must be trained in the use of AD dolls as an aid in child interviews about child sexual abuse. The interviewer should also establish initial rapport with the child before presenting a clothed doll. There is evidence that this is the practice followed by most professionals who use anatomical dolls and that most children aged 3 to 6 years undress dolls spontaneously or with little encouragement from an adult (Glaser and Collins, 1989). Not forgetting that at about the age of 5 years children are more likely to be able to communicate about (that is, name) body parts (Schor and Sivan, 1989), interviewers would be well advised not to give children names of body parts or to suggest functions for them (American Professional Society on the Abuse of Children [APSAC] Guidelines, 1990).[21]

One crucial question is whether the use of AD dolls as a demonstration/memory aid/diagnostic tool leads young children to make false allegations of sexual abuse (see DeLoache, 1995). Some authors (for example, Bruck and Ceci, 1995; Koocher et al., 1995; Raskin and Yuille, 1989) have argued that using AD dolls, especially with preschoolers, increases children's suggestibility. Boat and Everson (1993: 56–9), however, cite a number of studies (for example, Goodman and Aman, 1990; Saywitz, Goodman, Nicholas and Moan, 1991a) that appear to allay this concern. Saywitz et al. (1991a) used free recall, anatomical dolls and direct, and misleading questions to investigate the memories of non-refereed 5- to 7-year-old girls a week after experiencing a medical check-up by a paediatrician that involved medical touch. It was found that not only does the use of dolls not stimulate false reports of genital contact but it also helps children to remember more information about the event. However, since children younger than 5 years of age are known to be more suggestible, the results of Saywitz et al. (1991a) cannot be generalised to younger children. Boat and Everson (1993) conclude their discussion of relevant studies stating that, as far as the question of the use of anatomical dolls as a diagnostic tool is concerned: 'The preponderance of research supports the use of anatomical dolls as an interview tool but not as a litmus test for sexual abuse. It is important to remember that the effectiveness of any tool is contingent upon the skill of its user' (p. 65). Similarly, on the basis of their literature review, Koocher et al. (1995) conclude that 'research to date mainly supports use of AD dolls as a communication or memory aid for children 5 years or older, albeit with a certain risk of contributing to some children's errors if misleading questions are used' (p. 217). Their assessment of the available empirical evidence leads Koocher et al. to recommend that 'APA reconsider whether valid "doll-centered assessment" techniques exist and whether they still "may be the best available practical solution" (APA, 1991, p. 722) for the pressing and frequent problem of investigation of child sexual abuse' (p. 218).

Bruck and Ceci (1995) speak for most authors in this area when they state that because anatomically detailed dolls are suggestive and because one cannot draw definitive conclusions about whether or not children have been sexually abused on the basis of how they play with such dolls, 'The use of anatomically detailed dolls has raised skepticism, ... among researchers and professionals' (p. 290). Those professionals who prefer to err on the side of caution should heed Yuille, Hunter, Joffe, and Zaparniuk's (1993:109) advice that anatomical dolls 'are to be used only after the child has disclosed details of the abuse. The dolls should never be used to obtain the disclosure, only to clarify it'. Extreme caution in the use of anatomically detailed dolls in legal contexts is also urged by Skinner and Berry (1993) on the basis of their literature review. In the last week of September 1993 a group of experts from North America, Europe and the Middle East gathered in Satra Bruk in Sweden to assess what was known about how to effectively investigate child sexual abuse (Lamb, 1994). Twenty of the participants (interestingly none of them from the Middle East) signed a consensus statement which, *inter alia*, recommended that interviews utilising dolls should, as much as possible, be video-taped, and reminded potential consumers of investigative interviews that 'there is no anatomically detailed doll "test" yielding conclusive scores quantifying the probability that a child has been sexually abused' (Lamb, 1994:154). DeLoache (1995) argues convincingly against the use of dolls with children 3 years of age or younger. Finally, whether or not anatomically detailed dolls are used in child sexual abuse investigative interviews, one cannot but agree with McGough (1995) that, while the law in the US and in other common law countries does not require it, it is imperative that such interviews be video-taped. Such a practice will help to improve 'the quality of the child abuse investigations, the reliability of child witness testimony, and ultimately the justice of the American [and other countries'] civil trial' (p. 386).

10 Conclusions

The empirical evidence considered in this chapter shows there is no justification for considering children incompetent as witnesses by virtue of their age. In order to improve children's testimony it is important that attention is focused on elucidating jurors', judicial officers' and police officers' perceptions of children's and adolescents' credibility as eyewitnesses as well as identifying children's strengths and weaknesses and how they are treated by the legal system, the legal agents and other professionals who interact with child witnesses. There is a need for police personnel, lawyers and judicial officers to communicate with children in age-appropriate language. In view of the increasing number of children testifying in courts, relevant psychological knowledge should inform police, legal and judicial training as well as other professionals (for example, child protective services workers) whose work involves them in interviewing children in the context of abuse allegations having been made. As Doris et al. (1995) point out, however, implementing a training program for such professionals does not of itself mean they become competent interviewers. Similarly, reforming legislation is simply not enough. As Flin (1993:296) points out, closed-circuit television can save a child the trauma of having to confront an offender in court face-to-face but it does nothing about long pre-trial delays, the use of inappropriate language by lawyers in communicating with children (see Walker, 1993; Wilson, 1995), the cross-examination of a child by a lawyer who aims to intimidate and discredit a child as a witness (Westcott, 1995) or, finally, preventing the defendant or his/her associates intimidating a child in the environs of the courthouse. It is interesting to note in this context that one of the recommendations by Judge Pigot's committee was for a specialist child examiner to interview the child on behalf of both parties and for the benefit of the court. It was the representative of the bar who dissented from that suggestion (Flin, 1993:296).

As far as the use of AD dolls in child sexual abuse assessments is concerned, they can be a useful communication aid when used by an adequately trained professional interviewer with children of 5 years of age or older when the interviewer also remembers that 'many pressing questions about the impact of AD dolls on children's memory and suggestibility remain to be explored or have received insufficient research attention' (Koocher et al., 1995:218).

The legal system in western English-speaking common law countries can create a better sociolegal context for children's testimony by adopting some features of inquisitorial legal systems on mainland Europe, such as court-appointed child examiners. The need for innovation when it comes to hearing and testing children's evidence on both sides of the Atlantic and in the Antipodes is long overdue. Such reforms should utilise both top-down and bottom-up solutions. Meanwhile some researchers have shifted their attention to examining the importance in children's identification accuracy of children's secrets (see Pipe and Goodman, 1991), multiple interviewing (Davies, 1994:179) and ways in which judges regulate the questioning of children in court by lawyers (Carson, 1995). For many other researchers the behaviour of jurors/juries, the concern of the next chapter, continues to be the focus of their attention. Research into juridic decision-making is another pillar on which the edifice of legal psychology has been built.

Chapter 5

The Jury

•*Historical background.*
•*Notion of an impartial and fair jury.*
•*Arguments for and against the jury.*
•*Methods for studying juries/jurors.*
•*Selecting jurors.*
•*Importance of juror characteristics.*
•*Juror competence.*
•*Understanding and following the judge's instructions.*
•*Jury foreperson.*
•*Jury deliberation.*
•*Models of jury decision-making.*
•*Alternatives to jury trial.*

'*No freeman shall be seized, or imprisoned, or disposed or outlawed, or in any way destroyed; nor will we condemn him, nor will we commit him to prison, excepting by the lawful judgement of his peers, or by the law of the land.*' *(Clause 39, Magna Carta 1215)*

'*A better instrument could scarcely be imagined for achieving uncertainty, capriciousness, lack of uniformity, disregard of former decisions – utter unpredictability.*' *(Judge Jerome Frank, 1949:172)*

'*The verdicts juries give may sometimes seem wilfully perverse ... Stories provide answers to the pressing questions of identity, mental state, actions and circumstances that are required to establish blame. There is a story behind every verdict.*' *(Stephenson, 1992:196)*

Introduction

In *The Book of Magna Carta*, Hindley (1990:ix–x) comments that the words in the above quotation from clause 39, which has been the basis for the institution of trial by jury, were 'coined by a distant society in a half forgotten language, have been treasured by generations of men and women in the English-speaking world as a safeguard of individual liberty'. Darbyshire (1991:742), however, reminds us that, contrary to popular belief, legal historians (for example, Holdsworth, 1903:59) have pointed out (but their comments have gone largely unnoticed by students of the jury) that clause 39 has nothing to do with trial by jury. The notion of being tried by one's peers existed long before the Magna Carta. The conclusion reached in the pages that follow is that the weight of the evidence from both experimental simulation and studies of actual juries/jurors is that the jury system is not a reliable, sound method of determining whether a defendant is guilty or innocent. In view of the fact, however, that the jury is highly unlikely to be abolished in western common law countries in the foreseeable future, a number of reforms are suggested to improve jury decision-making. While the focus in this chapter is primarily on the psycholegal implications of jury research, some background information is necessary in order to place the issues considered in a broader context.

1 A Jury of Twelve: Historical Background

An early documented example of a system of jury existed in ancient Egypt 4000 years ago (Moore, 1973).[1] However, the idea and 'The right to trial by a jury of ordinary citizens (not persons having any special position or expertise)' was invented in Athens (McDowell, 1978:34). Allotting jurors by lottery and the number of jurors used meant that 'An Athenian jury was the Athenian people' (McDowell, 1978:40). From ancient Greece the concept of a jury was adopted across Europe in one form or another and was introduced to Britain in the middle of the 11th century by the Normans (Kerr, 1987:64).[2] Trial by ordeal was abolished by the Pope in 1215 and the idea of twelve jurors developed over many centuries (Cockburn and Green, 1988; New South Wales Law Reform Commission (NSWLRC), 1985:14). While the requirement that a jury's verdict be unanimous was established in 1367, until 1670 juries were often fined or even imprisoned if their verdict was not what the judge thought it should be. Furthermore, it was only relatively recently that women and indigenous peoples in Australia, for example, became eligible for jury service (NSWLRC, 1985:16). In western common law jurisdictions with a jury system the usual qualification for jury service is:

(a) being on the electoral role; and/or (b) being a licensed driver; and/or (c) not coming under any of the categories of disqualified or ineligible persons detailed in statutory provisions.

2 The Notion of an Impartial and Fair Jury: A Critical Appraisal

Many civil law countries (for example, Israel, Spain, the Netherlands) have no community participation in the guilt-determining process in serious criminal matters. Those common law and civil law countries that have a jury system differ regarding various aspects of their jury system (Osner et al., 1993). Such differences pertain to whether, for example, a jury comprises just lay persons (as in England and Wales, the US, New Zealand, Canada and Australia) or a combination of lay persons and judges (as in Denmark, Belgium, France, Italy, Germany and Sweden) and the types of legal cases they decide; how lists of potential jurors are compiled;[3] who is disqualified from or is ineligible for jury service; the categories of individuals who can be excused from service as of right; how many peremptory challenges and how many challenges for cause are allowed each side at a trial. Other important features are what information about potential jurors is divulged in court for either side to challenge (in England a lawyer knows only a potential juror's name and, therefore, unlike in the US, the scope for 'choosing' jurors is very limited – but see below for a judge's ruling that changes this) and whether a judge has discretion to exclude a juror even without a challenge having been made (as is the position in England and Wales – Buxton, 1990a, 1990b). In addition, the size of the jury varies between different countries and often depends on whether it is a civil or a criminal trial. While the public in western common law countries is well accustomed to twelve-member juries for criminal trials, the number of lay persons sitting with judges to decide serious criminal matters varies in civil law countries: in France, nine jurors deliberate with three judges; in Italy, six lay assessors sit with two judges; in Germany, three career judges adjudicate with lay judges and, finally, in Sweden, one professional judge sits with three lay judges (Osner et al., 1993). Furthermore, while some jurisdictions require a unanimous verdict others are content with a majority one. Other differences concern whether there is a requirement that a jury be segregated once it has commenced its deliberations[4] and whether the judge sums up to the jury on the facts (as happens in England and Wales, though not in the US (Evans, 1995:95)). A crucial characteristic of some jury systems is that a jury's verdict is final while in others it is merely a recommendation to the judge, as in some parts in the US. Finally, in some jurisdictions it is prohibited to interview jurors after a trial has been completed, as is the position in England under the Contempt of Court Act (1981) and in Australia, but this is not so in the US. Such differences between jurisdictions mean that one should not unquestionably generalise findings about juror decision-making across jurisdictions. Despite its great significance to so many people, it has been said that the jury is 'probably the least understood branch of our system of government' (Stanton Krauss, 1995:921). Drawing, in part, on Darbyshire (1991) concerning the very concept of the jury, let us next take a close and critical look at the jury, this 'quaint institution that reflects the apotheosis of amateurism' (Blom-Cooper, 1974).

A thorough dissection of the jury idea reveals that, sentimental attachments aside, the very concept of the jury itself is problematic and a strong case can be made for at least drastically reforming the jury system in western common law countries. To begin with, as already mentioned above, trial by one's peers is not provided in clause 39 of the Magna Carta. The fact is the Latin words '*judicium parium*' do not refer to 'a trial by jury', *judicium* 'implies the decision of a judge, not a jury verdict' (Darbyshire, 1991:743)[5] and *liber homo* (translated as 'freeman' or 'freeholder') 'did not mean what it does today' and 'we should remember from school history, freemen were a limited class in the feudal system' (p. 743). Thus, the long-held belief by legal scholars (for example, Blackstone, 1776; Devlin, 1956) that *judicium parium* referred to trial by one's peers is based on a misconception (Forsyth, 1852:108). It has also been pointed out that one cannot assert, in jurisprudential terms, that there is a right to jury trial (Darbyshire, 1991:743). The simple truth is that many criminal defendants charged with indictable offences/felonies simply do not have the choice of being tried by a magistrate/judge alone – they have to be tried by judge and jury. The view that it is desirable to be tried by one's 'peers' is based on the arguments that: (a) it is good to be tried by a group of individuals who are representative of one's community; and (b) that 'representativeness' makes for impartial, objective, just and fair jury verdicts. Marshall (1975) has argued that 'the right to trial by an impartial jury' is not an ideal that can be achieved because trial by one's 'peers', 'representativeness' and 'impartiality' do not go together and, even if they did, they would not guarantee that a jury's verdict would be a fair one. For example, fairness and impartiality may not be a feature of the general public which the jury represents (see Rosen, 1992).[6]

Such arguments, however, are unlikely to be taken seriously by staunch supporters of the jury. According to Cammack (1995:407), in the US where, historically, the jury has symbolised and embodied American democracy, the Supreme Court in *Powers v. Ohio* 499 US 400, 407 (1991) stated that, 'jury service is second only to voting in the implementation of participatory government' (p. 483) and the right to an 'impartial jury' in criminal cases is explicitly guaranteed in the Sixth Amendment (p. 428). In *Wainwright v. Witt* 469 US at 423 (1985) the Supreme Court provided a definition of a constitutionally impartial juror as someone 'who will conscientiously apply the law and find the facts' (Cammack, 1995:458). Finally, the Supreme Court stated clearly in *Holland v. Illinois* 493 US at 482 (1990) that the constitutional requirement of juror impartiality is to be achieved by means of per-emptory challenges (p. 447) but which are not to be exercised on the basis of the juror's sex (*J. E. B. v. Alabama* ex rel.T.B. 114 S.Ct 1419 (1994)) or race (*Batson v. Kentucky* 476 US 79 (1986)) because to do so violates the Equal Protection Clause of the Fourteenth Amendment (p. 406). Cammack maintains that definitions of juror impartiality such as that provided by the Supreme Court have their origin in and reflect the mind-body dualism of the Enlightenment, the belief that funda-mentally we can distinguish the subjective mind from the objective world and that, because there exists neutral objective reality, truth is something objective – beliefs that have been seriously questioned in linguistics, cognitive psychology and sociology (pp. 410, 463–6). As for the crucial term 'trial by one's peers', its meaning is by no means clear for the indigenous peoples of New Zealand (Dunstan et al., 1995:172). The very same comment can be made about indigenous people in the US, Canada and Australia. In order to provide a sufficient backdrop for the discussion of empirical studies that follows pertaining to a broad range of jury controversies, let us also consider what defenders and critics of the jury have said about it.

2.1 Arguments For and Against Jury Trials

The following is a list of arguments against jury trials:

- Trial by jury is not the cornerstone of the criminal justice system.[7]
- Juries are not representative of the wider community.
- In some jurisdictions jury trial is very nearly extinct.[8]
- A jury does not give reasons nor is it accountable for its verdict.[9]
- A jury deliberates in secret.
- A jury establishes no precedent.[10]
- Juries are unpredictable.
- For all intents and purposes, a jury verdict is final.
- A significant number of jury trials end up in mistrials.[11]
- Compared to a judge-alone trial, a jury trial is costly and time-consuming.[12]
- In a significant number of trials there is a hung jury.[13]

- Some jury verdicts reflect jurors' emotional involvement rather than rational decision-making.[14]
- A jury can be interfered with.[15]
- Non-legal factors such as inadmissible evidence and pretrial publicity impact on jury verdicts.[16]
- Juries are influenced by pretrial publicity of both non-legal[17] and legally-relevant[18] issues and neither judicial instructions nor deliberation reduce its impact.[19]
- Often jury verdicts are the result of persuasion tempering reason.[20]
- Many potential jurors try to avoid jury service and many of those who serve on juries report being disenchanted with the whole experience and lose confidence in the administration of justice.[21]
- In England and Wales the jury does not have to wait until the defence has finished presenting its case but can acquit the accused at any time after the prosecution has finished presenting its case.[22]
- Jury service can be a very traumatic experience.[23]
- Jurors often lack the ability to understand and judge a legal case adequately.[24]
- Jurors frequently cannot remember all the relevant facts of a case.[25]
- Juries acquit too readily.[26]
- Juries have been shown not to defy public opinion and, by failing to identify serious weaknesses in the prosecution case, convict innocent defendants.[27]
- Perverse jury verdicts are not uncommon.[28]
- Any form of *voir dire* is incompatible with both randomness and representativeness.[29]
- Allowing juries to rewrite the law has the potential for wrongful convictions.[30]
- Changing the law is the province of parliament.[31]
- Juries do not necessarily safeguard defendants' civil liberties.[32]
- There is no longer a need for perverse jury verdicts to counter the extreme severity of penal sanctions – thieves are no longer being sent to the gallows.[33]
- There is no big difference in the verdict of a jury of twelve and a judge deciding alone.[34]
- The jury's task is one for professionals, not amateurs.[35]

Interestingly, despite such a long list of serious criticisms against the jury, Sanborn (1993) has argued that the juvenile peer jury that exists in youth courts in the US (see Williamson et al., 1993) should be extended to all juvenile courts. In contrast to this, in England and Wales it has been suggested that the minimum age for jurors be raised to twenty-one years (Stone, 1990).

The following are arguments in favour of jury trials:

- Jury service is an important civic experience.
- Jurors discharge their duty with a strong sense of responsibility.[36]
- A decision by a jury of one's peers is more acceptable to most defendants than the decision of a single judge.
- The jury is an antidote to tyranny.[37]
- Twelve heads are better than one.
- Unlike an experienced judge, a jury brings a fresh perception to each trial.
- Jurors make up in common sense and experience what they do not possess in professional knowledge and training.
- Jurors generally stick to the evidence and are not swayed by irrelevant considerations.[38]
- It is not true that juries take too long to reach a verdict.[39]
- Jury deliberations iron out any idiosyncrasies of individual jurors.
- Jurors are able to decide complex legal cases.[40]
- Jury damages awards are not biased against businesses and high-status defendants.[41]
- Unlike a judge, a jury can counter strict and unfair legal rules by deviating from them, motivated by its own social and ethical standards.[42]
- Whether a jury's verdict is 'perverse' depends on whose opinion is sought.[43]
- Most jury trial protagonists believe the jury system is a 'good system'.[44]

Defenders of the jury in the UK (see Harman and Griffith, 1979) have pointed with great concern to the onslaught on the jury in the form, for example, of the abolition of unanimous verdicts (1978), restrictions of the right to question jurors (1973), restriction on the cases to be tried by the jury (1977), restriction of the right of defence counsel to challenge jurors (1977), as well as the legitimisation of jury vetting (1978).

In the light of so many, and often conflicting and entrenched, views held by both advocates and critics of the jury system, it would seem that no amount of research evidence as to how juries behave in real life or as to how they compare with judges or some other tribunal will resolve the jury controversy. Findings reported by psycholegal researchers may abound but at the end of the day important value judgements remain to be made. One thing is certain: the jury trial on both sides of the Atlantic and in Australia may well undergo further reforms (see below) but it will be with us for a long time to come. Its abolition 'will come only after long reflection and in the context of a complete overhaul of the administration of criminal justice' (Blom-Cooper, 1974).

Jury verdicts impact not only on individual criminal and civil defendants but can also have a significant effect on a whole community, as when, for example, at the end of the Rodney King trial in Los Angeles the jury's verdict triggered the riots. As Levine (1992) reminds us, the jury is a political institution, a jury verdict can also have dire economic consequences for companies made to pay large amounts in damages, can ruin a political party's popularity by finding a leading politician guilty and, finally, a jury's decision can send a strong message to a community regarding what behaviour is or is not tolerated.

The jury has been a very popular research topic for psychologists. Kadane (1993:234), however, draws attention to the fact that psychologists have devoted a disproportionate amount of time to studying juries and have neglected a host of other decisions in the criminal justice system: such as the decision to report a crime; the police deciding to record what has been reported; the police deciding to use their firearms; to stop and search someone; to arrest them; deciding what to charge them with and plea-bargaining decision-making processes and so forth which impact on a far greater number of individuals within most western societies than do jury decisions. The fact is that the great majority of legal cases are not decided by juries but by tribunals, Magistrates' Courts and judges sitting alone, and most criminal defendants plead guilty while most civil cases are settled outside courts (Baldwin and McConville, 1979; Hans, 1992:56; Willis, 1983). It should also be noted in this context that as judicial discretion at the sentencing stage is reduced (see Chapter 6) and sentences become more predictable, the scope for prosecutorial discretion increases as does the practice of plea-bargaining, thus reducing the importance of jury trials even further. In this chapter an attempt will be made to show that the jury's symbolic importance far outweighs its practical significance, that systematic jury selection is conceptually problematic and does not appear to be as 'scientific' as its advocates would have us believe and, finally, that there exists a strong case for drastically reforming the jury as it exists on both sides of the Atlantic and in Australia in both a legal and psycholegal sense. On the basis of the available behavioural research into jurors and juries some authors have argued that there is already a substantial body of knowledge relevant to attempts to improve the jury system (Pennington and Hastie, 1990).

Of course, as Hastie (1993b:6–10) and Hans (1992:56–8) point out, there are very good reasons for the popularity of jury studies, namely, the very nature of jury cases, the fact that the jury's task is clear, it appeals not only to cognitive psychologists interested in higher processes but also to psychologists with other interests, because of the symbolic importance and actual impact of jury decisions on people and, last but not least, because 'research on jury decisions can be profitable' (Hastie, 1993b:10). The practice of jury consulting firms, retained by wealthy defendants and their defence attorneys to construct ideal profiles of jurors who would be favourable or opposed to a defendant that are used to reject jurors during *voir dire* (a largely American phenomenon), can be criticised as being unethical.

3 Methods For Studying Juries/Jurors

Research into both jury verdicts and individual jurors has been bedevilled by the apparently insurmountable difficulty that there is no consensus about what constitutes a 'good juror' or a 'good verdict' (Cammack, 1995; Mungham and Bankowski, 1976). This fact has not prevented jury/juror research becoming one of the most popular topics for psycholegal researchers during the last three decades.

3.1 Archival Research

Archival research enables one to collect data on real jury verdicts and is the method used, for example, by a group of Rand Corporation researchers in the US who analysed jury verdict reporters over a twenty-year period.[45] Two limitations of archival research are: that important information of interest to a researcher may well be missing; and it is not possible to draw convincing causal inferences on the basis of such data. Of course, hypotheses developed from archival research can be tested under simulated conditions.

3.2 Questionnaire Surveys

The best known study using this method is Chicago Law School's Kalven and Zeisel's (1966) pioneering study, *The American Jury*, which 'was a remarkable contribution and stimulated generations of scholars to undertake empirical work on the jury' (Hans, 1995:1233). Because of the great impact this study has had on psychological studies of juries/ jurors, let us consider it in some detail.[46] Kalven and Zeisel sent a questionnaire to a total of 3500 judges in the US. Of those, 555 (15.8 per cent) cooperated, providing data on 3576 trials. This oft-cited study which provided the basis for a lot of the jury/juror research, however, suffers a number of very serious limitations (Law Reform Commission of Victoria, 1985; Pennington and Hastie, 1990; Stephenson, 1992). To illustrate, according to the Law Reform Commission of Victoria, the sample of cases surveyed comprised 3 per cent out of the total number of jury trials (60 000) during the two-year period in question in the

1950s; 50 per cent of 3576 cases were provided by only 15 per cent of the judges; the reliability and validity of the study was grossly undermined by the fact that 'at first a broadly worded questionnaire was used (2385 cases), which was changed midway to a more specific questionnaire, whilst lumping them together for the findings' (Law Reform Commission of Victoria, 1985:82).

Another major limitation of the same study is that judges, and not jurors themselves, were asked to assess the jurors' competence in understanding the content of a trial. The finding, therefore, that 'by and large the jury understand the facts and get the case straight' (Kalven and Zeisel, 1966:149) can only be viewed with a lot of scepticism since we would not expect a judge to admit that he/she gave a poor summing up for the jury before they retired to deliberate their verdict (LRCV, 1985:83). At best, Kalven and Zeisel's conclusions 'about the motivations and psychological conditions underlying individual jurors' decisions ... must be hypothetical rather than conclusive' (Pennington and Hastie, 1990:93). It is interesting to note that even though Kalven and Zeisel also carried out post-trial juror interviews in 225 cases and, in addition, went as far as to tape actual jury deliberations in five civil cases (it was legally still possible to do so then),[47] they provide no figures on jurors' responses regarding what they thought of the judges' summing up, or how far the jurors were influenced by the weight of the evidence as they perceived it, instead of how they were said to have been influenced by it on the basis of what the judges who took part in the postal survey led the researchers to conclude.

Two very significant findings reported by Kalven and Zeisel were: firstly, and contrary to what films like 'Twelve Angry Men' might lead us to believe, most jurors decide on their verdict before they retire to deliberate and the majority view prevails. If accepted, this finding has serious policy implications, not the least in emphasising the importance of screening potential jurors during *voir dire* so as to have as many jurors as possible who will favour one's client (see below). The same finding has also led many juror researchers (see Hastie, 1993a) to concern themselves with how jurors behave *before* they retire to deliberate. The wisdom of so doing, however, has been challenged (see Ellsworth, 1993). Secondly, the judge agreed with the jury in 75 per cent of the cases.

Stephenson (1992:180–2) has analysed the figures on judge–jury agreement provided by the Chicago researchers and shows convincingly that the conclusion that jurors' verdicts are not significantly different from what trial judges themselves would decide is not justified. Stephenson concludes that:

In effect, Kalven and Zeisel's work suggests that if the judges' views are taken to be the criterion against which the validity of jury decision-making is evaluated, then juries are very poor performers, and vice versa. Judges and juries agree that a majority of defendants is guilty. Unfortunately they do not agree on whom to find not guilty. (p. 181)

Stephenson shows that the judges in Kalven and Zeisel's study would have convicted 57 per cent of the 1083 defendants the juries would have acquitted (p. 180), and concludes that the police are apparently right in assuming that many criminal defendants should consider themselves lucky for having been tried by a jury and not by a more legally informed panel (p. 181).

Unlike the US, in the UK, Australia, New Zealand and Canada the function of the jury in criminal trials is confined to deciding whether a defendant is guilty or not. It is the judge who decides what sentence to impose. British researchers have also reported questionnaire surveys. The Oxford study by McCabe and Purves (1972b) surveyed judges, counsel and solicitors involved in 266 contested trials and reported a rate of 12.5 per cent 'perverse acquittals', that is, cases where the jury verdict is against the weight of the evidence. Zander's (1974) study of jury trials at the Old Bailey and the Inner London Crown Court reported that perverse acquittals comprised 6 per cent of the total. Finally, the well-known Birmingham jury study of 500 trials by Baldwin and McConville (1979) surveyed defence solicitors and judges (with a response rate of 84 per cent and 94 per cent respectively) as well as police and found that about one in four of the prosecuting solicitors and one-third of the judges were dissatisfied with the jury's verdict, with 12 per cent of such verdicts being considered as 'perverse'. The more recent questionnaire survey of jurors and other trial protagonists in Britain by Zander and Henderson (1994), however, found that the percentage of verdict acquittals considered 'surprising' varied depending on the category of respondents (see above). The same survey reported relatively high response rates except by defendants. Contrary to what the majority of American mock-jury researchers have reported (see below), Baldwin and McConville (1979:104) found no relationship between the social composition of juries in terms of age, social class, gender and race and their verdicts, indicating that jury verdicts are perhaps largely unpredictable. Dunstan et al.'s (1995) assessment of the relevant literature similarly concluded that jurors' sex, age and occupation do not seem to play any important role in jury deliberations (p. 55). Negative results from studies of actual juries (see also below) challenge the external validity of a lot of mock-juror/jury studies.

3.3 Mock Juries

This has been the most commonly used method by students of juridic behaviour, especially in the US, and has attracted a great deal of criticism. Such studies have reported a significant amount of experimental evidence suggesting that characteristics of both the defendant and the jurors impact on jury decisions about verdict and (in the US) severity of sentence. Since the early 1980s the quality of mock-jury studies has improved in terms of its sensitivity to the social and legal context of jury decision-making, methodological subtlety and legal sophistication (Hans, 1992:60). The maturity of the field of jury research is evidenced in the use, for example, of filmed trials based on transcripts of real cases (instead of brief descriptions of fictional cases), sampling jurors from actual court jury pools (instead of using psychology undergraduates), and having them deliberate as a group under conditions that are comparable to what goes on in real trials (see Hastie et al., 1983; Hastie, 1993b).

Such improvement has come about in the wake of criticism of jury simulation research by both psychologists (for example, Konečni and Ebbesen, 1979, 1992) and judges, such as Chief Justice Rehnquist in the US in the case of *Lockhart v. McCree* 106 S.Ct. 1758 (1986). Commenting on simulation research on the death penalty and jury verdicts (see below) Konečni and Ebbesen (1992:418) stated that:

> One is tempted to conclude that some psychologists and justices have behaved as they claim jurors do: their private attitudes against capital punishment have caused them to ignore the strength of the evidence and to assert external validity for a conclusion the truth of which as a scientific fact has been far from being established.

It would be true to say that while, generally, mock-jury research is characterised by high internal validity, a lot of it appears to be short on external validity. In addition to the problem of artificiality in many jury simulation studies, Hans (1995b:1234) has criticised the almost exclusive reliance on one research method – experimental simulation. There is also the problem that jury researchers have failed to consider what type of case or juror they want to use to extrapolate their experimental simulation findings (Kadane, 1993:233). This is not to suggest that the types of variables examined in mock-jury studies are irrelevant but, rather, that actual jury decision-making processes are more complex than laboratory studies would seem to suggest. Most mock-jury research is largely American (see Strodtbeck et al., 1957, and Chicago Law School's Jury Project – Simon, 1967 – for early examples) but jury experiments were also carried out at the London School of

Economics in the late 1960s and early 1970s utilising members of the public as jurors (see Cornish, 1968; Sealy and Cornish, 1973).

3.4 Shadow Juries

Given that juries deliberate in secrecy and it would be illegal to interview jurors at the end of a trial in England, McCabe and Purves (1974) of Oxford University's Penal Research Unit, as it was then known, studied thirty 'shadow juries' sitting in on actual trials. Whilst shadow jurors' verdicts were not binding on the defendants involved, the fact that they were recruited utilising the electoral roll, they listened to the same information being presented in the course of a trial as the real jury, and left the court at the same time as the real jury during *voir dires*, means that it is the closest one could get in simulating juries. Their deliberations were, of course, recorded and transcribed, and shadow jurors were interviewed subsequently. McCabe and Purves found that the verdicts of the real and shadow jury were very similar indeed. Both shadow and real jury decided on a conviction (30 per cent) and on an acquittal (30 per cent) but shadow juries opted to convict and real juries to acquit 13 per cent and, finally, shadow juries decided to acquit but real juries to convict 7 per cent, with the remaining juries being 'hung'. While the significant similarity in verdicts between the two juries supports the validity of conclusions to be drawn from this Oxford study, according to Stephenson (1992) this shadow jury study by itself does not constitute convincing evidence that juries decide whether defendants are guilty or, at least, not consistent and reliable evidence (p. 185).

3.5 Post-Trial Juror Interviews

Post-trial interviews have been used, for example, to ascertain jurors' understanding of judges' instructions (see Costanzo and Costanzo, 1994; Reifman et al., 1992).

In jurisdictions such as Australia (but see Cadzow, 1995), Canada and England it is against the law to interview ex-jurors, and even where it is allowed (as in the US) jurors themselves may agree not to talk about their deliberations to anybody and/or the judge may discourage jurors from speaking to journalists or researchers. Limitations of the interview method include the fact that verbal reports of mental events are often incomplete (Nisbett and Wilson, 1977) and, furthermore, people generally find it difficult to determine the effect different factors have had on their thinking processes. As Hans (1992:59) points out, such interviews are increasingly common but they still tend to be used with jurors in celebrated cases; jurors' memories of what was said in the retiring room are bound to be limited; different jurors may well disagree about the content of the deliberation; and, finally, publicising jury deliberations will impact adversely on actual jurors' participation and freedom of expression during deliberation. Like eyewitnesses generally, jurors' recall will normally get worse over time and be susceptible to 'contamination'; their answers may well be influenced by the 'hindsight bias' (Casper et al., 1989) and the social desirability factor. To illustrate, Doob (1977) reported that even though the great majority (97 per cent) of jurors surveyed said they had found judicial instructions easy to understand, about 25 per cent could not define 'burden of proof' and in cases where this applied half of them were unable to remember what the judge had instructed them about the defendant's criminal record.

Despite its limitations, by giving jurors a voice the interview method can be fruitful in yielding very significant findings, including revelations about phenomena not initially known, especially in terms of how jurors cope with the knowledge that they are responsible for someone's execution (Hans, 1995b:1235). Lengthy in-person interviews with capital jurors carried out by university students is the chief source of data in the national Capital Jury Project (CJP) currently underway in the US.[48] According to Bowers (1995:1057), the objectives of the CJP have been to: (a) examine and systematically describe jurors' exercise of capital sentencing discretion; (b) identify the sources and assess the extent of arbitrariness in jurors' exercise of capital discretion; and (c) assess the efficacy of the principal forms of capital statutes in controlling arbitrariness in capital sentencing.

3.6 Books by Ex-Jurors

Jurors in celebrated cases are not only constantly the object of widespread media coverage (as in the O. J. Simpson trial) but individual jurors on both sides of the Atlantic have published their experiences (see Barber and Gordon, 1976; Zerman, 1977). The major limitation of such books is that they are about the experience of one or a few individuals in isolated cases. Nevertheless, books by ex-jurors can still provide an insight into the experience of serving on the jury.

4 What Do We Know About Juries?

4.1 Selecting Jurors

As already mentioned, the scope for selecting jurors is very limited in Great Britain, Australia and New Zealand. Before a trial starts, during the *voir dire* hearing both the defendant and the prosecution can reject a number of prospective jurors without giving reason other than they do not like the look of them. The number of peremptory challenges, as this is known, varies from jurisdiction to jurisdiction. At the time of writing, in Australia each side is allowed six peremptory challenges in Victoria but three only in New South Wales. In the two States, the two sides can also challenge a number of jurors for cause. By comparison, in England and Wales, s.118(1) of the Criminal Justice Act (1988) abolished peremptory challenge, but the Juries Act (1974) preserves both statutory and common law grounds for challenging individual prospective jurors mainly on the basis of presumed or actual partiality (see Buxton, 1990a, 1990b). Baldwin and McConville (1980a) reported that challenging jurors was a rather uncommon practice in their Birmingham study since in only one trial in seven was the right to challenge potential jurors exercised; furthermore, where there was a challenge it generally meant challenging one single potential juror. It thus came as no surprise to find that 'the final composition of the juries had in effect been largely unaffected by the use of challenges' (p. 39). Recently, however, in England in the *R. v. Maxwell* trial,[49] which received a lot of pretrial publicity, Phillips J. directed that a questionnaire be administered to potential jurors by court officials to ascertain both their availability and any possibility they were unduly prejudiced against the defendant because of pretrial publicity. His Lordship ruled that the information thus collected would be of help to him in deciding if jurors ought not to sit on that case and would also be helpful to counsel when considering challenging potential jurors for cause (Victoria Law Reform Committee, 1995:8).

By using the juror challenge procedure and such instruments as the 'Juror Bias Scale' (see Kassin and Wrightsman, 1983) an accused in the US, especially one with a lot of money, can influence significantly the composition of the jury who will try the case and pass sentence. Both the length of the *voir dire* selection hearing, and the extent to which attorneys will go in questioning potential jurors, varies and often reflects the socioeconomic status of the defendant. As far as it has been possible to ascertain, in the much-publicised O. J. Simpson trial, for example, prospective jurors had to respond to a seventy-five-page questionnaire comprising 294 questions. The whole *voir dire* process is predicated on the assumption that jurors give honest answers. However, the validity of this assumption is questionable in light of evidence reported that between 25 and 30 per cent of real ex-jurors surveyed in one study admitted to having concealed relevant information about themselves when questioned in court (Seltzer et al., 1991).

The cases that are decided by juries in English-speaking western common law countries cannot be said to be representative of criminal cases as a number of processes negate this and, similarly, the individuals who serve as jurors cannot be said to be representative of their community (Kadane, 1993). Furthermore, every jury case is unique in terms of the defendant, the victim, the attorneys and the quality of their advocacy skills, the type and strength of the evidence against the defendant, the composition of the jury, and the way in which the attorney will frame his/her arguments. The question, therefore, arises of whether 'scientific', systematic jury selection is as possible as some maintain and, if so, is it done so successfully that it significantly influences the trial outcome as some psychologists and jury selection experts claim? After all, such experts have a vested interest since they make a lot of money offering their services and advising attorneys about the *voir dire* selection hearing. As Lloyd-Bostock (1988:52) points out: 'Systematic jury selection has coincided with winning in a growing number of cases. However, there are good reasons to remain sceptical about some of the more extravagant claims made for it'. The use of the term 'scientific jury selection' has been criticised by Hans and Vidmar (1986) on the basis that it conveys an impression of accuracy and precision not justified by existing knowledge and methods.

The very notion of systematic jury selection is also controversial for other reasons. Its supporters maintain that jury selection *per se* is a justifiable practice and should be empirically based. Its critics, on the other hand, maintain that selecting jurors is incompatible with the ideal of a representative jury chosen by a random process. The controversy is one that is unlikely to be resolved in the foreseeable future. Meanwhile, students of legal psychology should note that a lot of juror research has concerned itself with how individual jurors in serious criminal cases behave before they retire to deliberate (see Hastie, 1993b and section 4.5 below). This focus stems from a belief that: (a) most jurors have decided on a verdict before they retire to deliberate; and (b) the pre-deliberation distribution of individual jurors' verdict preferences is the best predictor of the final jury verdict (Kalven and Zeisel, 1966; McCabe and Purves, 1974). In considering the alleged importance of pre-deliberation distribution of individual juror verdict preferences, the reader should also remember that it is the strength of the evidence against the defendant that plays the most important role in determining trial outcome; that such characteristics of jurors as their personality and attitudes impact significantly on trial outcome if the evidence against the defendant is weak; jury deliberation tends to iron out individual juror preconceptions and, consequently, we are 'looking at quite a minor aspect of courtroom processes in looking at individual juror bias' (Lloyd-Bostock, 1988:48).

Ellsworth (1993:42) is similarly of the opinion that individual differences among jurors are not very good predictors of jury decision-
making. However, Ellsworth goes on to point to a paradox in this
context, namely, that 'In most cases the weight of the evidence is
insufficient to produce first-ballot unanimity in the jury ... Different
jurors draw different conclusions about the right verdict on the basis of
exactly the same evidence', and, 'first-ballot splits are the best-known
predictor of final jury verdict ... The inescapable conclusion is that
individual differences among jurors make a difference'. Examination of
jury literature shows that: (a) some enduring characteristics of jurors
are important in understanding the jury verdict; and (b) it is the
interaction of juror and case characteristics that should be the focus of
the jury researcher since neither set of variables can be said to be
operating alone. In the absence of sufficient such research, a certain
amount of scepticism is therefore warranted when considering research
findings concerning the relationship between juror characteristics and
verdict. In fact, such scepticism is further supported by studies of real
juries, such as that by Baldwin and McConville (1979) who found that
in 500 non-guilty pleas dealt with by the Birmingham Crown Court in
England during the period from February 1975 to September 1976 'no
single social factor [class, age, sex and race] nor as far as we could
detect, any groups of factors operating in combination, produced any
significant variation in the verdicts returned across the board' (p. 104).

A few studies have examined the impact on jury decisions of both the
strength of the evidence against the defendant and extralegal factors.
On the basis of such research it would appear that, as already mentioned, when the evidence against the defendant is weak jurors will
focus on legally irrelevant factors, such as a rape victim's physical
appearance, in order to agree on the verdict (Reskin and Visher, 1986).

Juror empanelling in celebrated cases often provides ample material
for the sensationalist print and electronic media, but the simple truth is
that if there is good, hard evidence against the defendant, the likelihood
is that it will be legal argument during the trial and not the composition
of the jury that will win the day (see Visher, 1987). Despite their
limitations, a significant contribution of mock-jury studies has been to
highlight the importance of non-legal characteristics of the defendant
in jury decision-making about the verdict (Stephenson, 1992:200).
Before considering the reported significance of individual juror
characteristics, it needs to be emphasised that their importance lies
more in the fact that different jurors choose to focus on and utilise
different information from what is presented to them during the trial in
order to construct different narratives justifying one verdict or another.

What, then, is the evidence that a number of characteristics of jurors, alone or in combination, which can be identified during *voir dire* impact significantly on jury verdicts?

4.2 The Reported Importance of Juror Characteristics

One book on trial advocacy contains reference to 'time-honoured selection criteria which counsel have used in years past' (Mauet and McCrimmon, 1993:25). The same authors, however, doubt the utility of generalising theories of jury selection from the US to Australia because of the 'cultural mosaic which characterises contemporary Australian society' (p. 26). Without reference to any supporting empirical research, Mauet and McCrimmon: emphasise the importance of having jurors with similar characteristics and backgrounds as one's client's; point out that prosecutors in a criminal case and defence counsel in a civil case prefer 'middle-aged or retired jurors who have average incomes, stable marriages, work in blue-collar or white-collar jobs, are in business or generally can hold jobs which demonstrate an adherence to the traditional work ethic' (p. 26); refer to the alleged importance of potential jurors' body language and physical appearance as a source of useful indicators in selecting jurors (p. 27); and, finally, they note the dichotomy between 'strong' and 'weak' jurors, with the latter said to be favoured by the party that has the onus of proof in a criminal or civil case (p. 27).

Studies have reported conflicting findings regarding the relationship between jurors' *gender* and verdict (Arce, 1995:566). However, the weight of the evidence shows that *female* jurors are more likely to convict a defendant charged with rape (Bagby et al., 1994; Brekke and Borgida, 1988; Hans and Vidmar, 1982) or child sexual abuse (Crowley et al., 1994; Gabora et al., 1993) and especially if there had been no eye-contact between the rape victim and the offender during the attack (Weir and Wrightsman, 1990). Interestingly, Brekke and Borgida reported that juror deliberation narrows such gender verdict differences. As one might have expected, *younger* jurors have been found to be more likely to acquit, but those of a *higher educational standard* have been reported as more likely to convict (Hans and Vidmar, 1982).

As far as *race* is concerned, the US Supreme Court has stated that peremptory challenges on the basis of a juror's race are unconstitutional (see above). In the first Rodney King trial, an all-white jury in Ventura County, Los Angeles, a predominantly white suburb, acquitted the four white policemen of the charge (under State legislation) of assaulting King, an African-American. In the aftermath of the Los Angeles riots, a racially mixed jury in Los Angeles County found two of the officers guilty of civil rights crimes the following year, casting doubt on the Supreme Court's sense of realism in pushing for sexless and colourblind jury decision-making (Hans, 1995a).

The well-known study of actual jury trials in Birmingham by Baldwin and McConville (1979) found that the racial composition of a jury was not important in explaining the verdict. It was the race of the defendant that emerged as significant, even when a jury was predominantly black a black defendant was more likely to feature among perverse convictions than acquittals. Evidence for juror prejudice and racial discrimination has also been reported in Canada (Avio, 1988; Bagby et al., 1994). According to Stephenson (1992:198): 'Little consistent effects of race have been demonstrated'. Of course, if a criminal defendant in England, Australia or in the US is black the chances are he/she is also of low socioeconomic status which, in turn, correlates with having a court-appointed counsel rather than a private one. Very few scholars of the criminal justice system in western countries doubt that, to a significant degree, a defendant's wealth can buy 'justice' in the courts. A juror's *authoritarianism* correlates with imposing a severer sentence but not with conviction proneness (Stephenson, 1992:198). Regarding jurors' *conservatism*, studies have reported conflicting findings (Arce et al., 1992:435). The presence on a jury of jurors with *previous experience* correlates with a greater likelihood of a guilty verdict (Dillehay and Nietzel, 1985) and severer sentences in both criminal and civil trials (Himelein et al., 1991).

Defence lawyers often advise their clients to look presentable in court and to watch their demeanour. But does research support such common-sense beliefs? A number of studies have reported that a defendant's *attractiveness* is a good predictor of defendant guilt in mock-jury studies (Bagby et al., 1994)[50] and whether mock jurors will apply the reasonable doubt standard (MacCoun, 1990). Interestingly, jurors have been shown to be harsher on an attractive defendant whose good looks enabled them to commit a deception offence (Sigall and Ostrove, 1975). Of course, as Sealy (1989:164) has pointed out, a defendant's attractiveness is not a variable that can be controlled in a trial. Furthermore, in an actual trial a perception by jurors that a defendant is 'attractive' is the result of a process, sometimes over weeks or even months, of watching and listening to him/her and not on the basis of subjects being allowed a brief look at a photograph as part of an experiment.

The relationship between one's attitudes and behaviour is one of the most researched, but remains a controversial topic in social psychology (see Jonas et al., 1995, for an excellent discussion). Attitudes, Ellsworth (1993:49) reminds us, 'rarely exist in isolation. Rather they come as bundles or constellations of related beliefs, and a scientifically ineffable but intuitively sensible consistency seems to apply locally to constellations of closely related attitudes'. The available evidence on the relationship between jurors' attitudes and their decision-making indicates that it is jurors' attitudes to the specific case at hand that are more important from an attorney's point of view and not who the jurors are or their general attitudes. A recent meta-analysis of the relevant empirical literature by Stephen Krauss (1995) concluded that attitudes do predict behaviour. Baldwin and McConville (1980a) concluded that it is not so much personal or social characteristics of the foreperson or of jurors that explain the verdict but 'individual attitudes, beliefs and prejudices, as they are brought out in discussions of the particular point at issue' (p. 41).

Capital juries are unique in American jurisprudence and in human experience generally because nowhere else does a group of ordinary members of the public, acting under legal authority, rationally discuss taking the life of another human being (Haney et al., 1994:149). For Weisberg (1983)[51] death penalty jurors are reminiscent of subjects in Stanley Milgram's (1974) famous obedience experiments because they are placed in a situation which is both novel and disorienting for them, experience stress, confront a moral dilemma and may well resort to 'a professional, symbolic interpretation of the situation' to get oriented.

There exists a sizeable body of literature on attitudes towards the death penalty and jury verdicts, and interesting findings have already been reported by researchers participating in the Capital Jury Project (see Bowers, 1995). According to Ellsworth (1993), attitudes towards the death penalty are generally strongly held and closely related to other attitudes about the criminal justice system (p. 48). More importantly, however, any potential jurors in the US who are found during *voir dire* to be opposed to the death penalty in principle and thus unable to return a fair verdict would be eliminated from jury service, as stated by the US Supreme Court in *Witherspoon v. Illinois* (1968). It has been reported that death-qualified jury candidates are influenced more by defendant characteristics than are death-penalty-excludable candidates (Williams and McShane, 1990).

However, conflicting views have been expressed about whether death-qualified juries are conviction prone (see Konečni et al., 1996). The American Psychological Association's *amicus* brief, submitted on behalf of the defendant in *Lockhart v. McCree* 106 S.Ct. 1758 (1986) concluded, on the basis of existing experimental evidence, that such juries are conviction prone. Subsequent researchers reached the same conclusion.[52] Further experimental evidence from jury simulation has been reported by Ellsworth (1993) and Mauro (1991). Chief Justice

Rehnquist was very critical of the methodology of mock-jury research and did not accept the view expressed in the APA's *amicus* brief. Criticising the US Supreme Court for mistrusting 'social scientific evidence', Mauro (1991:252) has claimed that in *Lockhart v. McCree*: 'The Supreme Court clearly did not appreciate the social scientific evidence of the biasing effects of death qualification'. Elliott's (1991) literature review of studies using brief written cases, studies based on the recall of real jurors and studies using audio-taped or video-taped trial presentation, concluded that the main assertion in the APA's *amicus* brief about the conviction proneness of death-qualified juries is not supported by the available research data; rather, 'There is support for the proposition that a weak relationship exists between death penalty attitude and predeliberation verdict preferences' (p. 263). It should be noted in this context that a potential juror's attitude towards the death penalty does not seem to exist in isolation but is part of a cluster of attitudes towards other criminal justice issues, such as how trustworthy are the prosecutors or the desirability of a crime control approach generally across the board in criminal justice (Fitzgerald and Ellsworth, 1984). In light of the contradictory conclusions reported, the jury is still out on the alleged prosecution proneness of death-qualified jurors. This conclusion should not surprise the reader because, as Arce (1995) points out, research into the relationship between individual charac-teristics of jurors and their verdicts have generally overlooked the inter-action between personality and such important variables as the type of legal case and the strength of the evidence against the defend-ant/plaintiff (see also, Konečni et al., 1996).

4.3 Juror Competence

In the context of a trial, 'competence' normally refers to whether a witness understands the difference between lying and telling the truth and the importance of telling the truth in court. We saw in Chapter 4 that child witnesses routinely have their competence assessed by the courts.[53] Also, statutory provisions in many jurisdictions make the accused a competent witness at his/her trial. While both sides in a trial can and do challenge jurors on a number of grounds, there is no requirement that the court be satisfied that a juror has the capacity to understand a legal case, let alone to judge it adequately. Not surprisingly, therefore, critics of the jury have charged that jurors are often incompetent in more ways than one.

4.3.1 Comprehending Evidence

Whilst there is evidence from shadow jury research (McCabe and Purves, 1974) that jurors are conscientious about the task, their initial enthusiasm and vigilance fades away in the course of the trial (Stephenson, 1992:187). Also, jurors are not selected because they have any special qualifications. It therefore should come as no surprise to find that jurors have been shown to have serious difficulty comprehending fine semantic differences between different legal concepts (Severance et al., 1992), have poor recall of important trial information (Hastie et al., 1983), especially in such complex trials as those involving fraud, for example (see Nathanson, 1995, for a discussion of relevant empirical studies). In fact, such was the concern of the Roskill Committee (1986) it recommended that a special tribunal should replace the jury in complex fraud cases. Some authors, however, have defended most jurors' competence to decide complex legal cases (Harding, 1988).

Zander and Henderson (1994) reported that 90 per cent of the more than 8000 Crown Court jurors themselves who took part in national British study over a two-week period in 1992 for the Royal Commission on Criminal Justice as individuals, and the jury as a group, had been able to understand and remember the evidence in the 3191 cases involved. Furthermore, in most cases prosecution and defence barristers were of the view that the jury would have had no trouble understanding or remembering the evidence. Zander and Henderson's findings, however, do not establish that the jurors surveyed actually understood and remembered the evidence since no test for that was included. Using a composite measure of case complexity based on data collected from ninety-four judges, Heuer and Penrod (1994b) surveyed 81 per cent of jurors in 160 trials (75 civil, 85 criminal). They found that as the amount of information in a case increased, the jurors admitted to greater difficulty deciding the case (p. 536). Rather alarming in this context is the finding from the Capital Jury Project that, while capital jurors could remember well details about the defendant, they admitted to having hardly comprehended and could barely recall the legal rules pertinent to their decision to impose the death penalty (Luginbuhl and Howe, 1995; Sarat, 1995).

4.3.2 Understanding and Following the Judge's Instructions

Given that jurors tend to rely on the judge's instructions to guide them in their deliberation (Costanzo and Costanzo, 1994), it is essential that jurors first of all understand such instructions. While it would be unfair to always blame jurors for not following instructions from the bench as if all judges and counsel were well versed in the art of clear verbal communication, there is evidence that jurors do have difficulty both understanding as well as following judges' legal instructions (Coyle, 1995).[54] Heuer and Penrod (1995:536) found that, as the complexity of the evidence in a case increased, jurors were less confident that their verdict reflected a proper understanding of the judge's instructions. Suggestions to ameliorate this problem have included rewriting and standardising judges' instructions to juries (Hans, 1992), allowing jurors to take notes in order to assist their memory of important trial details (see Forster Lee et al., 1994; Heuer and Penrod, 1988, 1994a) and to ask questions during the trial in order to clarify issues (Hollin, 1989). However, such reforms do not solve the problem that jurors may well decide not to follow the judge's instruction to ignore pre-trial publicity and/or other extra legal evidence that should not have been presented during the trial, such as a defendant's prior convictions (Casper and Benedict, 1993:66). Strong support for this concern has been provided recently by the CJP in the US.

The US Supreme Court in *Gregg* stated a requirement that capital jurors must decide guilt and punishment separately. However, Sandys (1995:1221) found that interviews with sixty-seven capital jurors in Kentucky revealed they made the decision concurrently, before the penalty stage of the trial, thus rendering irrelevant any subsequent evaluation of information about the defendant's mitigating and aggravating factors in order to decide on the right sentence. Emanating from the CJP, Bowers (1995) has also reported evidence for the same undesirable practice by capital jurors, adding that such decisions are made 'on the bases of their unguided feelings or reactions to the crime'; that the findings also show that sentencing guidelines provide 'legal cover' to many who have already decided on their verdict, and 'legal leverage' for convincing those jurors who have not made up their minds. Bowers concluded that, in either case, the guidelines 'appear to lessen the sense of responsibility for imposing an awful punishment' (p. 1102). Such findings show that lay persons are perhaps not competent to decide guilt in serious criminal cases, let alone decide the appropriate sanction and whether to impose the death penalty on a defendant.

4.4 The Jury Foreperson

When the *voir dire* process is completed the first task of the jurors is to elect a foreperson, unless the trial is in a jurisdiction which provides that this be done by the drawing of lots or that the first juror selected becomes the foreperson. The general public, practising attorneys, academic lawyers and researchers consider the foreperson a key figure in the courtroom. In his book *The Chosen Ones*, Bryan (1971) stated: 'It is a great general rule to say, "One cannot be too careful about the foreman". The foreman regulates discussion in the jury room and hence holds a great deal of power' (p. 388). This view is shared by Deosoran (1993) who maintains that 'all jurors are equal but the foreperson is first among equals ... any person who is elected to preside over a group must exert some influence in the development and conclusions of the deliberations' (p. 71).

The Morris Committee (1965) in England was of the view that the foreperson should, in principle, be no different from other jury members but considered it a good idea that he/she should, as far as possible, possess the qualities of a good chairperson. According to Saks and Hastie (1978:190), the juror characteristics that predict foreperson election are: male sex, high socioeconomic status, sitting at the end of the jury table and initiating discussion. Baldwin and McConville (1980a: 40–1) found that the forepersons in their study were disproportionately male, forty years or older and in managerial, professional and intermediate occupations. Similar findings were reported by Deosoran (1993). However, Baldwin and McConville found no relationship between the social characteristics of forepersons and jury verdicts. The shadow jury research by McCabe and Purves (1974) similarly found that the foreperson did not seem to unduly influence jury members. This is in contrast to mock-jury findings by Bevan et al. (1958) that the personality of forepersons can impact on jury deliberations to the extent that they frequently change the opinions of individual jurors regarding what constitutes equitable damages in negligence cases. It may very well be the case that individual juror variables identified as important in a well-controlled experiment are not as important in the context of an actual jury where a host of factors are operating at the same time. The foreperson can, of course, influence the outcome of the deliberation by directing discussion, timing poll votes and influencing whether poll votes will be public or secret (see below).

4.5 Jury Deliberation

At the end of a criminal trial the judge will normally instruct the jury on both procedures and verdicts and the jury will then retire to the jury room to discuss the case at hand and reach a verdict. The underlying belief is that 'jury deliberation is a reliable way of establishing the truth in a contentious matter' (Stephenson, 1992:179). What we know today about jury deliberation is from mock- and shadow-jury studies as well as from accounts by ex-jurors. None of the researchers in this area has observed real juries at their task. Whilst accounts by ex-jurors are idiosyncratic and biased (Baldwin and McConville, 1980a), most of the mock research into jury decision-making (see Hastie, 1993a; Levine, 1992, for reviews) focuses on juror behaviour at the pre-deliberation stage, in the belief that most jurors have already decided on a verdict before they retire to deliberate and that first-ballot majority verdict preferences predict the final verdict reliably. This belief can be traced back to Kalven and Zeisel's (1966) reported finding that in nine out of ten juries the deliberation task is concerned with convincing a minority of jurors to change their mind and embrace the verdict of the majority. This is referred to as Kalven and Zeisel's 'liberation hypothesis'. It is established that jurors generally enter the deliberation room without a unanimous verdict and there is support for Kalven and Zeisel's liberation hypothesis. Using six-member juries, Tanford and Penrod (1986) found that in approximately 95 per cent of the time the side that had most of the votes at first ballot had the final verdict. However, the relationship between predeliberation distribution of juror preferences and jury verdict is not as simple as Kalven and Zeisel suggested (see also section 4.1 above).

Ellsworth (1993:58) disagrees with Kalven and Zeisel's generalisation about jury deliberation – that it is in only 10 per cent of the cases that the distribution of individual jurors' predeliberation verdict preferences does not predict the final jury verdict – and points to the finding by Hastie et al. (1983) from their mock-jury research that the verdict of one-quarter of the juries who were in a minority before deliberation managed to prevail. It is worth noting in this context that, as Ellsworth (1993:58) points out, Kalven and Zeisel provide no details of how they came to their 'liberation hypothesis' conclusion. On the basis of their own work, the well-known American researchers Pennington and Hastie (1990:102) concluded that the relationship between individual jurors' initial verdicts and the final jury verdict is more complex than the simple one proposed by Kalven and Zeisel (1966). It would appear that many a jury researcher has been unaware or has downplayed, if not ignored outright, the importance of jury research contradicting Kalven and Zeisel's much-quoted nine out of ten predeliberation distribution of individual juror verdict preferences. Seriously considering such contradictory evidence would call into question the usefulness of a great deal of research into the relationship between juror characteristics and verdict.

Available empirical evidence (Hastie et al., 1983) indicates that we need to distinguish between: (a) deliberations where jurors announce their verdict preferences before discussion begins in the jury room (known as 'verdict-driven' deliberations); and (b) deliberations in which jurors' verdict preferences are expressed later in the deliberation process (known as 'evidence-driven' deliberations). In other words, with the latter there will be discussion before jurors have their first ballot and, consequently, first-ballot preferences may not reflect the jurors' predeliberation preferences. In addition, there is the possibility, for example, that jury discussion may reduce an initial majority verdict that the defendant is guilty of first-degree murder to a final verdict of guilty of second-degree murder (Hastie et al., 1983:59).

Additional evidence that predeliberation juror preferences are not equivalent to first-ballot votes was reported by Davis et al. (1988), who found that the timing of a straw poll on individual first-ballot votes (that is, whether before any discussion or after five minutes of discussion) makes a significant difference in how individual jurors will change their initial verdict preferences to their first-ballot votes. The findings by Hastie et al. (1983) and Davis et al. (1988), as well as findings reported regarding the importance of jury size (see below), whether jurors are instructed to reach a unanimous as opposed to a majority verdict (Hastie et al., 1983; Kerr and MacCoun, 1985) indicate that: (a) jurors' predeliberation verdict preferences do not necessarily predict their first-ballot votes; and (b) the process by which jurors' predeliberation verdict preferences are somehow synthesised to yield a jury verdict is a complex one, probably more complex than Kalven and Zeisel or some jury researchers would like us to think. Sandys and Dillehay (1995) tested Kalven and Zeisel's 'liberation hypothesis' utilising 142 telephone interviews of a representative sample of ex-jurors who had decided felony cases in Lexington, Kentucky. Ex-jurors were asked what they did first and, second, upon retiring to deliberate, how much time they spent discussing the case before having their first ballot and, finally, the outcome of the first ballot. Sandy and Dillehay reported: (a) in support of Kalven and Zeisel, a significant relationship was found between first-ballot votes and final jury verdict (p. 184); (b) that in most of the trials concerned the juries spent an average of 45 minutes discussing the case before having their first ballot; and (c) in only 11 per cent of the trials the jurors had a ballot without any discussion taking place (p. 191). Sandys and Dillehay concluded that their results suggest deliberation plays a more significant role in shaping the verdicts of real juries than was conjectured by Kalven and Zeisel (1966) in the 'liberation hypothesis'. The same view was expressed by Baldwin and McConville (1980a) on the basis of their study.

A number of factors have been found to influence the deliberation process and to impact on the jury's verdict. Recognising the crucial importance of jurors feeling responsible for their verdict, the Eighth Amendment in the US prohibits providing capital jurors with misleading information that undermines their sense of personal moral responsibility for imposing the death penalty (Hoffmann, 1995:1138). Given that, for most people, deciding to sentence someone to death is a negative consequence, the less responsible capital jurors feel for the decision the more likely they are to impose the death penalty (Sherman, 1995). In order to lessen their responsibility capital jurors may well attribute responsibility to the relevant guided discretion, the judge, the defendant, the appeal process, they may perceive themselves as mere conduits of community values and/or finally, may feel a diffusion of responsibility to other members of the jury (Sherman, 1995:1244–5). Findings from the CJP indicate that capital jurors try hard to distance themselves from the decision (Hans, 1995b:1235).

Socially 'successful' jurors have been found to talk more than less successful ones, men talk more than women and the foreperson talks a disproportionate amount of time (Ellsworth, 1993:59). It has also been reported by Hastie et al. (1983) that if a jury is required to return a majority instead of an unanimous verdict, then minority jurors will participate less and will be paid less attention by the rest of the jury and that taking a vote very early on speeds up the deliberation process. Jury deliberation will take longer if the jury is evidence-driven rather than verdict-driven (Hastie et al., 1983), but this will not necessarily result in a different verdict. However, studies of real juries have found that the longer the retirement the more likely it will lead to an acquittal (Baldwin and McConville, 1980a:42). More specifically, Baldwin and McConville reported that the chances of acquittal virtually doubled with juries that were out for more than three hours (p. 42). Multiple charges against the defendant correlate with a greater likelihood of a guilty verdict (Tanford et al., 1985) as is knowledge that the defendant has a prior conviction (Greene and Dodge, 1995). It has also been found that if a reasonable doubt standard of proof is emphasised then jurors are more likely to acquit (McCabe and Purves, 1974). As a jury proceeds with its discussion, the tendency is for minority jurors to move closer to the majority view and for leniency to prevail (Kerr and Bray, 1982). Osborne et al. (1986), however, found that, following deliberation, jurors shift to a severer decision if the jury is heterogeneous rather than homogeneous. In this sense, the composition of a jury can be said to be related to its verdict.

In the 1970s the Supreme Court in the US upheld the use of six-person juries in criminal (*Williams v. Florida* 399 US 78, 86 (1970)) and civil (*Colgrove v. Battin* 413 US 149, 156 (1973)) cases (Cammack, 1995:435). Thomas and Pollack (1992) applied probability theory to assess how far jury size and majority verdicts could be reduced without impacting adversely on the jury as a microcosm of the general community from which it is drawn. Their findings provided support for the Supreme Court's decisions in *Williams* and *Colgrove*. However, as Stephen Krauss (1995) points out, Thomas and Pollack's results are based on the assumption that juries comprise a random sample of the relevant community of potential jurors. Real jurors cannot be said to constitute such representative bodies of their parent communities, a factor that renders Thomas and Pollack's findings 'meaningless' (Stephen Krauss, 1995:924). The sad reality is that the US Supreme Court, like the judiciary and legislatures in other western common law, has as yet to come to grips with the contradictions that are inherent in the jury concept itself.

Smaller juries such as six-member ones can only be less representative of the broader community than the conventional twelve-member jury and their verdicts are likely to be different (Hans and Vidmar, 1986; Zeisel and Diamond, 1987). In fact, small juries involve less communication per unit time, are less likely to recall evidence accurately or to examine the evidence thoroughly or to result in a hung jury (Saks, 1977). There are conflicting views on whether jurors in a smaller jury participate less (Saks, 1977) or more (Arce, 1995:567). Small juries are more likely to hold secret ballots and to convict (Hans and Vidmar, 1986, cited in Hollin, 1989:168). It becomes clear that the real reason for introducing small-size juries have been economic concerns (Zeisel and Diamond, 1987:204). The fact is, of course, that the courts' wish to increase the jury's efficiency and to reduce its monetary cost inevitably has meant tampering with the psychological processes that take place during deliberation. As Wrightsman (1987:260) pointed out, what is also of particular concern is the fact that the US Supreme Court's decision in *Williams v. Florida* 399 US 78 (1970) – that six-member juries were constitutionally acceptable (that is, could discharge their responsibility as successfully as twelve-member juries) – was handed down on the basis of a misreading of the psychological research results available. In a country with the death penalty such practices by some of its most senior judges are definitely a worry. Equally worrying is the practice of politicians who legislate to change aspects of the criminal justice system that are vital to the defendant's rights in the name of expediency alone, as was the case with the change to the ten out of twelve majority in jury verdicts in Great Britain thirty years ago.

A perception that a small jury is 'okay' because many jurors are not active has justified having smaller juries. However, as Arce (1995:568) points out, there is empirical evidence that ' "non-active" jurors play a more decisive role in the dynamics of the jury ... than is commonly conceived' (p. 568). For example, non-active jurors have been found to accept arguments contrary to their initial position (pro guilty or pro not guilty) which in turn produces disequilibrium in the jury by finally swaying the more active members of the group towards a consensus (p. 568).

Regarding how jurors reach agreement, there has been report of at least one US jury (in the *Oliver North* case) who resorted to prayer to break an impasse in their deliberation (Rosenbaum, 1989).[55] Levine (1992) sums it up well when he states: 'Social and psychological pressure usually suffices to bring dissenters into line ... [but] this generalization is too broad; minorities within the jury are not so powerless as they have been made to seem' (p. 155), and it is not unheard of for 'holdouts' to cause a hung jury. According to Levine, jurors have also been found to reach a compromise verdict, to indulge in 'log rolling' (that is, split jurors trade-off convictions involving multiple defendants) and, in one case he quotes, a juror took it upon herself to mediate between two opposing groups of fellow jurors (p. 169). Of course, a juror with leadership qualities (and he/she does not have to be the foreperson), can sway even a majority to his/her point of view.

As to the question of why jurors change their minds about the appropriate verdict, according to Pennington and Hastie (1990:100) jurors do so primarily because they are influenced by information about legal issues or how legal definitions or instructions should be applied to the evidence, rather than information about the evidence and its implications for what had happened during the crime events. The trial judge can influence the verdict of the jury by, for example, sending the jury back to the jury room repeatedly until it reaches a unanimous verdict, or even by giving the jury a sermon (known in some parts of the US as 'Allen Charge') on the importance of reaching a verdict if it seems unable to do so (Levine, 1992:165).

5 Models of Jury Decision-Making[56]

According to Hastie (1993b) there are basically four descriptive models of jury decision-making: (a) the Bayesian probability theory model (see Hastie, 1993b:11–17); (b) the algebraic weighted average model (Hastie, 1993b); (c) the stochastic Poisson process model (Kerr, 1993); and (d) the cognitive story model (see Pennington and Hastie, 1993). The algebraic model (Ostrom et al., 1978) draws on the information integration theory and posits that jurors assess and weigh each item of evidence presented during the trial and decide on guilt in a criminal or liability in a civil trial by averaging their evaluations of the different pieces of evidence. According to Kerr (1993): 'The word stochastic derives from a Greek root that means random, chance, or haphazard' and 'Stochastic models ... characterize processes as probabilistic or chance events ...' and 'predict a set of possible responses weighted by their probability of occurrence' (p. 116). One limitation of mathematical models of jury decision-making is that they do not cater for jurors' own 'explanation' that mediates between evidence and verdict (Pennington and Hastie, 1990:95).

In contrast to mathematical models, the story model (see Hastie et al., 1983; Pennington and Hastie, 1986) assumes that jurors actively construct explanations for the evidence presented to them and decide on a verdict accordingly. It is thus possible for two members of the same jury, exposed to the same evidence, to arrive at a different verdict because of differences in how they have understood and interpreted the same evidence. In other words, the process by which jurors selectively pay attention to, interpret and remember evidence and justify their verdict is an active and dynamic one. Consequently, if a juror's gut feeling is that the defendant is guilty, he/she will construct a story that will be consistent with the preferred verdict, or as Stephenson (1992) puts it, a juror's perception of the evidence, their preferred verdict and story construction 'reciprocally influence one another', and 'There is a story behind every verdict' (p. 196). As might be expected, the more stories put forward early on in a jury's discussion the longer the deliberation will take to reach a verdict, and the greater the likelihood that there may be a hung jury (p. 197). Finally, in so far as the media construct narratives of celebrated trials before, during and after trials, they have the potential to influence jurors' own stories of the trials and, ultimately, the verdict (Stephenson, 1992:200).

6 Alternatives to Trial by Jury

In the light of some of the arguments against the jury mentioned earlier in this chapter, an obvious alternative to trial by jury is trial by a single judge. This is already available in the US. A second alternative is a combination of judge and jury as it exists in Germany, where a judge sits with two lay persons. Some commentators have questioned whether the laypersons would out-vote the judge often enough (Knittel and Seiler, 1972). Arce et al. (1996) have reported a study of one such jury system in Spain (the *escabinato* jury) which concluded that the loss of a jury of peers only implies the dominance of the judge's opinion. Of course, the number of laypersons can be greater to counter any undue influence of the judge, as is the case in Russia. As there are arguments for and against a judge sitting alone, another possibility is to have a Bench of judges deciding serious cases, as happens in Spain. Once again, it is debatable whether a panel of judges can compensate for not having a jury. Finally, another option is to take note of both criticisms that have been levelled against the jury as well as conclusions that can be drawn from the voluminous empirical literature on the workings of juries/juror and to reform the existing system. What type of trial one prefers would seem to depend on a number of assumptions. While psychologists can enlighten such debates by testing the validity of assumptions about jurors and judges deciding under different conditions, which alternative to jury trials a community might decide to adopt one day is a serious matter that should, perhaps, be resolved by a referendum.

7 Conclusions

The evidence discussed in this chapter indicates that: 'scientific' jury selection, in itself a controversial practice, is not as possible and success- ful in influencing trial outcome as some authors would have us believe; inconsistent findings have been reported by experimental studies on the one hand and research into actual jurors on the other; scepticism is warranted in considering research findings about the relationship between juror characteristics and sentence; juror/jury research should focus more on the interaction between juror and case characteristics; the empirical evidence casts doubt on the wisdom of having six-member juries; the deliberation process plays a more significant role than was reported by Kalven and Zeisel's (1966) 'liberation hypothesis' in their influential pioneering study; and, finally, the 'cognitive story model' of jury decision-making is potentially a very useful one in focusing on juror characteristics, the deliberation process and features of the case under consideration. Juridic decision-making is an area where psychologists have contributed, and will continue to contribute, useful knowledge to a vital debate in society.

Levine's (1992:185) verdict on the American jury is that: it is not representative of the public at large but does inject social values into the decision-making process, finds the law confusing at times and it inevit- ably reflects 'stains of the society'; under the circumstances it is doing a reasonable job in deciding trials; and, finally, 'it is a good institution that could be better'. For their part, Duff and Findlay (1988) conclude: 'It seems unlikely that its total abolition will be suggested by its critics or seriously considered by any government in the near future' (p. 226). The jury is far from perfect and needs to be reformed if it is to be improved (Byrne, 1988).

As far as suggestions for reforming the jury are concerned, Levine (1992:185–92) argues for: allowing jurors to take notes and to question witnesses; providing jurors with trial video-tapes; using plain language in instructing them; permitting jury nullification; allowing them to pass sentences in more categories of criminal cases than at present; to eliminate judges' control over verdicts; increased juror pay; and elimin- ation of peremptory challenges. A final proposal that has been put forward is for an alternative to jury trial that consists of jurors sitting with judges, as is the case on continental Europe. However, some authors have expressed a concern that the judge will dominate the lay participants (Jackson, 1994).

It is unlikely we shall see judges and lay persons deciding criminal cases together in US, English or Australian courts in the near future. The notion of the jury has miraculously survived thus far despite its inherent contradictions and waves of attacks by influential opponents. As we approach the next millennium, the jury means different things in common law and civil law countries and in some common law jurisdictions it is almost extinct. Reforms to the jury along the lines advocated by Levine (1992) are urgently needed if we want juries to live up to the jury ideals. Two additional reforms that would appear to be imperative in this context are: (a) make juries as representative as possible of the whole community as far as jury pools are concerned; (b) introduce higher pay for jurors; (c) provide child care; and (d) 'educate' potential jurors for their task, both through adult programs and through the teaching of a common curriculum subject in the last year of secondary school, as well as by making available to them a short but informative induction course on how to shoulder the responsibility and cope with the demands of being a juror. Psychologists would, no doubt, as this chapter shows, have a lot to contribute to such a course. If the jury is not reformed, there is a real danger that the trial of serious cases by a judge without a jury will become the norm, given, on the one hand, the current climate of economic rationalism and managerialism that permeates the administration of criminal justice in the west (see Chapter 6) and, on the other, a strong argument that: 'The jury is an anti-democratic, irrational and haphazard legislator, whose erratic and secret decisions run counter to the rule of law' (Darbyshire, 1991:750).

Chapter 6

Sentencing As A Human Process

- *Reasons for disparities.*
- *Methods used to research disparities.*
- *A defendant's gender, race, attractiveness.*
- *The capital punishment debate.*
- *The individual sentencer.*
- *Models of judicial decision-making.*

'Sentencing cannot be an exact science; indeed, Lady Wootton likened the sentencer to a small boy adding up his sums but with no one to correct his answers.' (His Honour Judge P. K. Cooke, OBE, 1987:57)

'Sentencing is part of a very complex system. Many events and agencies influence the decision, and sentencing can cause anything from a ripple to a tidal wave throughout the system. And so sentencing, in common with other stages in the criminal justice process, cannot be viewed in isolation.' (Morgan et al., 1987:169)

Introduction

The judiciary worldwide enjoy a great deal of discretion when it comes to imposing sentences on convicted criminal defendants. Historically, sentencing discretion and the availability of a broad range of sentencing options, both non-custodial and custodial, has been largely justified in the name of attempts to rehabilitate offenders (Kapardis, 1985; Sentencing Committee [Victoria], 1988). By definition, rehabilitation as a penal aim requires sentences that are tailored to an offender's needs. This is in contrast to a more structured approach in sentencing known as 'just deserts', where the emphasis is on fixing a custodial sentence that almost exclusively reflects the seriousness of the crime committed, that is, the offender's deed/s (von Hirsch, 1995).

The existence of wide judicial discretion, however, should not be taken to mean that judicial discretion is not subject to a number of important constraints and influences (Shapland, 1987). To illustrate, statutes normally provide a maximum sentence for a given offence;[1] courts in common law countries are obliged to follow precedent and to adhere to certain principles of sentencing (Thomas, 1979); in many jurisdictions judges and magistrates are provided with sentencing guidelines,[2] which, in England and Wales, for example, make it clear which are normally the mitigating (for example, a guilty plea – see Douglas, 1988; Willis, 1995) and aggravating factors to be taken into consideration, while in the US there exist specific sentencing guidelines (Doob, 1995; Frase, 1995); in Magistrates' Courts in England and Wales, the court clerk plays an important role in the form of advice he/she gives the Bench (Kapardis, 1985; Corbett, 1987); there is the possibility of appeal against the sentence; members of the judiciary in various jurisdictions participate in sentencing conferences aimed at reducing unjustifiable inconsistencies and, finally, sentencers are expected to provide reasons for their choice of sentence.

Sentencing has been termed the 'cornerstone of the criminal justice system' (Sallmann and Willis, 1984) and the 'visible pinnacle of criminal justice decision-making' (Morgan and Clarkson, 1995:7). The fact is, however, that a lot of negotiation precedes a guilty plea, sometimes even during the trial.[3] The reader should also note in this context that: (a) plea-bargaining is a practice that is more prevalent in the US than in the UK, Australia, or New Zealand (Curran, 1991; Willis, 1995); and (b) there has been enormous growth in non-court penalties, such as the infringement notice system with its powerful technological overlay (for example, speed cameras) which has transformed the very concept of sentencing itself (Fox, 1995).

1 Disparities in Sentencing

While acknowledging that a large number of criminal cases are routinely processed and disposed of in the lower courts, the task of the sentencer is often not an easy one. There are numerous reasons for this: there exist conflicting penal philosophies (for example, retribution, rehabilitation, deterrence, just deserts, social protection, denunciation – see Braithwaite, 1989; Walker, 1980, for a discussion) and unsatisfactory guidance on how they are to be applied; the judiciary are expected to process cases at a fast rate; the volume of the cases coming before the courts has increased over the years (Thomas, 1987); particular pieces of sentencing legislation turn out to be problematic as far as implementing them is concerned (Thomas, 1987); there is public demand for harsher penalties; and, finally, the field of sentencing is plagued by a lack of consensus on what is meant by a 'right' sentence.[4] This state of affairs is no consolation for judges and magistrates or judges who are often criticised for either being 'too soft on criminals' or for imposing unjustifiably harsh penalties on defendants who have already been victimised enough by an unjust society and its criminal justice system. Taking an empirical approach to the question, Farrington (1978) suggests that the 'right sentence' is the one that achieves a given penal aim for a given type of offender most effectively and efficiently, providing a challenge for researchers to enlighten judicial officers and the public alike on the issue of 'right' sentences. Sentencing researchers, however, have a long way to go before they are in a position to provide judicial officers with such specific advice. From a traditional, narrow (and cynical) legal point of view, the 'right' sentence is the one of the judicial authority that spoke last and highest on the matter.

Disparities in sentencing criminal defendants are endemic in the system. This is because it is a human system that involves both large numbers of cases and magistrates (about 30 000 magistrates in England and Wales – Lawrence, 1993:279), judges, and (in the US) jurors – see Chapter 6. In addition, there are regional variations as between urban vs. rural courts (Douglas, 1992; Hogarth, 1971:370); there are differences in the input to sentencers, that is, the type of information about a case that sentencers are provided with (for example, whether there is a pre-sentence report and whether a recommendation about sentence is made by a probation officer/social worker/psychiatrist); and, finally, sentencers differ in how they perceive and how much importance they attribute to particular kinds of case information as well as in how they justify their decision about disposition of the defendant (Hood and Sparks, 1970:154). Not surprisingly, therefore, inconsistencies in sentencing have been a cause for concern and attracted researchers' interest since the last century (Galton, 1985).

Unjustifiable inconsistencies in sentencing, a ground for appeal against a sentence (Thomas, 1979), are referred to in the literature as 'disparities'. One of the criticisms levelled against judicial discretion is that it often results in disparities in sentencing (Skyrme, 1979). The concern about disparities in sentencing has been one factor in the shift away from rehabilitation in favour of just deserts, as the dominant penal philosophy in some western countries has resulted in attempts to structure judicial discretion. According to Fox (1987) such attempts fall into two main categories: judicial self-regulation (appellate review, guideline judgements, sentencing councils or panels, judicial training, information services); and statutory regulation (restructuring penalties, presumptive sentencing, guideline sentencing). Despite such attempts (see NSWLRC, 1996, for a discussion), sentencing disparities continue to be a cause for concern. Evidence for variations in sentencing policy that simply cannot go unnoticed are to be found in British Home Office figures for the 411 Magistrates' Courts in England and Wales. They reveal that: 'despite sentencing guidelines laid down by the Magistrates' Association [1993], serious discrepancies still arise' (*Sunday Times*, 19 November 1995, p. 7).

Writing about the role of the sentencing scholar, Ashworth (1995) outlines the following six roles: (a) reminding politicians and the judiciary that their decisions have an impact on real people and their liberty; (b) ensuring that the sentencing system does not lose sight of the fact that it must remain committed to the principles of natural justice and to the rule of law (for example, by contributing to attempts to structure judicial discretion and to minimise disparities in sentencing); (c) informing the sentencing-effectiveness debate; (d) contributing to the development of sentencing theory; (e) researching sentencing in both theory and practice; and, finally, (f) providing a framework within which to discuss the role of sentencing in society. The empirical studies discussed in this chapter have been concerned with throwing some light on the factors that underpin disparities in sentencing and can thus be said to fulfil Ashworth's roles (b) and (d). The discussion of empirical evidence that follows concentrates on studies of actual sentencers.

There is a rather voluminous empirical literature on inconsistencies in sentencing and the importance of both legal and extra-legal factors in accounting for such inconsistencies. The *legal factors* identified by Kapardis' (1985:154) literature review of 140 studies as important (that is, that attracted an evaluation score of 2 ('of some importance'), 3 ('important') or 4 ('very important')) in explaining sentencing variation are: type of charge; defendant's criminal record, recency of last conviction, past interaction with the criminal justice system, type of plea, age, gender, community ties; provocation by the victim; whether a court is in an urban or rural area, and probation officer's recommendation about sentence. Such a literature review today would also need to include some courts' use of Victim Impact Statements when considering sentence (see NSWLRC, 1996:418–45). The *extra-legal factors* likewise identified are: a defendant's pre-trial status, socioeconomic status (see also Douglas, 1994), race, and attractiveness; the victim's race; a sentencer's age, religion, education, social background, cognitive complexity, constructs, politics and, finally, penological orientation (that is, whether offence- or offender-focused). There is no doubt that it is the interaction of both specific legal and extra-legal factors that best explains disparities in sentencing. Given regional differences in sentencing legislation and the large number of factors that have been found to have the potential to impact on sentence choice and severity, no generalisations are possible, especially not across different jurisdictions or over time. Some of the studies of sentencing go back almost eighty years and studies utilising court records preceded experimental simulation studies on both sides of the Atlantic. The sentencing stage in the criminal justice process provides a goldmine of opportunities for psychologists interested in decision-making. Furthermore, it is an area where organised psychology (for example, the American Psychological Association) has, on a number of occasions, attempted to influence judicial policy-making by filing *amicus curiae* ('friend of the court') briefs (Tremper, 1987b).

2 Studying Variations in Sentencing

Studies of sentencing can be grouped under the following categories on the basis of the research method used to study variations in sentencing (see Kapardis, 1984, 1985, for discussion of the merits and limitations of the different methods):

2.1. 'Crude Comparison' Studies

These studies have compared sentences passed by different courts in the same region (Warner and Cabot, 1936), by judges in different regions (Grunhut, 1956) or by different judges in the same court (Morse and Beattie, 1932) or, finally, between sentences imposed for the same offence (Ploscowe, 1951).

2.2. 'Random Sample' Studies

These studies have simply assumed a random distribution of offence and offender characteristics between different courts and or different judges, without any justification given for the assumption being made (for example, Chiricos and Waldo, 1975).[5]

2.3 'Matching-By-Item' Studies

For these studies, see Hood, 1962; Mannheim et al., 1957; Nagel, 1961; and Wolfgang and Riedel, 1973. The number of variables used to match criminal cases in order to compare sentences imposed has varied, for example, from one (Nagel, 1961) to twenty-seven (Wolfgang and Riedel, 1973).

2.4 'Prediction' Studies

See, for example, Hogarth, 1971.[6] In order to identify the best predictors of sentence severity, some researchers have controlled for a number of offences, offender, victim, court and community variables.

2.5 Observational Studies

Aware of the inadequacy of court records and of the importance in sentencing of information about courtroom interactions which is never recorded by court stenographers, a number of researchers have utilised the observational method (for example, Stewart, 1980).[7] A major attack against the observational method was launched by Konečni and Ebbesen (1979) who claimed to have shown: 'it is a completely inappropriate research tool to study sentencing'. The adequacy of their own findings, however, is impossible to evaluate as Konečni and Ebbesen failed to provide sufficient information about the number of judges involved in their observational study or the between-judge agreement in sentencing not significantly different cases (Kapardis, 1985:42–3).

2.6 Experimental Simulation Studies

It would appear the first such study of sentencing, using real sentencers as subjects, was by Rose (1965). Close examination of thirty-four such studies on both sides of the Atlantic by Kapardis (1985:44–57) revealed the following: in over half of them psychology students were used as subjects; British studies overall used actual sentencers as subjects but most of them suffered from low internal validity and, finally, only two (Devlin, 1971; Hood, 1972) compared sentence decision-making under simulated and real-life conditions. Hood (1972) reported no differences between the two conditions while Devlin's (1971) limited comparison cannot be said to provide a test of the external validity of experimental simulation.

A comparison of real vs. simulated sentencing using 168 magistrates from five different regions in England and deciding in groups of three with the most senior chairing the discussion, as they would normally do in real life, and nine criminal cases sentenced in the Cambridge Magistrates' Court, provided strong support for the external validity of experimental simulation (Kapardis and Farrington, 1981). It should also be noted that experimental simulation studies of inconsistencies in sentencing as a function of a large number of factors have generally failed to pay adequate attention to the legal context of actual sentencing; such researchers have demonstrated a reluctance, if not an inability, to locate such psycholegal research in the broad context of the contemporary sentencing reform debate.

In real life, sentences imposed on criminal defendants can vary from a fine, to a community-based order, to a suspended term of imprisonment or a term of imprisonment or a life-sentence. There is, therefore, a need for a scale to measure sentence severity (see Durham III, 1989; Fox and Freiberg, 1990). Such a scale was reported in the English study by Kapardis and Farrington (1981) who found significant consistency both within and between 168 magistrates in their ranking of twelve different disposals across nine cases, that is, the type of case did not seem to have much effect on their ranking of the severity of penalties (p. 113).

3 Some Extra-Legal Factors that Influence Sentences

In considering the empirical evidence for extra-legal factors, such as a defendant's gender and race, at the sentencing stage in criminal justice one must not lose sight of the fact that the very same factors influence decision-making earlier in the process through, for example, differential access to private legal representation and the existence of stereotypes among law-enforcement personnel, factors that can be expected to influence the charges laid against a defendant and/or a defendant's ability to bargain his/her plea for fewer and/or less serious charges. According to McCarthy and Smith (1986), therefore, there is a need to view and account for sentencing in a structural context. Let us take a close and critical look at the empirical evidence for the importance of a few interesting factors in sentencing disparities.

3.1 Defendant's Gender

Gender bias and the law and the administration of criminal justice has been an issue of concern for a number of years now. Feminist authors have argued that the theoretical underpinning of the law is, in many instances, biased in favour of men and that the judiciary are guilty of sexism. In the context of sentencing, it has been argued that sexism operates to reinforce traditional gender roles and manifests itself in a paternalistic approach that aims to protect the social institution of the family (Daly, 1987). It has also been suggested that while the judiciary takes into consideration the family circumstances of both male and female defendants, the way it does so differs: men are portrayed as breadwinners, in contrast to females who are seen as dependants and domestics, a perception that encourages gender inequality before the law; female defendants are perceived as psychologically disturbed deviants, even though the evidence for such assessment is often weak or questionable (Henning, 1995).

In an interesting study by Fontaine and Emily (1978) of judges' verbal statements in real courtroom settings it was found that judges gave reasons for their choice of sentence more often in the case of male than female defendants. In addition, judges sought information about the defendant's circumstances when having to sentence females but about the crime when dealing with males, an indication, perhaps, that the judges considered offences by females as out-of-role and, consequently, focused more on the type of woman she was and her motives. In the case of male offenders, judges considered their behaviour 'normal' and, consequently, focused more on the seriousness of the crime than on the type of individual involved and his circumstances. Judicial officers' own 'theories' of criminal behaviour and their penal philosophies would seem to bias how they perceive a case before them, what information about the case they emphasise, what additional information they seek and how they justify their decision about sentence (Hogarth, 1971; Kapardis, 1984; Oswald, 1992).

A defendant's gender is stated as a relevant consideration in deciding the sentence to be imposed in both statutes and in common law in the US, UK and Australia (Gillies, 1993; Odubekum, 1992; Thomas, 1979). The classic example of gender as a legally relevant factor in criminal law is infanticide, an offence that can only be committed by women (Laster, 1989) and which poses a serious difficulty for feminist criminological theory. It is, of course, questionable whether a criminal defendant's gender *per se* should be the basis for disparities in sentencing.

With one exception, British studies of gender differences in sentencing have reported that female defendants receive more lenient sentences (Allen 1987; Hedderman, 1994; Hood, 1992; Kapardis and Farrington, 1981; Mackay, 1993; Wilczynski and Morris, 1993). Kapardis' (1985:105–8) examination of three earlier British studies (Casburn, 1979; Mawby, 1977; Phillpots and Lancucki, 1979) came to a similar conclusion. Farrington and Morris' (1983) study of sentencing in the Cambridge Magistrates' Court used the penalty-severity scale developed by Kapardis and Farrington (1981) and is the only one to have found no gender differences when taking into account offence seriousness and previous convictions. In the absence of a study of other Magistrates' Courts using the same methodology as Farrington and Morris (1983), it is impossible to say whether their negative finding reflects idiosyncratic sentencing practices of the one particular Bench of magistrates in Cambridge. The British empirical evidence for gender disparities is all the more convincing when remembering that it has involved studies of both Magistrates' Courts and Crown Courts, a broad range of offences and offenders and, finally, different research methods. Wilczynski and Morris (1993) analysed data on 474 cases in which a child had been killed by a parent and found that female defendants were significantly more likely to be convicted of manslaughter rather than murder, to be dealt with on the basis of the defence of diminished responsibility, and to receive significantly more lenient sentences, especially non-custodial ones. The leniency of treatment was especially evident for the women convicted of infanticide – none of them was incarcerated. Wilczynski and Morris concluded that labelling such women's killings as 'abnormal' behaviour that contradicts sentencers' perception of women as 'inherently passive, gentle and tolerant ... nurturing, caring and altruistic' and that a woman 'must have been "mad" to kill her own child' (pp. 35–6), results in lenient treatment by the courts.

The relationship between gender and sentence severity has also proven problematic for American researchers. Regarding the disposition of civil cases, Goodman et al.'s (1991) jury simulation study of wrongful death awards found that male descendants were awarded substantially higher monetary damages than were their female counterparts. Goodman et al. explain their finding in terms of males enjoying a higher estimated lost income than females. Studies of the importance of gender at the sentencing stage in the US have reported rather contradictory findings. According to Kapardis (1985:105–9), while most of them have found female defendants to have been treated more leniently by the courts,[8] a number of other researchers have reported no significant gender differences in sentencing.[9] Finally, Feeley's (1979) study in Connecticut, like Hampton's (1979) in New Zealand, reported that female offenders were sentenced more severely. Taking into account the quality of the methodology used by researchers, Kapardis (1985) concluded that a defendant's gender is an important factor in sentencing on both sides of the Atlantic (p. 154).

3.2 Defendant's Race

It has been known for some time in criminology that blacks in the US, who are disproportionately represented in criminal statistics, are more likely to be questioned on the street (Piliavin and Briar, 1964); if questioned, they are more likely to be arrested and, if arrested, they are more likely to be prosecuted (Goldman, 1963), charged with more serious offences (Forslund, 1970) and to be remanded in custody awaiting trial and, finally, as this section shows, when sentenced, they are more likely to be given harsher sentences and less likely to be granted parole (Elion and Megargee, 1979). Blacks in Britain have also been shown to be more prone to be arrested than Asians or whites (Stevens and Willis, 1979). Research into race and sentencing has been reported in Canada (Hagan, 1975, 1977; Rector and Bagby, 1995), Australia (Eggleston, 1976; Walker and McDonald, 1995) and New Zealand (Mugford and Gronfors, 1978). Regarding the treatment of Aborigines in Australia by the criminal justice system, Aborigines have an imprisonment rate that is thirteen times higher than that of non-Aborigines. Walker and McDonald (1995) have claimed, on the basis of national prison data, that courts in Australia 'may have a lenient view of indigenous offenders, biasing sentence lengths in their favour to avoid accusations of racial biases in sentencing' (p. 4). However, taking into account prisoners' 'most serious offence' when comparing 'average aggregate sentences' of indigenous (that is, Aboriginal and Torres Strait islanders) and non-indigenous offenders does not establish that indigenous defendants are treated more leniently by the courts, as Walker and McDonald claim. While accepting that no single study can control all relevant legal factors, the fact is that in order to provide a satisfactory account of sentencing practices and whether racial discrimination (negative or positive) exists, a number of additional relevant and important legal variables (for example, criminal record, type of plea, etc.) should be taken into account as well as a broad range of personal and social characteristics that have been shown to impact on sentence severity (Kapardis, 1985:63–155).

British researchers did not start looking into the possibility of racial discrimination at the sentencing stage until the late 1970s. Most of the published empirical studies have failed to find a positive relationship between a defendant's race and penalty severity (Brown and Hullin, 1992; Crow and Cove, 1984; Hudson, 1989; Kapardis and Farrington, 1981; Jefferson and Walker, 1992). Mair (1986) did find, however, that blacks were less likely to be given probation than whites. Given that a recommendation is more likely to be made in the case of a defendant with community ties such as being in employment (Kapardis, 1985:154), Mair's tentative finding (due to his rather small sample) may well reflect black defendants' greater likelihood of being unemployed at the time of the trial (see Halevy, 1995:269).

Hood's (1992) study (in collaboration with Graca Cordovil) was undertaken for the Commision of Racial Equality and analysed data on all cases (2884 males and 433 females) tried in 1989 at five Crown Court Centres in the West Midlands. Taking into account sixteen factors related to both the offences and the offenders' criminal records, it was found that black men were 5 to 8 per cent more likely to be sentenced to a term of imprisonment than were white men with similar antecedents convicted of the same crimes; Asian men were slightly less likely to be incarcerated than similarly placed whites. Blacks and Asians were more likely than whites to have pleaded not guilty, and both groups were given significantly greater terms of imprisonment than whites in similar circumstances who had also pleaded not guilty. Hood claimed that 7 per cent of the over-representation of blacks amongst those imprisoned could be attributed to direct discrimination at the sentencing stage but did not contend that racial discrimination in sentencing occurs systematically and universally. Hood also compared the five Crown Court Centres and found that discrimination against blacks, in terms of the rate of custodial sentences, was much higher at three of them – Dudley, Warwick and Stafford. Despite the fact that some criticisms have been levelled against Hood's study (for example, for failing to control for personal and social characteristics of the defendants being compared – see Halevy, 1995), which Hood (1995) has vehemently refuted, the study can be said to have made a significant contribution to the debate about racial discrimination in criminal justice in Britain (see also Gelsthorpe and McWilliam, 1993; Smith, 1994). In her review of studies of discrimination against ethnic minorities in the criminal justice system in England and Wales for the Royal Commission on Criminal Justice, Fitzgerald (1994) points out: (a) researchers have tended to lump together people from the Indian subcontinent (Indians, Pakistanis and Bangladeshis) as a single 'Asian' group; and (b) that small direct and indirect racial discrimination effects at various stages in the criminal justice system can have a significant cumulative impact.

Research into racial discrimination at the sentencing stage in criminal justice has a much longer history in the US, where many jurisdictions provide for the death penalty for certain crimes. Blacks have consistently made up 11 per cent of the American population since 1930. The US Bureau of Justice Statistics show that during the period 1930 to 1984 the execution rate of blacks for murder and rape is five and nine times respectively that of whites (Aguirre and Baker, 1990:135). Such figures, of course, do not show that differences in the execution rate are due to racial discrimination. In an attempt to deal with inconsistent findings, Kapardis (1985) reviewed a total of thirty-seven studies and found that twenty-one of them reported evidence for racial discrimination but sixteen did not. Taking the quality of the research method used into account, it was concluded that 'the weight of the evidence supports the view that non-whites (in the main the research has been concerned with blacks) are discriminated against at the sentencing stage. However, this evidence is not as overwhelming as might be expected' (1985:122). That conclusion, however, should not be used to dismiss the argument that courts in the US discriminate against blacks in sentencing – even weak evidence should be a cause for concern, especially regarding the imposition of the death penalty. Spohn et al. (1981–82) had earlier concluded that black defendants received severer sentences than white defendants due to their more serious history of offending. Finally, a somewhat provocative view was expressed by Kleck (1985) who claimed that in the US there is no evidence that race influences sentencing, and that the problem lies not with members of the judiciary discriminating against blacks but with the researchers who distort and grossly exaggerate the importance of race in sentencing by selecting evidence that purports to show discrimination when, in fact, it does not. Since Kleck (1985), additional and well-controlled studies have reported evidence pointing to racial discriminatory practices against blacks by the judiciary. Nelson's (1992) New York State study found such evidence for both black and Hispanic defendants. Spohn (1992) found that in Detroit black non-jury defendants were treated more harshly than non-jury white defendants. The same study also found that racial discriminatory practices were also evident in judges' decision to incarcerate defendants who had pleaded guilty, and that such decisions in less serious cases reflected the impact of both legal and extra-legal factors (Spohn and Cederblom, 1991).

Walsh's (1991) Ohio study of 712 male felony offenders sentenced during the period 1978 to 1985 inclusive for crimes ranging from receiving stolen goods to murder, controlled for offence seriousness and prior record and reported that whites were treated more harshly by the courts than blacks. His failure, however, to take into account such very important legal variables as a defendant's type of plea and age casts serious doubt on his findings. Sweeney and Haney (1992) reported a meta-analytic review of nineteen simulation (experimental) studies that examined the effect of a defendant's race on mock-jurors' sentencing decisions. They found strong support for anti-black cross-racial punitive bias.

While there still remains the issue of the external validity of mock-juror studies (see Chapter 5), the studies reviewed and the conclusion by Sweeney and Haney (1992) add to the debate about (a) racial discrimination as well as (b) capital punishment, and strengthen the concern expressed by a number of authors (Aguirre and Baker, 1990; Applegate et al., 1994; Keil and Vito, 1990) that, controlling for legally relevant factors, a death sentence is more likely to be imposed on black offenders by juries in the US, especially when their victim is white. What is of particular concern in this context is the fact that racial discrimination in the use of capital punishment in the US continues unabated despite attempts by the Supreme Court to thwart it by providing guidelines (*Furman v. Georgia* (1972) 408 US 238; *Gregg v. Georgia* (1976)). Finally, the finding by so many researchers that a black offender is most likely to receive the death penalty if he/she victimises a white person adds credence to the claim that 'capital punishment serves the extra-legal function of majority group protection; namely, the death penalty acts to safeguard (through deterrence) that class of individuals (whites) who are least likely to be victimised' (Aguirre and Baker, 1990:147–8).

Regarding the controversy surrounding the use of *capital punishment* by the courts (see Cochran, 1994; Walker, 1987:84–93), it should be noted that supporters of capital punishment as the appropriate sanction in order to reduce the incidence of such crimes as murder, rape, and terrorist offences, basically assume – wrongly – that the serious violent offenders involved act rationally. To 'deter' means to discourage someone from offending through fear of consequences (Walker, 1980). In other words, deterrence theory assumes a rationally-thinking potential offender. However, as Walker (1980) points out, deterrence is inapplicable when: people do not commit certain crimes because it is against their moral scruples; the behaviour involved is impulsive (as is often the case in homicides and armed robberies (see Kapardis, 1989; Kapardis and Cole, 1988)) or compulsive; people intentionally commit a crime to defy the law or because they are desperate, or because they are prepared to die for a cause (as is the case with suicide bombers); or, finally, people believe they can commit a crime and remain unpunished. Penologists make a distinction between *individual deterrence* (that is, the penalty is directed at an individual offender convicted by the court in order to 'teach him a lesson') and *general deterrence* (that is, when it is hoped that by punishing severely those who are convicted and publicising the penalty imposed, others will be discouraged from perpetrating the same crime). Penologists also inform us that for a deterrent to be effective, a combination of penalty severity and high subjective probability of one being apprehended and convicted by the courts is required in most cases (Walker, 1980).

The available empirical evidence in criminology shows that capital punishment 'is no more effective as a general deterrent than long incarceration' (Walker, 1987:64). For their part, some advocates of the death penalty maintain that it is the deserved punishment for certain crimes and/or that it is the most effective way of preventing a serious violent offender from reoffending. Opponents of the death penalty, on the other hand, argue that: to allow that State to deliberately execute a convicted offender is no more justifiable than the crime he/she has committed; and 'it transforms assassins into martyrs, alienates ethnic communities who suspect discrimination and is bad for the morale of prisons' (Walker, 1987:64). Undoubtedly, one of the strongest arguments against capital punishment is that miscarriages of justice are known to have occurred and innocent persons have been executed. In addition, the previous chapter and this chapter show sentencing decisions, whether by magistrates, judges or juries, are influenced by non-legal factors, including the defendant's race. Finally, a question which many consider problematical is the extent to which, if at all, the judiciary (or juries in the US) should take public opinion into account in deciding sentence severity generally and the imposition of the death penalty in particular (see Harlow et al., 1995).

3.3 Defendant's Attractiveness

Defendants are often advised by the lawyers to look 'presentable' when appearing in court. Likewise, people are generally given the same type of advice when going for a job interview. The assumption is that magistrates', judges' and jurors' decision-making, like that of members of the public, is influenced by a person's appearance. From a legal point of view, of course, such considerations are irrelevant to decisions about guilt and sentence. The classic jury study by Kalven and Zeisel (1966) reported that American judges attributed 14 per cent of their disagreements with the jury to jurors' impression of the defendant, the impression itself alleged by the same judges to have been influenced by whether or not a defendant was 'attractive'. The term 'attractive' can refer to physical appearance or likeability, appeal of one's personality, or both.

Social psychologists have established that physical appearance is an important factor in impression formation. According to Bull (1974), people behave differently in the presence of a well-dressed, as opposed to poorly-dressed, individual. A respectable appearance can act as a buffer against imputations of deviance (Steffensmeier and Terry, 1973). Also, a physically attractive person will be perceived more positively on a broad range of personality attributes (Dion et al., 1972; Goldman and Lewis, 1977; Miller, 1970). But does a defendant's appearance impact significantly on the sentence he/she receives? As already mentioned in Chapter 5, experimental mock-juror studies indicate that a defendant's attractiveness will lessen harsh punishment but will have the reverse effect if the defendant exploited his/her attractiveness to perpetrate the crime.[10]

Some studies with real sentencers also suggest that highly physically attractive/socially respectable defendants promote sympathy and attract more lenient sentences. The observational studies of a minor traffic court in Ontario, Canada, by Finegan (1978) and Stewart's (1980) observational study in Philadelphia reported in the *Journal of Applied Social Psychology* showed a positive relationship between the defendant's attractiveness and leniency of sentence. The validity of Stewart's (1980) findings in Philadelphia, however, is questionable because he had no relevant information about the defendants in his sample. An Australian study of sentencing variations in Magistrates' Courts by Douglas et al. (1980) found a weak positive relationship between defendants' physical appearance (described as 'well dressed', 'average' and 'shabby') and likelihood of imprisonment, controlling for legally relevant variables. Douglas et al. (1980) and Konečni and Ebbesen (1979) indicate that attractive appearance does not necessarily correlate with being favourably treated by the courts. The inconsistent findings reported by studies of real sentencers do not allow any conclusions to be drawn about whether an attractive physical appearance is a positive asset for an offender at the sentencing stage in criminal justice, as experimental psychologists and practising lawyers would claim.

3.4 The Sentencer

Lawyers, convicted offenders and members of the judiciary all share a belief that the sentence imposed on a given defendant depends to a significant degree on who is the individual sentencer (Mather, 1979). It is also commonly known that lawyers indulge in 'magistrate/judge shopping' to get one who is likely to be favourably disposed to their case (Ericson and Baranek, 1982), while judges themselves allocate those of their brethren who are known for being tough on crime to courts that hear contested cases (Hagan and Bernstein, 1979). Early 'crude' studies of sentencing variations (for example, Everson, 1919) and more recent methodologically sophisticated ones (for example, Palys and Divorski, 1986) have claimed a relationship between sentencer and sentence severity. A few researchers, however, have reported negative findings (Konečni and Ebbesen, 1979; Rhodes, 1977). The role of the sentencer as a determinant of sentence has also received a great deal of attention by Australian researchers who have reported a positive relationship between the two (Anderson, 1987; Grabosky and Rizzo, 1983; Lawrence and Homel, 1987; Lovegrove, 1984; Polk and Tait, 1988). Douglas' (1989) study of Victorian Magistrates' Courts (ten in Melbourne and thirty-eight in the country) involving twenty-seven stipendiary magistrates also reported a positive, but weak, relationship between sentencer and sentence.

The importance of sentencer characteristics in sentencing was emphasised by Everson (1919) who concluded in his study of twenty-eight Magistrates' Courts in New York that: 'justice is a very personal thing, reflecting the temperament, the personality, the education, environment and personal traits of the magistrate' (p. 98). On the basis of Kapardis' (1987) literature review and more recent studies, the following conclusions emerge:

- Inconsistent findings have been reported concerning the relationship between a magistrate's social class and their sentencing (Hogarth, 1971; Hood, 1962);
- Lay magistrates in England from small towns are more punitive than their urban counterparts (Hood, 1972);
- Legally-trained, as opposed to lay, magistrates in Canada take a more flexible approach to law and focus on the offender in deciding on sentence (Hogarth, 1971);
- Older English magistrates impose severer sentences on motoring offenders (Hood, 1972) and older judges in Gibson's (1978) study discriminated against black defendants the most;
- Finally, inconsistent findings have been reported regarding a sentencer's gender,[11] religion,[12] politics,[13] and penal aims,[14] and his/her sentencing decisions.

The available empirical evidence shows that the sentencer plays an important role as a determinant of sentence. One way of reducing the individual sentencer as a source of disparity would be to reduce his/her discretion in what sentence to impose on a given type of defendant for a given offence. While the judiciary in the US is by now well accustomed to the 'just deserts' philosophy of sentencing curtailing their discretion, sentencers in Britain, Australia and New Zealand, however, are likely to resist such a restriction on their judicial independence; furthermore, restricting judicial discretion 'may produce reduced intra-legal disparity at the cost of reducing the ability of sentencers to make allowance for the distinctive features of particular cases' (Douglas, 1989:55). Two policy implications that would seem to follow from the findings reported about the sentencer as a source of disparities are: (a) educating sentencers about this knowledge; and (b) actively involving them in realistic sentencing exercises aimed at achieving uniformity of approach (Kapardis, 1985). Already such an approach has been used, amongst others, by the Judicial Studies Board in England and Wales and the Institute of Judicial Administration in Victoria, Australia, and, on the basis of feedback from magistrates and judges (personal communication), has proved very useful in achieving more uniformity in sentencing. A proper empirical evaluation of such attempts to reduce disparities in sentencing by targeting sentencers is long overdue.

4 Models of Judicial Decision-Making

A variety of models have been proposed for judicial decision-making by both psychologists and non-psychologists. Chambliss and Seidman (1971) presented a more sociological picture by identifying the effect of structural inputs (for example, court structure in appellate courts – see Coffin, 1994) and their impact on structural outcomes (that is, the court system). Two British criminologists, Hood and Sparks (1970:148–9), suggested a more social psychological viewpoint by focusing on the court system and identifying the flow of information in the courtroom.

Michon and Pakes (1995:510–11) draw attention to a distinction between 'normative' and 'descriptive' models. The latter describe optimal decision-making behaviour while the former describe how decisions are made in real life. Descriptive models assume that a decision-maker like a magistrate or a judge is limited as to the amount of information he/she can process and, consequently, uses information selectively (p. 511). Descriptive models focus on the heuristics (that is, the processes by which they find an answer to a question) and strategies real-life decision-makers use, and aim to describe the cognitive processes underpinning such decision-making. Michon and Pakes (1995) also distinguish six steps in the decision-making process: problem recognition, decision-making problem, identification of consequences, utility and likelihood assessment, long-term vs. short-term consequences and choosing between alternatives (pp. 512–13). They conclude that: (a) the complex task of judicial decision-making is performed rather well by human decision-makers, but not necessarily using methods that would be described by normative models; and (b) judicial decision-making cannot be 'rational' in a pure sense, as the term is used in economics, for example (p. 523).

Attribution theory is concerned with how people attribute traits, abilities and motives to people on the basis of observing their behaviour (Heider, 1958; Kelly, 1967). A basic distinction in attribution theory (see Schneider, 1995, for an excellent account) is that between internal (that is, dispositional) and external (that is, situational) causes of behaviour. Focusing on the sentencer as a source of variation, researchers in different countries have utilised attributional analysis (for example, Weiner 1979, 1980) in an attempt to understand how sentencers perceive a broad range of sentencing-relevant factors and how they are related to the sentence imposed (Ewart and Pennington, 1987; Oswald, 1992). According to Weiner's model, the psychological meaning of 'cause' (attribution of responsibility) results from the way an individual classifies another's behaviour in terms of locus of control, stability (that is, consistency over time) and controllability. Carroll and Payne (1977) reported that subjects imposed lenient sentences if they perceived the offender's criminal behaviour as resulting from external, unstable and uncontrollable causes. Ewart and Pennington (1987) tested Weiner's attributional model with British police officers and social workers and reported findings providing further support for the model. Bierhoff et al. (1989) also reported a significant relationship between causal attributions and punishment recommendation, with sentences becoming more lenient as situational (external) attribution increases (p. 204). Another German study by Oswald (1992) used questionnaires to survey thirty-six criminal court judges and concluded that sentencing decision-making can be usefully understood in terms of: (a) how a sentencer justifies punishments (retributive (that is, an end in itself) vs. utilitarian (a means to an end, such as crime-reduction)); and (b) whether sentencers act from the offender's or the victim's perspective. Oswald found that the more a judge adopted the perspective of the victim the more likely they were to attribute responsibility to the offender. Future research should test experimentally Oswald's findings and attempt to synthesise Weiner's (1979) model and Oswald's offender–victim perspective dimension.

5 Conclusions

The issue of disparity in sentencing is one of public concern and has attracted considerable research. A major contributing factor to disparities is the wide discretion enjoyed by magistrates, judges and, in the US, juries, as well as the existence of conflicting penal aims and lack of sufficient guidance on how judicial officers are to exercise their discretion. Researchers have used a range of different methods to disentangle disparities in sentencing. This chapter has focused on studies of actual sentencers and the importance of extra-legal factors, of which there are a few but these are controversial. The available empirical evidence shows that a criminal defendant's gender and race are significant determinants of sentence. Of particular concern is the failure of the US Supreme Court to thwart, by means of guidelines, apparently widespread racial discrimination by courts against black defendants when imposing the death penalty in cases where such defendants offend against whites. Such discriminatory practices by the courts add further support to the call for the abolition of the death penalty.

Inconsistent findings have been reported about the importance of a defendant's attractiveness. Finally, sentencers themselves have been shown to be a major source of disparity. Significantly reducing the range of sentencing options available to them, however, does not seem to be a commendable measure; educating sentencers about sources of disparity by focusing, perhaps, on how they perceive defendants and their circumstances, how they integrate different sources of information and how they attribute motives and traits to defendants who appear before them in order to select a particular sentence, and training them in how to achieve uniformity of approach by also making use of realistic sentencing exercises, appear much more promising. Both legal and extra-legal factors impact on sentencing and contribute to disparities. There is already ample empirical evidence that Justice herself is not as effectively blindfolded as some conservative lawyers and judges would have us believe. Members of the judiciary themselves, too, have come to accept this fact, and already proposals are under way in the US, UK, Australia, New Zealand and Canada to 're-educate' judges in the wake of a number of trials in which judges made rather sexist comments.

Chapter 7

The Psychologist As Expert Witness

- *Roles for psychologists as expert witnesses.*
- *Expert testimony and the law.*
- *Psychologists as expert witnesses in the US, England and Wales, Australia, New Zealand and Canada.*
- *The impact of expert testimony.*
- *Appearing as expert witnesses.*

'The law is hostage to the knowledge possessed by others; it needs data, good data. It can well do without the biases and prejudices of related disciplines – it has enough of its own to deal with.' (Allen and Miller, 1995:337)

'The use of expert witnesses in the courtroom has entered a dynamic era. Over the course of the next decade a great deal is likely to happen.' (Landsman, 1995:157)

'Expert witnesses do not just appear out of the blue. They are recommended by a city's "old boy" network over lunches, telephone calls and drinks. Or they are tried out by legal firms and insurance companies and, if successful, put onto their "panels" of suitable experts.' (Ragg, 1995)

'Psychology can play a valuable role in the criminal process, even if it must end at the door of the court.' (Sheldon and MacLeod, 1991:820)

Introduction

Experts, in the form of medical doctors, appear to have been first called upon to advise judges at the Old Bailey 600 years ago, but it was not until around 1620 that a jury was furnished with expert testimony for the first time. In 1721 there was the first challenge to an expert witness (a surgeon) testifying for the prosecution by another expert testifying on behalf of the defendant (Landsman, 1995). However, it was not until the latter part of the 18th century that the role of the expert witness (as the term is generally understood by lawyers on both sides of the Atlantic) was finally shaped, as counsel came to participate more and more in questioning and cross-examining expert witnesses (Landsman, 1995:139).[1] Lawyers' and other professionals' demand for expert evidence by psychologists has increased in the last two decades, reflecting growing recognition that psychologists 'have a unique contribution to make to judicial proceedings' (Gudjonsson, 1993:120). '[T]he specialty most involved in forensic psychology in practice is clinical psychology' (Blackburn, 1996:14). An area showing increasing involvement of psychologists as experts is family law. Psychologists, of course, are called as expert witnesses in both civil and criminal cases. As seen below, the range of cases has been broader in some jurisdictions than in others.

The terrain traversed is dotted with very significant developments in the courts' treatment of expect testimony by psychologists in a broad range of areas. It is noted that in a major judgement the US Supreme Court has reasoned its criteria for deciding whether expert evidence shall be admissible. Without abandoning the 22-year-old 'common knowledge and experience rule' (see below), the courts in England have opened the door to the psychologist as expert witness. Courts in Australia and New Zealand have been largely constrained by English precedent and have been rather restrictive in admitting expert evidence by psychologists, while Canadian courts seem to fall somewhere between the US pre-*Daubert* climate – conducive for admitting expert evidence – and the constrained English position that prevailed until very recently. This chapter does not purport to deal with the controversies about the adequacy of legal procedures for selecting or qualifying experts, whether expert testimony can be prejudicial, the objectivity of expert witnesses, the ethics of expert testimony by experimental psychologists (see McCloskey et al., 1986) or the scarcity of generally acceptable scientific methods and theories (Golding, 1992).

One of the basic assumptions in common law is that there exists a distinction between facts and the inferences that can be drawn from such facts. It is the function of the magistrate, judge and jury to draw inferences. The role of witnesses is to state the facts as they have directly observed them. In other words, witnesses do not give their opinions. However, the law makes an exception to this basic rule in the case of an expert in cases where a tribunal of fact decides that a specific issue calls for an expert witness because the particular expertise does not fall within the knowledge and experience of the magistrate, judge or jury, and a witness qualifies as an 'expert'. In some jurisdictions (for example, US) an expert witness is allowed to also express an opinion on the ultimate issue, the very question which the tribunal of fact itself has to answer. Hamlyn-Harris (1992), however, has pointed to the danger of courts coming to depend on experts' opinion on an ultimate issue before deciding the issue (p. 82). The cause for concern in this context becomes greater when one remembers that clinical psychologists and psychiatrists, for example, have been known to misrepresent their competence, falsely claiming they can predict dangerousness with a high degree of accuracy (see Faust and Ziskin, 1988, for a discussion).

A particular and special knowledge of a subject that has been acquired through scientific study or experience can qualify a witness as an expert (Cattermole, 1984:126). Haward (1979) identified four roles for forensic psychologists (using the term 'forensic' in a broad sense) appearing as expert witnesses:

- *Experimental:* this could involve a psychologist informing the court: (a) about the state of knowledge relevant to some cognitive process; and/or (b) carrying out an experiment (for example, involving eyewitness testimony, or a defendant's claim to be suffering from a phobia) directly relevant to the individual's case before the court (Gudjonsson and Sartory, 1983).
- *Clinical:* as already mentioned, this is the more common role for psychologists appearing in western English-speaking common law countries and involves testifying, for example, on their assessment of a client's personality, IQ, neuropsychological functioning, mental state or behaviour (Freckelton, 1990; Gudjonsson, 1985, 1995:62[2]).
- *Actuarial:* in a civil case involving, for example, a plaintiff claiming for damages for a psychological deficit caused by someone's negligence, a psychologist may be asked to estimate the probability that such an individual could live on their own and/or be gainfully employed (Haward, 1979).
- *Advisory:* in this role, a psychologist could be advising counsel before and/or during a trial about what questions to ask the other side's witnesses, including their expert witness/es. Knowing that there is another psychologist in court evaluating one's testimony has been reported to increase an expert's level of stress when testifying in court (Gudjonson, 1985).

More recently, Allen and Miller (1995) have argued that the likelihood of irrational verdicts increases the more fact-finders defer to experts and that expert witnesses become advocates too often. Then they propose an education-centred view of the expert's proper role at trial, very much along the lines of the *amicus* brief in *Michaels* (see Chapter 4).

Where parties to a dispute in a criminal or civil trial call their own expert witnesses, a 'battle' of experts can eventuate (Turnstall et al., 1982). A survey by Champagne et al. (1991) of forty-two experts (nearly half were physicians), seventy lawyers employing them, thirteen judges hearing cases involving them and 118 jurors who decided forty civil cases over a fourteen-week period in 1988 in Dallas County, Texas, reported that expert 'battles' occurred less frequently than had been suggested. The main limitations of such a postal survey, as Champagne et al. themselves acknowledge, is not knowing whether non-respondents differ from respondents – the average response rate was 37 per cent. Of course, given the high fees charged by most experts for their written or oral testimony, there is an incentive to avoid the possibility of the experts 'battling it out' in court 'by pre-trial agreements about the number of experts to be called, and pre-trial meetings of the experts. In England and Wales it is not unknown for the experts on both sides to come to court with a joint statement' (Nijboer, 1995:561–2).

Psychologists in the US have been appearing as experts more frequently and in a larger range of cases than their counterparts in other western English-speaking common law countries.[3] Kassin et al. (1989) surveyed sixty-three leading eyewitness testimony researchers in the US and found that over half of them (54 per cent) had testified on the subject at least once, with an average of 7.6 occasions. Kassin et al. also found that more had refused to testify at least once than those who said they had testified at least once. Reasons for refusing to testify included feeling that one did not have anything useful to say, having doubts about their expertise in a given case, and being concerned about not being allowed to qualify their answers. Kassin et al. also reported that experts were equally likely to testify for the prosecution as for the defence, and for both sides in a civil case. The same survey shows that although 'hired guns' exist in forensic psychology as they do in other fields, there is no justification for assuming that this is a common feature of such eyewitness experts.

There are differences between legal proceedings in different countries and this includes the precise roles of expertise and of expert witnesses (Nijboer, 1995:556). To illustrate, in western common law countries an expert witness testifies for the side that has retained him/her and pays his/her fees. In contrast to this practice, in continental European jurisdictions expert witnesses are normally appointed by the court to assist the court. In addition, there is a difference in status between court-appointed and privately retained expert witnesses, with the former enjoying a higher status (p. 557). Another important difference between continental European jurisdictions and England and Wales which Nijboer points out, for example, is the fact that the former (for example,

France, Switzerland, Holland, Belgium) are characterised by 'very low thresholds for the admissibility of expert evidence. They prefer to regulate how the expert evidence, which is admitted, is regulated' (p. 559). Expert witnesses, of course, may be involved in different stages during legal proceedings: pre-trial, trial and post-trial. This chapter is concerned with psychologists as expert witnesses in court-based legal disputes.

Importing non-legal knowledge into both criminal and civil trials has proven problematical in western common law countries with their adversary legal systems (Saks, 1992:185). There is no doubt that magistrates, be they stipendiary or justices of the peace, judges and jurors sometimes require assistance to establish the facts of a case before them. In this context, the expert witness can play a crucial role. In the words of Ian Freckelton, a well-known Australian practising lawyer and authority on expert testimony, 'The role of experts is vital. They supply information that can't be supplied elsewhere. They supply counter-intuitive information, myth-dispelling information, which may be essential to clear thinking' (quoted in Ragg, 1995:16). Alas, however, fact-finders have to also contend with the knowledge that expert 'evidence can be complex and hard for a jury to understand. Also, there's the danger of bias. These are hard financial times, and the forensic expert needs to be a repeat player. If they don't supply the information required, they will find they don't have as much work as they need to survive' (p. 16). Enough concern within the organised profession about the nature and the quality of expert testimony has resulted in forensic psychologists in the US, for example, being provided with formal guidelines.[4] According to Gudjonsson (1993): 'The main theme of these guidelines is that forensic psychologists have the responsibility of providing a service which is of the highest professional standard' (p. 120). Deviating from the present author's approach in the rest of the book, expert testimony is not dealt with here by structuring the discussion thematically but on a country-by-country basis. This is done for the benefit of the reader because there are significant differences in the common law position in different countries and in the fields in which psychologists are admitted as expert witnesses.

1 United States

The practice of providing expert testimony for a fee and as a means of earning a living did not become widespread in the US until the middle of the 19th century and the test for admitting expert testimony between 1850 and 1920 was 'whether the proffered expert was appropriately "qualified" to render an opinion on the issue before the court' (Landsman, 1995:150). In the landmark decision in the case of *Frye v.*

United States (293 F 1013 (1923)) the District of Columbia Court of Appeals rejected testimony by a lie-detector expert[5] that the defendant was telling the truth when he denied having committed the alleged offence on the ground that the scientific theory on which it was based was not generally accepted within the relevant professional community. Interestingly, it was not until the early 1980s that the *Frye* test came to be cited frequently in court decisions in the US (Landsman, 1995). *Frye* was a vague ruling that was instrumental in American courts admitting expert testimony in a rather broad range of fields without much scrutiny (Landsman, 1995:155). The US Supreme Court's unanimous decision in *Daubert v. Merrell Dow Pharmaceuticals* (113 S.Ct. 2786 (1993)) held that *Frye* had not been incorporated as part of federal evidence law but had, in fact, been rejected when the expert testimony rules of the Federal Rules of Evidence were proclaimed in 1975 (Landsman, 1995:155). According to the ruling in *Daubert*, the test for expert witnesses is 'vigorous cross-examination, presentation of contrary evidence, and careful instruction' (113 S.Ct, 2786, 2798 (1993)).[6] More specifically, the *Daubert* judgement stated, *inter alia*, that: 'The subject of an expert's testimony must be "scientific ... knowledge" ... [and] in order to qualify as "scientific knowledge", an inference or assertion must be derived by the scientific method' (p. 2795), and '[T]he criterion of the scientific status of a theory is its falsifiability, or refutability, or testability ... Another pertinent consideration is whether the theory or technique has been subjected to peer review and publication ...' (pp. 2796–7).

Landsman contends that the *Daubert* judgement embraced judicial managerialism, a trend evident in American courts for the last two decades, and 'increased trial judge authority to review challenges to scientific evidence at the expense of litigant control', and what remains to be seen is how far judges will go in exercising this authority and whether they will do so evenhandedly across litigants (p. 156). Landsman predicts that judges will favour well-established corporate or government defendants at the expense of civil rights, discrimination and product liability plaintiffs (p. 157). For their part, Penrod et al. (1995) have argued that the *Daubert* decision 'is likely to have minimal impact on the ways in which eyewitness expert admissibility decisions are made in the federal courts. *Daubert* will have less impact on states – the decision is not binding on the states and ... Several state supreme courts have explicitly rejected *Daubert*' (p. 244). Duncan (1996) concludes her discussion of expert testimony on psychological syndrome evidence after *Daubert* stating that, 'Examination of the scientific bases for most of the psychological evidence examined in this Note exposes as unfounded the fears of those apprehensive of the legitimacy of social science evidence' (p. 770). By handing down the *Daubert* ruling the US Supreme Court has indicated its confidence in judges adequately deciding the scientific status of a theory or technique in a civil or criminal case without scientific training; in fact, both advocates and the judiciary will need to be rather sophisticated in scientific matters (Freckelton, 1993:111). To achieve this, it will be necessary for lawyers to possess 'cross-disciplinary knowledge and understanding' (p. 113). The urgent need for legal psychology courses for practising lawyers provides psychologists with a great opportunity to communicate their expertise to the legal profession and move closer to bridging any remaining gap between the two disciplines.

2 England and Wales

Experts began to testify in English courts in the second half of the 19th century (see Hand, 1901). British courts, however, have been rather unenthusiastic about expert evidence by psychologists (Sheldon and MacLeod, 1991:818). The landmark decision in a provocation case, *R. v. Turner* (1975) QB 834, has meant that, unlike their American counterparts, their expert testimony has had to surmount a rather difficult impediment to admissibility, namely, the 'common knowledge and experience' rule of evidence. This common law principle can be traced to the case of *Folkes v. Chadd* in 1782 in which Lord Mansfield ruled that an expert's opinion is admissible if it provides the court with information which is likely to lie outside the common knowledge and experience of the jury. Lawton LJ stated in Turner:

> If on the proven facts a judge or jury can form their own conclusions without help, then opinion of an expert is unnecessary. In such a case if it is given dressed up in scientific jargon it may make judgement more difficult. The fact that an expert witness had impressive qualifications by that fact alone make his opinion on matters of humane nature any more helpful than the jurors themselves; but there is a danger that they may think it does. (at 841)

The gist of the *Turner* decision is that a court in England and Wales does not need a psychologist's or psychiatrist's expert knowledge when it comes to psychological processes except where mental abnormality is involved. As Colman and Mackay (1993) have argued, however, 'The *Turner* rule appears to be based on an interpretation of the relation between psychology and common sense that is sufficiently wrong-headed to be called a fallacy' (p. 47). One of the underlying assumptions in *Turner* is that normal human behaviour is essentially transparent and, consequently, a jury does not need a psychologist's opinion on such behaviour since it is within the jury's 'common knowledge and experience'. However, despite the fact that the ruling in *Turner* has largely restricted the admissibility of expert testimony, it also recognises the need for change (Thornton, 1995:147). Colman and Mackay (1993:48–9) argue convincingly that the human-behaviour-is-transparent assumption is undoubtedly false, citing psychological knowledge in the areas of the 'fundamental attribution error' (see Miller et al., 1990), obedience to authority (Milgram, 1974), group polarisation (Isenberg, 1986), cognitive dissonance (Wickland and Brehm, 1976) and bystander intervention (Latane and Naida, 1981). Colman and Mackay conclude their critique of *Turner* stating that 'expert psychological evidence should be admitted whenever it is both relevant and potentially helpful to the jury in explaining aspects of human behaviour that are not easily understood with common sense alone' (p. 49).

Examination of English authorities since *Turner* shows that psychiatric or psychological evidence which is not abnormal or does not directly concern the defendant's state of mind or the issue of intent has generally been excluded. However, there have been a number of encouraging decisions indicating greater readiness to admit psychological evidence (Thornton, 1995:144, 146). More recently, the restrictive interpretation of the rule in *Turner* was relaxed by the Court of Appeal in the case of *R. v. Sally Loraine Emery (and another)* [1993] 14 Cr.App.R.(S) 394. In the *Emery* case, an 11-month-old child died as a result of serious injuries inflicted over a period of weeks as a result of very severe physical abuse. Emery, the single mother of the child, was found guilty in the Peterborough Crown Court in January 1992 of failing to protect the child from its father and was acquitted of occasioning actual bodily harm on her child. She appealed against her sentence of four years' detention in a young offender institution and had it reduced to thirty months. The prosecution appealed against the trial judge's admitting expert evidence on post-traumatic stress disorder (PTSD), 'learned helplessness' and 'the battered woman syndrome' on the grounds that the evidence concerned fell within the common knowledge rule enunciated in *Turner*. However, the Court of Appeal upheld both the trial judge's decision to admit the expert evidence on behalf of the defendant as well as the justification offered for that decision.

The effect of *Emery* is that courts in England and Wales are no longer to assume that expert psychiatric evidence is called for to assist the jury only when it deals with mental disorder, mental handicap or automatism (Colman and Mackay, 1995). In delivering the Appeal Court's decision, Lord Taylor, Lord Chief Justice, upheld the decision of the trial judge to allow expert evidence by a psychologist and a psychiatrist that the defendant had been suffering from PTSD, 'learned helplessness' and the 'battered woman syndrome' on the grounds that such evidence was complex and not known by the general public and was necessary to assist the jury to determine the facts of the case. According to Colman and

Mackay (1995): 'The effect of the *Emery* judgement therefore appears to open the door to psychological evidence in a far wider range than has hitherto been the case' (p. 264).

Further evidence that courts in England and Wales are readier to admit expert evidence by psychologists on matters that do not fall within abnormal behaviour is also evidenced by the fact that in a small number of cases well-known legal psychologists have now testified on eyewitness testimony issues. One such British expert is Professor Ray Bull of Portsmouth University who in the last few years has provided expert testimony in three different cases (personal communication). One concerned the possibility of '*unconscious transference*' (see Chapter 10) by an eyewitness in an armed robbery trial. A newsagent proprietor had his back to the door near closing time when someone grabbed him from behind and demanded money, threatening him by sticking a knife to his face. The shop-owner saw the offender from behind as he was running away from the scene of the crime. One year earlier, the same shop-owner had been robbed in the street by someone with a knife. That offender was identified, tried, convicted and sentenced to a term of imprisonment. The issue on which Professor Bull was asked to provide expert testimony was whether the eyewitness might have assumed the identity of the second robber by being influenced by what he had seen of the first robber; in other words, might the second robber's identification have been the result of 'unconscious transference'? There was a hung jury and a re-trial with a different jury. The expert testimony provided was held helpful.

The second of Professor Bull's cases involved a rape trial in which the major source of evidence against the defendant was the female victim herself, and the fact that she had picked him after hearing his voice in a voice parade conducted by the police.[7] The expert was requested to express an opinion on the fairness of the parade for the benefit of the jury. The police carried out the voice parade after taking the trouble to seek the advice of a Cambridge University linguist to ensure that the suspect's voice did not differ from the rest of the voice parade in terms of accent. The voice parade constructed by the police contained segments of monologues by a number of speakers and the suspect's voice was the only one taken from an interview with the police. An experiment was carried out by Professor Bull in which subjects were asked to identify which of the voice samples came from a police interview. Subjects identified the suspect's voice at better than chance level. The testimony was admitted by the trial judge. That case ended up with a hung jury and, at the time of writing, there was to be a re-trial.

The final case in which the same expert has testified concerns an appeal, four years later, against a conviction by a prisoner serving a sentence for a murder on the grounds that he never committed the murder concerned and, furthermore, another person has confessed to the murder. At the time of the investigation, the police had no reason to suspect the person who has since confessed to the crime. The expert opinion requested of Professor Bull relates to the specific question of whether the *Cognitive Interview* technique (see Chapter 3) is likely to assist the witness to better remember the event in question. It can be seen that in a number of cases in recent years courts in England and Wales have opened the door to a broader range of cases than would have been possible under the restrictive interpretation of the rule in *Turner*. The common knowledge rule itself, of course, has not been abandoned but has been interpreted more broadly than in *Turner*. It will be interesting to see how far these significant developments in the Law of Evidence in England will impact on courts in Commonwealth countries like Australia, New Zealand and Canada, even though the English decisions are not directly binding on courts in the Commonwealth.

3 Australia, New Zealand and Canada

Expert testimony by mental health professionals in Australian and New Zealand courts has been allowed, for example, for sentencing, post-accident impairment, competence to stand trial, criminal responsibility, capacity to work, degree of mental retardation, trauma suffered by victims of crime, behaviour of victims, insanity defence, operation of memory, trademark infringement and fraudulent advertising, causation of death as a result of mental state, custodial and access arrangements and effects of discrimination (Freckelton, 1990:66). Some encouraging evidence that courts in Australia and New Zealand are readier to admit expert testimony by psychologists than allowed by a strict interpretation of the rule in *Turner* is to be found in the New Zealand case of *R. v. Taaka* ([1982] 2 NZLR 198) in which psychiatric evidence was admitted to show that the defendant had an 'obsessively compulsive personality, and in *R. v. Leilua* ((1985) NZ Recent Law 118) pertaining to chronic post-traumatic stress disorder. Despite such encouraging signs, the fact is that, as in England, rules of evidence in Australia and New Zealand (see *Murphy v. R.*, 1989, 86 ALJ 35; *Smith v. R.*, 1990, 64 ALJR 588), especially the 'common knowledge rule' from *Turner*, constrain the kinds of expert evidence that can be given by psychologists in Australian courts (Freckelton, 1990; see also, Freckelton and Selby, 1993). Thus, 'during the past decade evidence from mental health professionals has been disallowed on the working of memory [*R. v. Fong* [1981] Qd R 90], the dangers of eyewitness testimony [*R. v. Smith* [1987] VR 907; (1990) 64 ALJR 588], the typical behaviour of children after they have been molested [*R. v. B.* [1987] 1 NZLR 362] and on the likelihood of a defendant having made a particular record of interview to the police [*Murphy v. R.* (1989) 86 ALR 35]' (Freckelton, 1990:49).

Examination of relevant case law in both Australia and New Zealand by Freckelton (1990), including the leading case of *Murphy v. R.*, points to confusion about the application of the common knowledge rule and the kinds of expert testimony that can be given by psychologists and psychiatrists (pp. 49, 61). Regarding the likely impact, if any, of the *Daubert* case on the admissibility of scientific evidence in Australian and New Zealand courts, or English or Canadian courts for that matter, no prediction is possible. While the decision itself is not binding on courts in these countries, it is nevertheless a very significant decision by a superior court (Freckelton, 1993:111).

Two interesting developments in Australia are the Evidence Act 1995 (Cth) and Evidence Act 1995 (NSW). S.80 of the former and s.137 of the latter 'abolish the common knowledge exclusionary rule' (Freckelton, 1996) and the abolition is 'in the form of an opinion not being inadmissible "only because it is about" a matter of common knowledge' (p. 31). Writing about expert testimony in repressed memory syndrome (see Chapter 3), Freckelton (1996) has stated that, 'since the focus of the legislation is upon weighing the probative value of expert evidence against its potential for unfair prejudice', and 'Given the current profound division of opinion among psychiatrists and psychologists' the provisions of the new legislation 'should result in the exclusion of expert evidence concerning repressed memory syndrome' (p. 31).

Canadian courts have generally admitted expert testimony on a broader range of issues than focusing narrowly on mental illness, as has been the approach of courts in England, Australia and New Zealand.[8] While the impact of the *Daubert* decision on Canadian courts is difficult to predict, it is interesting to note that in *R. v. Johnston* ((1992) 69 CCC 395, (a DNA case)) it was held that the *Frye* test was not part of Canadian law and that the criteria for admissibility for 'novel scientific evidence' were relevance and helpfulness to the tribunal of fact, helpfulness to be decided by considering a list of fourteen factors. The factors in *Johnston* go beyond those stated in *Daubert*.[9]

4 The Impact of Expert Testimony by Psychologists

In his controversial critique of expert testimony about eyewitness identification Elliott (1993:433) argues that: 'we do not know very much about the factors contributing to eyewitness accuracy. We are also very far from knowing what the effect of expert testimony is, except that un-cross-examined experts for the defence have sometimes caused reductions in conviction rates (Loftus, 1980)'. Elliott also expressed the view that 'it remains premature to draw conclusions either about what we know or what our effect is on jurors or juries' (p. 433). Elliott concluded his critique by urging the adoption of three prudential rules on the basis that the present state of knowledge does not justify psychologists testifying as experts to the extent that they do. Kassin et al. (1994) have criticised Elliott (1993) both for: (a) the eyewitness literature and the experts who use it; and (b) 'because his critique merely parrots complaints of the past' (p. 203); as well as for (c) misrepresenting the results of the Kassin et al. (1989) survey of sixty-three eyewitness identification experts (p. 207). On the basis of the US Supreme Court's ruling in the *Daubert* case (that the general acceptance of a point of view within a particular field of expertise is a major criterion for admitting expert testimony in the US) it would appear that Elliott's (1993) conclusions are not shared by the majority of the experts in the eyewitness identification field (see Chapters 2, 3 and 10).

There is encouraging evidence that where expert testimony is provided it does influence cases. Available empirical evidence suggests that expert testimony pertaining to characteristics of sexually abused children does impact on jurors' decision-making (Cutler et al., 1989), that expert testimony in child sexual abuse cases has been generally admitted by courts in the US, and when challenged on appeal it is again admitted in more than half of the cases (Mason, 1991). Using data in trial court transcripts, Mason (1991) surveyed 122 appellate court decisions in both civil and criminal cases in which expert witness testimony on the characteristics of abused children, provided by a total of 160 experts, was challenged; 31 per cent of the experts concerned were clinical psychologists. It was found that in over half of the cases (55 per cent) the expert testimony was allowed on appeal and in 9 per cent the evidence was partly admitted; in those cases where the courts rejected the expert witness testimony they did so mainly on the grounds that the testimony went to the issue of the child's credibility, something which, in evidence law, is for the jury to decide and not for an expert witness. Mason concluded that expert testimony informing the court about the weight of the evidence in the relevant literature pertaining to sexually abused children's willingness to remember, the accuracy of their recall and vulnerability to suggestive questioning, can indeed assist the judge or jury to evaluate a child's testimony.

5 Appearing as an Expert Witness

Poor evidence by psychologists appearing as experts can be very damaging for psychologists in general, undermining the positive impact which psychologists can have on developments within the legal system and have a disastrous effect on individual cases, causing miscarriages of justice (Gudjonsson, 1993). For Gudjonsson, poor psychological evidence is testimony that, firstly, does not inform and, secondly, is misleading or incorrect. Furthermore, the characteristics of such poor evidence are: 'poor preparation, lack of knowledge and experience, low level of thoroughness, and inappropriate use or misinterpretation of test results' (p. 120).

Advice for psychologists who wish to avoid the embarrassing and unpleasant experience of seeing their expert testimony being distorted and their professional reputation damaged includes:

• Being very familiar with courtroom procedure, rules of evidence, and ways of presenting psychological data to a Bench or a jury, as well as being aware of the conduct expected of an expert witness (Wardlaw, 1984:135, 137).
• Having well-prepared reports and other evidence and, if inexperienced, to undertake some training in how to best handle lawyers' cross-examining (Carson, 1990; Nijboer, 1995).
• Stick to one's own area of expertise and be explicit and open (Nijboer, 1995).
• Novice expert witness psychologists can also benefit from having in mind a number of criteria by which to judge their testimony when preparing for it (see Newman, 1994) and, equally important, to be familiar with what advice is given lawyers about how to cross-examine a psychologist (see Mulroy, 1993).

Regarding cross-examination, Wardlaw (1984) lists a number of rules likely to prove helpful for the witness. *Inter alia*, these include:

• Answer all questions and do not allow counsel for the other side to put words in your mouth.
• Do not guess and take as much time as you need to reply to questions.
• If under attack keep calm and avoid getting angry or unreasonably defensive.
• Prepare for the cross-examination by trying to anticipate the questions by imagining that you are the one who is to cross-examine.

In providing advice on the art of advocacy, Evans (1995) reminds his readers that even experienced expert witnesses have been known to 'just come apart like wet cardboard toys when actually giving evidence' (p. 72) and urges them to remember that 'nobody – not even the ultimate leader in the field – knows everything about his subject' (p. 165). Mauet and McCrimmon (1993) are more specific in their advice on how to best cross-examine an expert witness. They suggest first to obtain from the expert admissions favourable to one's client, then to discredit unfavourable evidence and, finally, to impeach the expert him/herself (p. 203). The same authors list a number of cross-examination techniques, including:

- Building up the expert's field of expertise and then proceeding to show that it is not directly relevant to the issue facing the court.
- Using hypothetical situations to show either that the expert would, in fact, agree with your presentation of the facts of the case or that the expert's credibility is doubtful because of apparent rigidity in considering other possible interpretations of the fact at issue.
- Demystifying the expert's apparent self-importance by obtaining from him/her definitions of technical terms in simple, everyday language.
- Casting doubt on the thoroughness with which the expert has obtained his/her results.
- Getting the witness to admit that in the past other experts are known to have disagreed with him/her on the issue concerned (pp. 203–6).

6 Conclusions

The psychologist as expert witness has thus far had a luckier run in the US than in the UK, Australia, New Zealand or Canada, appearing in cases involving child sexual abuse (see Mason, 1991), child custody cases (Mulroy, 1993), the battered woman syndrome (Breyer, 1992) and eyewitness testimony (Elliott, 1993; Kassin et al., 1994; Loftus and Ketcham, 1991).

Gudjonsson (1995:56) reminds us that empirical research by psychologists has influenced 'legal structures, procedures and case law ' in the US in such areas as eyewitness testimony, prediction of dangerousness, forensic hypnosis and lie-detection. Similarly, legal researchers in the UK have influenced the development of police procedures in interviewing suspects and the admissibility of expert testimony on whether a witness is suggestible (pp. 56–7). In addition, a number of recent cases illustrate increased readiness by English courts to admit expert evidence by a psychologist on a broader range of issues, including eyewitness and earwitness identification, the battered woman syndrome, learned helplessness and the battered woman syndrome, than would normally have been allowed by a restrictive interpretation of the rule in the 1975 case of *Turner*. Unfortunately, an opportunity to reform the law of evidence in England regarding the admissibility of expert testimony by the Royal Commission on Criminal Justice (1993) – Runciman Report – has been missed. Despite the fact that the Commission called for a greater opportunity for experts to educate tribunals of fact, its report: (a) took a myopic view of the issue of court experts; and (b) by means of 'bizarre reasoning' – that such a move would 'lead to a confusion of roles' and prevent the cross-examination of expert witnesses – rejected a proposal for a Forensic Science Service that would be independent of both the prosecution and the defence and which would be appointed by the courts (Redmayne, 1994:157–8).

As far as Australian courts are concerned, by not admitting expert testimony by mental health professionals on the working of memory, pitfalls in identification evidence, the typical behaviour of children after they have been sexually abused or how likely it is that a record of interview presented by police was, in fact, made by the defendant, they deny 'the assistance of specialist information possessed by mental health professionals which may provide insights into a range of matters germane to the proof of a defendant's guilt or innocence' (Freckelton, 1990:49). The need for evidence law reform in Australia at state level (as in New South Wales) cannot be overstated. Explicitly abolishing the common knowledge rule in the rest of Australia's jurisdictions, in the UK and New Zealand would be a significant first step in the right direction. One cannot but agree with Freckelton that when a theory is sufficiently acknowledged by the experts in a given field to be reliable and characterised by scientific integrity 'surely it is only arrogance and foolhardiness for the law to close its eyes to knowledge and understanding which is germane to its decision-making practices' (p. 65).

For those sceptical of the need for expert testimony in court, Sheldon and MacLeod (1991) list three alternatives, namely: (a) making use of a psychologist's expert report on particular legal issues pertinent to a trial to cross-examine witnesses; (b) introducing independent forensic psychologists as part of an independent forensic science service; and (c) providing lawyers with much-needed training in psychology. Writing about the judiciary in England, Thornton (1995) has also canvassed the need for judicial training in areas of forensic psychology. In the future, judgements in individual cases in England, Australia, New Zealand, but less so in Canada where there is a lesser need, may well significantly reduce current restrictions to the admissibility of expert evidence. This, however, is a process that is likely to take a long time. An alternative would be to let the tribunal of fact decide whether a particular case calls for expert evidence or not. Finally, parliament could codify the new limits of admissibility (Thornton, 1995:148). As Landsman (1995) has stated, 'a great deal is likely to happen during the next decade' in the domain of expert evidence (p. 157).

Chapter 8

Persuasion In The Courtroom

- *Advocacy in perspective.*
- *Defining advocacy.*
- *Qualities of an advocate.*
- *Effective advocacy: opening address; examination-in-chief; cross-examination; re-examination; closing speeches.*
- *Psychology and courtroom persuasion.*

'*Appearing as an advocate in court is the most challenging thing a lawyer can do: it is the sharp end of lawyering and it calls not only for courage but a great deal of skill as well.*' *(Evans, 1995:vii)*

'*the feeling is [among practitioners] that the skills for the job of advocacy bear little or no relation to that knowledge most cherished by the law schools or by the Law Society's examining boards.*' *(Mungham and Thomas, 1979:174)*

Introduction

Law is a difficult course to get into at most universities. Being a practising lawyer confers social status in many countries and there is a strong tendency internationally to include judges on committees that are entrusted with important tasks in society. Such status seems to be synonymous with being a distinguished trial lawyer, a senior barrister in Great Britain and in the Commonwealth and, especially, becoming one of that elite group of Queen's Counsels who can command impressive fees. However, it should be remembered in this context that, as pointed out in Chapter 1, the aim of a trial in an adversary system of law is not to find the truth: 'The majority of cases are won or lost on their own facts despite the intervention of the finest advocacy' (Du Cann, 1964:183). Furthermore, there is also a popular perception of lawyers as liars and that enough skilled but unethical pleading by an advocate can see a patently guilty individual acquitted, causing a miscarriage of justice (p. 182).

A great deal of the perceived importance of the legal profession also comes from a perception of their main role as advocates and defenders of the innocent before the courts. Images of the lawyer as advocate, Mungham and Thomas (1979:170) pointed out, 'come down to us from reports and tales of the lives of the "great advocates"'.[1] In fact, many books on advocacy[2] give the impression that there has existed a 'golden age of advocacy' (p. 170), that the 'good old days' contain a lot of useful material for new and aspiring advocates and, finally, that 'things have changed' for the better for the novice advocate. During the last two decades a number of changes have taken place within society which have impacted on lawyering. These changes include: the introduction of legal aid in many jurisdictions which has expanded the practice of law and the concept of advocacy and has diversified the population of lawyers who appear in court; the increasingly heterogeneous population of law graduates; the introduction of formal teaching of advocacy; the introduction of state-initiated as well as community-based legal centres and mediation schemes; and, finally, the emphasis on conflict resolution rather than litigation. Since 'the myth that advocacy cannot be taught has been finally put to rest' (Hampel, 1993:xii), the system of pupillage for passing on advocacy skills has long been questioned and is rapidly being replaced by professional courses for barristers and solicitors in Britain (which, according to Evans (1995:vii), contribute to improving advocacy standards) as well as in Australia and New Zealand and for trial lawyers in the US. However, as practising lawyers are not tired of telling us, the skills needed to be an advocate bear hardly any relationship to that knowledge valued by law schools and the organised profession's examining boards (Mungham and Thomas, 1979:174).

The image of the advocate in a higher court as the epitome of what most practising lawyers do most of the time has more to do with popular television shows than reality.[3] A significant proportion of law graduates end up not practising law and for the majority of those who do, the reality is they will never appear before a higher court to defend someone charged with murder, they will not have the services of an expensive team of other lawyers and trial experts, including one or more psychologists, and finally, in Great Britain, Australia and New Zealand, the average lawyer is unlikely to ever find himself/herself addressing a jury. For most 'young' lawyers, practising law means appearing in very busy lower courts in large urban centres where most defendants plead guilty to minor charges, where the main skill required of a lawyer is to know how to plea-bargain with the police and/or the prosecutor along crowded corridors and where the blindfolded lady operates very routinely without much ritual and oratory preceding disposition by the Bench, irrespective of whether the Bench comprises two or more lay magistrates, more commonly known as 'Justices of the Peace' (as is the case in most Magistrates' Courts in England and Wales – see Kapardis, 1985), a stipendiary magistrate or a judge at a lower court. Lawyering means different things depending on whether one attends police stations (see Baldwin, 1994; Law Society, 1994), is dealing with private or public clients (Flemming, 1986), is a one-lawyer firm, or works within a small or a large law firm, as well as on whether one appears before a lower, higher or appeal court (see Glissan, 1991:149–57, on appellate advocacy) or a professional or non-professional court (see Evans, 1995:181–204), a juvenile court or, finally, whether one is cross-examining a social worker in the Family Court (see Moloney, 1986). A participant-observation study of a corporate law firm by Flood (1991) found that business lawyers are more involved in managing uncertainty for themselves and their clients and they do so through interaction with rather than through appeals to the law. To place advocacy in perspective, it should be remembered that the average lawyer spends most of his/her time drafting or advising on a variety of documents before a trial can even begin and not on advocacy (Du Cann, 1964:80). Psychologists interested in researching advocacy, therefore, need to address advocacy in context and to remember that winning a case is not objectively defined and can involve different strategies and outcomes in theory and practice.

In an interesting study in Britain, Mungham and Thomas (1979) interviewed sixty solicitor advocates over a period of eighteen months and also carried out observations of Magistrates' Courts in session. They found that, if working within a large practice, solicitors would most likely have a heavy case load, would read briefs at the last minute, had to juggle appointments and negotiate adjournments and would be rushing from one court to another. Such lawyers, whose criminal advocacy in Magistrates' Courts traditionally 'has had a low standing within the English legal profession' (p. 174), needed 'social skills and sheer physical energy' (p. 175) and would most often be called upon to argue questions of evidence rather than questions of law in contested cases. It can be seen that the concept of advocacy as the art of persuasion in the context of a trial at a higher court is too narrow and does not encompass the reality as experienced by the great majority of practising lawyers. For psychologists, a broader definition of 'advocacy' also means there is more they can offer the practising lawyer, including invaluable knowledge concerning interpersonal skills, negotiation and conflict resolution. In Britain the Law Society's (1994) training kit for legal advisers who attend police stations has been mostly written by Dr Eric Shepherd, a forensic psychologist who specialises in forensic interviewing techniques. It is not uncommon for a lawyer to know individual magistrates or judges, to be able to predict their sentencing, and adapt their advocacy accordingly.

Mauet and McCrimmon (1993:1–20)[4] point out the need for lawyers to demonstrate their advocacy skills in the courtroom does not exist in a vacuum but is often the climax of a process that has included attempts to settle the case without going to court and the amassing of trial material. It should also be remembered that advocacy manifests itself against the backdrop of a great deal of ritual, what authors on advocacy term 'etiquette'. Such rules (see Evans, 1995:7–17; Glissan, 1991:1–19) are more evident in the higher courts and vary from country to country. In considering advice on advocacy skills the reader should also bear in mind that there are significant differences between countries. For example, unlike the US, in Britain, Australia and New Zealand advocacy is very seldom conducted before a jury in a criminal trial and lawyers in Britain (where 'the civil jury has all but disappeared' – Evans, 1995:21) address the Bench, the jury or the witness from behind the bar table and do not enjoy the freedom to move about the floor that is enjoyed by trial lawyers in the US. Lawyers in these countries, for example, need permission from the Bench to cross the floor and approach a witness in the witness box. Also, the form advocacy takes depends on whether a lawyer is arguing about evidence or on a point of law.

1 Defining Advocacy

For Mungham and Thomas (1979) there is 'no generally agreed upon definition of what constitutes "good advocacy"' (p. 176) largely because it is context-specific and subjective and this makes even a market test (that is, whether a lawyer retains his/her clients or not) untenable. For the same authors, in fact, in one sense all solicitors' work is advocacy (p. 189). A well-known English QC has written that the task of the advocate is to be 'argumentative, inquisitive, indignant or apologetic – as the occasion demands – and always persuasive for his client' (Pannick, 1992:1). A definition of advocacy is not considered problematic for Justice Hampel, a well-known Australian judge for whom 'Advocacy is the art of persuasion in court' (Hampel, 1993:xi). In the same vein, Glissan (1991) offers a more elaborate definition of advocacy, stating that:

legal advocacy means the congeries of techniques which together make up the art of conducting cases in court ... The art of legal advocacy is in part one of communication and in part one of persuasion ... always remember they [the techniques] have to be varied (or ignored) according to time and circumstances and modified to suit one's own style. (p. 20)

Such a definition makes it possible for an author to provide novice advocates with 'a small bag of tools to get you started' (Evans, 1995:205). The reader should also note in this context that eyewitness testimony can be described as a persuasive communication.[5] Advocacy books tend to follow the same approach: offer advice, often accompanied by examples (sometimes extracts from famous trials) on how to best approach the different parts of a trial (that is, the opening address, examination-in-chief, cross-examination, re-examination and closing arguments), as well as advice on courtroom etiquette. Du Cann (1964) reminded his readers that 'Part of the art of advocacy lies in its concealment' (p. 180). Glissan (1991) asserts that 'advocates are born not made' (p. 21). This rather brave assertion is contradicted by the example of one famous advocate, namely 'John Philpot Curran, cruelly hampered by a stammer, was unable to utter a word the first time he got to his feet in court. Yet he too rose to great heights, dominating the Irish courts' (Du Cann, 1964:46). Accepting a nature, rather than nurture, position on advocacy would also render any notions of training for advocates largely irrelevant.

The picture of the successful advocate portrayed in books on advocacy is a composite of natural talent combined with a range of skills and effective techniques. It should therefore come as no surprise to be told that the prevailing view among legal writers on advocacy is that persuasion in the courtroom is an *art*. Such authors, in effect, provide numerous assertions, some of them giving actual examples of good (and sometimes also bad) advocacy in practice in the higher courts. Such books do not, as a rule, contain empirical support, as such, for the assertions made, and consequently, do not advance their subject matter to the level of arguments. They do, however, provide psychologists with a large number of testable hypotheses. There is a need for psychological research into the types of individuals who, after opting to study law, go into practice, what characterises their advocacy in a broad range of sociolegal contexts and how and why some lawyers come to be regarded by their peers as 'good advocates'. Such research could take the form of both a longitudinal study that follows a cohort of law graduates and also tests experimentally some of the assertions made by practising lawyers about persuasive communication in the courtroom and qualities said to characterise notable advocates.

2 Qualities of An Advocate: Lawyers Writing About Lawyers

Du Cann (1964:47) emphasises that eloquence is but one quality that is essential for an advocate, and provides aspiring young advocates with some food for thought when he reminds the reader that: 'The qualities essential to the successful practice of the art of advocacy cannot be acquired like pieces of furniture' (p. 46). He also considers it of crucial importance that advocates possess the right qualities (p. 183) and argues that failure to do so 'should arouse professional and public concern, for it is the lack of these which leads to incompetence and it is incompetence which leads to miscarriages of justice' (p. 183). What, then, are some of the basic qualities desired of a good advocate? In his book *The Seven Lamps of Advocacy*, His Honour Judge Parry (1923)[6] listed honesty, courage, industry, wit, eloquence, judgement and fellowship. For Lord Birkett (1962), however, 'presence' is the defining attribute of a successful advocate.

The qualities listed as essential by Du Cann are: honesty, judgement, courage, control of one's feelings, tenacity, sincerity and industry. Unlike Parry (1923), Du Cann does not consider wit a vital asset for an advocate. Those solicitor–advocates interviewed by Mungham and Thomas (1979:171–2) emphasised the following attributes: 'personality', 'projection', 'skills of persuasion', being able 'to take command of a court' and having a 'firm grasp of legal principle'. Glissan (1991:21) cites a number of qualities, mentioned in Munkman's book *The Technique of Advocacy*, that should characterise an advocate: 'voice' (that is, 'A clear, distinct and interesting voice'), 'command of language', 'confidence', 'persistence' and 'mileage' (that is, experience). Finally, in addition to an advocate's acquiring preparation and technical performance skills, His Honour Justice Hampel (1993:xi–xii) considers the most important truth about advocacy is that 'a good advocate must be a good communicator'.

3 Effective Advocacy: Some Practical Advice by Lawyers

3.1 Opening Address

Regarding a counsel's *position and delivery* during a trial, Mauet and McCrimmon (1993:37) emphasise maintaining eye contact with the jury and avoiding mannerisms and fidgeting so as not to distract the jurors. As far as the opening address is concerned, despite the fact that it can, and often does, play a key role in the outcome of cases it has been rather neglected by advocates, writers and researchers alike (Glissan, 1991:32). Regarding how the opening address is best delivered, Mauet and McCrimmon remind the reader that those advocates who can make the opening speech without using notes come across as confident and have a significant advantage over the other party (p. 37).

In trials in ancient Athens speeches by advocates were subject to a time limit, the same for both sides, measured by a water-clock known as 'clepsydra' (McDowell, 1978:249). Contemporary lawyers similarly agree that an opening address should be as brief as possible. Evans (1995:66) is specific about this – no more than 10 minutes – because a short address is more likely to be remembered by the jury and the counsel will appear more confident (p. 66). Writing for advocates addressing a jury, Evans advises prosecuting counsel to also attract the attention of the jury and gain their sympathy, to present him/herself as an 'honest guide', to give the jury 'a few phrases to hold on to' (p. 66) and, finally, 'Above all talk to them and not at them' (p. 64). Mauet and McCrimmon (1993:31–7) offer a rather long list of suggestions they regard as essential if one wishes to launch a case 'on the right footing'. With one omission,[7] the following is their advice:

- State the facts and be clear.
- Be forceful and positive.
- Do not be argumentative.
- 'It is essential that your opening address is delivered smoothly, without interruption.'
- Do not state personal opinions and do not overstate.
- Personalise your client and depersonalise the other side so as to reduce the likelihood of jurors identifying with them.
- Use exhibits and develop the theory of your case.
- Volunteer a weakness which is apparent and known to the other side (p. 35).
- In the case of a defence counsel, consider whether to waive the right to make an opening address at the close of the plaintiff's or the Crown's case 'If a decision has been made to move for a non-suit in a civil case, or a discharge on the basis that there is no case to answer in a criminal case' (p. 37). There is disagreement among advocates as to whether one should end an opening address reiterating the facts or arguments on which the case is based or to bring home to a jury the importance of a single issue (Du Cann, 1964:78).

3.2 Examination-in-Chief

While examination-in-chief 'has become an endangered species' in civil cases in Britain (Evans, 1995:124), if successfully conducted (that is, to present the facts of the case logically and forcefully), it will significantly influence the outcome of a case (Mauet and McCrimmon, 1993:59).

Glissan (1991:39) states that the aim of examination-in-chief is to prove the various elements of one's case by adducing all relevant and material evidence before judge and jury that the witness can give about the case. It is, therefore, of paramount importance that the witness be the centre of attention during this stage of the trial and be perceived and remembered as credible (see also Chapter 3). Consequently, advocates would do well to remember that the credibility of a witness does not evolve around how eloquent the advocate is as a speaker and, also, that it is the strength of the case-in-chief which is more likely to determine whether one side will win the case or not rather than weaknesses in the case presented by the other side (Mauet and McCrimmon, 1993:59–60). Before commencing to elicit evidence from a witness in examination-in-chief an advocate should first consider a range of preliminary questions, such as the issues which must be proved, how many and which witnesses to call and in what order.[8] Glissan maintains that whereas one can be taught how to cross-examine witnesses effectively, conducting an examination-in-chief calls for a 'natural talent' which is in rather short supply (p. 45). Mastering this difficult art of conducting an examination-in-chief, however, is considered by Glissan a precondition if an advocate is to really establish him/herself as a trial lawyer (p. 45). Interestingly, Glissan considers the art of examining witnesses an almost lost art.

Mauet and McCrimmon (1993:59–127) provide a comprehensive account of a long list of elements deemed important to an effective examination-in-chief, also illustrating with examples. Briefly stated these elements are:

- Keep the examination simple and elicit evidence from the witness in a logical sequence.
- Get the witness to first provide detailed information about a scene and then about what took place.
- Proceed with the examination at varying speed as deemed appropriate for the issue in question.
- Do not lead the witness but ask open-ended questions to encourage the witness to give descriptive and narrative accounts.
- Only ask leading questions about matters that are not being disputed.
- If confusion arises, get the witness to clarify it at once.
- Ensure the witness is the centre of attention throughout.
- Pay attention both to your own witnesses during the examination as well as to the witnesses of the other side during cross-examination (see below).
- Use a variety of exhibits effectively.

When a witness has been examined by the party who produced him/her (after first being sworn or affirmed) the other party or parties each cross-examine him/her in turn.

3.3 Cross-Examination

Mauet and McCrimmon (1993) maintain that the term 'cross-examination' 'still commands respect ... no other area of court work generates as much uncertainty, or is shrouded in as much mystery', and that: 'Texts on the subject often point out that cross-examination is an "art" or "an intuitive skill"' (p. 163). Regarding the question of what cross-examination is, Du Cann (1964:95) cites Lord Hanworth's, Master of the Rolls, statement that: 'Cross-examination is a powerful and valuable weapon for the purpose of testing the veracity of a witness and the accuracy and completeness of his story'. Du Cann also cites Lord Macmillan's (1952) view that when 'properly used' in a court in England cross-examination 'is the finest method of eliciting and establishing the truth yet devised' (pp. 95–6). Put simply, the aim of cross-examination is to elicit evidence favourable to one's side and to cast doubt on the credibility of the witnesses of the other side. To achieve this twofold aim, Mauet and McCrimmon (1993) advise that a cross-examination should be carried out according to a predetermined structure of questioning that is logical as well as persuasive (pp. 166–7). The same authors provide a number of rather useful questions advocates should ask themselves before embarking on a cross-examination in order to think clearly and to minimise risks inherent in this part of the trial (pp. 163–4).

Evans (1995:149–50) lists four objectives of cross-examination: laying the foundation; putting your case; eliciting extra and useful facts; and discrediting the evidence. He does remind advocates, however, that they are to discredit the evidence, not the witness. One way of discrediting the evidence mentioned by Evans is by 'driving the wedge', that is, by eliciting inconsistent answers from two witnesses, a task that should not be very difficult given the limitations of eyewitness testimony discussed in Chapters 2 and 3. Mauet and McCrimmon (1993) indicate that a witness' evidence can be discredited in cross-examination by casting doubt on their perception, memory or their ability to communicate.

A number of general, specific and cautionary rules to provide the advocate with some guidance in how to best carry out a cross-examination are outlined by Evans (1995:137–41). The *general rules* are: be kind to the other side's witnesses; every question must have a specific purpose; do not ask witnesses questions in a hostile manner but in a spirit of enquiry; do not look to a witness for assistance; and always try to give the impression that you are succeeding in your task. Evans' *specific rules* for the advocate (pp. 140–1) are: ask precise questions; avoid composite questions; and ask short questions that will elicit short and specific answers, thus enabling control of the witness. The *cautionary rules* (pp. 141–2) are: do not ask a question unless you know what the answer will be (p. 141); 'Do not suddenly draw back with a start' (p. 142); and, finally, 'ride the bumps' (p. 142). Du Cann (1964), Evans (1995), Glissan (1991) and Mauet and McCrimmon (1993) all agree that when cross-examining an advocate would be rather unwise and seriously risk losing the case to ask the witness a leading question.

Mauet and McCrimmon (1993) also furnish advocates with guidance on how to structure and conduct a cross-examination that is similar in many respects to what Evans (1995) provides. They do, however, also emphasise the principles of primacy and recency (that is, making one's strongest points at the beginning and at the end because this is what the jury will most likely remember). The *primacy effect* is well documented in social psychology (Schneider, 1995:45). This basically refers to the phenomenon that the first information we get about others is more important than information we get later. Mauet and McCrimmon also advise varying the order of the subject when cross-examining and, in contrast to Du Cann (1964:128), draw attention to the importance of an advocate projecting a confident, commanding attitude but in a natural way and, finally, they stress the importance of maintaining eye contact with the witness. Whilst some legal writers disagree about the importance of an advocate's style during cross-examination, as discussed below, the advice on keeping control of the witness by asking short precise questions is at variance with what has been reported by O'Barr (1982). Concerning the allegedly misplaced importance on style, Du Cann blames authors of legal biography who eulogise 'the subjects of their work [for] their virtues and not their questions' and is in no doubt that what matters is effect; that, in fact, 'the possession of a particular style can be a distinct handicap' since style is not adaptable, and adaptability is the most essential quality for the advocate who has to cross-examine people from very diverse backgrounds (pp. 128–9).

3.4 Re-Examination

At common law, after a witness has been cross-examined the party who has examined may re-examine about matters raised in cross-examination or about other matters with leave from the judge (Glissan, 1991:109). Glissan gives the aim of re-examination as 'to explain, to complete any matter left incomplete, and to countervail the damaging effect of the cross-examination' (p. 110). As re-examination 'must be prepared "on the run"' (p. 118), Glissan suggests that an advocate should first consider whether there is a real need to re-examine at all because of risks involved, and if re-examination is deemed necessary, to do so aiming to 'mend fences, not holes' and to avoid letting in material that will enable the other party to cross-examine the witness again (p. 119). Evans (1995) advises advocates to take advantage of the opportunity and to go ahead and re-examine a witness in cases where, during examination-in-chief or cross-examination (at the discretion of the judge for the latter), evidence was adduced that was inadmissible (pp. 173–6). Mauet and McCrimmon (1993) argue strongly against the view that an advocate should always re-examine and ask the witness at least one question so as to have the advantage of having the last word and show this belief to be an unsubstantiated myth (p. 124).

3.5 Closing Speeches

Following re-examination, each party in a trial has a last chance to address and communicate directly with the jury (or the presiding judge or magistrate/s) if it is a non-jury trial, in a last opportunity to provide a convincing argument for why they should accept the case as presented by one side rather than the other (see Mauet and McCrimmon, 1993:211–45; Glissan, 1991:130–48). Mauet and McCrimmon point out that the importance of closing arguments lies in the fact that they 'are the chronological and psychological culmination of a trial' (p. 211). Du Cann (1964) highlights the importance of an advocate's style which, unlike in the cross-examination, plays a significant part in closing speeches; more specifically, Du Cann maintains that 'A dose of good thumping sarcasm, spiced with a short, sharp rhetorical question or two, has always been one of the most effective weapons in the advocate's armoury' (p. 171). For psychologists, of course, such a view remains an empirical proposition. Additional guidance offered by Du Cann is that an advocate should first summarise the points of argument before dealing with each one separately, showing how the arguments fit into the facts and how they paint a more persuasive picture than the other side's arguments in order to have more of an impact on any tribunal (p. 176). To achieve the same goal, Mauet and McCrimmon provide detailed guidance on how an advocate should go about the closing argument, illustrating their suggestions with examples.

Mauet and McCrimmon urge advocates to:

• Use a logical structure and argue the theory of your case.
• Argue the facts and avoid personal opinions.
• Use exhibits and weave the judge's instructions into the advocate's argument.

- Use themes and rhetorical questions.
- Use analogies and stories and make the opening and closing points without referring to notes.
- Use understatement as well as overstatement.
- Argue strengths (that is, argue one's own strengths, not the other side's weaknesses).
- Volunteer a weakness (this helps the jury to like the counsel and this is important because jurors are inclined to favour those they like. The advocate should ensure that the jury or the Bench comes to like him/her and his/her client).
- Force the other side to argue its weaknesses, for example, by asking rhetorical questions.

4 Effective Advocacy in the Courtroom: Empirical Psychologists' Contribution

Trial advocacy is largely about argument-based persuasion. Advocates will be disappointed to find that while psychological research in this area has addressed Lasswell's (1948) question about 'who says what in which manner to who with what effect' (p. 37), it 'has not produced "laws of persuasion" in the form of general relationships between particular independent variables and amount of persuasion' (Jonas et al., 1995:11). Psychologists have therefore concentrated on identifying the processes underlying persuasion and have put forward a number of models (see Jonas et al., 1995, for a discussion). Drawing on Jonas et al.'s discussion, it can be said that such models emphasise the importance of systematic processing. McGuire's (1972) *information-processing model* suggested that persuasion requires the following processes: presentation, attention, comprehension, yielding (or acceptance), retention and behaviour (Jonas et al., 1995:12). Thus, this model highlights the importance of an audience having the intelligence to understand the content of a message in order to be persuaded. The message for advocates here is to tailor the complexities of their arguments according to the apparent intellectual abilities of the jurors.

The *cognitive-response model* stresses the importance of a message evoking favourable thoughts for the recipient in order for it to be persuasive (Petty et al., 1981). According to Jonas et al. (1995), more recent theories of argument-based persuasion maintain that people often decide to accept or reject a persuasive message, not as a result of having thought about the message, for the motivation to do so is frequently not there, but on the basis of peripheral processes, including heuristic cues (Chaiken et al., 1989). Advocates, of course, have the task of attempting to persuade the fact-finder in a trial, knowing only too well that if their arguments are not well thought out and logically consistent, the other side will capitalise on it. Unlike persuasive attempts at changing people's attitudes in order to impact on their behaviour – as happens, for example, in television advertising and which is a paradigm that has attracted a great deal of research by social psychologists – a trial is often a dynamic persuasion contest where strategies and tactics are crucial. Relevant psychological literature is, in this sense, of limited practical use to the advocate. However, what is known about how a speaker's credibility is assessed is of use to the advocate.

Drawing on Lloyd-Bostock (1988:37) and Zimbardo and Leippe (1991), the following factors appear to influence positively the credibility and persuasiveness of the source of a communication (message), namely:

- If it is perceived as being objective and having particular expertise in the matter at hand (Hurwitz et al., 1992; Petty et al., 1981).
- Supporting a position which is against one's own interest.
- If the person providing the communication is familiar to the audience or is similar to the audience in terms of social background and attitudes.
- If the communicator is likeable and considered physically attractive by the audience (Chaiken, 1979).

The psychological literature also supports the view that it is a good idea to admit weaknesses in one's evidence, thus 'inoculating' the jury or the Bench against the other side's cashing in on the weaknesses, and having variety in the channels of communication that are used to put a message across (Lloyd-Bostock, 1988:45–7). Other factors that may influence acceptance of a message include such characteristics of the audience as knowledge about the subject-matter of the communication (Wood, 1982) and pre-existing attitudes towards it (Lord et al., 1979). The psychological literature endorses the advice given advocates to deliver a logically-structured speech in a forceful style (Petty and Cacioppo, 1984) and to maintain eye contact with their audience (Mehrabian and Williams, 1969). Finally, a fast speech rate has also been shown to correlate with persuasion (Miller et al., 1976).

Jurors themselves or the judge or magistrate/s in a non-jury trial, like ordinary members of the public, have techniques for resisting persuasive communication by witnesses or by counsel. According to Avery et al. (1984:406–7), such techniques include: selective attention (that is, tuning out when not wanting to hear a given communication); rejecting a communication outright (that is, a 'blanket rejection' such as 'rubbish!'); distorting what is being communicated (for example, misperceiving a message as more extreme than it really is and hence it is not worth thinking about); discrediting the source (for example, during jury deliberation a juror attacks what defence counsel said about the defendant by claiming to the rest of the jury that defence counsels are notorious for lying about their clients). Avery et al. remind us that 'Attitudes and beliefs can be surprisingly resistant to change' (p. 407).

Books on advocacy and training courses for trial lawyers reiterate the importance for advocates to plan in advance and structure the arguments they will put to fact-finders, whether a jury or the Bench in non-jury trial. However, in considering advice on how to present arguments and evidence strategically, an advocate would be in some serious difficulty as to how to make best use of such advice, for every jury trial is unique. As Kadane (1993) so rightly points out: 'Attorneys will frame their arguments differently depending on who is on the jury and who they think will influence whom on the jury' (p. 233). Kadane's rather mundane but crucial observation would seem to 'throw a spanner into the works' of jury researchers and legal writers on advocacy alike, most of whom will most likely choose to ignore it!

Schum (1993) has reported interesting research into how arguments are structured and also how such evidence is evaluated by fact-finders. He has identified and examined two types of structuring: *temporary* (that is, one whereby 'its major ingredient is the believed ordering over time of events of significance to matters at issue' (p. 176)) and *relational* (that is, one which is meant 'to show how one's evidence items are related to these facts-in-issue and to each other' (p. 178)). Schum has found that it is not clear how people go about these two structuring tasks and how performing one impacts on the other (p. 189). In the light of this conclusion and the limited abilities fact-finders can bring to bear on large masses of evidence, Schum and his collaborators have been working on computer-based systems that will make easier the process of structuring arguments in rather difficult inferential problems involving large amounts of evidence (pp. 189–90).

Bartlett and Memon (1995) cite interesting ethnographic research by Bennet and Feldman (1981) concerning criminal trials in Seattle, which reported that trial protagonists rearrange, update, compare and interpret information utilising 'stories'(see also Chapter 5). As far as closing speeches are concerned, it appears that how much time has elapsed between the prosecution's opening speech and the judge's summing up influences whether the fact that the prosecution which is first to make a closing address (the *primacy* effect) is believed more than the defence which is the last to make a closing speech (the *recency* effect) before the judge's summing up (Lind and Ke, 1985). This finding is of importance in view of the fact that sometimes a criminal or civil trial can last for weeks, months or even more than a year. Making it possible for the jury or the Bench in non-jury trials to view a video of the prosecution's/complainant's opening address would seem to be one way of not disadvantaging some defendants/plaintiffs.

We have seen that while the advocate's language style is considered important in closing arguments, there is disagreement about its importance in cross-examination. At the risk of repetition, authors on advocacy, like the ones mentioned in this chapter, provide their readers with guidance about the different stages of a trial, in effect with lists of 'do's' and 'don'ts', accompanied with examples to illustrate. How useful such advice (for example, to control the witness in cross-examination by means of short, precise questions) is in practice can only be determined empirically. O'Barr (1982) reported a very interesting field simulation study of language styles ('powerful' [characteristic of male speakers], narrative, 'hypercorrect', and simultaneous speech) which were identified by analysing tape-recordings of actual trials. O'Barr subsequently found that subjects in experiments who had been presented with the same facts of a case rated witnesses as more truthful and convincing if they spoke in a powerful rather than in a 'powerless' style, and generally perceived witnesses more favourably if they spoke in narratives. As might have been expected, witnesses were assessed less favourably (that is, less intelligent, convincing, and less competent) if they spoke in a 'hypercorrect' style (for example, speaking in rather formal English one is not accustomed to in order to impress and thus making mistakes in the process). O'Barr also found that advocates should not try to dominate the witness, as various authors on advocacy recommend (see above), nor should they be trying to dominate the witness by 'hogging the floor' significantly more than the witness, because they are likely to be perceived negatively by a jury.

5 Conclusions

Various developments in recent years which have changed the practice of law do not seem to have impacted on the rather narrow way many legal writers conceive of advocacy as synonymous with lawyering in the higher courts nor, it should be said, have such developments impacted on how psychologists study persuasion as it relates to legal practitioners. This is not to deny the fact that for the minority of advocates who do appear in the higher courts there is ample advice on how to handle the different parts of a trial. A lot of the practical advice given, however, is generally in the form of assertions. The empirical social psychological literature on argument-based persuasion offers some useful findings for advocates. However, there is an obvious need for persuasion research done under forensically-relevant conditions, as well as for guidance on advocacy skills for all those lawyers appearing in the lower courts and in a broad range of sociolegal contexts. As a corollary, legal psychologists should take up the challenge and test, under forensically-relevant conditions and with a representative sample of lawyers' clients as subjects, the wisdom of advice given by legal writers about techniques of persuasion, both at different stages of a trial and in a variety of sociolegal contexts outside the courtroom. O'Barr's (1982) work is a limited indication that advice given advocates in how to treat and question witnesses may well be misguided.

Chapter 9

Detecting Deception

'*Human beings hate to be deceived. It makes us feel violated, used and stupid . . . The intellectual and moral traditions of Western culture have been shaped and driven by an explicit and consistent fear of deception . . . but . . . without such lies humanity cannot survive.*' *(Rue, 1994:4–5)*

'*Not every deception involves emotion, but those who do may cause special problems for the liar. When emotions occur, physiological changes happen automatically without choice or deliberation.*' *(Ekman and O'Sullivan, 1989:299)*

Introduction

A moment's reflection tells us that deception implies that someone intentionally does or says something in order to induce a false belief in someone else (Ekman, 1985; Miller and Stiff, 1993:16–31). Miller and Stiff have argued persuasively that a useful approach to studying deceptive communication is to conceptualise it as a general persuasive strategy, that is, as a means to an end and not an end in itself. Others, however, advocate using a discourse-centred definition rather than the intent criterion (Bavelas et al., 1990). Deception, as old as human existence, is a social phenomenon that permeates human life, irrespective of context, or one's age, gender, education or occupation. The Internet provides endless opportunity for deception. 'Deception includes practical jokes, forgery, imposture, conjuring, confidence games, consumer and health fraud, military and strategic deception, white lies, feints and ploys in games and sport, gambling scams, psychic hoaxes, and much more' (Hyman, 1989:133). Deception makes possible sale swindles and export scandals and can cause political scandals that bring about the downfall of politicians. Deception in the form of fraudulent reporting of research data and findings has been perpetrated by well-known scientists (see Humphrey, 1992) and routine use of deception in psychological experiments has increased in popularity and given rise to ethical debate (Fisher and Fyrberg, 1994). The use of an alias is a common practice among incarcerated offenders (Harry, 1986). Deception in the form of undercover operatives is standard practice by police and security services as is disinformation (see Marx, 1988; Wright, 1991).[1] In fact, 'Lying and other deceptive practices are an integral part of the police officer's working environment' (Barker and Carter, 1994:139). Lying is obviously necessary in covert policing and has been known to be tolerated by police when used to justify police practices or to ensure the conviction of a defendant who the investigators believe to be guilty. Barker and Carter cite the example of a Boston detective who committed perjury by 'inventing' an informant. Police lying, however, 'contributes to police misconduct and corruption and undermines the organisation's discipline system' (p. 150).

The law generally defines a number of both criminal and civil offences that involve deception and provides for sanctions. Criminal offences include obtaining property by deception and obtaining a financial advantage by deception. The Corporations Law also provides for such offences as fraudulent trading. Making a false complaint to the police or lying in court, if found out, are criminal offences. Most countries also have consumer-protection legislation that prohibits deceptive advertising while the use of deceit could render a contract invalid. Deception and its detection is, without doubt, a topic of great interest to psychologists, lawyers and law-enforcement personnel alike. Whilst deception offences are not responsible for people's paralysing fear in big cities, the financial cost is astronomical.

According to Hyman (1989): 'The early years of psychology's existence as an independent science offered the strong possibility of a psychology of deception' (p. 134). However, the rise and dominance of behaviourism in the US at the turn of the century left no room for associationist, mentalistic psychology and eclipsed the promising work of pioneers like Binet (1896), Dessoir (1893), Jastrow (1900) and Triplett (1900). The focus of these early deception scholars focused exclusively on demystifying conjuring tricks.[2] Despite the significance, the enormity and heterogeneity of deception, it is disheartening to find that we cannot, as yet, speak of a psychology of deception in the same sense as we can talk about a psychology of memory. No single, coherent framework has been put forward that can adequately account for the broad range of psychological issues involved in the plethora of deception contexts 'in terms of a coherent set of interrelated psychological propositions' (Hyman, 1989:143). As this chapter shows, most of the attention by psychologists has been focused on lying (see Ekman, 1985) and lie-detection, and detection can be assisted by drawing on sub-areas within psychology such as physiological, clinical, developmental, cognitive and social psychology.[3] Interrogation techniques are discussed in Chapter 11 as an example of psychology's contribution to law-enforcement.

1 Paper-and-Pencil Tests

It is well-established in criminology that theft by employees costs both the private and public sector all over the world a great deal of money, sometimes resulting in the collapse of companies. There is, therefore, a big incentive for employers to try to screen out potential thieves among job applicants. This practice is very widespread in western countries. In the US, the Employee Polygraph Protection Act (1988) prohibits the use of the polygraph (see below) in screening applicants for jobs except for local, state and federal personnel, members of the armed forces and the various secret services, security personnel guarding nuclear power stations, water supply facilities and those working in financial security businesses (Camara and Schneider, 1994). Since the Act was introduced there has been a lot of interest in what are commonly referred to as *integrity* or *honesty tests*. Such paper-and-pencil tests are used at the selection stage in an attempt to identify and minimise risks pertaining to employee theft, for example. In other words, they are said to be tests of potential employee trustworthiness (Goldberg et al., 1991).

Integrity tests are also used, though to a lesser degree, in post-employment investigations of employee misbehaviour such as theft. Whether it is used in a pre- or post-employment context, some authors assume that certain characteristics of individuals are stable over time and are useful in determining whether an individual is capable of dis-honest behaviour (Sackett, 1985). Other authors, however, assume that situational factors are more important in understanding why people cheat and so forth, than are characteristics of their personality (Harts-horne and May, 1928). It seems unlikely that the person vs. situation debate will be resolved in the near future, a factor that would appear to undermine the future of integrity testing.

There are two main types of integrity tests: overt and personality-based ones. The former measure attitudes towards theft. Personality-based ones, on the other hand, are supposed to measure traits such as conscientiousness (Wooley and Hakstian, 1992). Of course, paper-and-pencil tests are but one method of testing for integrity that can be supplemented with a face-to-face interview, applicant background checks or, finally, graphology (that is, hand-writing analysis, see Ben-Shakhar, 1989). The predictive utility of graphology in the pre-employment context is rather doubtful (Murphy, 1995:223–4).

According to Camara and Schneider (1994:113), a survey of pub-lishers of integrity tests carried out as part of the Goldberg et al. (1991) study by the American Psychological Association found that the con-structs measured by twenty-four such tests were: counter-productivity (15), honesty (9), job performance (9), attitudes (8), integrity (6), reliability (4) and 'other' (12). The last category, *inter alia*, includes: absenteeism/tardiness, admissions of dishonesty and drug abuse, credi-bility, dependability/conscientiousness, emotional stability, managerial/ sales/clerical potential, probability of short-term turnover, stress toler-ance, and substance abuse resistance. Bernardin and Cooke (1993) inform us that different overt tests contain an honesty subscale that is based on five universal constructs, namely:

1 Thinking about stealing more often than others.
2 Being more tolerant to those who steal than other people.
3 Believing most people commit theft regularly.
4 Believing in loyalty amongst thieves.
5 Accepting rationalisations for theft.

Bernardin and Cooke maintain that these five constructs exist in all the overt tests but different ones measure different areas in addition to honesty. The use of integrity tests raises questions about their reliability and validity but also broader questions about civil liberty concerns such as one's right to privacy. The validity of integrity tests is very difficult to determine irrespective of whether one validates them against background checks, self-reports of dishonest acts, contrasting those who appear to be honest with persons known to have been dishonest by virtue of their criminal records or, finally, by carrying out before-and-after testing comparisons of a company's losses (Murphy, 1995:212–15).

Given the very wide use of and the controversy surrounding integrity tests, the US Congress Office of Technology Assessment (OTA) (1990) undertook a close and critical look at these tests, as has the American Psychological Association (Goldberg et al., 1991). Not surprisingly, perhaps, the two bodies used different levels of validity, focused on different studies and arrived at different conclusions regarding the validity and usefulness of such tests. The OTA concentrated on five predictive validity studies. The APA report provides a review of 300 studies covering a broad range of criteria of validity. The OTA report evaluated integrity tests against 'absolute levels of validity' (Goldberg et al., 1991:7) using a detected theft or a close approximation to it as their external criterion of validity. The APA report assessed test validity in comparison, for example, with structured integrity interviews. Finally, neither of the reports examined whether such tests accurately predict total job performance (Camara and Schneider, 1994).

The OTA concluded that integrity tests over-predict dishonesty. More specifically, it found that 95.6 per cent of people who are given such tests and fail are incorrectly labelled as dishonest. In fact, the mean average percentage in the five studies examined that was detected for theft was 3 per cent. Camara and Schneider (1994:115) cite studies that used self-reported data and found theft base rates from 28 per cent to 62 per cent (see Hollinger and Clark, 1983, Slora, 1989, respectively). Consequently (and not surprisingly, the cynics might retort!), it is not possible to reach any definitive conclusions about the predictive utility of integrity tests. Camara and Schneider (1994:115) identify three major difficulties in evaluating integrity tests:

1 There is no consensus on what is meant by integrity.
2 There is an over-reliance on cut scores without the standard error of measurement and overlapping score ranges being reported.
3 Publishers are unlikely to encourage independent research into their integrity tests.

Camara and Schneider (1994)[4] conclude that: 'there is general agreement that integrity tests can predict a number of outcomes to employers and that they have levels of validity comparable to many other kinds of tests used in employment settings' (p. 117). Murphy (1995) lists the following caveats to the conclusion that integrity tests are useful: definition of integrity is problematic; the distinction between personality-based tests of integrity and other personality tests is not clear-cut; not informing examinees of integrity test scores when they are unsuccessful in their job applications poses serious ethical problems; from a psychometrician's point of view, the scoring procedure of some integrity tests is a cause for concern; and, finally, while integrity tests may help to identify high-risks among applicants they are not useful in screening the very honest individuals (pp. 215–17). Camara and Schneider (1994) remind the reader that legislation and the judiciary may one day decide what becomes of paper-and-pencil tests in general, be it personality or pre-employment tests, and that 'psychologists should wilfully participate in such public policy debates' (p. 117). One of the debates concerns the question of whether integrity tests should continue to be used in the employment setting in light of their limited predictive utility and invasion of an individual's privacy (see Stone and Stone, 1990).

2 The Social Psychological Approach

The demeanour of witnesses is relevant in judging their credibility in British courts (Stone, 1991:822): 'Hence, appeal courts are reluctant to interfere with decisions on veracity by the trial courts which saw and heard the witnesses' (p. 822). Apparently, the distinguished English judge, Lord Devlin, unlike many of his brethren on the Bench, did not have much faith in his ability to determine whether a witness was lying from his demeanour (Stone, 1991:828). Of course, the judiciary is not alone in believing that lying can be detected from a person's demeanour (that is, verbal and non-verbal communication) – the general public and many leading psychologists share the same belief.

In his article in the *Police Review* Oxford (1991), a serving detective in Cambridgeshire, England, had enough confidence as a 'human polygraph' to offer advice regarding both non-verbal and verbal cues to deception, which included delayed responses and the use of phrases like 'If I remember correctly' and 'Now let me see'. Alas, the provider of this advice betrays a rather dangerous assumption that the majority of suspects routinely lie when questioned by the police. But is such confidence in one's ability to distinguish the innocent but nervous individual (who has just been brought to a police station for questioning) from the guilty suspect on the basis of verbal and non-verbal cues to deceptive communication justified in the light of the existing empirical literature? Can 'human polygraphs' achieve the high deception-detection accuracy claimed by Oxford (1991)? As this chapter shows, wishing to emulate the polygraph is based on a grossly exaggerated belief in its effectiveness as a method of lie-detection as well as apparent absence of concern about false positive errors of judgement in this context.

2.1 Non-Verbal Cues to Deception

A number of different feelings may accompany deception, including detection apprehension and detection guilt. Some categories of individuals may well feel no guilt about having to lie to conceal their deceptive communication. Persons diagnosed with antisocial personality disorder (previously termed psychopathy) lack remorse and shame (Hare, 1970). Many diplomats are well versed in the art of lying, as are hardened career criminals. However, for many people lying is stressful. Strong deception guilt undermines attempts at lying because it produces non-verbal leakage or some other clues to deception (Ekman and Friesen, 1972). To choose when to feel emotions and to control whether others become aware of them is a most uncommon skill possessed only by the most accomplished of actors.

Deception, of course, may be accompanied by detection apprehension. Ekman and O'Sullivan (1989:305–6) list the following conditions that increase detection apprehension. These are: when the person to be lied to has a reputation for being difficult to deceive; is initially suspicious; when the deceiver has limited practice or no previous success; is particularly vulnerable to the fear of being caught out; is not particularly talented; possesses no special skill at lying; when the consequences of being found out are serious, or serious punishment awaits the deceiver upon being found lying; when the deceiver has not much incentive to confess because 'the punishment for the concealed act is so great'; and, finally, the person being lied to gains no benefit from the deceiver's lie.

A broad range of paradigms has been used by deception researchers to study the non-verbal and verbal leakage that normally occurs when people lie (see Miller and Stiff, 1993:39–49). These have included: uninterrupted message presentations, asking subjects to provide truthful and deceptive reactions to stimuli (known as '*reaction assessment*') and implicating subjects in a cheating incident during an experimental task. The last paradigm is known as the 'Exline procedure' (Exline et al., 1970) and has the advantage of both producing deceptive behaviour not sanctioned by the experimenter and motivating deceivers not to get detected (Miller and Stiff, 1993:43). Few researchers, however, have integrated correlates of deception with deception judgement accuracy (p. 65).

According to Ekman and O'Sullivan (1989), psychological studies of deception have tended to use college students as subjects who lie or tell the truth about liking or not liking their friends and who are sometimes offered trivial incentives to take seriously what they are asked to do in experiments. Such mock studies are generally very low on external validity, a far cry from the real world of deception detection in a law-enforcement context.

Reviews of the empirical literature on deception have reported that a number of vocal characteristics are indicative of deception. These include taking longer to answer a question, shorter speech duration and slower rate of speech (Ekman and O'Sullivan, 1989). Ekman and Friesen (1972) found that deceptive communication correlates with an increase in hand movements of the touching or stroking kind, as well as an increase in shrugs. DePaulo et al. (1985) reported that deception is accompanied by simultaneously reducing head movements, shifts in posture and leg and foot movements. There is a tendency for people to blink more when experiencing sudden emotional arousal. The meta-analytic review by Zuckerman and Driver (1985) reported that the frequency of eye-blinks correlates with deception. Ekman and O'Sullivan (1989) point out, however, that it is unwise to place too much reliance on such clues to deception for the simple reason they may be indicative of other emotions. As far as eye gaze is concerned, Ekman and O'Sullivan state that, contrary to popular belief, 'the overall tendency is for eye contact to increase during deception' (p. 299). Regarding smiles, in deceptive interviews it is smiles that 'leak' negative emotions that occur more often and not smiles that characterise positive emotions (pp. 298–9). Finally, Zuckerman and Driver (1985) reported that the amount of time subjects have to plan and rehearse their deceptions bears no relationship to verbal cues to deception.

2.2 Verbal Cues to Deception

The cognitive perspective on deception cues posits that producing a deceptive statement requires more cognitive effort than producing a truthful one (Cody et al., 1984), and results in a number of verbal cues such as number of specific references, and vocal cues to deception like how long one waits before answering a question and the number and duration of pauses. Unfortunately, research into verbal correlates of deception has reported contradictory findings. This unsatisfactory state of affairs is largely attributable to different researchers using different paradigms. A number of studies has found evidence supporting Yerkes and Berry's (1909) hypothesis that 'pauses are associated with lying'. Alonso-Quecuty (1992) reported that the number of pauses is greater in delayed false statements. Harrison et al. (1978) and Alonso-Quecuty have also found that false statements are longer (that is, have more words) than truthful ones.

According to Miller and Stiff (1993:65), however, 'The most consistent verbal correlate of deception is the number of words in a response' and, compared to truthful statements, deceptive ones tend to be shorter, more general, to contain a smaller number of specific references about people, places and the sequence in which events took place and, also, to over-generalise using words like 'all', 'every', 'none', 'nobody'. Stiff and Miller (1986) reported a significant relationship between deception and a composite measure of verbal content consisting of the following interrelated factors: clarity, consistency, concreteness and plausibility of one's verbal response.

An interesting new approach to detecting deception has been reported by two Spanish psychologists. Hernandez-Fernaud and Alonso-Quecuty (1995) carried out experimental work aimed at differentiating between true and false statements by eyewitnesses who watched a videotape of a simulated incident involving attempted car theft and threatening behaviour against the car-owner and a witness. Student subjects were instructed to give a true statement of what happened or a false one (a fabricated version to exempt one of the robbers). Subjects were interviewed using the traditional interview (TI) technique used by the Spanish police or the cognitive interview (CI) technique (Fisher and Geiselman, 1992). It was hypothesised that: (a) truthful statements would be more accurate and contain more contextual and more sensory information; (b) false accounts would contain more references to cognitive processes; and (c) the CI would enable a greater discrimination between truthful and false accounts by witnesses than the TI. It was found that witness accounts of events, persons and objects were more accurate in the CI condition (see Chapter 3). It was also found that: (a) true statements contained more contextual information and more sensory details than the false ones; and (b) the CI produced greater differences between truthful and false accounts than the TI by amplifying the differences between the types of account. Finally, Hernandez-Fernaud and Alonso-Quecuty reported that false statements did not differ from true ones in terms of number of references to internal information/processes (feelings, thoughts and opinions). These findings indicate the CI is potentially very useful to those social workers and police interviewing crime victims/crime witnesses – it not only produces significantly more accurate witness accounts but it also appears to differentiate reliably between true and false statements intentionally made by witnesses to a crime.

2.3 Humans as Lie-Detectors: How Accurate?

The available empirical literature shows that humans, though successful in deceiving others more often than not, are generally poor lie-detectors (DePaulo et al., 1980; Kalbfleisch, 1985).[5] Furthermore, even professionals supposedly trained to be good at detecting deception turn out to be no better than ordinary folk. In an interesting field study, Kraut and Poe (1980) conducted mock customs inspections in which 110 volunteer subjects who were domestic passengers waiting for their departure from Hancock Airport in New York were randomly assigned to the role of a 'smuggler' or innocent passenger and asked to try and smuggle contraband past a US customs inspector. The contraband was a miniature camera, a small pouch containing white powder and so on and the subjects had to hide it in their person. Subjects were offered a prize of $100 if they appeared honest. The questioning of passengers by the customs inspector was video-taped. Judges watched the video-tapes and decided whether to search a traveller. Kraut and Poe found that travellers were more likely to be searched if they were young and lower class, appeared nervous, hesitated before answering, gave short answers, avoided eye contact with the inspector, shifted their posture and were returning from holiday trips. In other words, the decision to search a traveller was based on their comportment. Interestingly, the researchers also found that customs inspectors were no better at detecting deceiving travellers than members of the public.

In another interesting study, Ekman and O'Sullivan (1991) investigated the deception-detection accuracy of US Secret Service, CIA, FBI, and National Security agents, armed forces personnel, federal polygraph examiners, robbery investigators, judges, psychiatrists, college students and working adults. They reported: (a) no relationship was found between one's confidence and deceit detection accuracy; and (b) with the exception of the secret agents (whose accuracy was 64 per cent), there were no significant differences between the members of the various law-enforcement agencies and the students. When occupational group was disregarded it was found that those who were accurate were more likely to use non-verbal or non-verbal plus speech clues to decide whether someone was lying in describing their feeling than did inaccurate observers, who seemed to have relied on speech clues alone. Regarding explanations why members of the US Secret Service were better than the rest, Ekman and O'Sullivan allude to the fact that many of them had done protection work that involved guarding important government officials from potential attackers and such work may have predisposed them to pay more attention to non-verbal behaviour. Also, such agents would have had experience questioning people who threaten to harm government officials and tend to be truthful when answering questions. By contrast, criminal justice personnel would have had experience questioning people who would have good reason for lying, leading these law-enforcement personnel to form the view that most of the people they question are liars, resulting in over-prediction of deceit and low accuracy.

Vrij and Winkel (1993) in the Netherlands showed eighty male and eleven female detectives with an average of seventeen years' experience in the Dutch police video fragments depicting subjects who had been instructed and given a monetary reward to lie about whether they were in possession of a pair of headphones. The detectives had 15 seconds to make their decision and to also indicate their degree of confidence in so doing. Given that 92 per cent of them indicated they had a lot of experience interviewing people, they were found, predictably, perhaps, to be very confident in their assessments and to agree significantly with each other about who was lying and who was telling the truth. Alas, the detectives' accuracy was less than chance (49 per cent) and, in fact, they turned out to be as inaccurate as subjects in other studies without any experience in questioning suspects. Vrij and Winkel reported that the detectives based their judgement on six criteria: less public self-consciousness, untidy dressing, less smiling, more social anxiety, less co-operative behaviour and more hand and arm movements during the communication the detectives deemed deceptive (p. 55). In other words, they were apparently judging on the basis of stereotypes.

However, caution is warranted in generalising from the results of both Vrij and Winkel (1993) and Ekman and O'Sullivan (1991) to real life because both studies would seem to be low on external validity. On the basis of the present author's personal experience in the field and intimate knowledge of the routine work of police detectives in more than one country it can be said confidently that the paradigms used in both these studies do not reflect the circumstances under which operational detectives make decisions about the truthfulness of a suspect's answers to questions. Such judgements are made in the context of dynamic interaction with the suspect. Showing subjects brief video fragments is convenient for the researchers and enables them to have control over what each subject is exposed to but it seriously detracts from the external validity of such research. It would have been interesting if the researchers in these two studies had also asked the law enforcement personnel how often they make such assessments in a matter of seconds based on such limited information about a person's demeanour, without asking any further questions. Let us not make the same mistake in studying deception-detection skills by law-enforcement personnel that Ebbinghaus made in studying memory – let us use sentences, not syllables. Also, using law-enforcement personnel instead of psychology students does not in itself justify calling such research a 'field' study. Once again, the need for ecologically-valid research cannot be overemphasised.

Being able to make an accurate judgement about whether a child is lying in what he/she is communicating would be of great help to all those professionals who work with children – parents, nursery school and primary school teachers, social workers and police. Without ignoring the importance of age differences for children (for example,

3 vs. 7 years) as far as the use of deception strategies is concerned, the available empirical evidence shows that adults believe they can detect reliably when children are lying. The fact is, however, that the performance accuracy of adults in this context is only slightly better than chance (59 per cent, reported by Westcott et al., 1991). Vrij and van Wijngaarden (1994) reported two experiments in schools in which students were shown video-clips depicting children (aged 5 and 6, or 8 and 9) giving either a true or a false report. Unlike earlier studies in this area, the children were completely visible, the false statement they made was their own decision (that is, they were not instructed to do so as in other studies) and the researchers also investigated the importance of children's social skills in successfully making a false statement. In support of earlier research both experiments found that, despite subjects' confidence, the accuracy rate was little better than chance – 57 per cent in the one experiment and 58 per cent in the other against a chance level of 50 per cent. Vrij and van Wijngaarden also found that observers showed higher accuracy scores for younger than for older children. One possible explanation put forward by them for the observers' apparent inability to accurately differentiate true from false statements by the children is that their student subjects had not been trained in detecting false statements by children and they speculated that nursery school teachers or child psychologists who have more experience in dealing with children might be more accurate.

Their prediction has, in fact, been borne out in a study by Chahal and Cassidy (1995) who examined how accurately social workers in the final year of their training, trainee primary school teachers and student controls could detect deception in male and female children in video-tapes that focused on the child's face in a close-up but also showed the child's upper body in another shot by a different camera. It was found that no group of subjects showed overall superiority in accuracy scores, but those subjects who were parents did significantly better than non-parents. One policy implication of the latter finding is that in real-life situations calling for decisions to be made about a child's allegations, more recognition should be given to the decision-maker having had real-life experience in dealing with children (p. 243).

Stone (1991) is in no doubt about the futility of attempting to decide in the courtroom context whether someone is lying by observing their behaviour and on the basis of their apparent anxiety or calmness (pp. 827–8). He concludes that 'There is no sound basis for assessing credibility from demeanour' (p. 829). Wellborn III (1991) surveyed the social science literature on the subject and concluded that demeanour evidence does not help in detecting deception or witness errors. Ekman and O'Sullivan (1989) suggest two ways to reduce making mistakes in detecting deceit when observing a person:

1 Take account of individual differences and base one's judgement on a suspect's observed behaviour.
2 Endeavour to become aware of one's own preconceptions about the suspect (p. 319) and to consider the possibility that a person may exhibit a particular emotion not because they are lying but because they are upset by being disbelieved (p. 320). This strategy should help one to avoid committing what Ekman and O'Sullivan call the 'Othello error', that is, that a person who is telling the truth under stress may appear to be lying.

Finally, the same authors provide a very useful lying checklist, containing thirty-eight questions to be considered in evaluating or checking a lie (see pp. 324–7).

3 Physiological and Neurological Correlates of Deception

3.1 Voice Characteristics: The Psychological Stress Evaluator

Mention has already been made that changes in voice pitch have been reported as a correlate of deceptive communication. The Psychological Stress Evaluator (PSE) is a commercially available instrument which its advocates claim detects and records low frequency stress changes in the voice (Horvath, 1979). The stress changes result in micro-tremors in the vocal muscles which the PSE is said to detect. The voice sample is recorded and played back at reduced speed to the PSE which plots a graph of the speech (Brenner et al., 1979). One obvious advantage of the PSE over the polygraph (see below) is that (if we accept what its supporters claim) it can be used to detect lying without the person physically being there or being hooked up to any machine. Thus, it could be used while someone is speaking on the phone, or it can be used to examine a tape-recorded or video-recorded message and, furthermore, it can be used to analyse sentences and statements, not just 'yes' and 'no' responses. These potential uses sound very impressive but what do we know about its accuracy in identifying lying?

Brenner et al. (1979) used two conditions (stressful situations), one involving an arithmetic problem and the other the guilty knowledge task. The subjects in the guilty knowledge task were motivated to conceal the correct answer. The accuracy of the PSE was no better than chance in the guilty knowledge task, casting serious doubt on its ability to accurately detect lying. PSE detection rates not exceeding chance level were also reported by Horvath (1979) and Hollien (1980). The research mentioned can be said to be limited due to low external validity but, according to Podlesny and Raskin (1977), negative findings about the PSE were reported by researchers utilising a mock-crime situation and a sample of criminal subjects. The available limited empirical evidence does not support the claims made about the PSE as a reliable means of identifying lying through voice-stress analysis (Bartol and Bartol, 1994:259). The possibility of using the PSE without someone being aware of it raises serious ethical questions about its use.

3.2 The Polygraph

As everybody knows, anxiety is normally accompanied by physiological changes – sweating, dryness of the mouth, the heart beating faster. The belief that most people feel anxious when lying and this, in turn, is betrayed by measurable physiological changes, is as old as human existence itself, is widely held today and forms the basis of the polygraph. In one English police force a detective superintendent has been advising his officers attending training courses that when questioning suspects they should look out for useful cues to lying like getting uncomfortable and fidgeting and, more importantly, when their blood pressure builds up to a level when the veins in their necks start protruding.[6] Noticing that when a person is anxious or afraid they do not salivate resulting in mouth dryness, the ancient Hindus would give a suspect rice to chew and spit it out. Failure to do so was taken as evidence of guilt (Harnon, 1982:341). The assumption that when people lie is evidenced in physiological changes which they do not control underpins the polygraph test for detecting deceit. The idea that changes in blood pressure and pulse accompany lying was first put forward by the pioneer Italian criminologist, Cesare Lombroso, in the 19th century (see Palmiotto, 1983). The polygraph itself has been available for almost eighty years now. It basically measures changes in: (a) blood pressure; (b) electrodermal activity (that is, the galvanic skin reflex (GSR)); and (c) respiration. The polygraph has been traditionally used in criminal investigation, employment screening, and for security screening (OTA, 1983). The GSR refers to the electrical resistance of one's skin, especially that on the palm or other hairless surfaces. The GSR varies with the activity of the sweat glands and is a convenient measure of sympathetic activity. Use of the polygraph in the US is provided in the Employee Polygraph Protection Act (1988). The polygraph is not used in a number of countries such as Australia, the UK (except by the security service – see Russell, 1986), Germany and France but it is used in a number of countries in addition to the US, namely Turkey, Israel, Canada, South Korea, Philippines and Japan (Barland, 1988). In the US, where the federal government's Department of Defence Polygraph Institute trains 100 new federal examiners each year, and where such evidence is admissible in court in thirty-two of the fifty States (see Honts and Perry, 1992), the polygraph is widely used by law-enforcement agencies as an investigative tool to verify witness statements, to clear suspects and to provide leads for interrogations (Honts and Perry, 1992). Its wide use in some countries should not, however, blind us to the controversy surrounding its reliability as a method of detecting deception as well as a number of ethical concerns about its use.

3.2.1 Deception Detection with the Polygraph: Techniques Used

The *relevant–irrelevant question test* was used in the early days of the polygraph and is nowadays used in pre-employment screening. A person who is lying is here expected to show stronger reactions to the relevant questions. The simple fact that an innocent person who is anxious about the outcome of the questioning would be labelled as a liar means that it is a technique that produces an unacceptable number of false positive identifications and 'is seldom used in federal law enforcement investigations in the US' (Raskin, 1989b:252).

To overcome limitations of the relevant–irrelevant test researchers developed the *control question test*. This technique is commonly used in criminal investigations and involves asking three types of questions: (a) relevant, 'hot', questions (for example, 'Did you drive the getaway car used in the robbery?'); (b) irrelevant, 'cold', questions (for example, 'Is your full name John Simon Smith?'); and (c) control questions (for example, 'During the first twenty years of your life, did you ever take something that did not belong to you?' (Raskin, 1989b:257)) which 'are designed to give an innocent suspect an opportunity to become more concerned about questions other than the relevant questions, thereby causing the innocent suspect to react more strongly to the control than to the relevant questions' (p. 253). The polygraph examiner compares a suspect's responses to the relevant and control questions and decides whether they indicate truthfulness or lying.[7] Strong supporters of the polygraph, such as Raskin (1989b), cite laboratory studies reporting polygraph examination accuracy of between 93 per cent and 97 per cent and a relatively high rate (30 to 80 per cent) of confessions by criminal suspects questioned by law-enforcement personnel using this technique. The OTA (1983) reported that acceptable field studies examined pointed to a 90 per cent and 80 per cent overall accuracy of the polygraph on criterion-guilty and criterion-innocent suspects respectively. In other words, at best, a polygraph examination risks labelling 20 per cent of suspects as liars who are later found to be innocent.

Raskin (1989b) reported a major field study that used data from criminal investigations conducted by the US Secret Service over a three-year period beginning in 1983. Polygraph examinations were only included in the sample if they involved: (a) a confession that inculpated or exculpated a suspect; and (b) if there was corroboration of the confession by physical evidence. The polygraphed suspects were thus 'classified as either confirmed truthful or confirmed deceptive on one or more relevant questions in the test' (p. 267). Different Secret Service polygraph examiners re-evaluated the polygraph charts blindly. It was found that the original examiners had a false negative rate of 5 per cent and a false positive rate of 4 per cent. The blind re-evaluations were found to have a 6 per cent false negative and 15 per cent false positive rate. The difference in the false positive rate was attributable to the fact that the original examiners were in a position to make judgements about deception also utilising information about the case concerned and about the demeanour of the suspect, information that was not available to the blind examiners. Raskin concluded that: 'Taken as a whole, these data provide strong support for the accuracy of control question polygraph tests when properly used in criminal investigations' (pp. 268–9).

However, caution is warranted in accepting Raskin's conclusion because: (a) a confession by a person as a result of having been given a polygraph test by an agent of the Secret Service is not a satisfactory criterion due to the likelihood that the suggestibility factor operated in a number of cases; (b) guilt had not been established beyond reasonable doubt by a properly constituted court of law; and, finally, (c) the vast majority of polygraph examiners do not possess the qualifications, do not receive the in-depth training and do not have the practical experience which apparently characterise Secret Service agents and explains their relative success at detecting deceit with and without the aid of the polygraph (Ekman and O'Sullivan, 1991). Raskin's field study is, nevertheless, a significant improvement on earlier attempts to test the effectiveness of the control question technique. Raskin (1989b) himself concedes: 'It is clear that the major weakness of the traditional control question test is its susceptibility to false positive errors'. Given that such mistakes by Secret Service agents may well be used by them to justify keeping a citizen under surveillance and so forth, false positive polygraph tests are a cause for concern.

Persons diagnosed as psychopaths (in contemporary clinical diagnosis the preferred term is 'suffering from an anti-social personality disorder') are known to have a propensity to lie, not to experience anxiety and to feel no remorse. Parrick and Iacono (1989) offered prison inmates $20 to beat the polygraph. They had forty-eight subjects, half of whom had been diagnosed as psychopaths. Half of each of each of those groups were instructed to steal money from a coat from a prison doctor's office and the rest in each group who were not involved in committing the theft served as controls (the innocent comparison group). Polygraph control question tests were conducted by professional polygraph examiners with over thirty years' experience between them and they scored each other's chart blindly using a semi-objective scoring method. It was found that the psychopaths had no advantage on the polygraph test. The accuracy of the control question technique with both psychopathic and non-psychopathic groups of inmates was slightly better than chance for the innocent (55 per cent) and 86 per cent for the guilty. In other words, using the control question technique polygraph examiners wrongly classified 45 per cent of the innocent subjects as guilty of the theft.

In another field study Parrick and Iacono (1991) collaborated with the polygraph division of the Royal Canadian Mounted Police (RCMP). Using information in police investigative files they identified persons who had taken a polygraph test but were subsequently shown to be innocent of a crime. The researchers had RCMP polygraph examiners score those persons' polygraph charts blindly and found that 55 per cent of them were classified as truthful. It was also reported that the RCMP conducts polygraphs tests when the investigation fails to unearth evidence incriminating a suspect. The two studies by Parrick and Iacono leave no doubt that the control question technique misidentifies almost half of innocent suspects as liars.

To overcome weaknesses of the control question technique the *directed lie control test* has been suggested (Honts and Raskin, 1988). A typical lie question might be 'Before the age of 18 did you ever lie to anyone about anything?' and a suspect is instructed to answer 'No' to each such question and is also told by the polygraph examiner that to deny ever having lied in the past means that he/she is lying. The assumption is that someone who is innocent and telling the truth will show stronger physiological reactions to the directed lie questions than to the relevant questions, while guilty ones will show stronger reactions to the relevant questions.

A field study by Honts and Raskin (1988) examined the validity of the directed lie test. Honts and Raskin carried out polygraph tests of criminal suspects over a four-year period and obtained twenty-five confirmed tests in which one personal directed lie was included with traditional control questions. Each of the polygraph examiners then scored blindly the charts obtained by the other examiners, including or not including the directed lie question. Honts and Raskin reported that including one directed lie question completely eliminated false positives. Raskin (1989b) concluded that the findings from experimental simulation and field studies support the view that the directed lie test has a number of advantages over the traditional control question test, namely that:

> It is more standardized in its structure; it is easier to administer; it requires less manipulation of the subject and creates fewer problems for the subject; it is more readily explained to lawyers, judges and juries; and most important, it reduces the problem of false positives inherent in the traditional control question test. (pp. 274–5)

3.2.2 Scoring the Polygraph Chart

There are three approaches to scoring the polygraph chart (Raskin, 1989b):

Global Evaluation: This is a subjective impression based on an examiner's overall inspection of the chart showing how an examinee answered different questions, as well as information about the case at hand and observations of the examinee's behaviour during the test. This scoring method has been shown to be inferior to the next two approaches (Raskin, 1989b:259).

Numerical Evaluation: This involves assigning a score ranging from -3 to $+3$ to each of an examinee's three physiological responses (GSR, blood pressure and respiration) to indicate the difference between the response to a control question and its nearby relevant question. If the reaction to the control question is greater and the magnitude of the response is a dramatic difference then a score of $+3$ is assigned to that response. A -3 would indicate the response to the relevant question was greater. According to Raskin (1989b:260), a zero score indicates no observed difference, 1 a noticeable difference, 2 a strong difference and 3 a dramatic difference, but a score of 3 is very rarely given.

Computer scoring: Using mathematics, Kircher and Raskin (1988) developed a computer method for scoring the chart that yields a probability value (ranging from 0 to $+1$) that an examinee was truthful on the basis of the test. According to Raskin (1989b), laboratory studies 'indicate that computer evaluations are extremely useful and are worthy of field implementation at this time' (p. 262).

3.2.3 The Polygraph and Ascertaining a Suspect has Direct Knowledge of Specific Information

An early method used to investigate whether a suspect has direct knowledge of particular items of information was the *peak of tension test*. This involves comparing a suspect's physiological responses to a number of alternative answers (usually five) to a particular question such as the type of knife used to stab a victim to death. One of the alternative answers is the correct one. What is known as the searching peak of tension test can be used to establish a fact a criminal investigator does not know but is keen to find out such as where a body is buried or a kidnapped victim is kept (Raskin, 1989b:276).

Building on the peak of tension test, Lykken (1959) proposed the *guilty knowledge test* (GKT). This basically tests a suspect's reactions to specific items of information, in the form of multiple choice questions, directly relevant to the commission of a crime of the kind that only the perpetrator would know. According to Podlesny and Raskin (1978) and Iacono et al. (1987), the galvanic skin response is the most useful measure in determining the outcome of a concealed knowledge test. Laboratory studies of the guilty knowledge technique have generally reported accuracy of approximately 84 per cent with guilty and 99 per cent with innocent subjects. Elaad (1990) reported a field study of detection of guilty knowledge in a random sample of ninety-eight real-life criminal investigations conducted during 1979–1985 in which the guilt and innocence of the suspects had been verified by the confession of the person who had committed the crime in question. Elaad found that 98 per cent of the innocent and 42 per cent of the guilty subjects on the basis of an a priori decision rule, while an optimal decision rule yielded correct classifications for 94 per cent of the innocent and 65 per cent of the guilty subjects. Elaad's study shows that the GKT can be a useful tool in criminal investigations and that it protects innocent suspects from being falsely classified as guilty. There is undoubtedly a need for more research in this area.

3.2.4 Factors Impacting on Polygraph Test Accuracy and Outcome

A number of factors can justifiably be said to influence lie-detection using the polygraph. Who the examiner is has been shown to be an important factor. Elaad and Kleiner (1990) reported an interesting field study that compared one group of examiners (N=5) with at least three years' experience in chart interpretation and a second group (N=5) of trainees in the seventh and eighth month of a ten-month training program. A random sample of fifty real-life polygraph records from the Israel Scientific Interrogation Unit were used to examine the perform-ance of the two groups of examiners. Half the records were of innocent suspects verified by the confession of another person and the other half were of guilty suspects verified by their own confession. It was found that an examiner's length of experience correlated positively with accuracy detection rate when scoring the respiration channel but not when scoring the skin resistance or blood pressure channels.

As far as the personality of the suspect is concerned, there is some evidence that emotional stability, also known as trait anxiety, can impact on the polygraph's accuracy (Gudjonsson, 1992a:186). More specifically: 'stable subjects may react in a way that leads the examiner to make false negative errors, whereas emotionally labile subjects more commonly react in a way that results in false positive errors' (p. 186). The potential of countermeasures to influence a polygraph test outcome has attracted a certain amount of research interest.[8] In brief, the available evidence shows that it is possible, using countermeasures (for example, of the kind that augment the examinee's response to the control questions) to seriously undermine the accuracy of the polygraph (Gudjonsson, 1992a:187). For one to use such countermeasures effectively, however, special training is required (p. 187). Apparently, an easy and effective countermeasure that can be used by guilty suspects against a control question polygraph test is to serially subtract 7 from a number greater than 200 (Honts et al., 1994). Anybody wishing to attempt to beat the polygraph should remember that examiners themselves get schooled in counter-countermeasures (Gudjonsson, 1988:133–4). However, there have been no field studies on the question of how effective different countermeasures and counter-countermeasures are (Gudjonsson, 1988:134).

From the point of view of the general public, an easy countermeasure to use would seem to be to take some drugs that will interfere with a polygraph test. Raskin (1989b) concluded his discussion of laboratory studies of the potential effects of such drugs as tranquillisers, beta blockers, stimulants and alcohol (see Iacono et al., 1987; O'Toole, 1988; Waid et al., 1981) by stating that there is no convincing evidence for such effects either with the control question or the GKT procedure (p. 285). Support for this view was more recently provided by Iacono et al.'s (1992) laboratory study finding that anti-anxiety drugs are not effective countermeasures to be used against the GKT. Countermeasures would seem to take on another interesting twist in the light of attempts by some researchers in recent years to infer the possession of information in persons attempting to conceal it measuring 'event-related brain potentials' (see Bashore and Rapp, 1993).

A number of bodies have carried out assessments of the polygraph and have published reports (Irving and Hilgendorf, 1980; OTA, 1983; Department of Defence, 1984; House of Commons Employment Committee, 1985; British Psychological Society's [BPS] Working Group, 1986). The Royal Commission on Criminal Procedure in Britain devoted nine lines to the polygraph in its report and rejected the idea of polygraph evidence in the courts, but did not deny its value as an investigative tool for police forces. Predictably, perhaps, the US Department of Defence (1984) report claimed that: 'Without the polygraph as an investigative tool, a number of espionage cases never would have been solved' (p. 13). Two years later, the BPS Working Group Report on the use of the polygraph in criminal investigation and personnel screening, prepared under the chairmanship of Professor Anthony Gale at the request of the Society's Scientific Affairs Board, concluded that polygraph tests are unlikely to be used in personnel selection generally in Britain; they raise serious efficacy concerns in the context of criminal investigations which need to be addressed by future research; they are irrelevant in the context of the security services and, finally, the Working Group seriously doubted whether such evidence would ever be admissible in British courts of law (pp. 80–1).

One of the strongest criticisms levelled against the polygraph by its opponents is that 'Unlike the fictional Pinocchio, we are not equipped with a distinctive physiological response that we emit involuntarily when, and only when, we lie' (Lykken, 1989:124). Lykken, perhaps the best-known critic of the polygraph, does nevertheless accept that: 'Polygraphic detection of guilty knowledge, based on entirely different and more plausible assumptions, has proved itself in the laboratory and deserves control study in the field of criminal investigation' (p. 125).

Opponents of the polygraph also repeatedly point to its bias against the innocent, that jurors are likely to be influenced by its results (but see Cavoukian and Heslegrave, 1979; Honts and Perry, 1992), that it constitutes an invasion of people's privacy, and that while in western countries the tendency is for police storage and so forth of criminal record information to be regulated by standing orders and legislation and in some jurisdictions members of the public can apply to access such information under freedom of information provisions, the storage and potential use of polygraph charts and the information that accompanies them is wide open to abuse. Meanwhile, there is no doubt that the polygraph will continue to be used in countries like the US and Israel in the context of criminal investigation and national security. The hope is that the courts will play a more effective role in regulating its use and enforcing strict ethical standards on its practitioners.

4 Brainwaves as Indicators of Deceitful Communication

Presenting the brain with a discrete stimulus generates an electrical signal known as *event-related potential* which is approximately a few millionths of a volt in size (Iacono, 1995:168–70). This takes place against the brain's background electrical activity. By presenting a stimulus repeatedly about thirty times and averaging the brain's responses to the repetitions it is possible to extract the event-related potential. P3 or P300 brainwave is one particular type of event-related potential which is evoked by relatively uncommon stimuli but which have special significance for a person. A number of laboratory studies have reported using P3 waves to distinguish guilty and innocent alternatives in guilty knowledge experiments (Allen et al., 1992; Boaz et al., 1991; Farewell and Donchin, 1991; Rosenfeld et al., 1991). Field studies of the accuracy of event-related potential recordings is the next logical step.

5 Stylometry

Drawing on Gudjonsson (1992a), stylometry is a branch of linguistics and literary studies that tries to authenticate the creator of a written or even spoken language text. It is assumed that a person's stylometric features do not change with time. Thus, the argument goes, no two individuals are significantly the same in how they express themselves through language: how often they use particular vocabulary, combinations of words, or how they structure their sentences. Stylometry can also be used to comment on the mental state of a person when he/she made a statement to the police, for example. To illustrate, it is known that people's use of the verb–adjective ratio changes according to one's emotional arousal (Gudjonsson, 1992a:194). To authenticate a document, a stylometrist might decide to count the most frequent linguistic characteristics in a document, quantitatively analyse the language structure used in terms of its vocabulary, grammar, syntax and spelling (see Morton, 1978; Morton and Michaelson, 1990).

Robertson et al. (1994) discuss case law pertaining to the admissibility of stylometric evidence in the UK and Australia and show that stylometry has had a mixed reception in the courts. It was not admitted in the well-known case of Patty Hearst[9] (*US v. Hearst*, 418, F Sup 893 (1976)) on the grounds that it failed the *Frye* test (*Frye v. United States*, 293 FR 1013 (1923) now superseded by the *Daubert* criteria – see Chapter 7). Stylometric evidence was admitted in England in *The Queen v. McCrossen* (unreported, 10 July 1991 CA (Cr.D.)) and in *Mitchell* (unreported, 82/2419/E2). In Australia, stylometric evidence was rejected in *Tilley* ([1985] VR 505), in which Justice Beach rejected the argument that 'a person's oral utterances would be stylometrically consistent with his or her written work' (Robertson et al., 1994:646). The British forensic psychologist, Professor David Canter (1992), has argued that there is no empirical evidence showing that an individual's stylometric features are consistent over a long period of time. The future of stylometric evidence does not seem optimistic either in the UK or in Australia and we need to wait and see how courts in the US will treat expert stylometry testimony on the basis of the *Daubert* decision, that is, whether they will regard the theory underpinning it as scientific.

6 Statement Reality Analysis

Following a West German Supreme Court decision in 1954, German psychologists came to play an important part appearing as expert witnesses in court testifying on the truthfulness of witness statements, especially in sex cases, utilising a method known as 'statement reality analysis', developed by Undeutsch and known widely as statement analysis.[10] The theoretical basis of this technique is that people's accounts of events actually experienced are both quantitatively and qualitatively different from fictitious accounts whether invented or coached. Undeutsch (1982) lists eight reality criteria (features) for deciding the objective reality, truthfulness, of a statement. The criteria are: 'Originality; Clarity; Vividness; Internal consistency; Detailed descriptions which are specific to the type of offence alleged; A reference to specific detail that would under normal circumstances be outside the experience of the witness or victim; The reporting of subjective feelings' and, finally, 'spontaneous corrections or additional information' (Gudjonsson, 1992a:201). Steller and Koehnken (1989) have been critical of earlier work on this technique and have proposed using a total of nineteen criteria instead of Undeutsch's nine[11] which are more likely to be found in truthful than in deceptive statements. The first five criteria (see Marxsen et al., 1995, for details) are considered the minimum necessary for a statement to be coded as truthful. If any of the remaining fourteen criteria are also present, this adds to the credibility of the statement but their absence does not render a statement untruthful. At least two additional criteria are considered sufficient for a statement to be classified as credible (Marxsen et al., 1995:455).

Using statement reality analysis, Undeutsch has claimed to have found victims to be truthful in 90 per cent of 1500 cases he examined. This finding is of interest in view of the fact that 95 per cent of the defendants involved in those cases were, in fact, convicted. Empirical support for the 'Undeutsch hypothesis' has also been reported by Yuille (1988) and Steller and Boychuk (1992) with children. Yuille found that statement analysis identified correctly 74 per cent of false and 91 per cent of true stories by children aged 6 and 8 years. Further support for statement analysis was reported by Esplin et al. (1988, cited in Raskin and Esplin, 1991) who examined forty statements, of which twenty involved child sexual abuse which had been confirmed either by a confession or medical evidence or a combination of the two, and twenty 'doubtful' (that is, there was no confession, the children withdrew the allegation, the case did not get to a court, the case was dismissed by the judge or the defendant was acquitted). Esplin et al. reported that a single person coding the statements without knowing which belonged to which category was able to differentiate perfectly between true and false cases of child sexual abuse. Marxsen et al. (1995) point out that researchers have neglected statement analysis as a useful technique with which to assess the credibility of children's statements.

Most of the validation studies of Undeutsch's theory have been with children, but Zaparniuk et al. (1995) reported that statement reality analysis distinguished reliably (mean accuracy rate of 76 per cent) between true and false statements by adult witnesses. Porter and Yuille (1995) examined ten of the statement analysis criteria in a mock-crime paradigm and found three (coherence, sufficient detail and admitting lack of memory) differentiated reliably between truthful and false accounts. Landry and Brigham (1992) showed the potential of training individuals to use the technique effectively with a video-tape of adults who were instructed to make true or false statements of a personal traumatic experience. Joffe (1992) and Yuille et al. (1993), however, reported difficulty in training field workers to perform statement analysis.

Some weaknesses of statement analysis have also been reported: its subjectivity, differing according to criteria have been shown; possible differences between statement analysis carried out 'post hoc from a transcript or video-tape of an interview and statement analysis done during the interview by the interviewer' and the fact that brief narrations (often a characteristic of rather young children) are not amenable to analysis (Marxsen et al., 1995). In addition, expert raters, using one only aspect of the statement analysis (criterion-based content analysis) have difficulty differentiating actual events in statements by children from events in their statements persistently suggested to them during interviews over a long period of time (Huffman, 1995, cited by Ceci et al., 1995:514).

The available empirical literature provides strong support for Undeutsch's hypothesis and validation findings for his technique. However, given the current state of knowledge about the reliability of statement analysis, 'it must be applied in a context of pursuing multiple hypotheses and is not a sort of "no tech" lie-detector. The individual criteria must be examined further, and there is no guarantee that what will work for younger children will work with older' (Marxsen et al., 1995:458). As far as it has been possible to ascertain, there has been no legal test of the question of the admissibility of expert statement analysis testimony in British, US or Australian courts. The results of such analysis would be particularly useful to both judges and juries in alleged sexual abuse cases.

7 Scientific Content Analysis

Another method of statement analysis that has been suggested as useful in detecting deceptive communication is Scientific Content Analysis (SCAN). This is a technique more familiar to an elite number of secret services personnel, law enforcement, armed forces and private sector investigators who have been introduced to it than to psychologists (Driscoll, 1994). The assumptions of SCAN are that: (a) there are significant differences between truthful and deceptive accounts; (b) the suspect's words must be produced without any help from the interrogator; and (c) every individual has his/her unique linguistic code, with the exception of pronouns. SCAN utilises a number of criteria to analyse the transcript or written statement of an individual. According to Driscoll (1994: 80–1),[12] these criteria include the following and show how they point to a deceptive communication: pronouns (a change or absence), spontaneous corrections (their use), emotion (if located near the peak of the story rather than throughout), connections (their use, for example, 'later on', 'the next thing I remember'), first person singular, past tense (deviations from these), time (a deceptive statement will have more lines written before the key issue or offence than after it) and, finally, changes in language use (inconsistent use of language indicates deception, as when 'a nice guy' becomes 'that man'). Driscoll reported SCAN analysis of thirty written statements given voluntarily by crime suspects prior to being given a polygraph test by the same examiner. Scoring of the statements indicated that the technique 'is capable, within limits, of differentiating between probably accurate statements and likely false statements' and compares well with the polygraph in effectiveness (p. 86). More research is needed, however, before definitive conclusions can be drawn about the forensic utility of SCAN in detecting written deceptive communication.

8 Conclusions

Despite the importance of deception as a social phenomenon, we cannot as yet speak of a psychology of deception. Early psychological research into deception was largely concerned with explaining conjuring tricks but was eclipsed by the rise of behaviourism. The wide use of integrity tests in pre-employment screening remains controversial, as different evaluations of the validity of such tests have reached rather different conclusions. There still remain serious difficulties in attempting to evaluate integrity tests, such as the absence of consensus on what is meant by 'integrity'.

A lot of research has been carried out into both non-verbal and verbal cues to deception. While studies have established a number of non-verbal correlates of deceptive communication, research into verbal cues appears to be more bedevilled by conflicting findings. Humans, including trained and experienced law-enforcement personnel (but apparently with the notable exception of US Secret Service agents), turn out to be as good as chance in detecting deception. The consolation is that most people are better than chance in deceiving others. The external validity of studies of deception-detection by law-enforcement personnel is questionable. As far as the psychological stress evaluator is concerned, research results do not support claims made for it.

Regarding the much-researched and talked-about polygraph, the main issue is its accuracy in general and the false positive rate in particular, as well as ethical concerns about its wide use. Researchers have reported false positive rates ranging from 4 per cent to 20 per cent and false negatives ones from 4 per cent to 15 per cent. The directed lie control test appears more accurate than the control question test and thus reduces even more the percentage of false positive errors. The directed lie control test, however, awaits evaluation in the field. The guilty-knowledge technique has been shown by Israeli researchers to be a useful tool in criminal investigations and to protect innocent suspects from being labelled as guilty.

In considering the accuracy of the polygraph with whichever technique, it is important to remember that such factors as how experienced the examiner is, the trait anxiety of the examinee, and the use of certain countermeasures (for example, that augment one's responses to control questions) can influence the test outcome. Even strong opponents of the polygraph, like Professor Lykken, accept that, properly used, the polygraph can be a useful tool in criminal investigations. Whether a police force should be allowed to use it, let alone whether such evidence should be admissible in court, is a question entirely left to the legal systems of different countries and their parliaments to decide. The answer would seem to depend on how a society decides to balance the rights of the individual citizen on the one hand and police powers on the other. The usefulness in the field of the event-related potential method is yet to be determined by studies that will attempt to replicate the rather impressive results obtained in the laboratory. The guilty-knowledge technique has been shown to have more merits than the control question technique, especially when it is used with event-related potential recordings.

As far as stylometry is concerned, despite some researchers' awarding it good marks as an effective method for authenticating the authorship of a given text, Australian courts, unlike courts in England, have shown a reluctance to allow such expert testimony, and the research that has given rise to the technique has come under attack.

Rather impressive results have been reported over the years from Germany and elsewhere regarding the usefulness of statement reality analysis in determining the truthfulness of both a child's or an adult witness' statement. It is a technique which, despite its limitations, undoubtedly deserves more attention from psychologists, lawyers and the judicial profession in common law countries. Finally, the SCAN technique appears to deserve more field testing before it is recommended for use by law enforcement investigators. Future research should also examine the comparative effectiveness of different techniques available for identifying deceptive communication, both oral and written, and the merits of their theoretical underpinnings. Meanwhile, the search for new methods continues. A method which has been suggested as potentially useful in detecting deception uses electronic noses to sniff and measure differences in a person's body smells that take place when people are under stress, such as when they are lying (Coghlan et al., 1995).

Chapter 10

Witness Recognition Procedures

- *Face misidentification and wrongful convictions.*
- *Photographs and person identification.*
- *Unconscious transference.*
- *Showups.*
- *Police face-composites utility.*
- *Line-ups, sources of bias: police, composition, size, instructions, presentation style, test medium.*
- *Factors that impact on voice identification.*

'Few problems can pose a greater threat to free, democratic societies than that of wrongful conviction – the conviction of an innocent person.' (Huff et al., 1986)

'In a democracy, the presumption of innocence is of paramount importance. Although there is sometimes a natural desire among police officers to seek to prove cases well beyond a reasonable doubt, there is very real need to ensure that such desires do not lead to behaviours that are manifestly unfair and add unjustifiable strength to the prosecution case.' (McKenzie, 1995)

Introduction

Very often, the identity of the perpetrator of a crime is not an issue or it can readily be established by the prosecution. In such cases, the primary concern of police investigators is to establish the necessary points of proof regarding the charges laid against the defendant. However, in those cases where a criminal offence has been committed and the issue is whether the defendant has been identified by a witness as the person who committed it, visual identification may involve one of the following: single confrontation identification, photograph identification, photo-board identification, video-film identification and, finally, identification by means of a line-up (that is, an identification parade). Courts have discretion to exclude witness identification evidence which has been obtained illegally, unfairly or improperly, as when a suspect was forced into taking part in a line-up or a police officer somehow communicated to a witness who the suspect was before a line-up is conducted, or when a line-up should have been conducted but was not, or finally, when the suspect's photograph 'stands out' in a photo-board or video-frame.

We saw in Chapter 2 that the issue of person identification has been of central concern to eyewitness researchers for over two decades. At the same time, there is widespread concern about biases in police identification practices and procedures that result in the false identification of innocent citizens. Wells et al. (1994:224) list three sources of support for the basis assumption 'that there is an identification problem': empirical studies reporting high rates of false identifications; the 'sincerity' and confidence of subjects in such studies reporting false identifications; and actual cases of wrongful convictions.

Recognising the dangers inherent in person identification, trial judges in Britain are required to warn the jury about identification evidence of witnesses in the terms required by *Turnbull* ([1977] QB 224).[1] Such warnings are also to be taken into account by magistrates. There are differences, of course, in what police officers in different countries can do legally as far as witness identification procedures are concerned. To illustrate, according to Wells and Turtle (1986) as many as a quarter of the cases in the mid-West of the US involve a procedure whereby the police create a line-up comprising only all the suspects in a crime. As Wells et al. (1994:228) put it, this procedure 'is like giving the witness a multiple choice test in which there can be no wrong answer'. Under the rules in the Code of Practice D made under s.66 of the Police and Criminal Evidence Act (1984), such a practice is prohibited in Britain.[2] The same practice is also prohibited in Australia. Differences in the law of evidence and police procedures need to be borne in mind when generalising some research findings from one country to another.

Police person identification procedures, which most often involve the use of photographs, do not, of course, take place in a vacuum but in a social context. The witness has his/her memory of the event in question, of which often one particular face is of special importance. At the same time, witnesses have their own expectations about the criminal investigation process they are contributing to, and the evidence is overwhelming that mock witnesses are more than ready to select a suspect from a line-up that contains only innocent foils. For their part, law-enforcement officers, often under a lot of pressure to detect (that is, clear up) crimes, are likely to have their suspicions who the culprit is and would like the witness to confirm their suspicions. Consequently, some police officers may inadvertently and in a rather subtle, non-verbal way, such as by smiling and showing approval (see Fanselow, 1975), or even quite openly (for example, in terms of the verbal instruction they give a witness to point out the criminal in the line-up), indicate to the witness who he/she should pick out from a photo-array or in a live line-up. The analogy between a methodologically sound social psychology experiment and a properly conducted line-up has guided eyewitness identification research implicitly and proven very fruitful (Wells and Luus, 1990a).

Estimates of the percentage of cases involving wrongful conviction vary. In an attempt to obtain a more reliable estimate of the size of the problem, Huff et al. (1986) surveyed State attorneys-general (fifty States, District of Colombia, American Samoa, Guam, and Puerto Rico) and an Ohio sample which included all presiding judges of common plea courts, all county prosecutors, all county public defenders, all county sheriffs and the chiefs of police of Ohio's seven major cities. On the basis of a 65 per cent response rate, they reported that 71.8 per cent of those surveyed believed that wrongful felony convictions in the US was less than 1 per cent. Taking the 1981 US figure for persons arrested and charged with index offences (2 291 560) and on the basis of a 50 per cent conviction rate, Huff et al. estimated that approximately 6000 are wrongly convicted annually (p. 523). This estimate, however, is rather crude as different crimes have different conviction rates. While it is impossible to have an accurate estimate of the number of wrongful convictions,[3] the concern is twofold: an innocent person is wrongly convicted and suffers the consequences while the real criminal is at large. Of particular interest to psychologists is the general view that eyewitness identification is considered the single most important factor leading to wrongful conviction (Brandon and Davies, 1973; Huff et al., 1986). Most members of the public would be concerned about falsely identifying an innocent person as the perpetrator of a crime. We also know that it is rather common in criminal trials for the defence and the prosecution to disagree about the fairness of police-conducted identification procedures.

Before taking a close and critical look at some well-known witness identification procedures, it is important to remember the following about the use of photographs as a means of identification, which mean that both police identification procedures and empirical research using photographs sacrifice a great deal of the memory potential of witnesses asked to perform a recognition task:

- Subjects in simulation studies using photographs are asked to recognise a target person by looking at static images of different faces.
- What such studies are actually studying is picture recognition rather than face recognition (Bruce, 1988).
- Unlike a static picture, motion (for example, rotating a picture of a face 360 degrees) gives information about a face from a variety of views as well as detailed information about the effects of illumination, and can thus 'provide information that can be used to increase identification accuracy' (Pike and Kemp, 1995:26).
- The recognition involved in such a task is based on familiarity and is not identification as such because it takes place in the absence of contextual information, such as details of the culprit's body and the crime scene (Davies, 1989). As Davies pointed out, a crime victim/witness at a live identification parade must both recognise the suspect and place him/her in the appropriate context (p. 557). Furthermore, reinstating the context of an event improves eyewitnesses' recognition accuracy (see Chapter 3).
- Recognition accuracy is higher for persons seen as actors in a film showing a robbery than for static, motionless pictures depicting faces devoid of bodies (Schiff et al., 1986).
- For understandable ethical reasons, most simulation identification studies involve student subjects who have witnessed a staged crime or who are shown a video of such an incident and subsequently are asked to pick the culprit from a set of photographs under different conditions. This is a major limitation because it has been shown that real crime victims generally produce much more information than bystanders (MacLeod, 1987).[4]

In the light of such serious limitations of a great deal of the empirical literature on face identification, one cannot but agree with Davies (1989) that relying on photo identification does not do eyewitnesses justice and empirical studies focusing exclusively on this identification procedure have very limited forensic relevance (p. 559). Davies' grave warning should not go unnoticed by psychology researchers and police alike (see also Laughery and Wogalter, 1989).

In view of the pressures under which police investigators work in busy police departments in large cities, and irrespective of the identification procedure used, they would no doubt appreciate psychologists enabling them to distinguish accurate from inaccurate eyewitness identification. Drawing on the existing literature on reality monitoring (Johnson et al., 1993), facial recognition (Sporer, 1993) and eyewitness identification, Dunning and Stern (1994) describe a test of eyewitness accuracy that could be applied to specific witnesses at the time they make their identifications of suspect. They hypothesised that different cognitive processes would be reported by witnesses when making accurate, as opposed to inaccurate, positive identification judgements. Individual mock witnesses in four studies were shown a 3-minute video-tape depicting a staged theft of money from a teacher's purse that had been left on a table. After spending 5 to 10 minutes completing a questionnaire about the scenes shown in the video (but not including the theft), the subjects were asked to pick out the perpetrator in a five-photo line-up. Subjects were also instructed to say aloud what they were thinking or doing, what sort of processes went on in their head, and they were tape-recorded while making/thinking aloud their judgements. It was found that, of those making positive identifications, accurate witnesses were significantly more likely than inaccurate ones to describe their judgements as resulting from *automatic recognition* (for example, 'His face just "popped out" at me'); in other words, they were relatively unable to articulate any explicit cognitive strategy that underpinned their identification judgement. A process of *elimination strategy*, that is, comparing the photos in a line-up to short-list suspects and so narrow their choices, was the process significantly more frequently used by inaccurate witnesses. Dunning and Stern also reported that by telling subjects about the strategy found to characterise accurate and inaccurate identifications it improved their identification performance.

1 Person Identification from Photographs

In western common law countries identification of a suspect by photograph is a lawful means of identification during a police investigation of a criminal offence, or as an alternative when a suspect refuses to take part in an identification parade. The most commonly used photo identification procedure is where a witness identifies a suspect from a photo-board, comprising in Victoria, for example, one photograph of the suspect and eleven others, such ordinary photographs (that is, not police ones) only showing facial features and which are, as much as possible, similar to the suspect's. Photo-board identification is used in criminal investigations when the identity of the suspect is not known, and at the evidence-gathering stage when the suspect has been identified (*Alexander v. R.* (1981) 145 CLR 395). Recently, there has been a trend towards identifying a suspect by means of video-frames or a video-film. With this form of identification, a witness views separate video-frames of twelve individuals, one of whom is the suspect. Unlike photo identification, video identification provides a coloured three-dimensional photograph of a suspect instead of a two-dimensional image allowed in a photo-board. Video-frame and video-film identification, like photo and photo-board identification, is admissible evidence.

Photographs of offenders known to the police are routinely kept at police stations and are used in local criminal investigations in an attempt to identify a culprit. In addition, within police forces there usually exists a criminal identification unit that keeps and updates State/national collections of such photographs. A large proportion of them go back a number of years. Such photographs are carefully indexed and catalogued and kept in albums and are sometimes also available on computers for police personnel and crime witnesses to search. Unlike witnesses in simulation or staged event studies, actual witnesses to different crimes who look (browse?) through police photo albums of offenders known to the police can expect to encounter different numbers of offenders because different crimes have different clear-up rates. For some crimes, even taking age and gender into account, there will be thousands of photographs of potential suspects a witness to a crime could be asked to look at and try to select the culprit, whereas for other crimes there will be at most a few dozen. To illustrate, police photo albums would contain fewer photographs of pedophiles and arsonists than burglars or armed robbers. In addition, the proportion of different ethnic groups in the community varies as does their involvement in different crimes, and there are fewer offenders known to the police with red hair because there are fewer such individuals among the population at large and there is no reason whatsoever why one should expect such individuals to be over-represented among offenders.

Identification from police photographs is admissible evidence in most jurisdictions even though defence attorneys might like to argue that such evidence should be inadmissible because it implies that the defendant has a criminal record (see *Bleakley* [1993] Crim. LR 203). On the basis that photographic evidence has its dangers from the defendant's point of view, trial judges in Britain, for example, are required by *Dodson* ([1984] 1 WLR 971) to warn the jury about such evidence.[5]

Research into the use of mugshots has considered them mainly as an independent variable, a source of interference, in a subsequent line-up identification task accuracy (the dependent variable). Such studies have generally found that showing subjects photographs of suspects significantly increases the number of false positive identifications, that is, under these circumstances witnesses tend to mistake for the culprit someone whose face they have seen before a line-up and despite the fact that such a person was not present near the original incident.[6] Such *unconscious transference* (UT) (originally a Freudian concept) is a byproduct of a human memory that is dynamic, integrative and malleable (Loftus, 1974, 1976) but which means it is possible for a witness to misidentify a familiar but innocent person from a police line-up who is subsequently charged, tried, convicted, and even sentenced to death and executed.

Ross et al. (1994:80) cite a case that illustrates UT. A railway station ticket clerk was held up and picked a sailor from the police line-up believing him to be the armed robber who victimised him. Fortunately, the sailor had an irrefutable alibi. The ticket clerk remembered him because he lived near the station and had bought tickets from the clerk a few times before the robbery. It is interesting to note in this context that most identification experts surveyed by Kassin et al. (1989) felt the available empirical support for UT was good enough for an expert witness to testify about the phenomenon in court.

In fact, it turns out few researchers have concerned themselves with UT and they have reported mixed results (see Ross et al., 1994b, 1994c, for a literature review). As far as it has been possible to ascertain, Buckhout (1974) was the first to do a study of UT (that did not include a control group) and found support for its existence. Additional support for UT has also been reported by Brown et al. (1977), Gorenstein and Ellsworth (1980), Loftus (1976), Peters (1985, in Ross et al., 1994b), Read et al. (1990, Experiment 5) and Ross et al. (1994b). Negative findings regarding UT have been reported by Read et al. (1990, Experiments 1–4) and Geiselman et al. (1996).

Regarding theoretical approaches to UT, Ross et al. (1994b) identify the following three:

1 *Automatic processing* (Hasher and Zacks, 1979) that maintains the witness is not aware of having seen the bystander previously but the presence of the bystander in the line-up makes the witness' unconscious memory of the bystander a familiar one and so predisposes him/her to misidentify.
2 *Source monitoring* (Lindsay, D. S., 1994) according to which, even though the witness remembers both the real offender and the bystander separately, he/she confuses the two because of some characteristic/s they have in common.
3 *Memory blending* (Ross et al., 1994b) posits that even though the witness remembers having encountered both the real offender and the bystander, he/she thinks they are the same individual.

In considering the empirical literature on UT it should be remembered that support for it is weak and the studies concerned are low on ecological validity. Also, it would be most unusual for police to conduct a line-up that does not include a crime suspect (Wells and Turtle, 1986). UT is undoubtedly an 'intriguing and important topic' (Ross et al., 1994b:99) but the available evidence indicates it is a rare phenomenon under simulated conditions and high self-monitors appear to be more vulnerable to it (Geiselman et al., 1996:207). Nevertheless, the policy implication of the limited evidence that asking eyewitnesses to view mug-shots interferes dangerously with a subsequent identification task is that police should refrain from such a practice. Police investigators, however, cannot always decide in advance that a line-up will be conducted at a later stage in the investigation process.

While some researchers have concerned themselves with unconscious transference, others have examined identification accuracy from mug-shots. In such experiments, subjects would be shown/would see a target face which they would then try to find embedded in a number of photographs and the position of the target face in the list of photographs and the actual number of photographs would be varied. Laughery et al. (1971) found that the target's photograph was more likely to be selected if presented after fifty other photographs rather than 125 photographs. In the light of this finding, Wells (1988:52) recommended that eye-witnesses should not be shown more than fifty photographs at a time. This recommendation, however, is not practical from a police point of view because of the very large numbers of photographs of known offenders who may be potential suspects for a particular crime in a big city and the various constraints and pressures under which criminal investigations are normally carried out. One practical solution suggested by R. C. L. Lindsay et al. (1994b) is for witnesses to sort faces by des-cription. This would reduce the number of photographs of known offenders a witness would need to examine before coming across the target face (p. 128). As far as it has been possible to ascertain, despite some promising work by British researchers (see Ellis et al., 1989) and the existence of sophisticated video capture and retrieval procedures for recording the appearance of suspects (Davies, 1989, cites PROD – a system for picture recapture from optical disc already in use with one police force in the UK at the time), there is a noticeable lack of studies of suspect identification that would build on Ellis et al.'s work. This may well be explained by the fact that, as R. C. L. Lindsay et al. (1994b) remind us: 'Further research is needed to determine the best method of sorting mugshots to improve eyewitness identifications' (p. 129).

It is often the case that police investigators do not know who the likely culprit/s of a crime might be and have to rely on the eyewitness for useful clues. In three interesting experiments R. C. L. Lindsay et al. (1994b) used staged theft to examine the usefulness of mugshots as an investigative tool, that is, in finding crime suspects during the course of varying the number of photos viewed before presenting the target face, by controlling the form of instructions given to the witness and the type of clothing worn in a line-up, by sorting photographs by description and, finally, by controlling whether the photographs were presented in books or as computer images. They found that: 'Witnesses in all three experiments revealed the ability to eliminate a very high proportion of innocent people as suspects and to reduce initially large pools to manageable numbers' (p. 129). Lindsay et al. concluded that mugshots are a useful investigative tool. When used as an investigative tool, mugshots do not appear dangerous but have a number of advantages: (a) since they are presented sequentially, they avoid witnesses making relative judgements; (b) they do not pose any potential dangers for innocent persons because they are not to be used as an identification technique; and (c) a witness can select more than one photo (p. 122). Future research should examine pitfalls in police identification procedures utilising computer technology that largely overcomes the limitations of using static pictures.

Finally, regarding the problem of witnesses having to leaf through too many photos of known offenders and, consequently, often failing to choose the target one, Israeli police researchers at the National Police Headquarters in Jerusalem (Dr Avraham M. Levi, personal communication) have reported an interesting new approach to identification using mugshots. Building on the work of Ellis et al. (1989), they first create a similarity network between the album photographs and then code each album photo in terms of its dissimilarity to reference photos. Witnesses first enter into a personal computer a brief verbal description of the suspect. Each photo in the album is weighted by the computer in terms of its compatability to the witness' description from 0 to 1. Witnesses are asked to choose up to five photographs that are subjectively most similar to the target. Each photo chosen by a witness in this way increases the ranking of every photo in the album which is similar to it, as determined by the similarity network. The computer displays the photos with the best fit. Early findings using this method indicate that witnesses leaf through many fewer photos than if they use the conventional way.

2 Showups

The showup identification procedure (that is, a one-person line-up) involves a witness being taken to a location where the suspect is expected to be or might appear and the witness is asked to point him/her out when the suspect is sighted. This evidentially-hazardous procedure was used by Melbourne detectives when a suspect was apprehended in close proximity to an attempted pharmacy robbery. They returned the suspect to the scene of the crime where he was seated in the back of an unmarked police car. The time of the attempted robbery was the first time the witness had seen the offender. A single confrontation identification was then held with the witness. However, as would have been expected (see below), at a subsequent trial the identification evidence was ruled inadmissible on the basis that it involved a high risk of mistaken identification (*R. v. Burchielli*, 1981, VR 611). To comply with law of evidence relevant to identification the detectives should have conducted an identification parade with the suspect's consent.

The case of *Rogers* ([1993] *Criminal Law Review* 386) provides a British example of the use made of showups by police. Two witnesses reported to police seeing a person damaging cars, they tackled him and noticed he had slurred speech. Upon investigating the matter, the police found a person whose speech was slurred sleeping inside an industrial unit. The two witnesses attended and, through a window, recognised the person concerned. Clothing found in the defendant's car was also recognised by the same two witnesses as the same one worn by the defendant earlier. The defence appealed against conviction on the grounds that the identification was inadmissible because it had not been carried out in accordance with the Code Practice provided by the Police and Criminal Evidence Act (1984). The Court of Appeal dismissed the appeal on the grounds that it was not uncommon for the police to take a witness to attempt to identify a suspect and, also, it would have been rather difficult for the police to justify the arrest before having the defendant identified by witnesses. As the Court of Appeal put it: 'it would make criminal investigations of this sort quite impossible if the police had to arrest everybody who might answer the description, and arrange an identification parade thereafter'. One-person showups are also frequently offered as evidence that a suspect is indeed the perpetrator of the crime (that is, that he/she is guilty) in the Netherlands (Wagenaar and Veefkind, 1992:274).

The in-court (dock) identification of the defendant is required in all cases. In most cases, dock identification is supported by out-of-court-identification. In a small percentage of cases, however, dock identification of the defendant may be the only identification by a witness. In such cases, dock identification is not an adequate form of identification unless the witness previously knew the defendant. In the English case of *Thomas* ([1994] Crim. LR 128) a shop-keeper who had been the victim of a robbery first recognised the defendant in a group identification. Another shop-keeper did not recognise the defendant in the group identification but subsequently identified him in court when giving evidence in the dock. The trial judge told the jury that dock identifications are very rare for they are believed to be unfair but failed to also point out that the defendant may well have been recognised by the shop-keepers as a result of unconscious transference. The conviction was overturned on appeal on the grounds the judge's warning to the jury was insufficient.

In a number of cases the Supreme Court of the US has held that whilst there are more substantial risks of bias in showups than in line-ups (see *Stovall v. Denno* (1967) 388 US 293), the admissibility of such evidence is decided by considering not so much whether the showup was necessary but by considering the circumstances affecting the likely accuracy of the identification (Gonzalez et al., 1993:526). In the case of *Neil v. Biggers* ((1972) 409 US 188), the Supreme Court considered an appeal against conviction in a rape case in which the victim identified her assailant in a showup seven months after the crime on the grounds that she had spent 'up to half an hour' with the defendant, she had been under a great deal of stress, she was very confident, and had not identified anyone else in another identification procedure (Gonzalez et al., 1993:526). According to Gonzalez et al., in *Manson v. Braithwaite* ((1977) 432 US 98), however, the Supreme Court reaffirmed its view that the acceptability of any identification procedure must be evaluated on the basis of the totality of the circumstances surrounding it. Not surprisingly, therefore, 'The police are the strongest proponents of showups, and their argument is largely practical' (Gonzalez et al., 1993:525). Interestingly enough, however, Kassin et al.'s (1989) survey of eyewitness testimony experts in the US found that most (78 per cent) of them agreed that 'the use of a one-person showup instead of a full line-up increases the risk of misidentification' and the majority (65 per cent) were of the view that there was reliable or very reliable evidence for that position.

The concern of opponents about the use of showups[7] is based on the belief that showups are significantly more likely to lead to false identifications than line-ups because they are far more suggestive. Malpass and Devine (1983:85) argued that a 'line-up is in principle more fair than a showup because it distributes the probability of identification of an innocent suspect across the line-up foils, reducing the risk of an identification error'. According to Gonzalez et al. (1993), witnesses exercise greater caution because of the presence of foils in a line-up and this is another argument against showups (p. 527). Gonzalez et al. maintain, however, that showups and line-ups involve different decision-making strategies; more specifically, line-ups require 'comparative, relative strategies because the witness selects from several alternatives. Showups elicit absolute strategies because the witness must decide if the suspect is or is not the perpetrator' (p. 527). This argument leads the same authors to predict that showups are characterised by a higher frequency of 'no' responses. So, does the weight of the empirical evidence support the concern of opponents of police use of showups that they lead to witnesses making significantly more positive (and especially false) identifications than in line-ups?

Wagenaar and Veefkind (1992) compared witness' identification accuracy and false identifications in two experiments. In the first, they used colour slides and the number of foils in the colour picture line-ups was 1, 2, 6, or 10, the subjects were visitors to the University of Leyden in the Netherlands whose age varied from 6 to 75, who were run in groups of twenty-five or fifty, and the retention interval was 20 minutes. It was found that the hit rates in target-present line-ups were 35 per cent, 56 per cent, 50 per cent and 42 per cent for the showup, two, six and ten foils respectively. In the target-absent condition the false alarm rates were 11 per cent, 12 per cent, 7 per cent and 5 per cent respectively. In a second experiment Wagenaar and Veefkind staged a relatively harmless but still violent event in front of a class of psychology undergraduates and compared photographic showups and six-person line-ups. During the exposure the witnesses did not know that they were taking part in the experiment, the retention period was a week and during this time the subjects did not know they would be tested, and in the line-up test it was suggested to the students that the experimenter did not know the correct answer. It was found that in the target-present condition the hit rate was significantly worse statistically in the showup (50 per cent) than in the line-up (75 per cent); in other words, increasing the number of foils correlated with witnesses showing a greater ability to distinguish between innocent and guilty subjects (p. 282). Wagenaar and Veefkind (1992) concluded their results showed that 'one-person line-ups are to be avoided as they increase the likelihood of false identifications. It must be feared that in actual practice the danger of one-person line-ups is even greater, because the demand characteristics of a police investigation differ markedly from those of a psychological experiment' (p. 283). The same researchers also concluded that there is no strong argument for preferring a ten-person over a six-person line-up. Finally, they consider it a matter of major concern that witnesses' performance was found to be of such low absolute level – at best it was 5 per cent false identifications in their second experiment. As for their overall assessment of showup accuracy: they should be considered an 'unsafe practice' (p. 284).

Gonzalez et al. (1993) also compared identification performance in showups and line-ups. In one experiment (a staged theft in front of a class) they compared a live showup and a live line-up, while in another both identification procedures were carried out using photographs. They also analysed data on 172 actual live showups and fifty actual photo line-ups provided by a police detective. Gonzalez et al. allowed their experimental subjects the option of an 'I can't remember' response in addition to whether or not they recognised the target person. It was found that, contrary to what opponents of showups would have predicted, in both photographic and live identification procedures witnesses were more cautious in making an identification in a showup than in a line-up; in other words, one-person line-ups are no more suggestive than many-person line-ups. Gonzalez et al. concluded that 'police pressure on the witness to make an identification may be considerably less in the typical showup than in the typical line-up' (Gonzalez et al., 1993:535). The conflicting findings reported by these two studies may well reflect differences in the events staged and/or the subjects used and/or the length of the retention period used or, finally, the fact that the subjects in the Gonzalez et al. study had the option of responding with 'I don't remember'. Regarding the retention period variable in such studies, according to Yarmey et al. (1994), a short period of time (that is, 30 minutes or less) between the time an incident takes place and a showup confrontation has been stated by the courts in the US as contributing to accuracy identification (*People v. Brnja*, 1980; *Singletary v. United States*, 1978) (p. 454).

A Canadian study by Yarmey et al. (1994) used a 5-minute retention period in a field study comparing face and voice recognition in which 651 members of the public took part in one-person showups and 169 others did so in six-person line-ups. A female researcher approached a member of the public and asked for directions. A few minutes later researchers would ask that same person to participate in the research by taking part in a test. It was found that, taking into account guessing (which Wagenaar and Veefkind, 1992, and Gonzalez et al., 1993, did not), witnesses were more likely to identify a target in a six-person visual line-up than in a showup. In fact, accuracy in showups was little better than chance. Finally, there were no significant differences in the false identification rate in the two procedures. Lest this last finding encourages supporters of showups to conclude that they do not lead to more false identification of innocent suspects than do many-person line-ups, Yarmey et al. (1994:461) repeat the advice of Wells (1993) that this finding 'should not be interpreted as a green light for the use of showups'.

3 Line-ups

Police use biased line-ups due to one or more of the following reasons (Lindsay, R. C. L., 1994b): ignorance, sloppiness and intentional bias (p. 183). In a series of experiments Lindsay found that lack of special training in line-up construction, a belief that the suspect is guilty, or a wish to lead a witness to identify the suspect, result in foils (distractors) being selected that resemble the suspect in appearance (see below). Lindsay also reported that conversations he had with police officers, subsequent to completing the research concerned, confirmed his belief that 'highly biased line-ups are the result of intentional actions by the police' (p. 198). He also points out, however, that his criticism applies to a very small proportion of police officers who engage 'in outrageously unprofessional behaviour'.

It would appear that, as a proportion of criminal cases investigated annually, live line-ups are seldom used by police investigators in western English-speaking countries. As far as it has been possible to ascertain, police forces in Britain, Australia, New Zealand, Canada and the US do not keep systematic statistics on the use made of live line-ups and it is thus impossible to be precise about the percentage and type of criminal investigations that involve this particular identification procedure, let alone how often correct identification is made. Without wishing to downplay the seriousness of witness misidentification and the conviction of innocent suspects, the reader should note that psychologists' exclusive focus on misidentification of innocent suspects in line-up identification, and by presenting this phenomenon in a somewhat stereotypical way against an over-typical background, most probably distorts the picture, for there is generally a failure by researchers to locate the issue of misidentification in a broad psycholegal context. Consequently, police investigators would argue that eyewitnesses have been given a bad reputation that is not justified by their accuracy performance in actual cases. The need to also know about the incidence and factors underpinning accurate witness identification with different identification procedures cannot be overemphasised. Psychologists need to balance a concern for the innocent suspect with fairness towards crime victims and the police.

In recent years, increasing concern about the unreliability of evidence identification can be seen in the close scrutiny with which the courts treat such evidence. Line-up identification evidence is a case in point. Police can be criticised both for the way they conduct line-ups as well as for failing to hold a line-up. As in other countries, there is no rule of law in Australia and in England that there must be a police identification parade for the purpose of identification (*R. v. Preston* [1961], VR 762).[8] However, the courts have indicated that visual identification of an accused should take the form of an identification parade (line-up). The exception is where the offender is well-known to the witness (*Davies and Goody v. R.*, [1937] CrLR 181) or if the accused does not consent to an identification parade (*R. v. Clune* [1982] VR 1). In addition, a suspect may request an identification parade and/or ask for a lawyer or a friend to be present, and in some jurisdictions police standing orders provide for such requests. Police officers are provided with detailed instructions in how to conduct identification parades as well as other types of identification procedures.[9]

It is interesting to note in this context that in *Alexander v. R.* ([1981] ALR1, at 34), the High Court of Australia held that the identification parade is the best and fairest method of obtaining evidence of identification of suspects by witnesses. Such parades normally comprise a number of persons (eight or more in Australia and in the UK) of the same sex as the accused, being lined up with the accused placed amongst them to be viewed by the witness who will decide whether the offender seen in a previous incident is one of them. According to Wells et al. (1994:225), line-ups are conducted 'because verbal descriptions do not contain a level of information that allows us to definitely decide whether our suspect is the suspect or not'. This proposition is consistent with the empirical evidence showing little statistical relationship between such measure of verbal recall as accuracy, completeness, consistency and fluency and accuracy of witness recognition performance (Pigott and Brigham, 1985).[10]

A parade may occasionally involve a witness being asked to identify an object used in the commission of a crime, such as vehicles, premises, firearms and other weapons, tools or instruments or other physical objects or even an animal. The same legal principles apply to both person and object identification parades (*R. v. Turnbull* [1976] WLR 445). Interestingly, the experimental psychological literature on line-ups has been exclusively concerned with person identification. From the court's point of view, the line-up is used to make certain that the ability of the witness to recognise the suspect or an object has been fairly and adequately tested. Such parades in Australia are normally conducted at police stations for a number of reasons but occasionally there is a need to do so elsewhere, including inside a prison. In addition to providing identification evidence for the courts, identification parades can also be used by police investigators to eliminate a suspect from an investigation early on or to put pressure on a suspect to confess. In view of the fact that photo-board identification may be prejudicial to the accused and its use prior to a line-up may result in unconscious transference, a line-up is, therefore, generally preferred to photo identification since a line-up also means the accused is present and in a position to comment on its fairness. A line-up rather than photo identification should be used at the evidence-gathering stage.

The existing empirical literature (see Penrod and Cutler, 1995a, 1995b, and Ross et al. 1994, for literature reviews) has identified a range of factors that contribute to biases in line-up procedures that result in apparently alarmingly high rates of false identifications. In common law countries alleged offenders are presumed innocent until proven guilty in a court of law or until they, of their own volition, decide to plead guilty. Consequently, biased line-ups are just not acceptable. As mentioned in

Chapter 7, the calling of an expert to give evidence of the unreliability of identification evidence is not permitted in Australia (*R. v. Smith* [1987] VR 907). But what is meant by 'fair' line-up? Wells et al. (1993) offer the following definition: 'A good line-up task is one that minimises the likelihood that an innocent suspect will be (falsely) identified and maximises the likelihood that a guilty suspect will be (accurately) identified' (p. 835). There is, however, disagreement as to whether the distractors should resemble the suspect or match the eyewitnesses' description of the suspect (see below).

Before considering empirical evidence pertaining to sources of bias in identification performance, it is important to note that most of the studies concerned have misused the term 'false identification'. This is partly because of a certain amount of conceptual confusion about the meaning of the terms 'culprit', 'suspect' and 'distractor/foil', which appears to have led so many identification evidence researchers to confuse all three or two of the these three terms. By definition, a standard police line-up includes a suspect. The suspect who, of course, may be innocent, is suspected of being the culprit of the crime. Positive identification of the suspect has serious consequences. A distractor/foil is innocent and if the witness selects a distractor it has no consequences (Wells et al., 1994:227). In the same context, a distinction also needs to be made between 'false identification' and 'identification error' by a witness. Wells et al. (1994:228) 'reserve the term false identification for instances in which the eyewitness identifies an innocent *suspect*; if the eyewitness identifies a distractor we call this a foil identification or distractor identification', and, 'a false identification cannot occur when the actual culprit is a member of the line-up' (p. 228). Often researchers are actually reporting 'distractor identifications' that are of no real significance in real life other than a source of police frustration and disappointment. High rates of false identifications in the target-present condition have seldom been reported. In a real line-up, of course, a witness has no way of knowing for certain whether the one the police suspect of committing the crime is, in fact, the culprit. The distinctions made by Wells et al. (1994) have implications for how one decides the similarity between the suspect and the foils.

3.1 Sources of Bias

3.1.1 Police Practices, Knowledge, Attitudes and Intentions

It is standard police practice worldwide when a crime is being reported to them and/or when an eyewitness is available, to ask for a *verbal description* of the culprit/s. One of the techniques used by police in criminal investigations is to ask witnesses to assist them with *constructing a composite face image* of the suspect/s by verbally describing facial features or simply selecting them from a collection provided by the police. This task can be performed manually or with the aid of computers. In fact, such state-of-the-art software is fast making the police artist an endangered species. Some well-known examples of commercially available software of face composites are the American Identi-Kit III, the British Photo-Fit and E-Fit and the Australian FACE (Facial Composition and Editing). They all involve a witness selecting individual level characteristics from data bases of facial (hair, eyebrows, nose, chin, eyes, etc.) and other features (for example, hats, glasses) which are put together to construct a composite face. Individual characteristics are then exchanged or edited using computer graphics in order to reduce discrepancies between the composite and the image of a face in the witness' memory. Sometimes, publicising a face composite image of the suspect/s is the only avenue of enquiry available to detectives in their search for crime suspects. Of course, as far as the outcome of criminal investigations is concerned, the use of a face composite is but one of many factors that can contribute to a crime being cleared up. Also, there is evidence that, when not instructed to do so, only 4 per cent of witnesses report focusing on facial cues (Tooley et al., 1984, cited in Deffenbacher, 1989:566). Finally, likely difficulties in communication between the witness and the operator of the computer-witness interaction system mean that the hardcopy generated is, at best, a poor likeness of the suspect (Davies, 1981, 1983, 1986). Having witnesses directly producing the computer image would not be feasible because of the heterogeneity of crime victims, time considerations and implications for police resources.

Evaluation data on the operational effectiveness of face composites is rather scarce. Despite what some police members may think, the available empirical evidence indicates that such face composites only contribute to the apprehension of offenders in a small minority of cases. An early survey by the British Home Office (Darnborough, 1977, cited by Clifford and Davies, 1989:54) reported that the Photo-Fit proved significantly useful in solving a crime in 22 per cent of applicable cases. In the absence of data regarding the types of crimes involved and the time interval between the offence and when composites were constructed, it is impossible to evaluate Darnborough's finding. Bennett (1986) sent questionnaires to 512 police officers in one Metropolitan Police area in London who had been supplied with a Photo-Fit image. With a response rate of 70 per cent, it was found that only 3.8 per cent indicated the Photo-Fit had led to an arrest. In fact, in four of the fourteen cases cleared up, the image was judged a poor likeness of the person arrested. The present author has recently completed a study (in preparation) of 200 colour computer face composites (representing an 18 per cent response rate by detectives) using FACE provided to operational police in Melbourne by the force's specialist six-member Criminal Identification Squad from July 1995 to June 1996. The squad members had been trained in the cognitive interview technique six months prior to the commencement of the study.

It was found that the main crimes involved were theft (22 per cent), burglary (20 per cent), armed robbery (12 per cent) and assault (10 per cent). Fifty-four per cent of the witnesses were female, 21 per cent were aged 11 to 20, 44 per cent were 21 to 30 and 35 per cent were over 30 years. It was also found that utilising FACE, police were able to charge someone in 19 per cent of the cases, while in 23 per cent the FACE assisted in confirming a suspect. Out of fifty-two cases where it was possible for police to rate the face composite on a five-point scale in terms of its likeness to the offender, 46 per cent attracted a rating of 4 and 69 per cent a rating of 3 or greater. Finally, there were significant between-squad member differences regarding the proportion of their composite face images that contributed directly to an offender being arrested and charged – it ranged from 6.9 per cent to 33 per cent. The findings reported concerning the apparent usefulness of face composites should be treated with caution, however, due to the low response rate by detectives and the fact that the memory of many of the witnesses was probably adversely affected by the fact that witnesses were interviewed for a FACE more than three days after the offence had been committed and had, by then, been interviewed by different police members, and the memory of 25 per cent had been further interfered with by being asked to look through photo albums of suspects at a police station before being interviewed for face composite. Nevertheless, the study does provide limited support for police use of computer face composites. The need for more research in this area cannot be over-emphasised, especially concerning the interactive nature of the composite face interviews and how to enhance the interviewer–witness communication.

When asking a witness for a verbal description of the suspect/s, police are in no position to know whether a line-up will be required later, and a good physical description of the culprit/s is needed to be communicated to patrol units, unmarked cars and even to a police helicopter if an operation is to be mounted to apprehend one or more serious offenders making their getaway from the scene of the crime. Schooler and Engstler-Schooler (1990) reported that the very act of asking eye-witnesses for a verbal description of the culprit can impair performance on a delayed line-up identification test. The researchers termed this phenomenon '*verbal overshadowing*'. The identification impairment was not found, however, if the subjects did the line-up test soon after describing the culprit.

On the basis of Schooler and Engstler-Schooler's verbal over-shadowing hypothesis, we would expect this police practice to impact on an eyewitness line-up identification performance. Indeed, Comish (1987) found that the identification performance of subjects who had earlier tried to construct an Identi-kit composite image of a suspect showed more false identifications than for control subjects if the foils in the line-up resembled the experimental subjects' errors when attempting the Identi-kit image. According to D. S. Lindsay (1994:46), the effects reported by Schooler and Engstler-Schooler (1990) and Comish (1987) can be described in terms of source monitoring processes, that is, without being aware of it subjects draw on memories from different sources – at the encoding stage, when describing the face (the inter-polated material) and when seeing it in a photo line-up because of similarity in the information involved. D. S. Lindsay (1994) suggests, therefore, that warning witnesses about these effects may well help to avoid them.

3.1.2 The Composition of the Line-up

A basic proposition by Wells et al. (1994:225) in the context of their numerous constructive recommendations on how to properly conduct line-up identifications is that 'The purpose of a line-up is to uncover information in an eyewitness recognition memory that was not available in recall' (Luus and Wells, 1991). Line-ups can differ in terms of their size (see below) as well as the extent of similarity between the suspect and the foils. In the typical line-up procedure used in Britain and in Australia, for example, a suspect is included in a line together with seven foils (innocent 'distractors') side-by-side and the suspect can choose his or her position in the line. The witness gets to view the line-up simul-taneously. As Thomson (1995a:143) points out: 'the standard method of identification parades is not unlike multiple-choice exam questions'. Such a procedure, of course, means that there is scope for each foil to somehow 'let the witness know' that they are not the suspect and, if for some reason, all or some of the foils know who the suspect is, the poten-tial is there for them to communicate that knowledge to the witness in a subtle way, whether consciously or unconsciously (Thomson, 1995a).

A line-up may be 'unfair', 'biased' or 'suggestive' when one person stands out from the rest in such a way that anyone equipped with the original verbal description given by the witness can pick him/her out irrespective of whether they were present at the scene of the crime (Clifford, 1981:25). A person could stand out in a line-up because of the colour of their hair, their ethnic background, their clothing (especially if one of the line-up members happens to be wearing clothes similar to those worn by the offender when seen by the witness) or because other line-up members are not standing close to a particular person or they keep looking at him/her (Lloyd-Bostock, 1988:14).

The inclusion of reasonably look-alike foils in a line-up is meant to ensure that a witness identifies a suspect on the basis of his/her memory of what the suspect looks like and not by deduction (that is, by knowing who the police suspect of having committed the offence in question and thus identifying that same person as the perpetrator, as might be happening with showups). In Britain and Australia, line-ups (most of which were live ones until recently) are presented simultaneously. We saw in Chapters 2 to 4 that police investigators should expect that eyewitnesses will often only be able to furnish them with incomplete and inaccurate descriptions of culprits. If the police use the witness' description to select the foils it will probably mean that in a number of cases they will not be very similar in appearance to the suspect the police have. In Britain, however, whatever the description given by a witness, Annex A of the revised edition (effective from 1 April 1991) of Code of Practice D (Police and Criminal Evidence Act (1984)) specifically states that the members of a line-up selected by the police must 'as far as possible resemble the suspect in age, height, general appearance and position in life' (cited by McKenzie, 1995). In the case of *Quinn* (*The Times*, 15 March 1994) Lord Taylor CJ stated that the idea is not to produce a line-up comprising seven clones of the suspect (cited in McKenzie, 1995:203).

Psychologists have examined the impact on identification performance of the *degree of similarity* between the target and foils in a line-up, as well as whether the choice of foils should be on the basis of the description given by a witness (Luus and Wells, 1991; Wells et al., 1993) or is made on the basis of what the target person looks like (Doob and Kirschenbaum, 1973; Wells et al., 1979). Discussion of line-up composition issues inevitably raises the question of: what is meant by a 'good distractor'? Wells et al. (1994:226) offers the following definition: 'a good distractor is one who fits the verbal description but varies in appearance from the suspect on features that were not part of that description'. Luus and Wells (1991) have argued that the strategy of selecting for foils persons who match the suspect arrested by the police results in unnecessary similarity between the foils and the suspect. Wells et al. (1993:836) accept that a high degree of similarity between suspect and foils provides effective protection against witnesses selecting an innocent suspect. They maintain, however, that the protection afforded has its price – 'a loss in accurate identifications' (p. 836). Wells et al. suggest that selecting foils on the basis of the witnesses' description of the suspect protects innocent suspects from being selected by witnesses. A comparison of the two approaches to selecting line-up foils by Wells et al. (1993) found that the match-description strategy produced both a low rate of false identifications and a high rate of accurate identifications.

Similarity between the suspect and the foils in a line-up is one of the aspects of *line-up fairness* suggested by Malpass and Devine (1983:221), the other being line-up size. What, then, can psychologists tell lawyers about the impact on identification performance of *similarity between the suspect and foils* in a line-up? One intriguing finding reported by R. C. L. Lindsay (1994a) from mock-jury research (see Lindsay and Wells, 1980) suggests that potential jurors: do not consider line-up procedures as being of any great importance in determining witness accuracy; they are more convinced by more biased line-ups (foils similar to suspect); and appear impervious to expert testimony, if not negatively influenced by it! These perplexing findings definitely warrant further attention by legal psychologists interested in reducing the number of innocent people who get convicted.

Undergraduates who saw a staged theft take place in front of them were subsequently asked to identify the thief by Lindsay and Wells (1980), who manipulated degree of similarity by varying the racial composition of the foils (all whites or three whites and two Asians) in a target-present/target-absent six-person photo-array. Subjects made the most correct identifications in the low-similarity target-present condition. It was also found that both correct and false identifications were low in the high similarity condition. Finally, in the low-similarity target-absent condition subjects made significantly more false identifications.

In their efforts to apprehend offenders the police sometimes broadcast eyewitnesses' descriptions of suspects. Such descriptions normally include details of *clothing* worn at the time a crime was committed. But, is clothing important in the context of line-ups? R. C. L. Lindsay et al. (1987) reported an interesting study, comprising three experiments, in which subjects who witnessed a staged theft were asked to identify the thief in six-person thief-present and thief-absent photo-arrays. Keeping the suspect and the foils the same across the different conditions, the clothing worn by the suspect and the foils was varied as follows: (a) in the 'usual' condition all the members of the line-up wore different clothes; (b) in the 'biased' condition all the foils wore the same clothes as in the 'usual' condition except that the thief (the actual one in the thief-present condition and the replacement in the thief-absent condition) wore exactly the same clothes as the culprit when committing the theft; and, finally, (c) in the 'dressed alike' condition, all members of the line-up wore identical clothes to those worn by the perpetrator. It was found that in the thief-present conditions the rate of correct identification was not significantly affected by clothing. Interestingly, the false identifications rate was found to be 38 per cent in the biased, 21 per cent in the usual, and 10 per cent in the dressed-alike condition. The Lindsay et al. (1987) study indicates that when a perpetrator is in the line-up, the degree of similarity in terms of clothing worn between the suspect and the foils does not influence the amount of correct identifications but does lead to significantly less false identifications if foils are dressed in exactly the same clothes as the perpetrator. The practice used by police forces in Australia and in Britain is for foils to be dressed in order to look like the perpetrator. However, whilst this practice may discourage witnesses from identifying suspects by deduction (and one could also argue it can therefore be said to protect suspects' right to a fair line-up), it makes it unduly difficult to identify the suspect (Wells, 1993). Consequently, Wells warns against using line-ups consisting of look-alike foils and suspect.

3.1.3 The Size of the Line-up

The size of a line-up is one of the two aspects of line-up fairness proposed by Malpass and Devine (1983). Interestingly, however, as Wagenaar and Veefkind (1992:277) have pointed out: 'Few countries prescribe the number of foils by law, but in practice a number around five is usual. Smaller and larger numbers are also found, usually without any justification'. In a survey of potential jurors, R. C. L. Lindsay (1994a) found that out of twenty-five variables, the number of line-up foils was fourteenth in terms of its mean rated importance (p. 372). Using foils that were similar to the culprit rather than in terms of the witness' description of the culprit, Nosworthy and Lindsay (1990) concluded that increasing the line-up size to more than a nominal size of three does not significantly increase the protection afforded an innocent suspect from a false identification. Wells et al. (1994:229) recommend that, for properly conducted identifications: 'A line-up should contain at least five appropriate distractors for every one suspect', and, this 'specifies a ratio of suspects to distractors rather than a ratio of suspects to total line-up members' (p. 229). In such a line-up, there is a 16.6 per cent probability of chance identification of an innocent suspect. The same authors argue that, the fact that Nosworthy and Lindsay (1990) chose foils on the basis of foil-suspect similarity instead of matching them with witnesses' description of the suspect, 'might have implications for the shape of the function relating the number of good distractors to the risk of false identifications of the suspect' (p. 229)

As already mentioned above, line-up bias refers to how much the suspect stands out in the line-up. Line-up bias often overlaps with line-up size (Brigham and Pfeiffer, 1994:202). A psychologist could be used, as has been the case especially in the US, to inform the court about the fairness of a line-up. Doing so would require working out the likelihood of any line-up member being picked out by a witness by chance alone. The formula for this is $1/N$ where N=the size of the parade. This approach was, in fact, used by Buckhout (1976)[11] to inform the jury in *State of Florida v. Richard Campbell* that the line-up in which the defendant had been identified had been biased. Buckhout reported that college students, who had not seen the defendant before, selected him 52 per cent of the time when in a six-member line-up his chance level would be only 16.6 per cent.

Regarding the fairness of line-up size, a number of measures have been proposed, namely: the *effective size* (Malpass, 1981; Malpass and Devine, 1983); *acceptable foils* (Malpass and Devine, 1983); *defendant bias* (Malpass and Devine, 1983); *proportions* (Doob and Kirschenbaum, 1973) and, finally, the *functional size* technique (Wells et al., 1979). Brigham and Pfeiffer (1994) provide a good account of all these techniques, but Navon (1990a, 1990b) and Wells and Luus (1990b) would also be worth reading. Such techniques basically involve the use of mock witnesses who have not witnessed a crime and are asked to attempt to identify the suspect in a line-up. In a six-person line-up, there is a 16.6 per cent probability that a mock witness would pick the suspect by chance alone. The techniques below basically compare expected chance identifications we would expect with identifications by mock witnesses. On the basis of their empirical assessment, Brigham et al. (1990) opt for the proportions technique as the most useful of the five line-up bias measures, both in terms of discriminability and sensitivity. This post-hoc measure of line-up fairness developed by psychologists is also known as the '*diagnosticity ratio*'. This refers to the ratio of correct identifications in a target-present line-up to false identifications in a target-absent one.

The suggestion for a double line-up, only one of which contains the suspect (Wells, 1984), would also point to unreliable witnesses who select an innocent foil in the blank line-up because they are anxious to select anyone or because their memory of what the culprit looked like is poor. This procedure would also reduce the pressure on the witness to select the suspect from a line-up which the witness has been 'informed' contains the suspect. The witness would, of course, be told that only one of the line-ups contains the suspect. Research reported by Brigham and Pfeiffer (1994) found that three line-up fairness measures based on college students' mock witnesses were statistically related to direct evaluations of line-up fairness by forty law officers provide further support for the use of student subjects in developing such indices (pp. 216–17). Furthermore, such indices can form the basis of guidelines for the courts to decide the question of whether a particular line-up was fair or not (Wells et al., 1979).

3.1.4 Biased Instructions

An identification police officer can also influence the witness' identification of the suspect by the *instruction/s* he/she gives the witness. This was also the view of the sixty-three eyewitness experts surveyed by Kassin et al. (1989). The same experts also believed the effect was reliable enough for them to so testify about it in court. Relative to twenty other factors listed, line-up instructions were perceived by the same experts to be the second most reliable phenomenon in eyewitness research. It has long been reported by a number of researchers that telling a witness the culprit is in the line-up produces high rates of mistaken identification (Cutler et al., 1987; Foster et al., 1994; Paley and Geiselman, 1989). Köhnken and Maass (1988, Experiment 1) challenged generalising research on biased instructions to actual line-ups on the basis that their own findings indicate that 'the instructional bias effect observed in previous experiments is limited to subjects who are fully aware that they are participating in an experiment' and the fact they failed to find a significant increase in false identifications as a function of biased instructions 'suggests that eyewitnesses are better than their reputation' (p. 369).

Cutler and Penrod's (1995a) discussion of the evidence, including Paley and Geiselman (1989), led them to the conclusion that 'biased instructions influence identification performance even when subjects are given the option of providing no response (that is, "don't know")' (p. 122). Biased instruction studies, however, have not, as a rule, taken into account the gender of the witness and whether the line-up is presented simultaneously or sequentially. It should also be remembered in this context that the biased instructions effect which inflates the false identification rate has been found in target-absent line-ups (Paley and Geiselman, 1989). Furthermore, Foster et al. found that male witnesses were more influenced by such instructions than female ones. On the basis of the existing empirical evidence, we can conclude that a biased instructions effect has indeed been demonstrated but the way it operates is not as simple as first thought. Of course, the scope for the police to give biased line-up instructions is limited when the law specifies how a witness is to be instructed and what to be told. In Britain, for example, Code of Practice D (Annexe A, paragraph 14) states that the identification officer shall tell the eyewitness that 'the person he saw may or may not be in the parade and [that] if he cannot make a positive identification he should say so'. How far operational police comply with this requirement is not known. If they don't, it would be a ground for the defence counsel asking the court not to admit the identification evidence concerned, and if the court of first instance nevertheless admits such identification evidence, it would be a ground for an appeal against any subsequent conviction.

3.1.5 How a Line-up is Presented

The police are also in a position to bias the outcome of a line-up identification by the very *procedure* they use, that is, whether they present a line-up *simultaneously* or *sequentially*. A line-up can be presented live, as has been the practice within British and Australian police forces, or on video (this procedure is currently being introduced in Victoria, Australia, combined with the use of a one-way viewing facility) or using a set of photographs. A body of empirical studies has examined whether presenting a line-up simultaneously or sequentially influences identification accuracy[12] (see Cutler and Penrod, 1995a, and Ross et al., 1994, for literature reviews). Such studies have tended to use line-ups or photo-arrays usually consisting of a target and five to seven foils. It has been found consistently that identification performance is not influenced by the type of presentation in the target-present condition. By definition, of course, an identification parade/line-up contains a suspect. As mentioned above, however, there are jurisdictions where there are no guidelines regarding the composition, size and so forth of line-ups or how they are to be conducted. The empirical evidence shows that:

- Presentation style does not significantly affect identification accuracy in a target-present line-up or photo-array.
- It is only in target-absent line-ups that witnesses yield an alarmingly high rate of false identifications when a line-up or a photo-array is presented simultaneously.
- The high rate of false identifications in target-absent line-ups is significantly reduced in sequential presentations for both children and adult witnesses (Parker and Ryan, 1993; Cutler and Penrod, 1995a:135). Sequential presentations also reduce the impact of biased instructions and, finally, the beneficial effects of sequential presentation are reduced if subjects have the opportunity of a target-absent practice trial or get a second chance, especially with a simultaneous presentation, after they have been exposed to all the members of a line-up sequentially.

Thomson (1995a:142–3) lists four advantages of presenting line-ups sequentially: (a) it increases the witness' tendency to select the person who is positively recognised; (b) it makes it more difficult for others present to somehow cue a witness as to who the suspect is; (c) it allows the suspect to decide his/her position in the parade; and, finally, (d) it would allow a witness to view line-up members re-enacting what they are alleged to have been involved in.

Bearing in mind the need for standardisation of suspect-identification police procedures, Thomson's suggestion to vary the size of line-ups so that the witness does not know how many individuals will be presented and, consequently, his/her temptation to select any member or foil is reduced, would not be feasible. In addition, even if police were to accept such a suggestion, defence attorneys would most likely attack identification evidence so obtained in cross-examination and would appeal against a conviction based on witness identification evidence obtained by police using rather inconsistent procedures. The rest of the advantages listed by Thomson (1995a) and the policy recommendations that follow from them should be taken very seriously by law reform commissions and police alike when revising witness identification law and procedure.

3.1.6 Identification Test Medium

Given that there are different ways of presenting a suspect to a witness for identification – showups, live line-ups, video-taped live line-ups or photo-arrays – Cutler et al. (1994:164–6) mention a number of practical issues in choosing the identification test medium: a number of constraints operating in constructing a live line-up, namely, availability of suitable foils, the time it takes to construct it and where it can take place. Photo-arrays, however, allow a greater pool of persons to select foils from, are transportable, they prevent line-up members influencing the witness in any way while he/she is viewing the line-up, and avoid the anxiety which most crime victims/crime witnesses would naturally feel when confronting the perpetrator of a crime face-to-face. The video-tape is an increasingly more popular alternative to both live line-ups and photo-arrays and, as Cutler et al. point out, it can provide a witness with the same information as a live line-up, it is less expensive and time-consuming to construct, requires less personnel and, finally, it prevents the witness being cued by foils as to who the suspect is. Another advantage of the video-tape that can be added to the list is that it provides a record of the line-up for the purposes of the trial, and thus avoids frequent legal arguments about alleged police improprieties in conducting the line-up that delay the processing of criminal cases through the courts. There can be no doubt that the video-tape will eventually replace live line-ups, but do different identification test media produce different identification performance?

Turnbull and Thomson (1984)[13] compared the identification performance of subjects who witnessed an abrasive exchange between the lecturer and a stranger and whose memory of the perpetrator was tested in target-present and target-absent conditions using either a live line-up or a photo-display. They found that in the target-present condition there were no significant differences in identification accuracy. Similar findings had earlier been reported by Hilgendorf and Irving (1978) and Shepherd et al. (1982). Turnbull and Thomson, however, also found that in the target-absent condition, false identifications were three times higher in the photo-display than in the live line-up condition. Cutler et al. (1994) carried out a meta-analysis of eight studies comparing identification test media and found that the type of medium (live line-ups, video-taped line-ups, photo-arrays, slides and line drawings) produced comparable identification performances (p. 179). Consequently, they concluded that 'identifications from photo-arrays should therefore not be given less weight in investigations or in trials than identifications from live line-ups. Another conclusion is that, given the apparent comparability of live line-ups and photo-arrays, it is not worth the trouble and expense to use live line-ups' (p. 181). Cutler et al. do remind their readers, however, that in deciding which identification test medium to use, one should take into account relevant legal provisions requiring, for example, that the suspect's legal counsel be present at any of them (Wells and Cutler, 1990).[14] Cutler et al. do not, however, consider their meta-analytic findings the last word on the subject but urge future researchers to examine the effects of identification test media in field experiments that are more relevant forensically. Finally, on the basis that video-tape technology allows faces to be blown up larger than life, persons to be shown in motion, and a line-up to be shown repeatedly, the same authors maintain that 'it is conceivable that video-taped line-ups might improve identification accuracy rates in comparison to live line-ups'.

4 Voice Identification

People have stereotypes of what sort of individuals speak with what kind of voices, and this applies also to stereotypes of different kinds of criminals (Yarmey, 1995:268). It is on the basis of stereotypes that people try to visualise a stranger they talk to on the phone or hear on radio. There is no convincing empirical evidence, however, that supports the validity of such noble endeavours since, at best, people can recognise a speaker's gender (Lass et al., 1976, in Yarmey, 1995). Voice identification has been a neglected topic in witness testimony research.[15] This section draws partly on discussions of the relevant empirical literature by Bull and Clifford (1984), Hammersley and Read (1995), Thomson (1995a) and Yarmey (1995). Admittedly, voice identification is involved in a small minority of criminal cases. In some such cases, however, voice identification may constitute a vital aspect of the legal proceedings against an offender. Furthermore, it has been found that mock jurors are more likely to convict if the evidence against the defendant includes confident positive identification by an earwitness (Van Wallendael et al., 1994:672) than on the basis of circumstantial evidence only.

The voice of an offender/suspect over the phone (for example, in extortion or obscene calls) or during the commission of crimes such as rape or armed robbery by an offender who is well hidden by darkness or is well disguised or attacks the victim from behind or when someone overhears offenders planning their crime or reflecting on a crime they have just committed, may be the only identification evidence available. In such cases, the victim or the earwitness may later be asked to identify the offender's voice in a tape-recorded voice line-up. To illustrate with an English case, in *Johnson* (Kevin) (1994) *The Times*, 9 July, the victim and her boyfriend were asleep at night when they were both awaken by an intruder who was caressing the victim's stomach. Threatening them with a knife, the offender proceeded to tie and gag the boyfriend and to assault and attempt rape and buggery of the victim. The two victims reported to the police that the culprit had a deep voice and a slight London accent. The offender was arrested and the two victims selected his voice from nine tape-recorded extracts of voices. The offender's voice was third in line. Hearing the extract of her rapist's voice 'made her go cold and shaky'.[16] This is a far cry from the conditions under which simulation studies of voice identification are carried out.

Voice identification has been accepted in English courts since the case of *Hulet* in 1660 (Hollien et al., 1983), but the general public on both sides of the Atlantic became more aware of its importance in the baby Lindberg kidnapping case sixty years ago in the US.[17] In that case, Colonel Lindberg positively recognised the kidnapper's voice almost three years after the crime was committed, evidence that was very important in securing the conviction of the defendant. The *Lindberg* case also provided the stimulus for the early pioneering work into voice recognition by McGehee (1937). Courts in common law jurisdictions generally recognise that there is in existence expert study and knowledge of voice identification.[18]

How accurate, then, is voice identification by humans? Before turning our attention to the empirical literature it should be noted that, as far as voice identification by humans vs. voice identification by machine is concerned, in an early literature review Bull (1981:40–1) concluded: 'there is evidence that the performance of electro-mechanical spectrographic voice identification systems is no more accurate than that of human listeners. This being the case it is important that courts, and especially jurors, are not led to believe that apparently sophisticated electrical hardware and apparent experts are infallible'. However, more than a decade later, Hammersley and Read (1995)[19] stated in their literature review that computers can exceed human listeners in voice recognition accuracy, even achieving an error rate of 5 per cent.

The existing literature shows a remarkable degree of similarity between visual and voice identification, as the studies below testify. Earwitnesses, like eyewitnesses, are equally prone to error and thus potentially unreliable. It should be noted, however, that most of the studies on voice identification have been carried out under low conditions of ecological validity. For example, only a very small number of researchers have examined voice memory under conditions of unpreparedness and/or violence (see Clifford, 1980; Saslove and Yarmey, 1980; Yarmey, 1991). Let us next consider the reported impact on voice identification of a broad range of factors.

4.1 Circumstances Under Which a Voice is Heard

It is sometimes the case that a crime is perpetrated by more than one offender. It has been found that if witnesses initially hear a *number of voices* their subsequent voice recognition accuracy (VRA) is negatively affected (Goldstein and Chance, 1985, in Yarmey, 1995; Legge et al., 1984; McGehee, 1937). McGehee (1937) reported that VRA decreased significantly within 24 hours when subjects had to recognise three voices instead of one. Many offences against the person (for example, assault, mugging, sexual assault) involve the use of threat of violence, often backed up with possession of a firearm, or actual use of violence against the victim who no doubt finds the experience very stressful. Yarmey and Pauley (1993, in Yarmey, 1995) investigated the influence on VRA of the presence of a *weapon* and whether *abusive language* was used in a videotape of a hold-up by a masked offender. Neither variable was found to impact significantly on VRA or false identifications in a voice line-up but they were found to 'allow guilty suspects more easily to escape detection' (Yarmey, 1995:266). One possibility not considered by Yarmey and Pauley is the fact that the robber wore a mask and this may have influenced any weapon or abusive language effect on the listeners. If a speaker is under *stress* at the time of communicating a message or when being tested later on has been found to impact adversely on the accuracy with which his/her voice will be identified (Hecker et al., 1968).

In real life the victim of a crime often will converse with the offender/s even though they may exchange but a few words. Studies of earwitness accuracy, however, have only examined memory for a passively heard voice irrespective of whether the subjects have been warned. Hammersley and Read (1985) examined the effect of participation in a conversation on identification of the speaker's voice and found that passively heard voices were rarely selected at above-chance level. In other words, 'talking to someone leads one to recognise and identify their voice better than listening to someone' (p. 79). Voices heard over the *telephone* are little more difficult to recognise than voices heard directly from *tape-recorders* (Clifford et al., 1980:100).

4.2 Characteristics of the Voice

In contrast to Pollack et al. (1954), Clifford et al. (1980) reported that identification accuracy of adults is not related to the duration of the speech sample listened to, with the proviso that subjects hear at least one sentence. In the case of children, however, accuracy of voice identification correlates with the length of the speech sample, that is, with the length of exposure (p. 379). Brickner and Bruzansky (1966) looked at the effect of both *duration* and the *length of speech samples* on earwitness identification. They found that for the voices of people who worked together there were 98 per cent correct identifications for sentences spoken, 84 per cent for syllables and 56 per cent for vowel excerpts. Bull and Clifford (1984) reported that voice recognition is possible even with 2-second short-speech samples. The longer the duration of the speech sample, however, the better the accuracy.[20] Yarmey and Matthys (1992) also found, however, that as speech duration increases from 2 to 6 minutes so does the rate of false identifications, especially in a target-absent condition (see also Yarmey, 1991).

Many offenders attempt to disguise their voices to impede their identification. In addition, easily accessible advanced technology enables one to so transform salient features of a tape-recorded message as to disguise it. There is empirical support for the view that disguising one's voice (for example, by a change in pitch) means a witness cannot draw on voice characteristics that are crucial in its identification (Clifford, 1983). An easy way to disguise one's voice mentioned by Yarmey (1995:266) is to communicate in an *angry tone* of voice (Clifford and Denot, 1982;[21] Saslove and Yarmey, 1980) or to *whisper* a statement (Orchard, 1993).[22] A number of researchers have reported that subjects are significantly less likely to correctly identify a disguised than a non-disguised voice.[23]

Defendants in criminal trials involving voice identification are generally strangers to the victim. But how good are we in recognising *familiar voices?* Bartholomews (1973) reported that the VRA of nursery-school children was better than chance for tape-recorded speech samples of classmates and teachers they had known for five months. Adults in the same study did significantly better than children but had an inaccuracy rate of 19 per cent. Individual children's identification performance was as good as that of adults. As Yarmey (1995:263) puts it: how accurate we are in recognising a familiar voice depends on the context and our own expectations. To illustrate, Yarmey (1995:263) cites the following anecdotal evidence for familiar voice recognition accuracy: 'While driving to work in San Francisco, Doug Friday, 33, heard a woman tell a radio phone-in audience that she had taken a lover because her husband neglected her. Recognising the voice of the speaker as his wife, Joanna, Doug filed for divorce' (*Toronto Star*, 15 August 1982). Goldstein and Chance (1985) asked subjects to identify nine familiar voices from eleven unfamiliar ones and found that 40 per cent of the subjects were unable to recognise all familiar voices. In this sense, a voice line-up for a familiar speaker makes sense. It appears, therefore, that recognising voices familiar to us may not be as straightforward as many believe.

For those readers who are monolingual it probably comes as no surprise to be told that Anglophone-only subjects in the Thompson (1987) study recognised a voice with significantly greater accuracy when spoken in English than when the same voice was heard speaking in Spanish; in other words, *language familiarity* had a positive effect on VRA. In view of the extent to which unification has taken place in Europe, the fact that travel permeates contemporary life, and the increasing proportion of people who are at least bilingual if not polyglots, this is an area that deserves more attention by experimental psychologists. Furthermore, such research would be of practical interest to police forces in different parts of the world.

It is not uncommon for extortionists to aurally communicate their demands in a piecemeal fashion, out of a concern, perhaps, that the telephone they are calling from can be identified if they speak long enough. One hopes such criminals will continue this practice (unless they read this book!) because there is empirical support for the hypothesis that hearing the same voice *repeatedly* for short periods instead of hearing the whole voice sample on one single occasion correlates with high VRA (Goldstein and Chance, 1985; Yarmey and Matthys, 1992).

4.3 Retention Interval

How much time elapses between actual earwitnesses hearing a voice and when they are asked to identify it varies from case to case. There has been no consistency in the findings reported about the effect of retention interval on VRA. McGehee (1937) had subjects listen to a fifty-word passage read by an unseen speaker at different *time intervals*. Later subjects were asked to identify the speaker from among four others reading the same passage. It was found that identification accuracy was

83 per cent at two days, 68 per cent at two weeks, 35 per cent at three months, and 13 per cent at five months. Other researchers found no significant decrease in accuracy 24 hours later (Saslove and Yarmey, 1980) while others have reported a significant negative effect over 24 hours (Clifford et al., 1981; Hammersley and Read, 1985), one week (Thompson, 1985a) or two weeks (Goldstein and Chance, 1985). A week after subjects in the Thompson (1985a) study heard a reader's voice, they were asked to select the voice from an array of six voices. Some subjects' VRA was no better than chance. Van Wallendael et al. (1994) reported that retention interval (0 days, 7 days, and 14 days) had no detrimental effect on VRA in both target-present and target-absent conditions (pp. 666–7). Finally, Yarmey and Matthys (1992) found that while VRA did not differ significantly over a one-week period, the false alarm rate increased over the same delay. As Yarmey (1995) points out: 'forgetting over time depends upon the extent of original learning; some voices because of their distinctiveness may be more easily learned and less affected by delay in testing' (p. 267).

4.4 Listener Characteristics

As far as the *age* of the earwitness is concerned, it is known that infants under 6 months of age can differentiate their mother's voice from that of strangers (Friedlander, 1970). Conflicting findings have been reported about whether VRA in children increases with age. Peter's (1987) study of children aged 3 to 8 years found that identification performance was generally poor, irrespective of the age of the children, when their recognition was tested 24 and 48 hours following a visit to the dentist and conversing with the target speaker for 5 minutes. An earlier study by Mann et al. (1979) reported that VRA increases from age 6 to 10 years but declines during the ages 10 to 14 years. Differences have also been reported for different adult age-groups. Bull and Clifford (1984) reported that individuals under 21 years of age and those over 40 years showed inferior VRA than those aged between 21 to 40 years. Regarding the question of whether adults' VRA is significantly better than children's, Mann et al. (1979) found that accuracy among children aged 10 approached that of adults. More research into age differences in VRA is needed before definitive conclusions can be drawn about the children vs. adults issue.

As far as *gender* differences are concerned, McGehee (1937) found male subjects better only at recognising female voices. Clifford et al. (1980) reported that, in general, female listeners were better than male listeners. Thompson (1985a) had subjects identify a reader's voice from an array of six voices. One week later, no gender differences were found.

Finally, Yarmey and Matthys (1992:375) varied voice-sample duration (18 seconds, 36 seconds, 120 seconds and 6 minutes) and, like Yarmey (1986), found no gender differences, with one exception: 'Females were reliably inferior to males in hit scores with the 6-minute voice sample'. Yarmey and Matthys offer no theoretical reason for the one specific gender difference they found. Regarding the importance of the *race* of the speaker and the earwitness, Goldstein et al. (1981) could find no clear evidence of cross-racial difficulties in speaker identification. In their report to the British Home Office, Clifford et al. (1980:100) concluded that sighted listeners are not as accurate at recognising a voice as *blind* listeners.

Empirical studies of the nature of the relationship between earwitness *confidence* and accuracy have found some support for positive relationship. More specifically, a positive correlation was reported by Clifford and Bull (1984), a small but significant correlation by Saslove and Yarmey (1980), a significant correlation in the target-absent condition (Yarmey, 1991) and, finally, a significant positive relationship with voice-sample duration of 2 or 6 minutes but not 18 or 36 seconds (Yarmey and Matthys, 1992). Yarmey et al. (1994), however, found no significant relationship between confidence and VRA in showups and six-voice line-ups in both target-present and target-absent conditions. The nature of the relationship between these two factors, therefore, remains problematic.

Common sense would lead us to predict that highly skilled, experienced phoneticians would show significantly better VRA than non-voice experts. Ladefoged (1981, in Yarmey, 1995) appears the only study to have investigated this hypothesis and found that nine of the eleven phoneticians tested made correct identifications of all eleven familiar target speakers, but five of the 'experts' also falsely identified an unfamiliar speaker. Correct identification of unfamiliar voices poses difficulties even for phoneticians. The McGehee (1944) study reported some evidence that it might be possible to train people in voice recognition. Later research, however, has failed to find support for *trainability* (Clifford et al., 1980).

4.5 Post-event Interference

As in the case of eyewitness testimony, there is empirical support for post-event interference on subsequent voice recognition. Subjects in Thompson's (1985b) study listened to a tape-recorded message and two to seven days later they listened to another voice that was either the same as the original voice or a lure and had to identify it. One month later their VRA was tested with a six-voice line-up that included both the original and the lure voice. Thompson found that subjects who had been exposed to the lure were significantly more likely to falsely identify it as the original voice than those who had not been exposed to the lure between hearing the original voice and the test. The adverse effect of an interpolated test that plants new information in earwitnesses' memory (that is, contaminates it) for voices could easily be produced by police investigators who sometimes test witnesses' memory of a suspect's voice on more than one occasion for operational reasons. Such a practice should definitely be avoided.

4.6 Identification Procedure Used

In view of the fact that voice line-ups are more time-consuming to arrange than showups, police investigators might be interested in the finding that VRA has been found to be poor in both procedures by Yarmey et al. (1994). Clifford et al. (1980:100) reported that identification accuracy is decreased by the *size of the voice parade.*

4.7 Voice Identification Accuracy: Conclusions

On the basis of the available literature it can be concluded that, while in many situations human listeners are capable of accurate voice identification, the reliability of earwitness testimony is affected by a number of factors, namely, the duration of the verbal communication listened to and the number of voices listened to at the time a crime is being perpetrated. Additional factors are the pitch of the voice, delay in an earwitness being asked to identify the suspect's voice, whether the witness has been an unexpected earwitness and whether the earwitness has conversed with the speaker. Finally, the emotional state at the time of encoding as well as the age and the gender of the witness and whether the voice is disguised impact on VRA.

In view of the limitation of voice identification accuracy, Clifford et al. (1980:101) concluded: 'the complexities of criminal identification by voice are no greater than by visual means' and that 'While verbal identification like any evidence of identification will need to be treated with caution there is no evidence that it should be ignored'. Since then a great deal of research has been carried out. Hammersley and Read (1995) point out in their review of the literature that earwitness performance in experimental studies may have frequently been found to be poor because the researchers used recognition tasks that are intrinsically too difficult. They urge caution in interpreting earwitness accuracy findings from well-controlled laboratory studies. They also state that recognition of a familiar voice is a more feasible task but one that has attracted the attention of a few researchers. They conclude that while 'Generally, voice identification or recognition does not guarantee the speaker's identity and one should be pessimistic about the likelihood of recognition' (p. 147), they concede that such identification can be possible and can be tested in a voice line-up on the condition that the voice line-up is valid and the results are not misinterpreted. They suggest future research looks at the questions of how voice and speech processing interact, whether listeners develop a holistic representation of someone's voice with enough exposure to them and, finally, how does such exposure, its duration, how it is spaced out as well as its content influence the accuracy of subsequent voice recognition (p. 147).

5 Conclusions

The extent of similarity between visual and voice identification is exemplified by the finding that when listeners attending a voice parade were instructed that the target voice might be absent, they were still reluctant to indicate its absence, that is, earwitnesses, too, approach their task with a set to select someone (Clifford et al., 1980:101). As Wells et al. (1994:224) points out, no eyewitness author has yet proposed a coherent theoretical framework to account for the social and cognitive processes involved in deciding whether or not to select a particular line-up member as the suspect. The same authors refer to such social and cognitive processes as 'the eyewitness identification process' (p. 224).

Without ignoring limitations of psychological studies of identification procedures, undesirable police practices are a major cause of eyewitness misidentification. While there is some limited empirical evidence that police computer face-composite images appear to be useful to police hard-pressed to apprehend offenders, the range of identification procedures considered in this chapter are fraught with risks for the innocent. As McKenzie (1995) puts it, the question of fairness to the police, the accused and the victim is the issue in this context. Psychologists have already contributed a great deal in this controversial area and have helped to improve the fairness of police identification procedures. Psychologists still have much to contribute in this interesting area of law and law enforcement, and to prevent even more miscarriages of justice. To this end, psychologists should play a more active role in educating operational police, lawyers, jurors, the judiciary and the public at large about the need to strike a balance between, on the one hand, police investigators' wish to solve crimes reported to them and see the guilty convicted and, on the other, the need to minimise various dangers for the innocent suspect that are inherent in police identification procedures.

Chapter 11

Psychology and The Police

• *Introduction.*

• *Police selection.*

• *Predicting success as a police member.*

• *Encounters with the public.*

• *Stress.*

• *Questioning suspects.*

• *False confessions.*

'The public tends to forget, but nonetheless understands and will agree with the service, that officers are busy people, hard pressed, pressured by limited resources and pressing demands, often reflective of primitive emotions rather than considered reflection. The public, however, entrusts the police service – from top landing to the 'front line' – to keep its head and to observe society's moral guidelines to respect the person, to tell the truth and to converse accordingly.' (Shepherd, 1991b:55)

Introduction

The domain of policing offers ample opportunity for psychological research. As psychological research is appreciated more by police management and an evaluation component is included more often than it used to be when changes are introduced within police forces, psychologists will come to play a more significant part in contributing to knowledge about and influencing developments in a broad range of policing issues. However, psychologists need to be closely integrated into police forces if they are to perform their various roles constructively. This chapter does not consider many topics within criminological psychology of interest to law-enforcement personnel, such as theories of criminal behaviour,[1] empirical studies of particular types of violent offenders,[2] criminal investigative techniques like profiling (see Ainsworth, 1995:182–201; Canter, 1995; McCann, 1992), police decisions to prosecute (Grant et al., 1982; Tuohy et al., 1993), decision-making in violent or potentially violent confrontations or police use of firearms,[3] or police officers' perceptions of different offences.[4] The focus of this chapter is at the micro-level, encompassing both studies of police and psychological knowledge applied to police work.

Police psychology is a well-established discipline in a number of countries and psychology modules form an integral part of courses taught to new recruits, sub-officers and officers in many a police force and to university students worldwide. In considering the psychological literature in this chapter, the reader needs to note the country of origin of a particular study. While law-enforcement personnel in different countries have a lot in common, there exist significant differences between police forces in different countries regarding general cultural differences, the laws governing their powers, their structure and procedures, accountability, selection and training, police subculture, use of technology and, finally, the type of demands placed on the police. Such important differences mean that one should not readily generalise findings from one country to another. The reader should also note in this context that, as Yuille (1992) points out, some psychologists have been too eager to apply their research findings (for example, in eye-witness testimony) to policing 'without any apparent concern about the generalisability of the results' (p. 207). Overselling psychology to police management (as Münsterberg, 1908, tried to do with the legal profession) is likely to have negative consequences – in fact, such a practice is dangerous for the healthy development of the field of legal psychology in general.

1 Selection

Perusal of the annual reports of western police forces shows that the demographic composition of western police forces has changed over the last twenty years or so to include a greater proportion of females, university graduates and ethnic minority group members. At the same time, the role of police officers has become much broader and a lot more demanding (Dutton, 1986). It would not be an exaggeration to say that no other occupation calls for such a diversity of skills as being a police officer: responding to and investigating crime, dealing with distraught accident and crime victims and witnesses, coping with an angry crowd, diffusing a domestic dispute, having to knock on someone's door to tell them a loved one has been killed in a road accident. The sheer variety of police skills is probably a factor that explains the popularity of cop shows on television in crime-obsessed societies but it makes the task of reaching consensus on what qualities a police officer should possess and in selecting new recruits almost impossible.

Of course, there are significant differences in how different police forces, even in the same country, select their new recruits. Attractive salaries in some countries and/or high levels of unemployment means that it is no longer a case of screening applicants who meet the minimum criteria. One of the consequences of this has been a more sophisticated approach to police selection that aims to identify the 'right person for the job' (see Gowan and Gatewood, 1995, for a discussion of the literature on personnel selection). A number of interesting and methodologically good studies have been reported since Bull et al.'s (1983) book, Burbeck and Furnham's (1985) comprehensive review of the psychological literature on psychological testing, job analysis, and the selection interview and since Yuille (1986), Ainsworth and Pease (1987) and Hollin (1989) were published. Ainsworth's (1995) book provides a very good discussion of issues in police selection and training as well as other topics considered in this chapter. Mirrles-Black's (1992) assessment of the usefulness of psychometric personality tests in the selection of police officers who will carry firearms is very thorough and draws attention to the uncertainty that exists about the value of this method of selection as well as to some concomitant ethical problems. While this section deals with selection of recruits it needs to be remembered that police selection also includes selecting experienced police officers for such specialist roles as detectives, bomb disposal, covert policing or emergency operation teams (see Scrivner, 1986).

Supporters of the use of psychometric tests to screen in or screen out applicants for police forces, or police personnel to perform specialist functions, have to confront the argument that, generally speaking, scores of such tests do not predict future performance. This, of course, does not mean that psychometric tests do not say something about individuals; rather, it points to the importance of such factors as faking by test-takers and the possibility that what a police psychologist might be trying to predict may well be influenced by stress, physical exhaustion, and other factors present in an operational context, that militate against the predictive value of psychological tests.

The police selection field is also plagued by the simple fact that there is no general agreement on what qualities a good recruit should possess. Ainsworth (1993)[5] reported a study in which a small sample of British police officers attending a course at Manchester University listed the following qualities in order of importance: a sense of humour, communication skills, adaptability, common sense, resilience, assertiveness, sensitivity, tolerance, integrity, literacy, honesty, and problem-solving ability. As Ainsworth (1995) points out, while some of these traits can be reliably measured others cannot (p. 137). A key question in police psychology is whether some types of person (in terms of their values, attitudes or personality) are more likely to want to become police officers and it is this that explains characteristics of serving police personnel (the 'pre-dispositional' model), or whether such police characteristics reflect the impact of training and socialisation into the police role (the 'socialisation' model). This section draws partly on Burbeck and Furnham's (1985) review.

The selection process usually comprises medical and fitness tests, psychological testing and interview/s. On the basis of both US and British studies of police values, utilising, for example, the Rokeach Value Survey,[6] Burbeck and Furnham (1985) concluded that: 'police officers' values seem pretty representative of those of people from their own age and class, though these are not very close to the population at large. However, some of these values appear to change with the experience of being a police officer' (p. 60).

According to Worden (1993), the stereotypical police officer holds a jaundiced view of citizens and the insularity and isolation of the job is thought to encourage an 'us against them' mentality (pp. 210–11). At the same time, because the perceived role of police emphasises fighting crime and especially their prosecutorial role (Stephenson, 1992:114), operational police appear to have a 'concern for the truth: in what actually happens, rather than what they might wish to happen' (Brown, 1988).[7]

It does appear that police are generally perceived, especially by young people, as authoritarian and conservative. But are they? The answer to this question is important (Hollin, 1989) because, as Brown and Willis (1985) pointed out, authoritarianism is a recurring theme in police research and also because it relates to hostile police attitudes and behaviour which should not be tolerated and is also associated with unacceptable treatment of racial minorities (Scarman, 1981).

Research into police attitudes on both sides of the Atlantic[8] has been criticised for inadequate matching of controls, and results reported are difficult to interpret because of the likely possibility that subjects fake their responses to impress (Burbeck and Furnham, 1985). Not surprisingly, such studies have reported conflicting findings. In an interesting study by Brown and Willis (1985) a revised version of the F (fascism) scale was administered to two groups of police recruits, one in the north

(N=54Ms and 19Fs) and one in the south of England (N=30Ms and 6Fs). A third group of sixteen fire-service recruits was also administered the scale. Recruits completed the scale during the first week, after twelve to thirteen weeks upon completion of training and after three months in the job. The researchers also interviewed twenty-five police inspectors and chief inspectors about their reactions to the preliminary findings. Brown and Willis found support for the socialisation model, as recruits were low on authoritarianism during training but experience on the beat increased their authoritarianism. It was also found that the impact of operational policing experience was greater for those who worked in a high crime area and in a police force that used a more traditional approach to policing. Brown and Willis' findings emphasise the importance of the well-established practice whereby more experienced police members pass on the police subculture (also termed 'locker room culture' by Holdaway (1983), with its norms for malpractice and emphasis on excitement and taking risks) to the neophytes, who are in no position to question 'advice' given them by the station sergeant, for example. The Brown and Willis (1985) study has a number of weaknesses. However, as they themselves admit, the version of the F scale used means their results are not comparable with those of other studies; furthermore, sixteen fire-service recruits cannot be said to be an adequate control group.

Partial support for the socialisation model has more recently been reported by Australian researchers. Wortley and Homel (1995) administered the Beswick and Hills' (1972) Australian Ethnocentrism (E) scale to measure prejudice, as well as Ray's (1972) Balanced F (BF) scale and a shortened version of the Marlowe–Crowne Social Desirability (SD) scale to help control motivational distortion, to 412 recruits at the New South Wales Police Academy at recruitment, after six months' full-time academy training and after twelve months' police experience. There was some evidence that respondents would not acknowledge their ethnocentricism in order to give a good impression. Wortley and Homel found that:

- Ethnic recruits and females were generally less ethnocentric than Anglo and male recruits. Also, female recruits were less authoritarian than males.
- Recruit training reduced authoritarianism.
- Recruits became more ethnocentric and authoritarian during field experience. Ethnocentricism increased especially in those recruits sent to police districts with a large Aboriginal population.

Wortley and Homel concluded that police attributes develop as a function of particular policing experience and that training alone is unlikely to overcome the problem of police prejudice. It is unfortunate that Wortley and Homel did not have a control group to test the importation vs. socialisation hypothesis.

Worden (1993) did not focus on either ethnocentricism or authoritarianism in her survey of gender differences among 740 police officers (10 per cent females) who had been in the job for no more than seven years in twenty-four police departments in three metropolitan areas in the US. Worden reported that, taking relevant variables into account, the gender of a police officer was not related to his/her attitudes (pp. 228–9).

2 Predicting Success Within the Force

Burbeck and Furnham (1985) concluded that neither intelligence nor education guarantee success in the police; in fact, they allude to the possibility that: 'Higher levels of education may paradoxically give rise to more dissatisfaction and higher wastage' (p. 62), a hypothesis worth testing at a time when more university graduates are applying to join the police in western countries than a few years ago. To the disappointment, perhaps, of police psychologists, Burbeck and Furnham also concluded, like Lester (1983), that psychological testing does not predict a recruit's later performance and that part of the difficulty here may lie in the fact that there is so much variation in what being a police officer entails that, 'it is not necessary to be expected that one common denominator will be found' (p. 64). In addition, there is no consensus on what is meant by 'success' and 'failure' in this context and 'what is needed is a multidimensional, reliable and robust set of criterion measures on which police officers could be judged by superiors, peers and junior officers. Discriminant analysis can then be used to determine what factors discriminate between successful and unsuccessful police officers' (p. 64). The same argument can be made regarding selection of detectives, utilising already available knowledge about the skills and abilities required to carry out the role of a police detective successfully (see McGurk et al., 1994). The need for the kind of research advocated by Burbeck and Furnham (1985) cannot be overemphasised because psychological testing has also been shown not to be useful in predicting future performance of police officers, even in cases where candidates are selected for entry into a police force against recommendations based on psychological testing (Lester et al., 1980). In other words, psychological testing is not particularly useful at present in either screening in or screening out police applicants. This conclusion is at variance with Hollin's (1989) more optimistic conclusion on the basis of his review of the relevant literature, namely, that psychometric and interview data can predict success at police work but 'the exact predictors of success await definition' (p. 139).

Assuming that one can reliably detect deception in law-enforcement applicants using, for example, such widely used tests as the MMPI (see Borum and Stock, 1993), paper-and-pencil psychological tests are easy to administer and score, do not cost much money and are usually supplemented with interviews. Since both of these selection methods are shown to have no significant predictive utility, there is a strong argument for making greater use of *assessment centres* (see Reinke, 1977). This method is more commonly used to select officers in the armed forces and civil service personnel. It usually involves applicants spending two or three days at a centre where they undergo a range of exercises and tests, including job-simulation exercises to ascertain whether they possess qualities required for a particular position. More recent American research into the predictive utility of one such centre for police recruits (Pynes and Bernardin, 1992) found that whereas psychological testing predicted academy performance better than the centre, the latter was better at predicting on-the-job performance. Pynes and Bernardin used one-day assessment, three candidates at a time, a written examination on three role-play exercises and a multiple-choice test after viewing a crime-related video, and requiring applicants to speak to a home-owner who had reported vandalism. The assessment produced ratings on eight 'skill clusters': directing orders, interpersonal skills, perception, decision-making, decisiveness, adaptability, oral communication and written examination (p. 45). One limitation of the assessment centre is that because of its nature and financial cost, this method can only be used when selecting a small number of candidates. Nevertheless, given the cost to train a police recruit and the financial and other loss incurred when he/she resigns, or is advised to resign or is found to be corrupt and is prosecuted, more thought should be given by police executives to using assessment centres.

3 Encounters With the Public

Police public relations are problematic in many a country but especially in such multiracial societies as the US (Nietzel and Hartung, 1993), the UK (Ainsworth, 1995:130–4),[9] in Australia[10] and in New Zealand. In fact, 'Complaints arising from police-citizen contacts account for much of the attention police receive' (Goldstein, 1994:323). Some authors would argue that as psychologists come to play a bigger role in police training, such important skills as listening, counselling, stress awareness, communication, decision-making and conflict-resolution skills (Reiser and Klyver, 1987:453) on recruit, subofficer and officer courses can be transferred to the workplace and improve police encounters with the public (Bull and Horncastle, 1986; Bull et al., 1987). Bull and his co-workers evaluated the Human Awareness Training (HAT) program introduced into the Metropolitan Police's recruit training in June 1982 which was based on a skills-based model of police training. The focus of HAT has been threefold, namely: to improve 'interpersonal skills (comprising conversational skills and purposive encounter skills); self awareness (comprising self-knowledge through tests and participation in structured experience); and community relations – comprising race awareness and cultural awareness' (Bull, 1985:109).

The comprehensive five-year-long evaluation of the effectiveness of HAT by Bull and his co-workers (see Bull and Horncastle, 1994, for an overview) was carried out in three phases. Because this research is a very good example of how psychologists can contribute to improving police training by evaluating changes introduced, it will be described in some detail drawing on Bull and Horncastle (1994).

In phase 1, three groups of around thirty officers each completed three questionnaires in week 1 of recruit training, and at the end of recruit training (week 20), as well as at six months and at twelve months into their probationary period. The three questionnaires were: a social-evaluative anxiety questionnaire (measures social avoidance and distress); a self-esteem questionnaire (measures perceived interpersonal threat, self-esteem, faith in people, and sensitivity to criticism), and an interpersonal relations questionnaire (measures need to establish satisfactory relationships, need to control them and need for affection). In addition, a recruit training questionnaire (RTQ) was administered to two groups of officers (N=30) on the four testing occasions. The RTQ assesses attitudes and behaviours which HAT aimed the recruits to acquire.

In phase 2, the first three questionnaires as in phase 1 and a self-monitoring questionnaire (measures amount of self-observation and self-control) were administered to three cohorts of forty officers 20, 40 and 66 weeks after initial training, during which time the new recruits were into their probationer training program. In addition, a revised version of the RTQ (subsequently called district training questionnaire (DTQ)) was administered to two groups of officers (totalling sixty-one) on the same testing occasions. By now, HAT was retitled Policing Skills Training (PST). As part of phase 2, an observational study was carried out by one or two researchers of sixty-four police officers in eight police stations with 28 to 43 months' service while on patrol. Observers recorded data on 550 police–citizen encounters. On fifty occasions the observer/s also interviewed the constable concerned and the encountered member of the public separately at the end of the encounter.

Bull and his coworkers found that, generally, HAT trainees were more satisfied with training than were their predecessors and HAT-trained officers attracted fewer complaints during their first three years of service than a matched control group. Regarding the extent to which HAT-trained police officers use HAT skills in their work, Bull et al. (1987) reported a follow-up some 43 months after completing recruit training found some evidence for the transfer of HAT skills to the workplace resulting in improved police–public relations. Bull (1986) concluded that:

> of the three components of HAT, 'interpersonal skills' is clearly the best; the component described as 'self-awareness' is of a reasonable standard; and that described as 'community relations' is, as yet, rather poor ... HAT is a very substantial improvement over that which it preceded. HAT also compares very favourably indeed with training in other forces around the world. (p. 121)

Regarding the extent to which the effects of PST were manifested in police constables' behaviour, Bull and Horncastle (1994) reported phase 2 of their evaluation found 'little evidence to suggest that the concepts and skills which Policing Skills Training sought to impart to recruits were significantly undermined by those recruits' subsequent operational experience' (p. 149). Bull and Horncastle identified the following areas which needed to be addressed by the London Metropolitan Police command: (a) enhancement of the self-evaluation and self-awareness components of PST; (b) misunderstandings about the nature and objectives of PST within the force; (c) enhancement of officers' understanding and sympathy towards victims. It is encouraging to be told by Bull and Horncastle (1994) that 'Since receiving our final report the London Metropolitan Police has acted on all its recommendations' (p. 149). It remains to be seen how many of the police forces in England and Wales will benefit from the experience of the London Metropolitan Police experience with PST.

The research thus far shows that, unless a systematic program to minimise some negative influences by more experienced colleagues on probationary police officers in the process of being inducted into the police subculture and occupational deviance accompany steps taken to improve recruit training, any improvements in police attitudes and behaviour are likely to be ephemeral.

North-American and Australian tourists in the UK are often surprised to find that British police on the beat carry no firearms. While the explanation for this characteristic of the British 'bobby' is more historical, British police forces would be well advised to resist the call to be armed when on duty in view of the rather low risk of serious physical injury or death to which they are exposed, unlike their patrol officer counterparts in some parts of the US. Furthermore, there is empirical evidence that the presence of a firearm has an adverse effect on public perceptions of the police. Boyanowsky and Griffiths (1982) carried out a field experiment to examine weapon presence and eye contact as instigators or inhibitors of aggressive arousal in police–public encounters during the normal course of performing traffic patrol duties. Four constables were recruited in Surrey, British Columbia, for the study. They stopped eighty-seven men and forty-six women and told them they were either going to give them a traffic ticket or that they were merely making enquiries and/or making a records check. The constable would be wearing or not wearing a gun and sunglasses. The researcher observed the encounter and straight after gave the motorist a questionnaire to complete. It was found that: (a) a constable wearing sunglasses was perceived more negatively; and (b) motorists who were told they were getting a ticket expressed the most anger on their faces and reported more aggression when the police wore a gun than when no weapon was visible.

Stephenson (1992:121) points out that 'there are very few in-depth studies of the effects of police–citizen interaction on attitudes of citizens'. One such study by Cox and White (1988) surveyed 460 students who had received a traffic citation and compared their responses with those of 373 who had not. The former were found to have negative perceptions of the police as far as police demeanour (for example, brutality) but not as far as police competence is concerned. These findings point to the need to differentiate between specific and general public attitudes towards the police.

4 Stress

Police associations and police management worldwide are concerned about the long-term effects of stress on their members, including medical problems, absenteeism, alcohol abuse, marital problems and staff turnover. The available evidence indicates that it is not uncommon for police who stay in the job for their working career to continue to experience professional exhaustion, otherwise known as burnout (Oligny, 1994). Kroes' (1985) study of 2300 police officers from twenty-nine different stations or squads painted the following picture of stress indicators: marital problems (37 per cent), health problems (36 per cent), drinking problems (23 per cent), having children with emotional problems (20 per cent) and using tranquillisers (10 per cent). There is a large body of literature on the topic of police stress (Reiser and Klyver,

1987). What follows is an overview of what has been reported about the topic and draws partly on Hollin's (1989) review.[11]

Terry (1981) distinguished four categories of stress:[12]

1 *External* (for example, feeling under siege by an antagonistic public, seeing offenders convicted of serious offences receive very lenient sentences).
2 *Internal* (for example, a feeling that nepotism underpins promotion decisions, feeling there is no hope of promotion, having to be content with obsolete technology).
3 *Task-related* (for example, emotional burnout due to seeing the dark side of human nature too often).
4 Serious concerns about one's own personal safety (for example, knowing that there is a high risk of getting shot at in some areas one has to patrol and that there has been a significant number of both fatal and non-fatal shootings of colleagues already).

Police officers would appear vulnerable to stress because of the very nature of some of their duties (Bull et al., 1983:112–37) but also because one feature of police 'canteen culture' is the macho style that discourages officers from talking about causes of stress, preferring instead to 'keep a stiff upper lip' – a mechanism which is 'over-used and inadequate' (Manolias, 1991, see also, Pogrebin and Poole, 1991). Regarding the kind of officer most vulnerable to burnout, a Quebec study reported by Oligny (1994) identified the following characteristics: being a perfectionist and highly committed to one's duties; not confiding in others; having a very strong will; and, finally, the type who blames others for his/her problems (p. 23).

A British study by Cooper et al. (1982) of 200 police officers, ranging in rank from sergeant to superintendent, found that most significant causes of stress were: work overload; lack of personal recognition and unfulfilled work aspirations; perceived unnecessary obstacles that undermine the police function; and the consequences of autocratic management. Complaints about the police accounted for 2.6 per cent of the variance. A more recent study of perceptions of stress among random samples of 1125 chiefs and 302 sheriffs in the US found that: (a) sheriffs reported higher levels of stress than did chiefs; (b) chiefs with greater autonomy and with a perception that they had control over the hiring process reported less stress; and, finally, (c) chiefs with lower levels of education (especially those with a higher school diploma or less) were more likely to perceive stress (Crank, 1993). Utilising the Life Events Inventory and the Bodily Sensations Questionnaire, Gudjonsson (1983) investigated sources of stress experienced by 100 British police officers the previous year, comparing them with a sample of hospital administrators. The three most frequently reported causes of stress were promotion difficulties, difficulties with their own children as well as with their spouses. It was also found, however, that the police officers were no different to the hospital administrators in what they had experienced as stressful and what bodily sensations they had as a result.

Intuitively, one might expect stress to be related to how long one has been a police member but it turns out that the picture is not so straightforward. Gudjonsson and Adlam (1982) reported that senior ranks were more likely to point to work overload and paperwork as their sources of stress while the lower ranks cited having to deal with violent confrontations and having to respond to nasty car accidents. These findings show that British police officers, like their American counterparts, experience different sources of stress depending on their rank which correlates with length of service and type of duties performed.

In an Australian study, Evans et al. (1992) administered the Jenkins Activity Survey (Jenkins et al., 1979) and the State-trait Anxiety Inventory – Form Y (Spielberger et al., 1983) to 120 Victoria Police and 151 Federal Police officers. They found that officers with more than twelve years of service had significantly lower trait anxiety scores even though they scored higher on the Hard-driving and Competitive dimension of the Jenkins Activity Survey. As Evans et al. point out, these behavioural differences over length of service may reflect changes in how officers perceive their jobs and themselves (see also Perrot and Taylor, 1995), or they may reflect the fact that those who are not happy as police officers, or think of themselves as unsuitable for the job, simply leave. Interestingly, there is some evidence to suggest that years of experience in the job tend to render police officers 'more accepting of legal restrictions, but also more narrowly focused on crime fighting, more resistant to rules, more inclined to favour selective enforcement, and more motivated by money' (Worden, 1993:221).

In what appears to be a unique study, Alexander and Wells (1991) followed up ninety-one Scottish police officers involved in body-handling duties following the Piper Alpha disaster in the North Sea in 1988 when 167 men were killed, and compared them with a control group matched for age, sex, marital status, and band scores on the Hospital Anxiety Depression (HAD) Scale (Zigmond and Smith, 1983), pre-disaster data (HAD) and the Eysenck Personality Questionnaire (EPQ) (Eysenck and Eysenck, 1975); and post-disaster data (Revised Impact of Event (IES) Scale – Horowitz et al., 1979; a body-handling questionnaire, and a coping strategy scale). Alexander and Wells reported that the police officers concerned 'emerged relatively unscathed, and some even seem to have gained from the experience' (p. 551). It was also reported that 'over half of the officers found the anticipation of what was facing them more stressful than the work itself' (p. 553) and that humour and talking to colleagues were the ways most officers found useful in coping with the experience (p. 550). In accepting Alexander and Wells' findings, however, a certain degree of caution is warranted because of the lack of normative data for Eysenck's lie (L) scale. This means that the absence of significant evidence for stress as a result of the body-handling experience may be due to some police officers lying in accordance with the macho image but not being detected by the lie scale.

Regarding stress management, there is no shortage of advice on how to both recognise stress (Ainsworth and Pease, 1980) and how to cope with it (see Ainsworth and Pease, 1987; Stein, 1986). Counselling is discussed by Bull et al. (1983) who also recommend relaxation, meditation, dietary control and exercise. They also argue that: 'organizationally much can be done to reduce the risk of stress and strain by obviating role conflict and role ambiguity, and by managing job content and work loads' (p. 134). Both junior and senior officers made the following suggestions to police command on how to reduce stress (Gudjonsson and Adlam, 1982; Gudjonsson, 1983): (a) better training on how to cope with demanding situations; (b) greater support from senior colleagues; (c) better familiarity with police procedures; (d) improved police–community relations; (e) fewer bureaucratic obstacles. For such suggestions to be implemented, changes at an organisational level are needed (Ainsworth and Pease, 1987).

5 Questioning Suspects

The police clear-up rate for major/indictable/index crime is generally low in western countries. This is especially the case with property offences. In those jurisdictions with an adversarial system, the major role for the police is to construct the case for the prosecution (Sanders, 1987).[13] Historically, being a detective confers status on a police member, especially if he/she happens to belong to an elite squad of detectives. A recent British study by McGurk et al. (1994) used both questionnaires and interviews to collect data from 334 detectives in four police forces: the Metropolitan, Greater Manchester, Hertfordshire and Cambria Constabulary. They found that in 98 per cent of cases their work involved interviewing.

Not surprisingly, therefore, one of the core attributes expected of a good detective is detecting a lot of crime by being effective and efficient at questioning suspects. A significant number of criminal suspects confess and obtaining a confession is strategically important because police are more likely to formally charge a suspect and to end up with a conviction. Therefore, it comes as a surprise to be told that questioning suspects is a skill which, despite its importance and the availability of textbooks on how to go about the task (see, for example, Inbau et al., 1986; Yeschke, 1993), is apparently poorly taught to even detectives and that the whole process of suspect questioning is rather inadequately supervised (Irving and Hilgendorf, 1980; Stephenson, 1992). Dubious practices of police investigators are reduced when they are legally obliged to have the questioning tape-recorded, as is the case in England and in Australia (Heaton-Armstrong, 1995b; Shepherd, 1995). The Homicide Squad of the Victoria Police in Australia routinely conducts its questioning of suspects on video and such evidence is admissible in court. If there is a reasonable basis for suspecting that someone has committed an offence, police are required by law to caution the suspect before questioning. Such a legal requirement, of course, does not stop police questioning a suspect outside a police station (for example, in a police car, or before the tape-recorder or video-camera is switched on (see Torpy, 1994)). In the US an undercover officer in the prison context is not required to caution another inmate when asking questions (see Chapter 9). Gudjonsson (1992a) provides a good discussion of the literature on the broad topic of police questioning of suspects, as does Stephenson (1992). This section draws on both these reviews as well as on the work of other researchers.

Apparently, a high proportion (48 per cent) of suspects who are subsequently convicted and imprisoned initially deny their involvement in crime and a number (41 per cent) are unwilling to confess when first questioned (Gudjonsson and Bownes, 1992). However, a significant proportion of suspects questioned by police make full or partial admissions/confessions. Softley et al. (1980) reported that 47.6 per cent of the 218 suspects questioned at four police stations in England made full confessions, while an additional 13.4 per cent made partial confessions. A number of factors appear to be important in whether suspects confess. Research with prisoners in Iceland (Gudjonsson and Petursson, 1991) and in Northern Ireland (Gudjonsson and Bownes (1992) has identified three reasons why suspects confess: proof (that is, the strength of the evidence against the suspect); internal pressure (that is, a need to tell the investigator about the crime); and external pressure (that is, police persuasion, fear of confinement).

A significantly higher admission/confession rate for suspects without a criminal record has been reported by Neubauer (1974) and Softley et al. (1980) but Baldwin and McConville's (1980b) study of confessions in London and Birmingham reported the opposite trend. The likelihood of a confession decreases significantly as a suspect's age increases.[14] Moston et al. (1992) found that when there is strong evidence against a suspect, juveniles are more likely to deny an allegation while older suspects are more likely neither to admit nor to deny (p. 36). Finally, with the notable exception of Baldwin and McConville (1980b), it has generally been found that property offenders are significantly more likely to make an admission/confession than those charged with crimes against the person (Mitchell, 1983; Neubauer, 1974). It is quite possible that the higher confession rate of property offenders (whose criminal activity level is high) can be attributed to the practice whereby they confess on the understanding that the police will take other offences into consideration. In examining correlates of making a confession one needs to take into account whether a suspect has had legal advice before being questioned by police, which significantly reduces the likelihood of a confession (Moston et al., 1992, see below).

Horgan (1979)[15] defines the goals of interrogation as including: (a) to learn the truth of the crime and how it occurred; (b) to secure an admission/confession of guilt from the suspect; (c) to obtain all the facts to ascertain the *modus operandi* and the circumstances of the crime; (d) to collect information that will enable the investigators to draw logical conclusions; (e) to furnish the prosecutor with the evidence required.

In the light of recent criticisms levelled against the interviewing skills of British police, an attempt has been made to identify gaps in specialist investigative interviewing (see Bull and Cherryman, 1995). First, however, a working definition of specialist investigative interviewing (SII) was generally agreed. Bull and Cherryman analysed, quantitatively and qualitatively, data from 194 police officers from thirteen forces in England and Wales and reported of SII: 'The fair questioning or facilitative interviewing by a well trained, experienced officer with "in-depth" knowledge of a specific area, of a suspect, witness or victim in offences of a special nature or in unusual circumstances' (p. ii).

In recent years in western countries (in the US since *Miranda v. Arizona*, 384 US 436 (1966)) there has been a shift away from physically coercive to psychologically manipulative tactics in police questioning of suspects. Interrogation is now referred to as 'interviewing a suspect' to denote a shift which is part of a large change in policing: social control has become more subtle, more sophisticated, yet potentially more dominating. The shift has paralleled legislative changes and concomit-ant changes in police standing order/codes of practice. Leo (1994) informs us that police use four psychological techniques of influence: persuasion, deception, neutralisation and normalisation. On the basis of his participant observation field study of more than 500 hours in three police departments, Leo (1966) argues that contemporary US police interrogation 'can be best understood as a confidence game based on the manipulation and betrayal of trust' (p.259).

There is no shortage of advice on how to interrogate criminal suspects. According to Tousignant (1991), a prerequisite for a successful interrogation is for the interrogator to 'treat suspects in a civilised manner, no matter how vicious or serious the crime might have been' (p. 16). Another essential rule propounded by the same author is that 'investigators should adopt a compassionate attitude and attempt to establish a rapport with suspects' (p. 16). Such treatment is said to encourage suspects to be 'open, forthright and honest'. Tousignant's (1991) basic premises are:

• Committing a crime gives rise to psychological and physiological pressures in people which they are motivated to alleviate by communicating and explaining the circumstances under which the crime was committed. In other words, 'most suspects feel a need to confess' (p. 17). Empirical evidence supporting this view has been provided by Gudjonsson and Bownes (1992) who found that 56 per cent of the prisoners they surveyed in Northern Ireland had confessed to the police because of an internal need to 'get it off their chest'.

• Suspects confess when their internal anxiety caused by their deception is greater than their perceptions of the consequences of the crime (p. 17).[16]

• A guilty individual who confesses is, from the start, looking for the 'proper opening during the investigation to communicate their guilt to the interrogators' (p. 17).[17]

• Fear of punishment combined with a loss of pride in confessing to a crime inhibits suspects from communicating their guilt (p. 17).

• To communicate about the circumstances of the crime, suspects must feel comfortable during the interrogation and have confidence in the investigator.

• Two basic qualities of a good interrogator are being a good listener and allowing suspects to describe in their own time and words the circumstances surrounding the crime.

• To overcome a suspect's inhibitions about communicating the circumstances of a crime the interrogation should focus on what motivated the suspect to commit the crime and not on the crime itself. This encourages the suspect to begin to rationalise, to explain what made them do it.

• When a suspect makes an admission, however insignificant, it indicates a breakthrough in the interrogation because the suspect's 'defense mechanisms are diminished, and at this point, the investigators may push through to elicit the remaining elements of confession' (p. 17).

One basic assumption made by Tousignant (1991) is that: 'Both the hard-core criminals and first-time offenders suffer from the same pangs of conscience' (p. 17). The validity of this assumption, however, is questionable.

In the recently completed British study of SII by Bull and Cherryman (1995) a questionnaire was constructed on the basis of in-depth interviews with ninety-three police officers experienced in SII. The officers concerned were asked what skills they considered to be the most important in officers who conduct SII as well as in themselves. 'Listening' was found to be considered the most important in SII. Bull and Cherryman also found that the skills most often missing in police officers who conduct SII were said to be 'preparation', 'open-mindedness' and 'flexibility'.

Assuming we have a good interrogator (that is, one who possesses both good intelligence and understanding of human behaviour, is skilled at getting on with other people, is patient and persistent – Inbau et al., 1986, cited by Gudjonsson, 1992a:29) and a suspect who is willing to communicate with the investigator, what approach should one follow to secure a confession? Inbau et al. (1986) recommend the following steps:

- 'Direct positive confrontation'.
- 'Theme development' (for example, to reduce an emotional suspect's guilt or to assist a non-emotional suspect to see the futility of continuing to deny their part in the crime).
- 'Handling denials'.
- 'Overcoming objections'.
- 'Procurement and retention of a suspect's attention'.
- 'Handling the suspect's passive mood'.
- 'Presenting an alternative question'.
- 'Having suspect orally relate various details of the offence'.
- 'Converting an oral confession to a written confession'.

The last step would be unnecessary in jurisdictions which provide for the tape-recording of police interrogations, usually for the more serious crimes termed felonies/indictable offences. But what can psychologists tell police investigators about the process of questioning itself?

According to Stephenson (1992), interviewing is basically a question-and-answer information-gathering exercise and 'interviewing skill may be evaluated in terms of the interviewer's success in eliciting relevant and accurate information' (p. 125). It follows that the interviewer may be unsuccessful in obtaining relevant and accurate information and/or a confession if the interviewer conducts the interview on the basis of unfounded assumptions and/or does not allow the suspect enough opportunity to give a full account of their position *vis-à-vis* the crime. At the same time, a suspect who provides the interviewer with a plausible but untruthful account, or says very little or even says nothing, can undermine the success of the interview. To illustrate, Evans and Webb (1991), two serving British police officers, analysed a random sample of sixty tape-recorded interviews of male and female suspects aged 10 to 16 by police on Merseyside in May 1990. It was found that interviews of children and young persons, in which a parent, guardian or other responsible adult would often be present, take a lot less time – an average of 7 minutes compared with 21 to 22 minutes for adults. As Evans and Webb point out, this finding may well be due to the presence of others during the interview and/or the police having decided to caution the child or young person and, consequently, wanting to 'get it over and done with as quickly as possible'. The same researchers also found, however, that the police interviews in their sample exhibited 'a rather didactic, and dismissive handling of the interviewees who spoke for about a third of the woefully short period of time' (p. 45).

A common concern of detectives is having to cope with a suspect who simply refuses to answer their questions, and especially one who does so while being tape/video-recorded. What, then, can a detective do in response to the 'no comment' problem? How can he/she overcome the suspect's resistance? According to Shepherd (1991a), an investigator should remember that it is not only suspected offenders who resist questioning; the aetiology of resistance is much more complex. Shepherd argues that appropriate conversation and conversation management help an investigator to cope with resistance. This strategy entails: 'respect for the person, empathy, supportiveness, a non-judgemental attitude, straightforward talk and a conversational style signalling a commitment to talk across as equals, not up-down or as pseudo-equals' (pp. 6–7).

Shepherd maintains that the following are conducive for creating resistance in suspects: poor conversation management; inappropriate pacing (impatiently rushing in as soon as the suspect has answered a question); inappropriate forms of assertion and listening (that is, disruptive talk, overtalking, counterproductive questions, inappropriate listening – for example, assuming the answer before it is given); inappropriate content of assertions which lead the suspect to the conclusion that the interviewer does not have sufficient knowledge about the crime, or what he/she knows about it is rather vague. Such practices by the interviewer, Shepherd argues, result in 'Alienation, antipathy, mistrust, loss of confidence in the interviewer and loss of interviewer credibility and loss of self-confidence' (p. 9). One major reason why police investigators find it difficult to cope with a suspect who does not answer their questions is the fact that 'the general pattern of investigative training – as exemplified by CID training – is not training to develop skills but crash courses in the law and procedures' (p. 11). As Moston et al. (1992:38) point out, most British police officers receive no interview training and, in fact, training courses are a relatively new development 'which is still under-researched and under-resourced' (p. 38).

5.1 How Police Officers Approach the Task

Stephenson and Moston (1991, 1994) and Moston et al. (1992) reported a large study of police questioning of suspects at ten Metropolitan Police stations in London. The researchers investigated a consecutive series of fifty or more interviews of suspects by detectives at each police station, giving a total of 1067 cases, ranging in seriousness from minor offences to rape and murder. Each detective was asked to complete two short questionnaires – one before and one after the interview. It was found that in the majority of cases the detectives' aim was to secure a confession as either main evidence or additional evidence (Stephenson and Moston, 1991:30). It was also found that most interviewing officers (73 per cent) were sure of the guilt of the suspect they were interviewing before the interview got under way, largely on the basis of their perception of the strength of the evidence against the suspect. Officers were particularly prejudiced against suspects with previous convictions (p. 32).

In their research for the British Home Office, Bull and Cherryman (1995) analysed sixty-nine video-taped recordings of interviews with suspects provided by a number of different police forces which fell into the category of SII. Four experienced analysts rated independently each interview for the overall skill with which the police officers concerned carried out the interview, as well as whether the interview was or was not characterised by twenty-nine factors. Bull and Cherryman reported:

> The weaknesses most commonly observed in the interviews were the failure to use pauses and silences, the lack of rapport, the lack of empathy/compassion, inflexibility, and the use of leading questions. Comparison between those interviews rated as skilled with those not rated as skilled revealed several differences, with communication skills, flexibility and empathy/compassion showing the largest differences. (p. iii)

Regarding how effective British detectives are in getting suspects to confess, Stephenson and Moston (1991) reported that there was no statistical relationship between a detective's assumption of guilt and the outcome of the interrogation. Although London detectives would probably like us to think otherwise, 'few suspects were "persuaded" to confess' (p. 33). Furthermore, the decision to admit an allegation during the interrogation was, in the main, associated with three factors, namely: strength of evidence, legal advice and the criminal history of the suspect (Moston et al., 1992). Full admissions were found to drop 20 per cent in cases where a suspect had made contact with a solicitor (Moston et al., 1992:36). Further support for the importance of the strength of evidence against a suspect in whether he/she confesses to a crime has been reported by Gudjonsson and Bownes (1992). They found that proof was the factor most commonly (60 per cent) given by the prisoners they surveyed for making a confession to the police which they did not subsequently retract.

Whether a suspect has a criminal record is another relevant factor in this context. Suspects in the Moston et al. study with a criminal record were 20 per cent less likely to make an admission even in the face of strong evidence against them – 59 per cent of them did so compared with 78 per cent of the first offenders. There was also significant variation between different police stations in the percentage of suspects who admitted allegations put to them during questioning. This is an interesting finding that awaits an explanation. Virtually all of the suspects who confessed were charged, but detectives favoured female suspects in that they were significantly less likely to be charged (53 per cent compared with 66 per cent of male suspects). Finally, the same study also found that the style of questioning differed depending on the strength of the evidence against a suspect. In cases where the evidence was strong, detectives used accusatorial questioning strategies; where the evidence was weak, information-gathering strategies (for example, asking open-ended questions) were more likely to be used (Moston et al., 1992:38).

The experience of criminal suspects of police questioning methods internationally provides myriads of examples of sheer police brutality, more so in some countries than in others. It is generally the case that, for most suspects, the interrogation context is still rather coercive without the need for manacles, handcuffs and hoods (Gudjonsson, 1992a; Stephenson, 1992:129). They may be physically exhausted, embarrassed, harbouring a strong sense of guilt, very anxious and feeling at a disadvantage *vis-à-vis* the police investigators. Realistically speaking, the interrogator has control of the situation and can determine whether a suspect gets 'rewarded' or is 'punished', the interrogator is in a position to manipulate the information available to the suspect about the evidence against him/her in order to increase the suspect's level of anxiety and lead to the conclusion that there is no sense in continuing to deny his/her involvement in the crime. From the present author's knowledge of many hardened, career criminals, and on the basis of discussions with detectives in different police forces, there is a minority of criminal suspects who have had extensive experience in being interrogated, have read books on the subject, do not mind lying (and some of them can do so very convincingly) but may prefer to say as little as possible and, finally, the worst punishment if they are charged – prison – does not worry them in the least. Most people, however, would find the experience of being questioned by police as a suspect for a crime a rather unpleasant one. Legislation in the UK (Police and Criminal Evidence Act, 1984, and relevant Practice Codes) with the requirement that interrogations be tape-recorded, has been shown to reduce police use of coercive tactics (Irving and McKenzie, 1988).[18] Interestingly, the same researchers reported that such reduction does not lead to a reduction in the proportion of suspects who confess. Similar legislation has existed in Australian jurisdictions since the late 1980s but its impact on police questioning practices remains to be ascertained.

Interrogative pressure, of course, is a double-edged sword in the hands of the interviewer since it has been shown to sometimes have a boomerang effect. Gudjonsson (1995) describes four cases (two of incest, one of murder and one of conspiracy to commit sexual offences) which show that 'interrogative pressure can result in a marked shift in lowering subjects' suggestible behaviour' (p. 317). Utilising Ofshe and Christman's (1986) 'two-process theory', Gudjonsson states that his finding 'can be interpreted ... as an effective discontinuation of reactive behaviour and activation of strategic coping' (p. 317).

6 False Confessions

As mentioned in Chapter 9, some police investigators feel confident they know how to 'spot a liar' on the basis of 'obvious' clues, coupled with an assumption that most suspects routinely lie. Interviewer bias against the suspect and the coerciveness of the whole questioning context and process has been shown to result occasionally in false confessions, especially by suggestible suspects (Torpy, 1994). Ainsworth (1995:41) describes the case of George Heron in north-east England who in 1993 was cleared of the murder of a 7-year-old girl. He had confessed to the murder after four days of intensive police questioning and after other members of his family had also been arrested by the police. He claimed he decided to make a confession to the police to put an end to what the police were doing to him and members of his family. While the idea of interrogative suggestibility goes back to Binet (1900), the results of empirical studies and a number of highly publicised miscarriages of justice, like the Birmingham Six and the Guildford Four, in which defendants were convicted and served terms of imprisonment largely on the basis of having confessed to crimes while undergoing interrogation by police, have focused attention on pressures placed on police investigators to be successful and some dubious practices by police, as well as on the question of the voluntariness of confessions and some suspects' vulnerability to falsely confessing to a crime. Gudjonsson (1992a) provides a very comprehensive discussion of the topic of false confessions and this section partly draws on his work.

As far as how frequently false confessions occur, Richardson (1991)[19] reported that 23 per cent of sixty juveniles in a residential forensic unit, who apparently had no ulterior motive for such a claim, claimed to have made a false confession to the police largely out of loyalty and in order to protect a peer or a friend (48 per cent). More recently, Gudjonsson and Sigurdson (1994) approached all offenders admitted to prisons in Iceland (a country with an inquisitorial legal system) during the period August 1991 to July 1992 and 95 per cent of them (N=229) agreed to be interviewed. It was found that 12 per cent of the inmates claimed to have made a false confession in the past during police interview, and the majority of them (78 per cent) were subsequently convicted of the offence in question; female inmates were approximately three times more likely to have made such a claim; most (78 per cent) had not retracted their alleged false confession because they considered it futile; 52 per cent said they had made a false confession to avoid police pressure or in order to get out of police custody, while slightly less (48 per cent) did it to protect someone else. Gudjonsson and Sigurdson concluded that their findings 'corroborate the results of Richardson (1991) among adolescent delinquents in England and suggest that false confessions do occur with greater frequency than is commonly believed' (p. 24). Gudjonsson and Sigurdson point out, however, that their findings do tell us how frequently persons interviewed by the police in Iceland falsely confess in general and is an indication of the frequency of false confessions among prison inmates in Iceland. One crucial issue which Gudjonsson and Sigurdson do not really address is the truthfulness of the claims made by the inmates.

In the course of an interrogation an investigator is usually in control of the situation and in a position to place psychological demands on a suspect, communicate excessive expectations and, also, manipulate the suspect's emotions, especially since 'Suspects are never quite sure of exactly what information investigators possess' (Tousignant, 1991:15). Experimental evidence shows that being told that one should remember certain non-existent facts in a memory task results in some subjects accepting more false clues relating to those facts than if no such expectation is communicated and the interview contains no such demands (Gudjonsson and Hilton, 1989). A combination of the experimenter effect, the coercive circumstances of being questioned in a police station (Irving and Hilgendorf, 1980), a suggestible suspect (for example, one low on self-esteem and/or of low intelligence)[20] and investigators who are bent on securing a confession and a false confession becomes a real possibility. Some authors have expressed strong concern about the reliability of confessions made by drug users while intoxicated or under the influence of drugs or suffering from withdrawal symptoms or drug-induced illnesses (Davison and Forshaw, 1993). The same concern has been voiced about the reliability of confessions made by individuals of low cognitive ability when questioned by the police (Torpy, 1994).

Following the quashing by the Court of Appeal in England of the convictions for murder of the Birmingham Six in March 1991, the Royal Commission on Criminal Justice was established with a brief to scrutinise the operation of the criminal justice system, to examine how effective it was in securing the conviction of the guilty and the acquittal of the innocent against the backdrop of efficient use of resources. To assist the Commission in its task, the British Home Office funded twenty-two research reports.[21] One of the research projects was that by Gudjonsson et al. (1994) who investigated the psychological characteristics of adult subjects before being interviewed by the police in order to identify those vulnerable to interrogative suggestibility and thus at risk, and candidates for safeguards provided in the Police and Criminal Evidence Act (PACE), (1984). They interviewed an unbiased sample of 156 suspects at two London police stations. About two-thirds of the suspects had previous convictions and more than one in three had already served a prison sentence. Seven per cent of the suspects were found to be suffering from mental illness, 3 per cent from mental handicap, 3 per cent were illiterate and 2 per cent had language problems; in other words, 15 per cent were vulnerable to suggestibility. The police, who were somewhat unlikely to identify those suspects suffering from clinical depression, summoned an appropriate adult to be present during the questioning (as provided in PACE) in only 4 per cent of those cases. There was some evidence that Afro-Caribbean subjects were more suggestible than others. Gudjonsson et al.'s findings emphasise the need for operational police to be trained and to have clear criteria for identifying mental disorder and suggestibility to children.

Gudjonsson and McKeith (1988) distinguish three kinds of false confessions:

1 *Voluntary false confession:* in this case, one confesses falsely for one's own very good reason and without having been pressured to do so.

Possible reasons in this context might be a wish by an individual to be in the limelight, or to be punished or to cover up the real culprit.

2 *Coerced-compliant false confession:* here someone agrees to make a confession which they know to be untrue in order, for example, to avoid further physical pain, or to be allowed to sleep, or to go home, or on a promise that the investigator/s will 'have a word with the magistrate/judge' about a lenient sentence.

3 *Coerced-internalised false confessions:* in such cases, suspects come to believe that they are guilty because they no longer trust their own memory of certain details (see Ofshe, 1989, for details of how this kind of confession can be constructed by an interrogator).[22] Later on, of course, such a person may come to realise that they falsely confessed but it may be rather late because a retracted confession has been shown to still influence jurors.

Gudjonsson and Clark (1986) put forward a theory of suggestibility (see Gudjonsson, 1992a:116–30) which postulates that 'most people would be susceptible to suggestions if the necessary conditions of un-certainty, interpersonal trust and heightened expectations are present' (Gudjonsson, 1992a:121). Implicit in such a model is the assumption that interrogative suggestibility is a distinct type of suggestibility (Gudjonsson, 1992a:123). Gudjonsson also points out that: 'Sug-gestibility is, to a certain extent, influenced by situational factors and experience' (p. 163). Gudjonsson has constructed a suggestibility scale (Gudjonsson Suggestibility Scale (GSS)) but, as he himself acknow-ledges: 'One of the most difficult questions with regard to suggestibility relates to the extent to which one can generalise from a GSS test score to a trait concept of interrogative suggestibility' (p. 164).

Gudjonsson (1984) tested his scale by comparing the GSS score of twelve alleged confessors and eight resisters. The former group made confessions during police interrogation which they subsequently retracted. The latter group were defendants who continued denying their crime involvement even though there was forensic evidence linking them with the crime. Gudjonsson found that resisters scored less on the GSS. Gudjonsson admits two limitations of that study: the small number of subjects in each group; and that the differences in IQ between the two groups could have influenced their suggestibility scores. Stephenson (1992:132) has pointed out two more limitations: that 'the scores of the false confessors fell within the normal range of scores on this test'; and 'What has to be explained is the remarkably low scores of the deniers, most of whom, it almost has to be said, were found guilty of the offence with which they were charged'. When examining whether the GSS discriminates reliably between those who are high and those who are low on interrogative suggestibility, one needs to also take into account such relevant factors as whether suspects are first offenders or recidivists used to being questioned by the police, as well as whether suspects have received legal advice before being questioned. Moston et al. (1992) found that first offenders were twice as likely to be interviewed by police without having seen a solicitor (p. 33) and, furthermore, 50.4 per cent of those without legal advice made admissions to the police but only 29.4 per cent of those who had legal advice did so (p. 35).

Gudjonsson and Lebegue (1989) reported evidence supporting the validity of the GSS in the form of a higher score by a man who had confessed to the murder of a close friend he was subsequently shown not to have committed. Gudjonsson (1991) reported further evidence that the GSS reliably differentiates between resisters (N=20) and false confessors (N=20). He measured their suggestibility and compliance and controlled for age, sex, intelligence and memory capacity and found significant differences between the two groups on both suggestibility and compliance – two constructs which are theoretically constructed as overlapping. Gudjonsson (1989) also found that suggestibility assessment discriminated between the two groups independent of their level of intelligence. He also compared resisters and false confessors as groups but there were individual differences within each group. Gudjonsson (1991) does admit, however, that 'it is almost certain that not all of the alleged false confessors in the present study are innocent of the crime with which they were charged' (p. 151). It will be interesting to know what became of the four false confessors whose cases were pending at the time. It does seem that convincing evidence for the validity of the GSS has not yet been provided. At the time of writing his paper, five out of the twenty false confessors had, in fact, been convicted. Consequently, the question about the validity of the GSS remains unresolved. It needs to be remembered in this context that a suspect's suggestibility is not the only factor relevant to whether he/she successfully resists the interrogator's suggestions and pressures, but it 'is undoubtedly due to the combination of situational and interrogational factors on the one hand, and the suspect's mental state, motivation, personality and coping ability, on the other' (Gudjonsson, 1992a:157).

Shepherd (1991b) has argued that unethical police interviews of suspects are founded on valuing expediency (p. 48), has proposed a change of approach in how police interviews are conducted and has outlined the following six principles of ethical interviewing: the *prior investigation, sincerity, disclosure, open-mindedness, tolerance* and finally, the *integrity* principle.

Such moral principles, if adhered to by criminal investigators, would go a long way in eliminating improper practices during police questioning of suspects. However, it is unlikely that they will be embraced readily by a large proportion of criminal investigators who would have serious difficulties, for example, telling a suspect where some of their knowledge about a crime has come from. In the world of real, serious, violent crime and offenders (including organised crime), to divulge such information to a suspect could well result in the murder of a police informer, the compromise of an undercover operative or a long-term surveillance operation. Is Shepherd (1991b) suggesting that such police methods are unethical and should cease? Like changes in police procedures legislated in a number of countries in recent years, it remains to be seen whether the ethical style of interviewing proposed by Shepherd, appealing though it may be, has an effect on false confessions. Despite some pragmatic reservations about some of Shepherd's (1991b) moral principles, many would probably agree with him that: 'Doing the job in response to a call to cope with a rise in crime or to catch the perpetrator of an outrageous crime can never be taken to be a licence to act with expediency when dealing with information or with people' (p. 55).

7 Conclusions

Psychologists have a great deal to contribute in the area of law enforcement, as exemplified by the Human Awareness Training project by Ray Bull and his co-workers in England, the empirical literature on false confessions and on police stress. Psychologists, however, need to address seriously the limitations of tests used to select personnel. Of course, incorporating findings from the psychological literature into police training can help improve police–citizen encounters, but only to a certain degree. Traditional, and apparently not very effective, methods of questioning suspects need to give way to interviewing methods that are informed by psychological knowledge and safeguard the rights of suspects without jeopardising the effectiveness of the work of investigators. Reflecting on the contributions to police work thus far and taking note of some of the limitations is necessary if psychology is to contribute meaningfully to move police work generally into the next century. Law enforcement remains a goldmine for psycholegal researchers.

Chapter 12

Conclusions

The contents of this book show that a great deal has been happening at the interface of psychology and law. Especially over the last two decades, major advances have been made in our knowledge on a broad range of legal, psychological and psycholegal issues and the influence of psychology and law has been a two-way process. The maturity of legal psychology as a discipline in its own right and its contributions to society, both diverse and significant, are of special interest in view of a number of impediments to the process of bridging the gap between psychology and law.

As legal psychology continues to evolve, the indications are that psycholegal researchers are more cognisant than they used to be of the need to use a range of research methods and to conduct research that is ecologically valid. Of course, irrespective of how forensically relevant research might be, 'there is always some risk when generalising from scientific studies to real world analogs' (Bruck and Ceci, 1995:309).

The discussion of empirical studies in the preceding chapters also shows that legal psychology's advances are more evident in some areas than in others and some summits still await to be conquered. As Kadane (1993) has noted, there is undoubtedly an imbalance in the amount of attention psychologists have paid to different areas within law and legal process. This imbalance probably reflects the fact that: (a) some issues are more amenable to study by the experimental method (psychologists' preferred method); and (b) the contemporary sociolegal climate in a country is such as to make some research topics the focus of psycholegal researchers' attention. In the process, important topics such as legal advocacy in and out of court or how real crime victim/witnesses fare in their interaction with lawyers in their chambers, in busy court corridors or in the courtroom and/or operational police on the street or in police stations, have been neglected by psychologists.

Despite the limitations of some of the empirical literature discussed in the preceding chapters and the imbalance mentioned, euphoric about their successes, legal psychologists run the risk of overselling psychology to the lawyers and overlooking a few but major difficulties that remain in bridging what gap is left between the two disciplines. Such differences include their different models of anthropos and preferred methodology, difficulties within legal psychology and its relationship with both academic and practising lawyers and a tendency for many psycholegal researchers not to locate their work in a contemporary critical sociolegal context.

As legal psychology approaches its adulthood and draws closer to the next century and the discipline's centenary birthday, legal psychologists have a lot to be proud of. At the same time, there is reason to expect that the scope of psycholegal research will continue to be widened, psychologists' communication with academic and practising lawyers will become more frequent and more constructive, and the feeling of frustration that has characterised members of the legal and psychological professions will dissipate. Optimistic psychologists can, therefore, look forward to the day in the near future when, to borrow Carson and Bull's (1995a:3) words, 'the legitimacy of the offspring of the relationship between psychology and law' will cease to be an issue.

Discussion in the preceding chapters has identified a number of gaps in our knowledge about various psycholegal issues. They include the following, and tackling them poses a challenge for legal psychologists:

- To utilise a range of research methods (including follow-up studies of real crime victims/witnesses as they are processed through the criminal justice process system) to determine the interaction effects of key factors known to impact adversely on the accuracy of adult and child witnesses.
- To identify the merits and defects as far as jury decision-making is concerned of different alternatives in the jury reform debate, such as lay persons vs. professional judges alone or lay persons vs. a combination of lay persons and professional judges.
- To identify good predictors of successful legal advocacy in a variety of contexts and how to teach the skills involved efficiently and effectively to law students and legal practitioners.
- To ascertain the comparative effectiveness of different methods of detecting deception and to provide a theory that accounts for success at both deceiving others and at detecting deception.
- To contribute more to law enforcement by improving the predictive utility of different methods of selecting police personnel both generally and for specialist roles in operational policing.

- Finally, historical and sociological research into the development of legal psychology as a discipline and how and why some of its 'successes' and 'failures' have come about will be of great interest and practical use to all those legal psychologists who like to reflect on their discipline and to take stock.

All those with an interest in legal psychology can look forward to the discipline's increasing growth in terms of both the quantity and quality of the research conducted and courses taught at tertiary institutions.

Psychologists are not always able to provide definitive answers to questions posed by, *inter alia*, academic and practising lawyers, the judiciary, jurors, law-enforcement personnel or the general public. However, as this book shows, the results of their empirical work can throw very useful light on psycholegal issues that enables informed decisions to be made. At the same time, psycholegal research enriches the tapestries of contemporary law and psychology.

Notes

1 Psycholegal Research: An Introduction

1 See Haney (1980) – cited by Blackburn (1996).
2 Cited by Lösel (1992).
3 However, see Landy (1992).
4 Cited in Diamond (1992).
5 Sales (1977); Tapp and Levine (1977); Saks and Hastie (1978); Loftus (1979); Kerr and Bray (1982); Konečni and Ebbesen (1982); Wells and Loftus (1984); Monahan and Walker (1985); Hans and Vidmar (1986); Weiner and Hess (1987); Wrightsman (1987); Raskin (1989a); Kagehiro and Laufer (1992); Ogloff (1992); Goodman and Bottoms (1993); Ross et al. (1994a); Cutler and Penrod (1995a); Bartol and Bartol (1994); Levine (1995).
6 Clifford and Bull (1978); Farrington et al. (1979a); Haward (1981); Lloyd-Bostock (1981a, 1981b, 1984, 1988); Lloyd-Bostock and Clifford (1983); Müller et al. (1984); Fitzmaurice and Peace (1986); King (1986); Pennington and Lloyd-Bostock (1987); Gale (1988); Hollin (1989); Gudjonsson (1992); Bull and Carson (1995).
7 For example, Saks and Hastie (1978); Farrington et al. (1979b); Yarmey (1979); Lloyd-Bostock (1981a, 1981b, 1988); Diamond (1992); Lösel (1992).
8 See in Chapter 2 Tollestrup, Turtle and Yuille's (1994) finding concerning the relationship between arousal and accuracy with real-life victims and witnesses to robbery and fraud.
9 Cited by Lloyd-Bostock (1981a:XII).
10 See Law Reform Commission of New South Wales (1985) *The Jury in a Criminal Trial*; Law Reform Commission of Victoria (1985) *The Jury in a Criminal Trial*; Law Reform Committee [Vic] (1995) *Jury Service in Victoria*; Law Reform Commission of Western Australia (1991) *Report on Evidence of Children and Vulnerable Witnesses*.
11 See, for example, *Brown v. Board of Education*, 347 US 483, 494–5, n.11 (1954) [psychological effects of segregated education]; *Ballew v. Georgia*, 435 US 223, 231–44 (1978) [effects of jury size]; Bruck and Ceci (1995) [children's suggestibility].
12 See Irving and Hilgendorf (1980); Royal Commissions on: Civil Liability and Compensation for Personal Injury, 1978; Gambling, 1978; Criminal Procedure, 1980; Fraud Trials, 1986 (Medical Research Council (MRC) Applied Psychology Unit, Cambridge, 1986) and the Royal Commission on Criminal Justice, 1993 – Runciman Report.

2 Eyewitnesses: Key Issues and Event Characteristics

1 Burtt (1931), Gross (1911), Hutchins and Slesinger (1928), McCarty (1929), Münsterberg (1908), Stern (1939), Whipple (1909).
2 Cited by Gudjonsson (1992:98).
3 See Chapter 10 for witness accuracy with police identification procedures.
4 Cited by Lloyd-Bostock (1988).
5 Cited in Thomson (1995a:120–1).
6 Cited in Thomson (1995a:122).

3 Eyewitnesses: The Perpetrator and Interviewing

1 Cited by Hosch (1994:343).
2 Cited by Diges et al. (1992:317).
3 Cited by Hosch et al. (1994:332).
4 Cited by Hosch et al. (1994:338).
5 Cited by Hosch et al. (1994).
6 Cited by Gudjonsson (1992).
7 Cited by Ellis and Ashbrook (1991).
8 See *Davis v. R.*, Supreme Court, South Australia, Crt Crim App, 8 September 1995.
9 Cited by Light (1991:334).
10 These research findings have been reported by Williams et al. (1992:146).
11 See Bothwell et al. (1989), Brigham (1986), Brigham et al. (1982), Jalbert and Getting (1992), Lindsay and Wells (1983), Shapiro and Penrod (1986), Wells (1978).
12 Cited by Levine and Tapp (1973).
13 Cited by Leippe (1994:384–5).
14 Cases cited by Smith et al. (1989).
15 See Bothwell et al. (1987b), Brigham (1983), Cutler et al. (1987), Lindsay et al. (1981), Pigott et al. (1985), Smith et al. (1989), Wells et al. (1979), Wells and Murray (1984).
16 See Greuel (1992), Stone (1991), Vrij and Winkel (1992), Winkel and Koppelaar (1992).
17 Reported in the *Sunday Times* (Spectrum), 19 May 1974.
18 Cited by MacLeod et al. (1994:129).
19 Stated in Payne (1987).
20 Cited by Hoffman et al. (1992:293).
21 Cited by Yarmey (1990).

4 Children As Witnesses

1 See Howels (1994) regarding prevention of child sexual abuse.
2 See, for example, Police and Criminal Evidence Act, 1984, s.66, in Great Britain.
3 See Birch (1992), Brennan (1993), Bull (1992, 1995a, 1995b), Carson (1995c), Clifford (1993), Davies (1991, 1993b, 1994), Davies and Noon (1991, 1993), Dent and Flin (1992), Flin (1993), Lloyd-Bostock (1984), McEwan (1988, 1990), Milne and Bull (1995), Sattar and Bull (1994),

Morgan and Zedner (1992a, 1992b), Spencer and Flin (1990, 1993), Westcott (1995), Wilson (1995).

4   See Doris (1991), Goodman and Bottoms (1993), Moore et al. (1990), Perry and Wrightsman (1991), Schwalb (1991), Zaragoza et al. (1995).

5   See Brooks and Siegal (1991), Byrne (1988), Byrne and Maloney (1991), Cashmore (1991), Dent (1988), Law Reform Commission of Western Australia (1990, 1991), Naylor (1989), Parkinson (1991), Siegal and Peterson (1995), Thomson (1988), Tucker et al. (1990), Vernon (1991), Warner (1988).

6   See Davies (1991), Davies and Noon (1993), for a discussion of these reforms.

7   See s.37C Evidence Act (Vic.), 1958 (as amended by the Crimes (Sexual Offences) Act, 1991; Evidence (Closed Television) Act, 1989 (ACT); ss.405D and 405F Crimes (Child Victim Evidence) Amendment Act (1990) NSW ss.405D and 405E], and Acts Amendment (Evidence of Children and Others) Act, 1992 (WA)].

8   Fivush et al. (1987), Hamond and Fivush (1991), Hudson and Fivush (1987) cited by Fivush (1993), Pillemer and White (1989), Sheingold and Tenney (1982), Todd and Perlmutter (1980).

9   See Fivush and Hamond (1990), Fivush et al. (1991), Hudson (1990), Hudson and Fivush (1990).

10 See Schacter et al. (1995) for evidence that some aspects of memory development and cognitive development are associated with immature frontal functioning.

11 See *Thomas* [1994] *Criminal Law Review*, 745, for two witnesses to a murder aged 8 and 11.

12 See also Fitzpatrick and Boldizar (1993), Shakoor and Chalmers (1991).

13 Cited by Batterman-Faune and Goodman (1993).

14 See Myers (1995) and Lyon (1995) for criticisms of Bruck and Ceci's work but see also Ceci et al.'s (1995) response to those criticisms of their work and the *amicus* brief.

15 Cited by Batterman-Faune and Goodman (1993).

16 See also Goodman et al. (1991), Rudy and Goodman (1991).

17 Cited by Saywitz and Snyder (1993).

18 From Nelson et al. (1983).

19 Geiselman and Padilla (1988), Geiselman et al. (1990), Saywitz et al. (1993).

20 Cited by Memon et al. (1993).

21 Cited by Boat and Everson (1993).

5 The Jury

1   Cited by Kerr (1987:64).

2   See New South Wales Law Reform Commission [NSWLRC] (1985:13–17) for a more detailed historical account.

3   See Kadane (1993:232–3) who criticises voter registration lists, and Fukurai et al. (1991) who suggest using cluster sampling to select representative jurors.

4   See s.42(1) Criminal Justice and Public Order Act (1994) for England and Wales.

5 Darbyshire (1991:743) attributes her comments on these Latin terms to Cornish (1968:12).
6 Cited by Cammack (1995:481).
7 Darbyshire (1991:751).
8 Brown and Neal (1988:127–8), Darbyshire (1991:741, 746), Evans (1995).
9 Blom-Cooper (1974).
10 Blom-Cooper (1974).
11 Willis (1983).
12 Blom-Cooper (1974).
13 Willis (1983).
14 Bevan et al. (1958:447), Kerr (1987:63).
15 Queensland Criminal Justice Commission (1991).
16 Barber and Gordon (1976), Nathanson (1995), Pickel (1995).
17 Ogloff and Vidmar (1994), Sue et al. (1974).
18 Green (1990).
19 Kramer et al. (1990).
20 Bevan et al. (1958).
21 Darbyshire (1991:746), Dunstan et al. (1995:42).
22 See the case of *Kemp*, *The Times*, 25 April 1994.
23 Cadzow (1995:16), Margolic (1995), Slind-Flor (1992), Feldman and Bell (1991), Shuman et al. (1994).
24 Kerr (1987:63), Nathanson (1995), Severance et al. (1992), Williams (1963).
25 Kerr (1987:63).
26 Mark (1973) but see Zander (1974) for a rebuttal.
27 Stephenson (1992).
28 Baldwin and McConville (1979,1980a), Kalven and Zeisel (1966), McCabe and Purvis (1974), Stephenson (1992), Zander and Henderson (1994).
29 Darbyshire (1991:744), Dunstan (1995:33).
30 Darbyshire (1991:748).
31 Blom-Cooper (1974).
32 Darbyshire (1991:741).
33 Blom-Cooper (1974). An exception to this would be some jurisdictions in the US where long terms of incarceration can be imposed on even minor repeat offenders under the 'three-strikes-and-you-are-out' approach to keep them out of circulation.
34 Blom-Cooper (1974).
35 Kerr (1987:63), Roskill Committee (1986).
36 Duff and Findlay (1988).
37 Brett (1962:74), Devlin (1974).
38 McCabe (1975), Sealy (1975).
39 Zander and Henderson (1994).
40 Diamond and Casper (1992), Harding (1988), Thompson (1989).
41 Bornstein (1994), Hans and Lofquist (1992).
42 Galiber et al. (1993).
43 Zander and Henderson (1994:47).
44 Zander and Henderson (1994:46).
45 See Werner et al. (1985) for one of the reports from that project.
46 See also Hans and Vidmar (1991).
47 However, as far as it has been possible to ascertain, it would be illegal to tape jury deliberations in any western common law or civil law country.
48 See issues of *Indiana Law Review*, 1995, vol. 70 (3, 4).

49 *Maxwell* case proceeding at the time of writing. See Goldberg (1995).
50 See also Izzett and Leginski (1974), Landy and Aronson (1969), Ostrom et al. (1978).
51 Cited by Hoffmann (1995:1137).
52 See Bersoff and Ogden (1987), Hans and Vidmar (1986:233–4), Kassin and Wrightsman (1988:39).
53 See, for example, the English Criminal Evidence Act (1898) upon which are based such provisions in each Australian jurisdiction (Waight and Williams, 1995).
54 See also Hans and Vidmar (1986), Kassin and Wrightsman (1988), Potas and Rickwood (1984).
55 Cited by Levine (1992:152).
56 See Hastie (1993b) for a discussion.

6 Sentencing As A Human Process

1 See Freiberg and Ross (1995) for a discussion of the experience in recent years in Victoria, Australia, with sentencing legislation in theory and practice.
2 See, for example, the [British] Magistrates' Association's Sentencing Guidelines (1993), Harris (1987), Lovegrove (1995), Victorian Sentencing Manual (1993), Wasik and Pease (1987).
3 See McConville and Mirsky (1995) for an interesting ethnographic study of how guilty pleas are socially constructed.
4 See *Herald Sun*, 1995, for some interesting Australian cases that illustrate this difficulty.
5 See also Everson (1919), Frankel (1940–41), Patchett and McClean (1965).
6 See also Baab and Furgeson (1967), Green (1961), Hood (1972).
7 See also Darbyshire (1980), Konečni and Ebbesen (1979), Snel (1978).
8 See, for example, Atkinson and Newman (1970), Baab and Furgeson (1967), Pope (1975), Steffensmeier et al. (1993), Wilbanks (1986).
9 See, for example, Carter and Cleland (1979), Clarke and Koch (1980), Rapaport (1991), Unnever et al. (1980).
10 See, for example, Bierhoff et al. (1989), Efran (1974), Miller et al. (1986).
11 See, for example, Ho and Venus (1995), Rose (1965), Solimine and Wheatley (1995).
12 See Bowen (1965), Gibson (1978), Hogarth (1971).
13 See Schubert (1959), Walker (1972).
14 See Hogarth (1971), Kapardis (1984, 1985), Spreutels (1980).

7 The Psychologist As Expert Witness

1 See also Kargon (1986) regarding the historical development of the expert witness and the special issue of *Law and Human Behaviour* 16(3) on expert evidence.
2 Citing Hodgkinson (1990:52).
3 See Carson (1992), Edmondson (1995), Freckelton (1990, 1993), Gudjonsson (1992b, 1995) and Nijboer (1995) for discussions of this, and Loftus

and Ketcham (1991) regarding the experience of appearing as an expert witness for the defence in American courts.

4   See American Psychology Law Society (1991) and Committee on Ethical Guidelines for Forensic Psychologists (1991) for details.

5   The expert concerned was William Marston, a pioneer in the use of the polygraph to detect deception.

6   Quoted in Landsman (1995:155).

7   Voice identification is recognised as an expert field in England (see *R. v. Robb* (1991) 93 Cr.App.R. 161 at 165; EE, 1(1):20).

8   See Freckelton (1990:56) who cites *R. v. Holland* (1981) 6 WCB 177; *R. v. Scoppelliti* [1981] 34 OR (2d) 524 at 531; *R. v. Clark* (1983) 1 DLR (4d) 46.

9   See Freckelton (1993:111) for details.

8 Persuasion In The Courtroom

1   Examples of 'great advocates' mentioned by the same authors are: Lord Birkett (1962), Lord Macmillan (1952), Hastings (1923), Jackson (1959) and Parry (1923) (p. 190).

2   See Du Cann (1964), Evans (1995), Glissan (1991), Lubert (1993), Pannick (1992), Phillips (1985), Munkman (1951, 1986), Wells (1988).

3   See, however, Tronk and Dearden's (1993) *Advocacy Basics for Solicitors*, for a long-awaited focus on the humble solicitor and advocacy in the lower courts.

4   According to Mauet and McCrimmon (1993), courtroom advocacy skills are called for after: completing interrogatories; pre-trial motions; negotiations with the other party to achieve settlement of the dispute in question have failed; a case file has been compiled that contains court documents, evidence and counsel notes; a notebook is by now also available in the name of effectiveness and efficiency; the lawyer has constructed a 'theory of the case' (that is, the chosen position and approach to all the evidence the lawyer anticipates will be presented at trial; witnesses have been prepared for trial and, finally, a decision has been made which witnesses to call and in what order.

5   See Leippe (1994) for a model.

6   Cited in Du Cann (1964:47).

7   The one not included concerns counsel's position and delivery and has already been mentioned.

8   See Glissan (1991:39–44) for a detailed discussion of these issues and relevant Australian case law.

9 Detecting Deception

1   See also Block et al. (1992), Jacobs (1993a, 1993b), Pogrebin and Poole (1993) regarding the use of undercover agents by the police.

2   See Hyman (1989:140–3) for non-human deception.

3   See Hyman (1989:134–9) for a review.

4   Citing Goldberg et al. (1991), Ones et al. (1993) and Sackett et al. (1989).

5   Cited by Miller and Stiff (1993).

6 Personal communication, Sergeant Chris Ward, Nottingham, England.
7 See Raskin (1989b) and Iacono (1995) for details of the procedure used with this and the other techniques.
8 See Gudjonson (1988) for a good discussion of this topic.
9 Patty Hearst came from a wealthy family and was imprisoned for a number of crimes (including armed robbery) she committed while a member of the Symbionese Liberation Army. At her trial it was alleged she had been brainwashed into joining that terrorist organisation while she was its captive.
10 See Gudjonsson (1992a) for discussion of this technique.
11 The criteria are also listed in Marxsen et al. (1995:445).
12 Citing Sapir (1991, 1993).

10 Witness Recognition Procedures

1 See *R. v. Burchielli* [1981] VR 611 regarding similar guidelines for the judiciary in Victoria, Australia.
2 See Joyce (1993) for evidence that only a minority of the general public in England might be able properly to understand a lot of the information contained in the [1991] revised Codes of Practice, Police and Criminal Evidence Act (1984).
3 See Borchard (1932), Brandon and Davies (1973), Frank and Frank (1957), Rattner (1988).
4 Cited by Davies (1989).
5 See *Downey* (1994), *The Times*, 5 April, and *Fremantle v. R.* (1994), *The Times*, 7 July, for cases where the warning was not given but the appeal failed.
6 See Brown et al. (1977), Hilgendorf and Irving (1978), Loftus (1974, 1976).
7 See Brigham (1989), Malpass and Devine (1983), Wagenaar and Veefkind (1992).
8 See *R. v. Cormack* [1981] 5 CrLJ 163; *R. v. Kehagias, Leone and Durkic* [1985] VR 107.
9 Examples of such advice is to be found, for example, in: Victoria Police, Detective Training School (1994), *Identification*, Police Headquarters, Melbourne, Australia; Victoria Police (1995), *Prosecutor's Manual* (Chapter 43, 43.1–43.11) and, finally, in police standing orders worldwide.
10 Cited in Wells et al. (1994:225).
11 Cited in Clifford (1981).
12 See Cutler and Penrod (1988), Lindsay and Wells (1985), Lindsay et al., (1991a, 1991b), Parker and Ryan (1993) and Sporer (1993).
13 Cited in Thomson (1995a:142).
14 Cited by Cutler et al. (1994:181).
15 See Bull (1981), Bull and Clifford (1984), Clifford et al. (1980), Clifford and Davies (1989), Hammersley and Read (1995), Thomson (1995a:133–5) and Yarmey (1994, 1995) for literature reviews.
16 Reported in *Expert Evidence*, 1994, 3(2):87.
17 *United States v. Hauptman* [1935] *Atlantic Report*, 180, 809–29, cited in Yarmey (1995:262).
18 See *R. v. Gilmore* [1977] 2 NSWLR, 935; *R. v. McHaardie and Danilson* [1983] 2 NSWLR, 763.

19 See Hammersley and Read (1995) for a review of the empirical literature on earwitness identification.
20 Goldstein and Chance (1985), Hammersley and Read (1985), Yarmey and Matthys (1992).
21 Cited in Yarmey (1995).
22 Cited in Yarmey (1995).
23 Clifford (1980), Clifford and Denot (1982), Orchard (1993), Reich and Duke (1979, cited in Yarmey, 1995), Saslove and Yarmey (1980).

11 Psychology and The Police

1   See Blackburn (1993), Feldman (1993).
2   See Kapardis (1988, 1989, 1990).
3   See Blumberg (1994), Fridell and Binder (1992), Kapardis (1990a), Vrij et al. (1995).
4   Mortimer (1991), Stalans and Finn (1995).
5   Cited in Ainsworth (1995:136–7).
6   See Bennett and Greenstein (1975), Griffeth and Cafferty (1977), Teahan (1975).
7   Cited by Stephenson (1992:115–16).
8   See Bayley and Mendelsohn (1969), Carlson et al. (1971), Colman and Gorman (1982).
9   See, also, Feldman (1993: 98), Policy Studies Institute (1981), Scarman (1981).
10 See Cunneen (1990), Hazlehurst (1988), Johnston (1991).
11 See Bull et al. (1983), Ainsworth (1995), Stein (1986).
12 The examples given to illustrate are the present author's.
13 Cited in Stephenson (1992:126).
14 See Baldwin and McConville (1980b), Leiken (1970), Softley et al. (1980).
15 Cited by Tousignant (1991).
16 Citing Reid and Associates (1986:44).
17 Citing Swanson et al. (1988:210).
18 Cited in Stephenson (1992).
19 Cited in Gudjonsson and Sigurdson (1994).
20 See Richardson and Kelly (1995), Torpy (1994).
21 See Home Office Research and Planning Department (1994), *Research Bulletin*, vol. 35.
22 Cited in Ainsworth (1995).

Bibliography

Aguirre, A. and Baker, D. V. (1990). Empirical research on racial discrimination in the imposition of the death penalty. *Criminal Justice Abstracts*, 135–51.

Ainsworth, P. B. (1981). Incident perception by British police officers. *Law and Human Behavior*, 5, 231–6.

Ainsworth, P. B. (1995). *Psychology and Policing in a Changing World*. Chichester: Wiley.

Ainsworth, P. B. and Pease, K. (1987). *Police Work*. London: British Psychological Society and Methuen.

Alexander, D. A. and Wells, A. (1991). Reactions of police officers to body-handling after a major disaster: a before-and-after comparison. *British Journal of Psychiatry*, 159, 547–55.

Allen, H. (1987). The logic of gender in psychiatric reports to the courts. In D. C. Pennington and S. M. A. Lloyd–Bostock (eds), 104–16.

Allen, J. J., Iacono, W. G. and Danielson, K. D. (1992). The identification of concealed memories using the event-related potential and implicit behavioral measures: a methodology of prediction in the face of individual differences. *Psychophysiology*, 29, 504–22.

Allen, R. J. and Miller, J. S. (1995). The expert as educator: Enhancing the rationality of verdicts in child sex abuse prosecutions. *Psychology, Public Policy, and Law*, 1, 323–38.

Allport, G. W. and Postman, L. (1947). *The Psychology of Rumor*. New York: Henry Holt.

Alonso-Quecuty, M. (1992). Deception detection and reality monitoring. In F. Lösel et al. (eds), 328–32.

American Professional Society on the Abuse of Children (1990). *Guidelines for psychological evaluation of suspected sexual abuse in young children*. Unpublished manuscript.

American Psychiatric Association (1993). *Statement on Memories of Sexual Abuse.*

American Psychological Association (1990). *Craig v. Maryland: Brief of the American Psychological Association*. Washington, DC. (Reprinted as Goodman, G. S., Levine, M., Melton, G. B. and Ogden, D. W. (1990)). *Law and Human Behavior*, 15, 13–29.

American Psychological Association (1991). Minutes of the Council of Representatives. *American Psychologist*, 46, 722.

American Psychology Law Society (1991). Speciality guidelines for forensic psychologists. *American Psychology Law Society News*, 11, 8–11.

Anderson, K. (1987). Sentencing in Magistrates' Courts. In I. Potas (ed.), *Sentencing in Australia: Issues, Policy and Reform* (pp. 191–206). Canberra: Australian Institute of Criminology.

Applegate, B. K., Wright, J. P. and Dunaway, R. G. et al. (1994). Victim–offender race and support for capital punishment: a factorial design approach. *American Journal of Criminal Justice*, 18, 95–115.

Arce, R. (1995). Evidence evaluation in jury decision-making. In R. Bull and D. Carson (eds), 565–80.

Arce, R., Farina, F. and Real, S. (1996). Empirical assessment of the *escabinato* jury system. *Psychology, Crime and Law*, 2, 175–83.

Arce, R., Sobral, J., Farina, F. (1992). Verdicts of psychosocially biased juries. In F. Lösel et al. (eds), 435–9.

Arndt, B. (1995). Dark memories. In 'Focus', p. 28, *The Weekend Australian*, 1–2 July.

Aronson, E. (1980). *The Social Animal* (3rd edn). San Francisco: Freeman.

Ashworth, A. (1995). Reflections on the role of the sentencing scholar. In C. Clarkson and R. Morgan (eds), *The Politics of Sentencing Reform* (pp. 251–66). Oxford: Clarendon Press.

Atkinson, D. N. and Newman, D. A. (1970). Judicial attitudes and defendant attributes: some consequences of municipal court decision-making. *Journal of Public Law*, 19, 68–87.

Atkinson, J. and Walker, E. (1955). The affiliation motive and perceptual sensitivity to faces. *Journal of Abnormal Social Psychology*, 53, 38–41.

Australian Psychological Society (1995). *Guidelines Relating to Recovered Memories.* Melbourne.

Avery, G., Baker, E. and Kane, B. (1984). *Psychology at Work: Fundamental and Applications.* Sydney: Prentice-Hall.

Avio, K. L. (1988). Capital punishment in Canada: statistical evidence and constitutional issues. *Canadian Journal of Criminology*, 30, 331–45.

Baab, G. W. and Furgeson, W. R. (1967). Texas sentencing practices: a statistical study. *Texas Law Review*, 471–503.

Bagby, R. M., Parker, J. D., Rector, N. A. and Kalemba, V. (1994). Racial prejudice in the Canadian legal system: juror decisions in a simulated rape trial. *Law and Human Behavior*, 18, 339–50.

Baldwin, J. (1994). The role of legal representatives at police stations. Royal Commission on Criminal Justice, Study No. 3. *Research Bulletin*, No. 35, 11–12. London: Home Office Research and Statistics Department.

Baldwin, J. and McConville, M. (1979). *Jury Trials.* Oxford: Clarendon Press.

Baldwin, J. and McConville, M. (1980a). Juries, foremen and verdicts. *British Journal of Criminology*, 20, 35–44.

Baldwin, J. and McConville, M. (1980b). *Confessions in Crown Court Trials.* Royal Commission on Criminal Procedure, Research Study No. 5. London: HMSO.

Ballard, P. B. (1913). Obliviscence and reminiscence. *British Journal of Psychology Monograph Supplements*, 1, 1–82.

Bandura, A. (1986). *Social Foundations of Thought and Action: A Social Cognitive Theory.* Englewood Cliffs, NJ: Prentice–Hall.

Barber, D. and Gordon, G. (eds) (1976). *Members of the Jury.* London: Wildwood House.

Barclay, C. D., Cutting, J. E., and Kozlowski, L. T. (1978). Temporal and spatial factors in gait perceptions that influence gait recognition. *Perception and Psychophysics*, 23, 145–52.

Barker, T. and Carter, D. L. (1994). Police lies and perjury: a motivation-based taxonomy. In T. Barker. and D. L. Carter (eds), *Police Deviance* (3rd edn) (pp. 139–52). Cincinnati, OH: Anderson Publishing.

Barland, G. H. (1988). The polygraph test in the USA and elsewhere. In A. Gale (ed.), *The Polygraph Test: Lies, Truth and Science* (pp. 73–95). London: Sage.

Bartholomews, B. (1973). Voice identification by nursery-school children. *Canadian Journal of Psychology*, 27, 464–72.

Bartlett, D. and Memon, A. (1995). Advocacy. In R. Bull and D. Carson (eds), 543–54.

Bartlett, F. (1932). *Remembering: A Study in Experimental and Social Psychology*. Cambridge University Press.

Bartlett, J. C. and Leslie, J. E. (1986). Aging and memory for faces versus single views of faces. *Memory and Cognition*, 14, 371–81.

Bartol, C. R. and Bartol, A. M. (1994). *Psychology and Law: Research and Application* (2nd edn). Pacific Grove: Brooks/Cole.

Bashore, T. R. and Rapp, P. E. (1993). Are there alternatives to traditional polygraph procedures? *Psychological Bulletin*, 113, 3–22.

Bass, E. and Davis, L. (1988). *The Courage to Heal: A Guide for Women Survivors of Childhood Sexual Abuse*. New York: Harper and Row.

Batterman-Faune, J. M. and Goodman, G. S. (1993). Effects of context on the accuracy and suggestibility of child witnesses. In G. S. Goodman and B. L. Bottoms (eds), 301–30.

Bauer, P. J. (1996). What do infants recall of their lives? Memory for specific events by one- to two-year olds. *American Psychologist*, 51, 29–41.

Bavelas, J. B., Black, A., Chovil, N. and Mullett, J. (1990). *Equivocal Communication*. Newbury Park, CA: Sage.

Bayley, D. and Mendelsohn, H. (1969). *Minorities and the Police: Confrontation in America*. New York: The Free Press.

Bekerian, D. A. (1993). In search of the ideal eyewitness. *American Psychologist*, 48, 574–6.

Bell, B. E. and Loftus, E. F. (1988). Degree of detail of eyewitness testimony and mock juror judgement. *Journal of Applied Social Psychology*, 18, 1171–92.

Belli, R. F. (1989). Influences on misleading postevent information: misinformation interference and acceptance. *Journal of Experimental Psychology: General*, 118, 72–85.

Bennett, P. (1986). Face recall: a police perspective. *Human Learning*, 5, 197–202.

Bennett, P. and Gibling, F. (1989). Can we trust our eyes? *Policing*, 5, 313–21.

Bennett, R. R. and Greenstein, T. (1975). The police personality: a test of the predispositional model. *Journal of Police Science and Administration*, 3, 439–45.

Bennet, W. S. and Feldman, M. S. (1981). *Reconstructing Reality in the Courtroom*. New Brunswick: Rutgers University Press.

Ben-Shakhar, G. (1989). Non-conventional methods in personnel selection. In P. Herriott (ed.), *Assessment and Selection in Organizations* (pp. 469–85). Chichester: Wiley.

Berliner, L. and Williams, L. M. (1994). Memories of child sexual abuse: a response to Lindsay and Read. *Applied Cognitive Psychology*, 8, 379–87.

Berman, G. L. and Cutler, B. L. (1996). Effects of inconsistencies in eyewitness testimony on mock-juror decision-making. *Journal of Applied Psychology*, 81, 170–7.

Berman, G. L., Narby, D. J. and Cutler, B. L. (1995). Effects of inconsistent statements on mock jurors' evaluations of the eyewitness, perceptions of defendant culpability and verdicts. *Law and Human Behavior*, 19, 79–88.

Bernardin, H. J. and Cooke, D. K. (1993). Validity of an honesty test in predicting theft among convenience store employees. *Academy of Management Journal*, 36, 1097–108.

Bersoff, D. N. and Ogden, D. W. (1987). In the Supreme Court of the United States: *Lockhart v. McCree*. *American Psychologist*, 42, 59–68.

Beswick, D. G. and Hills, M. D. (1972). A survey of ethnocentricism in Australia. *Australian Journal of Psychology*, 24, 153–63.

Bevan, W., Albert, R., Loiseaux, P., Mayfield, P. and Wright, G. (1958). Jury behavior as a function of the prestige of the foreman and the nature of his leadership. *Journal of Public Law*, 7, 419–49.

Bierhoff, H. W., Buck, E. and Klein, R. (1989). Attractiveness and respectability of the offender as factors in the evaluation of criminal cases. In H. Wegener, F. Lösel and J. Haisch (eds), *Criminal Behavior and the Justice System: Psychological Perspectives* (pp. 192–207). New York: Springer-Verlag.

Billig, M. and Milner, D. (1976). A spade is a spade in the eyes of the law. *Psychology Today*, 21, 13–15, 62.

Binet, A. (1896). *Psychology of Postagitation. Annual Report of the Board of Regents of the Smithsonian Institution*, 1894, pp. 555–71. Washington, DC: GPO.

Binet, A. (1900). *La Suggestibilité*. Paris: Doin and Fils.

Binet, A. (1905). La science du témoigue. *Année Psychologique*, 1, 128–38.

Birch, D. J. (1992). Children's evidence. *Criminal Law Review*, 262–76.

Birkett, Lord (1962). *Six Great Advocates*. Harmondsworth, England: Penguin.

Blackburn, R. (1993). *The Psychology of Criminal Conduct: Theory, Research and Practice*. Chichester: Wiley.

Blackburn, R. (1996). What is forensic psychology? *Legal and Criminological Psychology*, 1, 3–16.

Blackstone, W. (1776). *Commentaries*, vol. IV.

Blaney, P. H. (1986). Affect and memory: a review. *Psychological Bulletin*, 99, 229–46.

Block, A., Marx, G., Leo, R. A. et al. (1992). Issues and theories on covert policing. *Crime, Law and Social Change*, 18, 1–217.

Blom-Cooper, L. (1974). The jury on trial. *The Guardian*, 10 June, p. 9.

Blumberg, M. (1994). Police use of deadly force: exploring some key issues. In T. Barker and D. L. Carter (eds), *Police Deviance* (3rd edn) (pp. 201–21). Cincinnati, OH: Anderson Publishing.

Boat, B. W. and Everson, M. D. (1993). The use of anatomical dolls in sexual abuse evaluations: current research and practice. In G. S. Goodman and B. L. Bottoms (eds), 47–69.

Boaz, T. L., Perry, W. P., Raney, G., Fischler, J. R. and Shuman, D. (1991). Detection of guilty knowledge with event-related potentials. *Journal of Applied Psychology*, 76, 788–95.

Bond, R. A. and Lemon, N. E. (1979). Changes in magistrates' attitudes during the first year on the Bench. In D. P. Farrington, K. Hawkins and S. Lloyd-Bostock (eds), 125–42.

Bonto, M. A. and Payne, D. G. (1991). Role of environmental context in eyewitness memory. *American Journal of Psychology*, 104, 117–34.

Boon, J. C. W. and Davies, G. M. (1987). Rumors greatly exaggerated: Allport and Postman's experimental study. *Canadian Journal of Behavioral Science*, 19, 430–40.

Boon, J. and Noon, E. (1994). Changing perspectives in cognitive interviewing. *Psychology, Crime and Law*, 1, 59–69.

Borchard, E. (1932). *Convicting the Innocent: Errors of Criminal Justice*. New Haven: Yale University Press.

Bornstein, B. H. (1994). David, Goliath, and Reverend Bayes: prior beliefs about defendants' status in personal injury cases. *Applied Cognitive Psychology*, 8, 233–58.

Bornstein, B. H. (1995). Memory processes in elderly eyewitnesses; what we know and what we don't know. *Behavioral Sciences and the Law*, 13, 337–48.

Borum, R. and Stock, H. V. (1993). Detection of deception in law enforcement applicants. *Law and Human Behavior*, 17, 157–66.

Bothwell, R. K., Brigham, J. C. and Malpass, R. S. (1989). Cross-racial identification. *Personality and Social Psychology Bulletin*, 15, 19–25.

Bothwell, R. K., Brigham, J. C. and Pigot, M. A. (1987a). An exploratory study of personality differences in eyewitness memory. *Journal of Social Behavior and Personality*, 2, 335–43.

Bothwell, R. K., Deffenbacher, K. A. and Brigham, J. C. (1987b). Correlations of eyewitness accuracy and confidence: optimality hypothesis revisited. *Journal of Applied Psychology*, 72, 691–5.

Botwinick, J. and Shock, N. W. (1972). Age differences in performance decrement with continuous work. *Journal of Gerontology*, 7, 41–6.

Bowen, R. A. (1965). The explanation of judicial voting behavior from sociological characteristics of judges. Unpublished PhD dissertation, Yale University, cited by Grossman, J. B. (1966), Social backgrounds and judicial decision-making. *Harvard Law Review*, 79, 1551–61, at 1561.

Bower, G. (1967). A multicomponent theory of memory trace. In K. W. Spence and J. T. Spence (eds), *The Psychology of Learning and Motivation*, vol. 1.

Bower, G. H. (1981). Mood and memory. *American Psychologist*, 36, 129–48.

Bowers, W. (1995). The capital jury project: rationale, design, and preview of early findings. *Indiana Law Review*, 70, 1043–102.

Boyanowsky, E. O. and Griffiths, C. T. (1982). Weapon and eye contact as instigators or inhibitors of aggressive arousal in police citizen interaction. *Journal of Applied Social Psychology*, 12, 398–407.

Bradley, B. P. and Baddley, A. D. (1990). Emotional factors in forgetting. *Psychological Medicine*, 20, 351–5.

Braithwaite, J. (1989). *Crime, Shame and Reintegration*. New York: Cambridge University Press.

Brandon, R. and Davies, C. (1973). *Wrongful Imprisonment: Mistaken Convictions and their Consequences*. London: George, Allen & Unwin.

Bray, R. M. and Kerr, N. L. (1982). Methodological considerations in the study of the psychology of the courtroom. In R. M. Bray and N. L. Kerr (eds), *The Psychology of the Courtroom* (pp. 287–323). New York: Academic Press.

Brekke, N. J. and Borgida, E. (1988). Expert psychological testimony in rape trials: a social cognitive analysis. *Journal of Personality and Social Psychology*, 55, 372–86.

Brennan, M. (1993). The battle for credibility. *New Law Journal*, 143, 623–6.

Brenner, M., Branscomb, H. H. and Schwartz, G. E. (1979). Psychological stress evaluator – two tests of vocal measure. *Psychophysiology*, 16, 351–7.

Brewer, S. and Wilson, C. (eds) (1995). *Psychology and Policing.* Hillsdale, NJ: Lawrence Erlbaum.

Breyer, H. (1992). The battered woman syndrome and the admissibility of expert testimony. *Criminal Law Bulletin*, 28, 99–115.

Brickner, P. and Bruzansky, S. (1966). Effects of stimulus context and duration on talker identification. *Journal of Acoustical Society of America*, 40, 1441–9.

Brigham, J. C. (1983). Psychological factors in eyewitness identifications. *Journal of Criminal Justice*, 11, 47–56.

Brigham, J. C. (1986). The influence of race on face recognition. In H. D. Ellis, M. A. Jeeves, F. Newcombe and A. Young (eds), *Aspects of Face Processing* (pp. 170–7). Dordrecht, The Netherlands: Martinus Nijhoff.

Brigham, J. C. (1989). Disputed eyewitness identifications: can experts help? *The Champion*, 8, 10–18.

Brigham, J. C. (1990). Target person distinctiveness and attractiveness as moderator variables in the confidence–accuracy relationship in eyewitness identifications. *Basic and Applied Social Psychology*, 11, 101–15.

Brigham, J. C. and Bothwell, R. K. (1983). The ability of prospective jurors to estimate the accuracy of eyewitness identifications. *Law and Human Behavior*, 7, 19–30.

Brigham, J. C., Maass, A., Snyder, L. D. and Spaulding, K. (1982). The accuracy of eyewitness identifications in a field setting. *Journal of Personality and Social Psychology*, 42, 673–81.

Brigham, J. C. and Pfeiffer, J. E. (1994). Evaluating the fairness of line–ups. In D. F. Ross, J. D. Read and M. P. Toglia (eds), *Adult Eyewitness Testimony: Current Trends and Developments* (pp. 201–22). New York: Cambridge University Press.

Brigham, J. C., Ready, D. J. and Spier, S. A. (1990). Standards for evaluating the fairness of photograph line–ups. *Basic and Applied Social Psychology*, 11, 149–63.

Brigham, J. C., Van Verst, M. and Bothwell, R. K. (1986). Accuracy of children's eyewitness identification in a field setting. *Basic and Applied Social Psychology*, 7, 295–306.

Brigham, J. C. and Wolfskiel, M. P. (1983). Opinions of attorneys and law enforcement personnel on the accuracy of eyewitness identifications. *Law and Human Behavior*, 7, 337–49.

British Psychological Society Working Group on the Use of the Polygraph in Criminal Investigation and Personnel Screening (1986). *Bulletin of the British Psychological Society*, 39, 81–94.

Brooks, K. and Siegal, M. (1991). Children as eyewitnesses: memory, suggestibility, and credibility. *Australian Psychologist*, 26, 84–8.

Brown, A. (1988). *Watching the Detectives.* London: Hodder and Stoughton.

Brown, D. and Neal, D. (1988). Show trials: the media and the gang of twelve. In M. Findlay and P. Duff (eds), *The Jury Under Attack* (pp. 126–39). Sydney: Butterworths.

Brown, E. L., Deffenbacher, K. and Sturgill, W. (1977). Memory for faces and the circumstances of the encounter. *Journal of Applied Psychology*, 62, 311–18.

Brown, I. and Hullin, R. (1992). A study of sentencing in the Leeds Magistrates' Courts: the treatment of ethnic minority and white offenders. *British Journal of Criminology*, 32, 41–53.

Brown, J. C., Deffenbacher, K. and Sturgill, W. (1977). Memory for faces and the circumstances of encounter. *Journal of Applied Psychology*, 62, 311–18.

Brown, L. and Willis, A. (1985). Authoritarianism in British police recruits: importation, socialization or myth? *Journal of Occupational Psychology*, 58, 97–108.

Brown, M. R. (1926). *Legal Psychology*. Indianapolis: Bobbs-Merrill.

Brown, R. and Kulik, J. (1977). Flashbulb memories. *Cognition*, 5, 73–93.

Bruce, V. (1988). *Recognising Faces*. London: LEA.

Bruck, M. and Ceci, S. J. (1995). Amicus brief for the case of *New Jersey v. Margaret Kelly Michaels* presented by committee of concerned social scientists. *Psychology, Public Policy, and Law*, 1, 272–322.

Bryan, W. J. (1971). *The Chosen Ones*. New York: Vantage Press.

Buckhout, R. (1974). Eyewitness testimony. *Scientific American*, 231, 23–31.

Buckhout, R. (1976). Expert testimony by psychologists. *Social Action and the Law*, Centre for Responsive Psychology, 3, 41–53.

Budai, P. (1995). Rehabilitation of child sexual assault cases. *Current Issues in Criminal Justice*, 7, 223–30.

Bulkley, J. A. and Horowitz, M. J. (1994). Adults sexually abused as children: legal actions and issues. *Behavioral Sciences and the Law*, 12, 65–87.

Bull, R. (1974). The importance of being beautiful. *New Society*, 30, 412–14.

Bull, R. (1979). The influence of stereotypes on person perception. In D. P. Farrington, K. Hawkins and S. Lloyd-Bostock (eds.), 184–93.

Bull, R. (1981). Voice identification by man and machine: a review of research. In S. Lloyd-Bostock (ed.), *Psychology in Legal Contexts: Applications and Limitations* (pp. 28–42). London: Macmillan.

Bull, R. (1985). Police awareness training. *Policing*, 1, 109–23.

Bull, R. (1992). Obtaining evidence expertly: the reliability of interviews with child witnesses. *Expert Evidence*, 1, 5–12.

Bull, R. (1995a). Interviewing children in legal contexts. In R. Bull and D. Carson (eds), 235–46.

Bull, R. (1995b). Interviewing children with learning disabilities. In R. Bull and D. Carson (eds), 247–60.

Bull, R., Bustin, B., Evans, P. and Gahagan, D. (1983). *Psychology for Police Officers*. Chichester: Wiley.

Bull, R. and Carson, D. (eds) (1995). *Handbook of Psychology in Legal Contexts*. Chichester: Wiley.

Bull, R. and Cherryman, J. (1995). *Helping to Identify Skills in Specialist Investigative Interviewing: Enhancement of Professional Skills*. London: Home Office, Police Department, Police Research Group.

Bull, R. and Clifford, B. R. (1984). Earwitness voice recognition accuracy. In G. L. Wells and E. F. Loftus (eds), 92–123.

Bull, R. and Davies. G. (in press). Child witness research in England. In B. Bottoms and G. Goodman (eds), *International Perspectives on Children's Testimony*. Newbury Park, CA: Sage.

Bull, R. and Green, J. (1980). The relationship between physical appearance and criminality. *Medicine, Science and the Law*, 20, 79–83.

Bull, R. and Horncastle, P. (1986). Metropolitan police recruit training: an independent evaluation. London: Police Foundation.

Bull, R. and Horncastle, P. (1994). Evaluation of police recruit training involving psychology. *Psychology, Crime and Law*, 1, 143–9.

Bull, R., Horncastle, P., Jones, C. and Mason, D. (1987). *Metropolitan Police Recruit Training in 'Policing Skills' (Phase 2): An Independent Evaluation. Executive Summary*. London: Police Foundation.

Bull, R. and Reid, R. (1975). Recall after briefing: television versus face-to-face presentation. *Journal of Occupational Psychology*, 48, 73–8.

Burbeck, E. and Furnham, A. (1985). Police officer selection: a critical review of the literature. *Journal of Police Science and Administration*, 13, 58–69.

Burman, S. and Allen-Meaves, P. (1994). Neglected children of murder: children's witness to parental homicide. *Social Work*, 39, 28–34.

Burtt, M. (1931). *Legal Psychology*. Englewood Cliffs: Prentice-Hall.

Bussey, K. (1995). Allegations of child sexual abuse: accurate and truthful disclosures, false allegations, and false denials. *Current Issues in Criminal Justice*, 7, 176–92.

Bussey, K., Lee, K., and Grimbeek, E. J. (1993). Lies and secrets: implications for children's reporting of sexual abuse. In G. S. Goodman and B. L. Bottoms (eds), 147–68.

Bussey, K., Ross, C. and Lee, K. (1991). The effect of the transgressor's presence on children's truthfulness. Manuscript in preparation.

Buxton, R. (1990a). Challenging and discharging jurors – 1. *Criminal Law Review*, 225–35.

Buxton, R. (1990b). Challenging and discharging jurors – 2. *Criminal Law Review*, 284–91.

Byrne, K. (1988). Distinguishing genuine from fabricated child sexual abuse. In D. Greig, and I. Freckelton (eds), 186–91.

Byrne, K. and Maloney, L. (1991). Brainwashing of children in family law cases: is there a cure? In I. Freckelton., D. D. Greig and M. McMahon (eds), 307–14.

Byrne, P. (1988). Jury reform and the future. In M. Findlay and P. Duff (eds), *The Jury Under Attack*, (pp. 190–208). Sydney: Butterworths.

Byrne, P. (1991). Children as witnesses – legal aspects. In J. Vernon (ed.), 3–18.

Cadzow, J. (1995). Witness to the prosecution. *Good Weekend (The Age)*, 4 February, pp. 14–20.

Camara, W. J. and Schneider, D. L. (1994). Integrity tests: facts and unresolved issues. *American Psychologist*, 49, 112–19.

Cammack, M. (1995). In search of the post-positivist jury. *Indiana Law Journal*, 70 (2), 405–89.

Canter, D. (1992). An evaluation of the 'cumsum' stylistic analysis of confessions. *Expert Evidence*, 1, 93–9.

Canter, D. (1995). Psychology of offender profiling. In R. Bull and D. Carson (eds), 345–456.

Cantor, C., Brodie, J. and McMillen, J. (1991). Firearms victims – who are they? *Medical Journal of Australia*, 155, 442–6.

Carey, S. (1981). The development of face perception. In G. M. Davies, H. Ellis and J. Shepherd (eds), *Perceiving and Remembering Faces* (pp. 9–38). London: Academic Press.

Carlson, H., Thayer, R. E. and Germann, A. C. (1971). Social attitudes and personality differences among members of two kinds of police departments (innovative vs. traditional) and students. *Journal of Criminal Law, Criminology and Police Science*, 62, 564–7.

Carroll, J. S. and Payne, J. W. (1977). Judgements about crime and the criminal: a model and a method for investigating parole decisions. In B. D. Sales (ed.), 191–239.

Carson, D. (1990). *Professionals and the Courts: A Handbook for Expert Witnesses*. Birmingham: Venture Press.

Carson, D. (1992). Beyond the ultimate issue. In F. Lösel et al. (eds), 447–64.

Carson, D. (1995a). Individualism: its importance in law and psychology. In R. Bull and D. Carson (eds), 43–53.

Carson, D. (1995b). Law's premises, methods and values. In R. Bull and D. Carson (eds), 29–40.

Carson, D. (1995c). Regulating the examination of children. *Expert Evidence*, 4, 2–9.

Carson, D. and Bull, R. (1995a). Psychology in legal contexts: idealism and realism. In R. Bull and D. Carson (eds), 3–11.

Carson, D. and Bull, R. (1995b). Psychology and law: future directions. In R. Bull and D. Carson (eds), 645–50.

Carter, T. and Cleland, D. (1979). A neo-Marxian critique, formulation and test of juvenile dispositions as a function of social class. *Social Problems*, 27, 96–108.

Casburn, M. (1979). *Girls will be Girls – Sexism and Juvenile Justice in a London Borough*. London: Women's Research and Resources Centre.

Cashmore, J. (1990). The use of video technology for child witnesses. *Monash Law Review*, 16, 228–50.

Cashmore, J. (1991). Problems and solutions in lawyer–child communication. *Criminal Law Journal*, 193–202.

Cashmore, J. (1992). The use of closed-circuit television for child witnesses in the ACT. Sydney: Australian Law Reform Commission.

Casper, J. D. and Benedict, K. M. (1993). The influence of outcome information and attitudes on juror decision-making in search and seizure cases. In R. Hastie (ed.), *Inside the Juror: The Psychology of Juror Decision-Making* (pp. 65–83). New York: Cambridge University Press.

Casper, J. D., Benedict, K. M. and Perry, J. L. (1989). Juror decision-making, attitudes and the hindsight bias. *Law and Human Behavior*, 13, 291–310.

Cassell, W. S. and Bjorklund, D. E. (1995). Developmental patterns of eyewitness memory and suggestibility: an ecologically-based short-term longitudinal study. *Law and Human Behavior*, 19, 507–32.

Cattermole, G. A. (1984). The psychologist as an expert witness. In M. Nixon (ed.), *Issues In Psychological Practice* (pp. 121–32). Melbourne: Longman Cheshire.

Cavoukian, A. and Heslegrave, R. J. (1979). The admissibility of polygraph evidence in court. Some empirical findings. *Law and Human Behavior*, 4, 117–31.

Ceci, S. J. and Bruck, M. (1993). Suggestibility of the child witness: a historical review and a synthesis. *Psychological Bulletin*, 113, 403–39.

Ceci, S. J., Bruck, M. and Rosenthal, R. (1995). Children's allegations of sexual abuse: forensic and scientific issues: a reply to commentators. *Psychology, Public Policy, and Law*, 1, 494–520.

Ceci, S. J. and Leichtman, M. (March 1992). Group distortion effects in preschoolers' reports. In D. Peters (chair), *Issues Related to the Witness Child*. Symposium presented at the American Psychology and Law Biennial Meeting, San Diego, CA.

Ceci, S. J. and Loftus, E. F. (1994). 'Memory work': a royal road to false memories? *Applied Cognitive Psychology*, 8, 351–64.

Cecil, J. S., Lind, E. A. and Bermant, G. (1987). *Jury Service in Lengthy Jury Trials*. Washington, DC: Federal Judicial Center.

Chahal, K. and Cassidy, T. (1995). Deception and its detection in children: a study of adult accuracy. *Psychology, Crime and Law*, 1, 237–45.

Chaiken, S. (1979). Communicator physical attractiveness and persuasion. *Journal of Personality and Social Psychology*, 37, 1387–97.

Chaiken, S., Liberman, A. and Eagly, A. H. (1989). Heuristic and systematic processing within and beyond the persuasion context. In J. S. Uleman and J. A. Bargh (eds), *Unintended Thought* (pp. 212–52). New York: Guilford.

Chambliss, W. J. and Seidman, R. B. (1971). *Law, Order, and Power*. Reading, Mass: Addison-Wesley.

Champagne, A., Shuman, D. and Whitaker, E. (1991). An empirical examination of the use of expert witnesses in American courts. *Jurimetrics Journal*, 31, 375–92.

Chance, J., Goldstein, A. and McBride, L. (1975). Differential experience and recognition memory for faces. *Journal Social Psychology*, 97, 243–53.

Chance, J., Turner, A. L. and Goldstein, A. G. (1982). Development of differential recognition of own- and other-race faces. *Journal of Psychology*, 112, 29–37.

Chappel, D., Grabosky, P., Wilson, P. and Mukherjee, S. (1988). Firearms and Violence in Australia. Report No. 10, Trends and Issues in Justice and Criminal Justice series. Canberra: Australian Institute of Criminology.

Chen, Y. Y. and Geiselman, R. E. (1993). Effects of ethnic stereotyping and ethnically-related cognitive biases on eyewitness recollections of height. *American Journal of Forensic Psychology*, 11, 1–7.

Chiricos, T. G. and Waldo, G. P. (1975). Socio-economic status and criminal sentencing: an empirical assessment of a conflict proposition. *American Sociological Review*, 40, 753–72.

Chisholm, R. and Nettheim, G. (1992). *Understanding Law: An Introduction to Australia's Legal System*. Sydney: Butterworths.

Christiansen, R. E., Sweeney, J. D., and Ochalek, K. (1983). Influencing eyewitness descriptions. *Law and Human Behavior*, 7, 59–65.

Christianson, S. A. (1984). The relationship between induced emotional arousal and amnesia. *Scandinavian Journal of Psychology*, 25, 147–60.

Christianson, S. A. (1989). Flashbulb memories: special, but not so special. *Memory and Cognition*, 17, 435–43.

Christianson, S. A. (1992). Emotional stress and eyewitness memory: a critical review. *Psychological Bulletin*, 112, 284–309.

Christianson, S. A., Goodman, J. and Loftus, E. F. (1992). Eyewitness memory for stressful events: methodological quandaries and ethical dilemmas. In S. A. Christianson (ed.), *The Handbook of Emotion and Memory: Research and Theory* (pp. 217–41). Hillsdale, NJ: Lawrence Erlbaum.

Christianson, S. A. and Hubinette, B. (1993). Hands up! A study of witnesses' emotional reactions and memories associated with bank robberies. *Applied Cognitive Psychology*, 7, 365–79.

Clark, N. K., Stephenson, G. M. and Rutter, D. R. (1986). Memory for a complex social discourse: the analysis and prediction of individual and group recall. *Journal of Memory and Language*, 25, 295–313.

Clarke, S. H. and Koch, G. G. (1976). The influence of income and other factors on whether criminal defendants go to prison. *Law and Society Review*, 11, 57–92.

Clifford, B. R. (1978). A critique of eyewitness research. In M. M. Gruneberg, P. E. Morris and R. W. Sykes (eds), *Practical Aspects of Memory*. New York: Academic Press.

Clifford, B. R. (1979). Eyewitness testimony: the bridging of a credibility gap. In D. P. Farrington, K. Hawkins and S. Lloyd-Bostock (eds), 167–83.

Clifford, B. R. (1980). Voice identification by human listeners: on earwitness reliability. *Law and Human Behavior*, 4, 373–94.

Clifford, B. R. (1981). Towards a more realistic appraisal of the psychology of testimony. In S. Lloyd-Bostock (ed.), 19–27.

Clifford, B. R. (1983). Memory for voices: the feasibility and quality of earwitness evidence. In S. M. A. Lloyd-Bostock and B. R. Clifford (eds), *Evaluating Witness Evidence* (pp. 189–218). Chichester: Wiley.

Clifford, B. R. (1993). Witnessing: a comparison of adults and children. *Issues in Criminological and Legal Psychology*, No. 20, 15–21.

Clifford, B. R. (1995). Psychology's premises, methods and values. In R. Bull and D. Carson (eds), 13–27.

Clifford, B. R. and Bull, R. (1978). *The Psychology of Person Identification*. London: Routledge & Kegan Paul.

Clifford, B. R., Bull, R. and Rathborn, H. (1980). Voice identification. The final report to the Home Office. (Res. 741/1/1). 207 pages, Department of Psychology, North-East London Polytechnic.

Clifford, B. R. and Davies, G. M. (1989). Procedures for obtaining identification evidence. In D. C. Raskin (ed.), 47–95.

Clifford, B. R. and Denot, H. (1982). Visual and verbal testimony and identification under conditions of stress. Unpublished manuscript, North East London Polytechnic, London, England.

Clifford, B. R. and George, R. (1995). A field evaluation of training in three methods of witness/victim investigative interviewing. *Psychology, Crime and Law*, 2, 1–18.

Clifford, B. R. and Hollin, C. R. (1981). Effects of the type of incident and the number of perpetrators on eyewitness memory. *Journal of Applied Psychology*, 66, 364–70.

Clifford, B. R., Rathborn, H. and Bull, R. (1981). The effects of delay on voice recognition accuracy. *Law and Human Behavior*, 5, 201–8.

Clifford, B. R. and Richards, G. (1977). Comparison of recall by policemen and civilians under conditions of long and short durations of exposure. *Perceptual Motor Skills*, 45, 39–45.

Clifford, B. R. and Scott, J. (1978). Individual and situational factors in eyewitness memory. *Journal of Applied Psychology*, 63, 352–9.

Cockburn, J. S. and Green, T. A. (eds) (1988). *Twelve Good Men and True: The Criminal Trial Jury in England, 1220–1800*. New Jersey: Princeton University Press.

Cody, M. J., Marston, P. J. and Foster, M. (1984). Deception: paralinguistic and verbal leakage. In R. N. Bostrom (ed.), *Communication Yearbook 8* (pp. 464–90). Beverly Hills, CA: Sage.

Coffin, F. M. (1994). *On Appeal: Courts, Lawyering, and Judging*. New York: W.W. Norton & Co.

Coghlan, A., Kiernan, V. and Mullins, J. (1995). Nowhere to hide. *Technospy* (*New Scientist* Supplement), 4 November, pp. 4–7.

Cohler, B. J. (1994). Memory recovery and the use of the past: a commentary on Lindsay and Read from psychoanalytic perspectives. *Applied Cognitive Psychology*, 8, 365–78.

Colgrove, F. W. (1899). Individual memories. *American Journal of Psychology*, 10, 228–55.

Colman, A. M. and Gorman, L. P. (1982). Conservatism, dogmatism, and authoritarianism in British police officers. *Sociology*, 16, 1–11.

Colman, A. M. and Mackay, R. D. (1993). Legal issues surrounding the admissibility of expert psychological and psychiatric testimony. *Issues in Criminological and Legal Psychology*, No. 20, 46–50.

Colman, A. M. and Mackay, R. D. (1995). Psychological evidence in court: legal developments in England and the United States. *Psychology, Crime and Law*, 1, 261–8.

Comish, S. E. (1987). Recognition of facial stimuli following an intervening task involving the identi-kit. *Journal of Applied Psychology*, 72, 488–91.

Committee on Ethical Guidelines for Forensic Psychologists (1991). Specialty guidelines for forensic psychologists. *Law and Human Behavior*, 15, 655–65.

Cook, P. J. (1983). The influence of gun availability on violent crime patterns. In M. Tonry and N. Morris (eds), *Crime and Justice: An Annual Review of Research*, vol. 2, 211–68. Chicago: University of Chicago Press.

Cooke, P. K., Judge (1987). The practical problems of the sentencer. In D. C. Pennington and S. M. A. Lloyd-Bostock (eds), 57–60.

Cooney, M. (1994). Evidence as partisanship. *Law and Society Review*, 28, 833–57.

Cooper, C. L., Davidson, M. J. and Robinson, P. (1982). Stress in the police service. *Journal of Occupational Medicine*, 24, 30–6.

Corbett, C. (1987). Magistrates' and court clerks' sentencing behaviour: an experimental study. In D. C. Pennington and S. M. A. Lloyd-Bostock (eds), 204–16.

Cornish, W. R. (1968). *The Jury*. London: Penguin.

Corso, J. F. (1981). *Aging Sensory Systems and Perception*. New York: Praeger.

Costanzo, S. and Costanzo, M. (1994). Life or death decisions: an analysis of capital jury decision-making under the special issues sentencing framework. *Law and Human Behavior*, 18, 151–70.

Cox, T. C. and White, M. F. (1988). Traffic citations and student attitudes toward the police: an examination of selected interaction dynamics. *Journal of Police Science and Administration*, 16, 105–21.

Coyle, M. (1995). Death juries get it wrong – study: survey reports they mishear judges. *National Law Journal*, 13 March, 17, A6.

Craik, F. I. M. (1977). Age differences in human memory. In J. E. Birren and K. W. Schaie (eds), *Handbook of the Psychology of Aging*. New York: Van Nostrand Reinhold.

Crank, J. P., Regoli, B., Hewitt, J. D. and Culbertson, R. G. (1993). An assessment of work stress among police executives. *Journal of Criminal Justice*, 21, 313–24.

Crombag, H. F. M. (1994). Law as a branch of applied psychology. *Psychology, Crime and Law*, 1, 1–9.

Cross, J., Cross, J. and Daly, J. (1971). Sex, race, age and beauty as factors in recognition of faces. *Perception and Psychophysics*, 10, 393–6.

Crow, I. and Cove, J. (1984). Ethnic minorities and the courts. *Criminal Law Review*, 413–17.

Crowley, M. J., O'Callaghan, M. G. and Ball, P. J. (1994). The juridical impact of psychological expert testimony in a simulated child sexual abuse trial. *Law and Human Behavior*, 18, 89–105.

Cunneen, C. (1990). Aboriginal–police relations in Redfern: with special reference to the 'police raid' of 8 February 1990 (Report commissioned by the National Inquiry into Racist Violence).

Cunningham, J. L. and Brightmann, W. G. (1986). A re-examination of William Stern's classic eyewitness research. *Perceptual and Motor Skills*, 63, 565–6.

Curran, P. (1991). Discussions in the judge's private room. *Criminal Law Review*, 79–86.

Cutler, B. L., Berman, G. L., Penrod, S. and Fisher, R. P. (1994). Conceptual, practical, and empirical issues associated with eyewitness identification test media. In D. F. Ross et al. (eds), 163–81.

Cutler, B. L. and Fisher, R. P. (1993). Identifying Ivan: some thoughts on the application of psychological research. *Expert Evidence*, 1, 119–26.

Cutler, B. L. and Penrod, S. D. (1988). Improving the reliability of eyewitness identification: line-up construction and presentation. *Journal of Applied Psychology*, 73, 281–90.

Cutler, B. L. and Penrod, S. D. (1995a). *Mistaken Identification: The Eyewitness, Psychology, and the Law*. New York: Cambridge University Press.

Cutler, B. L. and Penrod, S. D. (1995b). Assessing the accuracy of eyewitness identifications. In R. Bull and D. Carson (eds), 193–213.

Cutler, B. L., Penrod, S. D. and Dexter, H. R. (1989). The eyewitness, the expert psychologist, and the jury. *Law and Human Behavior*, 13, 311–32.

Cutler, B. L., Penrod, S. D. and Dexter, H. R. (1990). Juror sensitivity to eyewitness evidence. *Law and Human Behavior*, 14, 185–91.

Cutler, B. L., Penrod, S. D. and Martens, T. K. (1987). The reliability of eyewitness identification: the role of system and estimator variables. *Law and Human Behavior*, 11, 233–58.

Cutler, B. L., Penrod, S. D. and Stuve, T. E. (1988). Juror decision-making in eyewitness identification cases. *Law and Human Behavior*, 12, 41–56.

Cutting, J. E. and Proffitt, D. R. (1981). Gait perception as an example of how we may perceive events. In R. Walk and H. I. Pick (eds), *Intersensory Perceptions and Sensory Integration* (pp. 249–73). New York: Plenum Press.

Dahmen-Zimmer, K. and Kraus, M. (1992). 'Phenomenal causality' in eyewitness report. In F. Lösel et al. (eds), 321–7.

Daly, K. (1987). Structure and practice of familial-based justice in a criminal court. *Law and Society Review*, 21, 267–90.

Darbyshire, P. (1980). The role of the magistrates' clerk in summary proceedings. *Justice of the Peace*, 144, 186–8, 201–3, 219–21.

Darbyshire, P. (1991). The lamp that shows that freedom lives – is it worth the candle? *Criminal Law Review*, 740–52.

Darnborough, M. (1977). The use of facial reconstruction methods by the police. Paper presented at the Annual Conference of the British Psychological Society, Exeter, Devon, England.

Davenport, G. C. (1992). *Essential Psychology*. London: Collins Educational.

Davies, G. M. (1981). Face recall systems. In G. M. Davies, H. D. Ellis and J. W. Shepherd (eds), *Perceiving and Remembering Faces* (pp. 227–50). London: Academic Press.

Davies, G. M. (1983). Forensic free recall: The role of visual and verbal information. In S. M. A. Lloyd-Bostock and B. R. Clifford (eds), 103–23.

Davies, G. M. (1986a). Context effects on episodic memory: a review. *Cahiers de Psychologie Cognitive*, 6, 157–74.

Davies, G. M. (1986b). The recall and reconstruction of faces: implications for theory and practice. In H. D. Ellis, M. A. Jeeves, F. Newcomb and A. W. Young (eds), *Aspects of Face Processing* (pp. 388–97). Dodrecht: Martinus Nijhoff.

Davies, G. M. (1989). The applicability of facial memory research. In A. W. Young and H. D. Ellis (eds), 557–62.

Davies, G. M. (1991). Children on trial? Psychology, videotechnology and the law. *Howard Journal*, 30, 177–91.

Davies, G. M. (1992). Influencing public policy on eyewitnessing: problems and possibilities. In F. Lösel et al. (eds), 265–74.

Davies, G. M. (1993a). Witnessing events. In G. M. Davies and R. H. Logie (eds), *Memory in Everyday Life* (pp. 367–401). Amsterdam: Elsevier Science Publishers.

Davies, G. M. (1993b). Children's identification evidence. In S. L. Sporer, R. S. Malpass and G. Köhnken (eds), *Psychological Issues in Eyewitness Identification* (pp. 223–58). New York: Lawrence Erlbaum.

Davies, G. M. (1994). Children's testimony: research findings and policy implications. *Psychology, Crime and Law*, 1, 175–80.

Davies, G. M. (1995). Evidence: psychological perspective. In R. Bull and D. Carson (eds), 179–91.

Davies, G. M. (in press). Mistaken identification: where law meets psychology head on. *Howard Journal*.

Davies, G. M. and Noon, E. (1991). An evaluation of the live link for child witnesses. London: Home Office.

Davies, G. M. and Noon, E. (1993). Video links: their impact on child witness trials. *Issues in Criminological and Legal Psychology*, No. 20, 22–6.

Davies, G. M., Lloyd-Bostock, S., McMurray, M. and Wilson, C. (eds) (1996). *Psychology, Law and Criminal Justice: International Developments in Research and Practice*. New York: de Gruyter.

Davies, G. M., Stevenson-Robb, Y. and Flin, R. (1988). Tales out of school: children's memory for an unexpected event. In M. Gruneberg, P. E. Morris and R. N. Sykes (eds), *Practical Aspects of Memory: Current Research and Theory*. Chichester: Wiley.

Davies, G., Wilson, C., Mitchell, R. and Milsom, J. (1995). *Videotaping Children's Evidence: An Evaluation*. London: Home Office.

Davies, M. (1994). *Asking the Law Question*. Sydney: Law Book Company.

Davis, J. H., Stasson, M., Ono, K. and Zimmerman, S. (1988). Effects of straw polls on group decision-making: sequential voting pattern, timing and local majorities. *Journal of Personality and Social Psychology*, 55, 918–26.

Davison, G. C. and Neale, J. M. (1974). *Abnormal Psychology: An Experimental Approach*. Chichester: Wiley.

Davison, S. E. and Forshaw, D. M. (1993). Retracted confessions: through opiate withdrawal to a new conceptual framework. *Medicine, Science and the Law*, 33 (4), 285–90.

Deffenbacher, K. A. (1983). The influence of arousal on reliability of testimony. In S. M. A. Lloyd-Bostock and B. R. Clifford (eds), 235–51.

Deffenbacher, K. A. (1989). Forensic facial memory: time is of the essence. In A. W. Young and H. D. Ellis (eds), 563–70.

Deffenbacher, K. A. and Loftus, E. F. (1982). Do jurors share a common understanding concerning eyewitness behavior? *Law and Human Behavior*, 6, 15–30.

DeLoache, J. S. (1995). The use of dolls in interviewing young children. In M. S. Zaragoza, J. R. Graham, G. C. N. Hall, R. Hirschman and Y. S. Ben-Porath (eds), 160–78.

De Luca, J. R. (ed.) (1981). *Fourth Special Report to the US Congress on Alcohol and Health*. Rockville, Maryland: National Institute of Alcohol and Alcoholism.

Dent, H. (1988). *Children as Witnesses.* In H. Dent and R. Flin (eds), 1.1–1.17.

Dent, H. and Flin, R. (eds) (1992). *Children as Witnesses.* Seminar papers, Leo Cussen Institute and Law Institute of Victoria, Melbourne, Australia. Chichester: Wiley.

Dent, H. R. (1977). Stress as a factor influencing person recognition in identification parades. *Bulletin of the British Psychological Society,* 30, 339–40.

Deosoran, R. (1993). The social psychology of selecting jury forepersons. *British Journal of Psychology,* 33, 70–80.

Department of Defense, US (1984). *The Accuracy and Utility of Polygraph Testing.* Washington, DC.

DePaulo, B. M., Stone, J. I. and Lassiter, G. D. (1985). Deceiving and detecting deceit. In B. R. Schlenker (ed.), *The Self in Social Life* (pp. 323–70). New York: McGraw Hill.

DePaulo, B. M., Zuckerman, M. and Rosenthal, R. (1980). Humans as lie detectors. *Journal of Communication,* 30, 129–39.

Dessoir, M. (1893). The psychology of legerdemain. *The Open Court,* 7, 3599–602, 3608–11, 3616–19, 3633–4.

Devlin, K. (1971). Sentencing offenders in magistrates' courts: a study of legal factors affecting the sentencing process. Unpublished manuscript, School of Social Sciences, Brunel University, England.

Devlin, P. A., Sir (1956). *Trial by Jury.* Hamlyn Lecture Series. London: Stevens.

Devlin, P. A., Lord (1974). Trial by jury. *The Guardian,* 10 June, p. 9.

Devlin, P. A., Lord (1976). *Report to the Secretary of State for the Home Department of the Departmental Committee on Evidence on Identification in Criminal Cases.* London: HMSO.

Diamond, R. and Carey, S. (1977). Developmental changes in the representation of faces. *Journal of Experimental Child Psychology,* 23, 1–22.

Diamond, S. S. (1992). Foreword. In D. K. Kagehiro, and W. S. Laufer (eds), v–ix.

Diamond, S. S. and Casper, J. D. (1992). Blindfolding the jury to verdict consequences: damages, experts and the civil jury. *Law and Society Review,* 26, 513–63.

Dietze, P. M. and Thomson, D. M. (1993). Mental reinstatement of context: a technique for interviewing child witnesses. *Applied Cognitive Psychology,* 7, 97–108.

Diges, M., Rubio, M. E. and Rodriguez, M. C. (1992). Eyewitness memory and time of day. In F. Lösel et al. (eds), 317–20.

Dillehay, R. C. and Nietzel, M. T. (1985). Juror experience and jury verdicts. *Law and Human Behavior,* 9, 179–91.

Dion, K. E., Berscheld, E. and Walster, E. (1972). What is beautiful is good. *Journal of Personality and Social Psychology,* 24, 285–90.

Doob, A. N. (1977). Canadian jurors' view of the criminal jury trial. Law Reform Commission of Canada, *Studies on the Jury,* 29, 60–4.

Doob, A. N. (1995). The United States Sentencing Commission Guidelines: If you don't know where you are going you might not get there. In C. Clarkson and R. Morgan (eds), *The Politics of Sentencing Reform* (pp. 199–250). Oxford: Clarendon Press.

Doob, A. N. and Kirschenbaum, H. M. (1973). Bias in police line-ups – partial remembering. *Journal of Police Science and Administration,* 1, 287–93.

Doris, J., Mazur, R. and Thomas, M. (1995). Training in child protective services: a commentary on the amicus brief of Bruck and Ceci (1993/1995). *Psychology, Public Policy, and Law,* 1, 479–93.

Doris, J. (ed.) (1990). *The Suggestibility of Children's Recollections: Implications for Eyewitness Testimony.* Washington, DC: American Psychological Association.

Douglas, R. (1988). Tolerated contests: plea and sentence in the Victorian Magistrates' Courts. *Journal of Criminal Justice,* 16, 269–90.

Douglas, R. (1989). Does the magistrate matter? Sentencers and sentence in the Victorian Magistrates' Courts. *Australian and New Zealand Journal of Criminology,* 22, 40–59.

Douglas, R. (1992). A different kind of justice: trial and punishment in the rural Magistrates' Courts. *Law in Context,* 10, 63–90.

Douglas, R. (1994). Social class and court outcomes: making sense of the empirical literature. *Law in Context,* 12, 97–129.

Douglas, R., Weber, T. and Braybrook, E. K. (1980). *Guilty, Your Worship: A Study of Victoria's Magistrates' Courts.* Occasional Monograph No. 1, Legal Studies Department, La Trobe University, Melbourne, Australia.

Doyle, J. M. (1989). Legal issues in eyewitness evidence. In D. C. Raskin (ed.), 125–47.

Driscoll, L. N. (1994). A validity assessment of written statements from suspects in criminal investigations using the scan technique. *Police Studies,* vol. XVII, 77–87.

Dristas, W. J. and Hamilton, V. L. (1977). Evidence about evidence: effect of presupposition, item salience, stress, and perceived set on accident recall. Unpublished manuscript, University of Michigan.

Du Cann, R. (1964). *The Art of the Advocate.* Harmondsworth, England: Penguin.

Duff, P. and Findley, M. (1988). The politics of jury reform. In M. Findlay and P. Duff (eds), 209–26.

Duncan, K. L. (1996). 'Lies, damned lies, and statistics?' Psychological syndrome evidence in the courtroom after *Daubert. Indiana Law Journal,* 7, 753–71.

Dunstan, S., Paulin, J. and Atkinson, K. A. (1995). *Trial by Peers? The Composition of New Zealand Juries.* Wellington, New Zealand: Department of Justice.

Dunning, D. and Stern, L. (1992). Examining the generality of eyewitness hypermnesia: a close look at time delay and question type. *Applied Cognitive Psychology,* 6, 643–57.

Dunning, D. and Stern, L. B. (1994). Distinguishing accurate from inaccurate eyewitness identifications via inquiries about decision process. *Journal of Personality and Social Psychology,* 67, 818–35.

Durham III, A. M. (1989). Judgements of appropriate punishment: the effect of question type. *Journal of Criminal Justice,* 17, 75–85.

Durso, F. T., Reardon, R. and Jolly, E. J. (1985). Self-nonself segregation and reality monitoring. *Journal of Personality and Social Psychology,* 48, 447–55.

Dutton, D. G. (1986). The public and the police: training implications of the demand for a new model police officer. In J. C. Yuille (ed.), 141–57.

Easterbrook, J. A. (1959). The effects of emotion on the utilization and organization of behavior. *Psychological Review,* 66, 183–201.

Ebbinghaus, H. (1885). Uber das Gedachtnis. Leipzig. Dunker. H. Ruyer and C. E. Bussenins (translation), *Memory.* Teachers College Press, New York, 1913.

Edmondson, J. (1995). The psychologist as expert witness. *Forensic Update,* No. 42, 28–33.

Edwards, D. and Middleton, D. (1986). Joint remembering: constructing an account of shared experience through conversation discourse. *Discourse Processes,* 9, 423–59.

Efran, L. (1974). The effects of physical appearance on the judgement of guilt, interpersonal attraction and severity of recommended punishment in a simulated jury task. *Journal of Research in Personality*, 8, 44–54.

Egeth, H. E. (1993). What do we know about eyewitness identification? *American Psychologist*, 48, 577–80.

Eggleston, E. (1976). *Fear, Favour or Affection: Aborigines and the Criminal Law in Victoria, South Australia and Western Australia.* Canberra: Australian National University.

Ekman, P. (1985). *Telling Lies: Clues to Deceit in the Marketplace, Politics and Marriage.* New York: Norton & Co.

Ekman, P. and Friesen, W. V. (1972). Hand movements and deception. *Journal of Communication*, 22, 353–74.

Ekman, P. and O'Sullivan, M. (1989). Hazards in detecting deceit. In D. C. Raskin (ed.), 297–332.

Ekman, P. and O'Sullivan, M. (1991). Who can catch a liar? *American Psychologist*, 46, 913–20.

Elaad, E. (1990). Detection of guilty knowledge in real-life criminal investigations. *Journal of Applied Psychology*, 75, 521–9.

Elaad, E. and Kleiner, M. (1990). Effects of polygraph chart interpreter experience on psychophysiological detection of deception. *Journal of Police Science and Administration*, 17, 115–23.

Elion, V. H. and Megargee, E. I. (1979). Racial identity, length of incarceration, and parole decision-making. *Journal of Research in Crime and Delinquency*, 16, 232–45.

Elliott, R. (1991). On the alleged prosecution-proneness of death-qualified juries and jurors. In P. J. Suedfeld and P. E. Terlock (eds), *Psychology and Social Policy* (pp. 255–65). New York: Hemisphere Publishing Corporation.

Elliott, R. (1993). Expert testimony about eyewitness identification: a critique. *Law and Human Behavior*, 17, 423–37.

Elliott, R., Farrington, B. and Mannheim, H. (1988). Eyewitness credible and discredible. *Journal of Applied Social Psychology*, 18, 1411–22.

Ellis, H. D. (1975). Recognising faces. *British Journal of Psychology*, 66, 409–26.

Ellis, H. C. and Ashbrook, P. W. (1988). Resource allocation model of the effects of depressed mood states on memory. In K. Fielder and J. Forgas (eds), *Affect, Cognition and Social Behavior.* Toronto: Hogrefe.

Ellis, H. C. and Ashbrook, P. W. (1991). The 'state' of mood and memory research. In D. Kuiken (ed.), *Mood and Memory* (pp. 1–21). California: Sage Publications.

Ellis, H. D. (1984). Practical aspects in face memory. In G. L. Wells and E. F. Loftus (eds), 2–37.

Ellis, H. D., Shepherd, J. W., Flin, R. H. and Davies, G. M. (1989). Identification from a computer-driven retrieval system compared with a traditional mug-shot album search. *Ergonomics*, 32, 167–77.

Ellsworth, P. C. (1993). Some steps between attitudes and verdicts. In R. Hastie (ed.), 42–64.

Epstein, S. (1994). Integration of the cognitive and the psychodynamic unconscious. *American Psychologist*, 49, 709–24.

Ericson, R. and Baranek, P. M. (1982). *The Ordering of Justice: A Study of Accused Persons as Dependents in the Criminal Process.* Toronto: University of Toronto Press.

Esplin, P. W., Houed, T. and Raskin, D. C. (1988). Application of statement validity assessment. Paper presented at the meeting of the NATO Advanced Study Institute on Credibility Assessment, Maratea, Italy.

Estes, W. K. (1955). Statistical theory of spontaneous recovery and regression. *Psychological Review*, 62, 145–54.

Evans, B. J. (1994). Introduction. In B. J. Evans and R. O. Stanley (eds), 1–5.

Evans, B. J., Coman, G. J. and Stanley, R. O. (1992). The police personality: type A behavior and trait anxiety. *Journal of Criminal Justice*, 20, 429–41.

Evans, B. J. and Stanley, R. O. (eds) (1994). *Hypnosis and the Law: Principles and Practice. Australian Journal of Clinical and Experimental Hypnosis* (special issue). Melbourne.

Evans, G. and Webb, M. (1991). High profile – but not that high profile: interviewing of young persons. *Issues in Criminological and Legal Psychology*, 18, 37–46.

Evans, K. (1995). *Advocacy in Court: A Beginner's Guide* (2nd edn). London: Blackstone Press.

Everson, G. (1919). The human element in justice. *Journal of Criminal Law and Criminology*, 10, 90–9.

Ewart, B. and Pennington, D. C. (1987). An attributional approach to explaining sentencing disparity. In D. C. Pennington and S. M. A. Lloyd-Bostock (eds), 181–92.

Exline, R. E., Thibault, J., Hickey, C. B. and Gumpert, P. (1970). Visual interaction in relation to Machiavellianism and an unethical act. In R. Christie and F. L. Geis (eds), *Studies in Machiavellianism* (pp. 53–75). New York: Academic Press.

Eysenck, H. J. (1977). *Crime and Personality* (3rd edn). London: Paladin.

Eysenck, H. J. and Eysenck, S. B. (1975). *Manual of the Eysenck Personality Questionnaire*. Sevenoaks, Kent: Hodder & Stoughton.

Eysenck, M. (1982). *Attention and Arousal. Cognition and Performance*. Berlin: Springer-Verlag.

Fanselow, M. (1975). How to bias an eyewitness. *Social Action and the Law*, 2, 3–4.

Farewell, L. A. and Donchin, E. (1991). The truth will out: interrogative polygraphy ('lie detection') with event-related potentials. *Psychophysiology*, 28, 531–47.

Farrington, D. P. (1978). The effectiveness of sentences. *Justice of the Peace*, 4 February, 68–71.

Farrington, D. P., Hawkins, K. and Lloyd-Bostock, S. M. (eds) (1979a). *Psychology, Law and Legal Processes*. London: Macmillan.

Farrington, D. P., Hawkins, K. and Lloyd-Bostock, S. M. (1979b). Introduction: doing psycholegal research. In D. P. Farrington et al. (eds), xiii–xvii.

Farrington, D. P. and Lambert, S. (1993). Predicting violence and burglary offenders from victims, witness and offence data. Paper presented at the First Netherlands Institute for the Study of Criminality and Law Enforcement Workshop on Criminality and Law Enforcement, The Hague, Netherlands, October.

Farrington, D. P. and Morris, A. (1983). Sex, sentencing and reconviction. *British Journal of Criminology*, 23, 229–48.

Faust, D. and Ziskin, J. (1988). The expert witness in psychology and psychiatry. *Science*, 241, 31–5.

Feeley, M. M. (1979). *The Process is the Punishment: Handling Cases in a Lower Criminal Court*. New York: Russell Sage Foundation.

Feldman, P. (1993). *The Psychology of Crime.* New York: Cambridge University Press.

Feldman, T. and Bell, R. A. (1991). Crisis debriefing of jury after a murder trial. *Hospital and Community Psychiatry,* 42, 79–81.

Felson, R. B. (1981). Physical attractiveness and perceptions of deviance. *Journal of Social Psychology,* 114, 85–9.

Findlay, M. and Duff, P. (eds) (1988). The Jury Under Attack. Sydney: Butterworths.

Finegan, J. (1978). The effects of non-legal factors on the severity of sentence in traffic court. Unpublished MA thesis, University of Toronto.

Fischer, K. and Bullock, D. (1984). Cognitive development in school-age children: conclusions and new directions. In W. Collins (ed.), *Development During Middle Childhood: The Years from Six to Twelve* (pp. 70–146). Washington, DC: National Academy Press.

Fisher, C. B. and Fyrberg, D. (1994). Participant partners: college students weigh the costs and benefits of deceptive research. *American Psychologist,* 49, 417–27.

Fisher, R., McCauley, M. R. and Geiselman, R. E. (1994). Improving eyewitness testimony with the cognitive interview. In D. F. Ross et al. (eds), 245–69.

Fisher, R. P. and Geiselman, R. E. (1992). *Memory Enhancing Techniques for Investigative Interviewing: The Cognitive Interview.* Springfield, IL: Charles Thomas.

Fisher, R. P., Geiselman, R. E., Raymond, D. S., Jurkevitch, L. M. and Warhaftig, M. L. (1987). Enhancing enhanced eyewitness memory: refining the cognitive interview. *Journal of Police Science and Administration,* 15, 291–7.

Fitzgerald, M. (1994). Ethnic minorities and the criminal justice system. *Research Bulletin,* No. 35, 49–50.

Fitzgerald, R. and Ellsworth, P. C. (1984). Due process vs. crime control: death qualification and jury attitudes. *Law and Human Behavior,* 8, 31–51.

Fitzmaurice, C. and Pease, K. (1986). *The Psychology of Judicial Sentencing.* Manchester: Manchester University Press.

Fitzpatrick, K. M. and Boldizar, J. P. (1993). The prevalence and consequences of exposure to violence among African American Youth. *Journal of the American Academy of Child and Adolescent Psychiatry,* 32, 424–30.

Fivush, R. (1993). Developmental perspectives on autobiographical recall. In G. S. Goodman and B. L. Bottoms (eds), 1–24.

Fivush, R., Gray, J. T. and Fromhoff, F. A. (1987). Two-year-olds talk about the past. *Cognitive Development,* 2, 393–410.

Fivush, R. and Hamond, N. R. (1990). Autobiographical memory across the preschool years: toward reconceptualizing childhood amnesia. In R. Fivush and J. A. Hudson (eds), *Knowing and Remembering in Young Children* (pp. 223–48). New York: Cambridge University Press.

Fivush, R., Hamond, N. R., Harsch, N., Singer, N. and Wolf, A. (1991). Content and consistency in early autobiographical recall. *Discourse Processes,* 14, 373–88.

Fivush, R. and Shukat, J. R. (1995). Content, consistency and coherence of early autobiographical recall. In M. S. Zaragoza et al. (eds), 5–23.

Flemming, R. B. (1986). Client games: defense attorney perspectives on their relations with criminal clients. *American Bar Foundation Research Journal,* 2, 253–77.

Flin, R. H. (1992). Child witnesses in British courts. In F. Lösel et al. (eds), 365–73.

Flin, R. H. (1993). Hearing and testing children's evidence. In G. S. Goodman and B. L. Bottoms (eds), 279–99.

Flin, R. H. (1995). Children's testimony: psychology on trial. In M. S. Zaragoza et al. (eds), 214–54.

Flin, R. H., Davies, G. and Tarrant, A. (1988). *The Child Witness.* Report to the Scottish Home and Health Department. Aberdeen: Robert Gordon Institute of Technology.

Flin, R. H., and Shepherd, J. W. (1986). Tall stories: eyewitnesses' ability to estimate height and weight characteristics. *Human Learning,* 5, 29–38.

Flood, J. (1991). Doing business: the management of uncertainty in lawyers' work. *Law and Society Review,* 25, 41–71.

Fontaine, G. and Emily, C. (1978). Causal attribution and judicial discretion: a look at the verbal behavior of municipal court judges. *Law and Human Behavior,* 2, 323–37.

Forslund, M. A. (1970). A comparison of negro and white crime rates. *Journal of Criminal Law, Criminology and Police Science,* 61, 214–17.

Forster Lee, L., Horowitz, I. A. and Bourgeois, M. (1994). Effects of note taking on verdicts and evidence processing in a civil trial. *Law and Human Behavior,* 18, 567–78.

Forsyth, W. M. A. (1852). *History of Trial by Jury.*

Foster, R. A., Libkuman, T. M., Schooler, J. W. and Loftus, E. F. (1994). Consequentiality and eyewitness person identification. *Applied Cognitive Psychology,* 8, 107–21.

Fox, R. G. (1987). Controlling sentencers. *Australian and New Zealand Journal of Criminology,* 20, 218–46.

Fox, R. G. (1995). On punishing infringements. In A. Kapardis (ed.), *Sentencing. Law in Context* (special issue), 13, 7–38.

Fox, R. G. and Freiberg, A. (1990). Ranking offence seriousness in reviewing statutory maximum penalties. *Australian and New Zealand Journal of Criminology,* 23, 165–91.

Frank, J. and Frank, B. (1957). *Not Guilty.* London: Gollancz.

Frank, Judge J. (1949). *Law and the Modern Mind.* London: Stevens & Sons.

Frankel, E. (1940–41). The offender and the court: a statistical analysis of the sentencing of delinquents. *Journal of Criminal Law, Criminology and Political Science,* 31, 448–56.

Frase, R. S. (1995). Sentencing guidelines in Minnesota and other American States: a progress report. In C. Clarkson and R. Morgan (eds), *The Politics of Sentencing Reform* (pp. 169–98). Oxford: Clarendon Press.

Freckelton, I. (1987). *The Trial of the Expert.* Melbourne: Oxford University Press.

Freckelton, I. (1990). Psychiatry and psychology – mistrusted guests at the legal table: contemporary operation of the common knowledge rule. In D. Greig and I. Freckelton (eds), 49–68.

Freckelton, I. (1993). Science and the legal culture. *Expert Evidence,* 2, 107–14.

Freckelton, I. (1996). Repressed memory syndrome: counterintuitive or counterproductive? *Criminal Law Journal,* 20, 7–33.

Freckelton, I., Greig, D. and McMahon, M. (eds) (1991). *Forensic Issues in Mental Health. Proceedings of the 12th Annual Congress of the Australian and New Zealand Association of Psychiatry, Psychology and Law.* Melbourne.

Freckelton, I., Knowles, A. and Mulvany, J. (eds) (1992). *Current Controversies in Psychiatry, Psychology and Law. Proceedings of the 13th Annual Congress of the Australian and New Zealand Association of Psychiatry, Psychology and Law.* Melbourne.

Freckelton, I. and Selby, H. (eds) (1993–). *Expert Evidence.* Sydney: Law Book Co. (looseleaf service).

Freedman, J. L., Adam, E. K., Davey, S. A. and Koegl, C. J. (1996). The impact of a statement: more detail does not always help. *Legal and Criminological Psychology*, 1, 117–30.

Freeman, R. J. and Roesch, R. (1992). Psycholegal education: training for forum and function. In D. K. Kagehiro and W. S. Laufer (eds), 567–76.

Freud, S. (1940). An outline of psychoanalysis. In J. Stachey (ed.), *Standard Edition of the Complete Work of Sigmund Freud*, vol. 23. London: Hogarth.

Fridell, L. A. and Binder, A. (1992). Police officer decision-making in potentially violent confrontations. *Journal of Criminal Justice*, 20, 385–99.

Friedlander, B. Z. (1970). Receptive language development: issues and problems. *Merrill-Palmer Quarterly of Behavior and Development*, 16, 7–15.

Friedman, W. J. (1993). Memory for time of past events. *Psychological Bulletin*, 113, 44–66.

Fukurai, H., Butler, E. W., Krooth, R. (1991). Cross-sectional jury representation or systematic jury representation? Simple random and cluster sampling strategies in jury selection. *Journal of Criminal Justice*, 19, 31–48.

Gabora, N. J., Spanos, N. P. and Jacob, A. (1993). The effect of complainant age and expert psychological testimony in a simulated child sexual abuse trial. *Law and Human Behavior*, 17, 103–19.

Gale, A. G. (ed.) (1988). *The Polygraph Test: Lies, Truth and Science.* London: Sage Publications/British Psychological Society.

Galiber, J. L., Latzer, B. and Dwyer, M. et al. (1993). Law, justice, and jury nullification: a debate. *Criminal Law Bulletin*, 29, 40–69.

Galton, Sir F. (1985). Terms of imprisonment. *Nature*, 20 June, 174–6.

Gardner, D. (1933). The perception and memory of witnesses. *Cornell Law Quarterly*, 18, 391–409.

Gardner, R. W., Holzman, P. S., Klein, G. S., Linton, H. B. and Spence, D. P. (1959). Cognitive control: a study of individual consistencies in cognitive behavior. *Psychological Issues* (Monograph 4).

Garkawe, S. (1994). The role of the victim during criminal court proceedings. *University of New South Wales Law Journal*, 17, 595–616.

Garrido, V. and Redodo, S. (1992). Psychology and law in Spain. In F. Lösel et al. (eds), 526–34.

Geis, G. (1991). Sanctioning the selfish: the operation of Portugal's new 'bad Samaritan' statute. *International Review of Victimology*, 1, 297–313.

Geiselman, R. E., Fisher, R. P., Firstenberg, I., Hutton, L. A., Sullivan, S., Artisan, I. and Prosket, A. (1984). Enhancement of eyewitness memory: an empirical evaluation of the cognitive interview. *Journal of Police Science and Administration*, 12, 74–80.

Geiselman, R. E., Fisher, R. P., MacKinnon, D. P. and Holland, H. L. (1985). Eyewitness memory enhancement in the police interview: cognitive retrieval mnemonics versus hypnosis. *Journal of Applied Psychology*, 70, 401–12.

Geiselman, R. E., Fisher, R. P., MacKinnon, D. P. and Holland, H. L. (1986). Enhancement of eyewitness memory with the cognitive interview. *American Journal of Psychology*, 99, 385–401.

Geiselman, R. E., Haghighi, D. and Stown, R. (1996). Unconscious transference and characteristics of accurate and inaccurate eyewitnesses. *Psychology, Crime, and Law*, 2, 197–209.

Geiselman, R. E. and Padilla, J. (1988). Interviewing children witnesses with the cognitive interview. *Journal of Police Science and Administration*, 16, 236–42.

Geiselman, R. E., Saywitz, K. and Bornstein, G. K. (1990). Cognitive questioning techniques for child victims and witnesses of crime. (Unpublished technical report, SJI-88-11J-D-016.) State Justice Institute.

Geiselman, R. E., Saywitz, K. J. and Bornstein, G. K. (1993). Effects of cognitive questioning techniques on children's recall performance. In G. L. Goodman and B. L. Bottoms (eds), 71–93.

Gelsthorpe, L. and McWilliam, W. (eds) (1993). *Minority Ethnic Groups and the Criminal Justice System*. Cambridge: Institute of Criminology, University of Cambridge.

Gillies, P. (1987). *Law of Evidence in Australia* (1st edn). Sydney: Legal Books.

Gillies, P. (1993). *Criminal Law* (3rd edn). Sydney: Law Book Co.

Glaser, D. and Collins, C. (1989). The response of young, non-sexually abused children to anatomically correct dolls. *Journal of Child Psychology and Psychiatry*, 30, 547–60.

Glissan, J. L. (1991). *Cross-examination Practice and Procedure*. Sydney: Butterworths.

Goldberg, H. (1995). A random choice of jury? *The Times*, 13 June.

Goldberg, L. R., Grenier, J. R., Guion, R. M., Sechrest, L. B. and Wing, H. (1991). *Questionnaires Used in the Prediction of Trustworthiness in Pre-employment Selection Decisions: An APA Task Force Report*. Washington, DC: American Psychological Association.

Golding, S. L. (1992). Increasing the reliability, validity and relevance of psychological expert evidence: an introduction to the special issue on expert evidence. *Law and Human Behavior*, 16, 253–6.

Goldman, N. (1963). *The Differential Selection of Juvenile Offenders for Court Appearances*. US National Council on Crime and Delinquency.

Goldman, W. and Lewis, P. (1977). Beautiful is good: evidence that the physically attractive are more socially skilful. *Journal of Experimental Social Psychology*, 13, 125–30.

Goldstein, A. G., Knight, P., Bailis, K. and Conover, J. (1981). Recognition memory for accented and unaccented voices. *Bulletin of Psychonomic Society*, 17, 217–20.

Goldstein, A. G. and Chance, J. E. (1985). Voice recognition: the effects of faces, temporal distribution of 'practice', and social distance. Paper presented at the Midwestern Psychology Association meeting. Chicago, Illinois.

Goldstein, H. (1994). Controlling and reviewing police–citizen contacts. In T. Barker and D. C. Carter (eds), *Police Deviance* (3rd edn) (pp. 323–54). Cincinnati, OH: Anderson Publishing. Reprinted from Goldstein, H. (1977) *Policing a Free Society*.

Gonzalez, R., Ellsworth, P. C. and Pembroke, M. (1993). Response biases in line-ups and showups. *Journal of Personality and Social Psychology*, 64, 525–37.

Goodman, G. S. and Aman, C. J. (1990). Children's use of anatomically detailed dolls to recount an event. *Child Development*, 61, 1859–71.

Goodman, G. S., Aman, C. and Hirschman, J. (1987). Child sexual and physical abuse: children's testimony. In S. J. Ceci, M. P. Toglia, and D. F. Ross (eds), *Children's Eyewitness Memory* (pp. 1–23). New York: Springer-Verlag.

Goodman, G. S. and Bottoms, B. L. (eds) (1993). *Child Victims, Child Witnesses: Understanding and Improving Testimony*. New York: The Guildford Press.

Goodman, G. S., Bottoms, B. L., Schwartz-Kenney, B. and Rudy, L. (1991). Children's testimony about a stressful event: improving children's reports. *Journal of Narrative and Life History*, 7, 69–99.

Goodman, K. C. and Gareis, K. C. (1993). The influence of status on decisions to help. *Journal of Social Psychology*, 133, 23–31.

Goodman, G. S. and Hahn, A. (1987). Evaluating eyewitness testimony. In I. Weiner and A. Hess (eds), 258–92.

Goodman, G. S., Hirschman, J. E., Hepps, D. and Rudy, L. (1991). Children's memory for stressful events. *Merrill-Palmer Quarterly*, 37, 109–57.

Goodman, J., Loftus, E. F. and Greene, E. (1991). Money, sex, and death: gender bias in wrongful damage awards. *Law and Society Review*, 25, 263–85.

Goodman, G., Rudy, L., Bottoms, B. and Aman, C. (1990). Children's concerns and memory: ecological issues in the study of children's eyewitness testimony. In R. Fivush and J. Hudson (eds), *Knowing and Remembering in Children* (pp. 249–84). Cambridge: Cambridge University Press.

Goodman, G. S, Taub, E., Jones, D. P. H., England, P., Port, L. K., Rudy, L. and Prado, L. (1992). Testifying in criminal court: emotional effects on child sexual assault victims. *Monographs of the Society for Research in Child Development*, 57 (5), Serial No. 229.

Gorenstein, G. and Ellsworth, P. (1980). Effect of choosing an incorrect photograph on a later identification by an eyewitness. *Journal of Applied Psychology*, 5, 616–22.

Gowan, M. A. and Gatewood, R. D. (1995). Personnel selection. In N. Brewer and C. Wilson (eds), 205–28.

Grabosky, P. and Rizzo, C. (1983). Dispositional disparities in courts of summary jurisdiction: the conviction and sentencing of shoplifters in South Australia, 1980. *Australian and New Zealand Journal of Criminology*, 16, 146–62.

Grant, J. D., Grant, J. and Toch, H. G. (1982). Police–citizen conflict and decisions to arrest. In V. Konečni and E. Ebbesen (eds), 133–58.

Green, E. (1961). *Judicial Attitudes in Sentencing: A Study of the Factors Underlying the Sentencing Practice of the Criminal Court of Philadelphia*. London: Macmillan.

Green, E. (1990). Media effects on jurors. *Law and Human Behavior*, 14, 439–50.

Greene, E. and Dodge, M. (1995). The influence of prior record evidence on juror decision-making. *Law and Human Behavior*, 19, 67–78.

Greer, D. S. (1971). Anything but the truth: the reliability of testimony in criminal trials. *British Journal of Criminology*, 11, 131–54.

Greig, D. and Freckelton, I. (eds) (1988). *International Perspectives on Psychiatry, Psychology and Law. Proceedings of the 9th Annual Congress of the Australian and New Zealand Association of Psychiatry, Psychology and Law*. Melbourne, Australia.

Greig, D. and Freckelton, I. (eds) (1989). *Emerging Issues for the 1990s in Psychiatry, Psychology and Law. Proceedings of the 10th Annual Congress of the Australian and New Zealand Association of Psychiatry, Psychology and Law*. Melbourne, Australia.

Greig, D. and Freckelton, I. (eds) (1990). *The Patient, the Law and the Professional. Proceedings of the 11th Annual Congress of the Australian and New Zealand Association of Psychiatry, Psychology and the Law*. Melbourne, Australia.

Greuel, L. (1992). Police officers' beliefs about cues associated with deception in rape cases. In F. Lösel, D. Bender and T. Bliesener (eds), 234–9.

Griffeth, R. W. and Cafferty, T. P. (1977). Police and citizens value systems: some cross-sectional comparisons. *Journal of Applied Social Psychology*, 3, 191–204.

Gross, H. (1898). *Kriminalpsychologie*. Graz: Leuschner and Lubensky.

Gross, H. (1911). *Criminal Psychology* (4th edn). (Kallen, M., translation). Mount Claire, NJ: Paterson Smith.

Groth, A. N. (1979). The older rape victim and her assailant. *Journal of Geriatric Psychiatry*, 11, 203–15.

Grunhut, M. (1956). *Offenders Before the Courts*. Oxford: Pergamon Press.

Gudjonsson, G. H. (1983). Life events stressors and physical reactions in senior police officers. *Police Journal*, 56, 66–7.

Gudjonsson, G. H. (1984). A new scale of interrogative suggestibility. *Personality and Individual Differences*, 5, 303–14.

Gudjonsson, G. H. (1985). Psychological evidence in court: results from the BPS survey. *Bulletin of the British Psychological Society*, 38, 327–30.

Gudjonsson, G. H. (1988). How to defeat the polygraph tests. In A. G. Gale (ed.), 126–36.

Gudjonsson, G. H. (1989). Compliance in an interrogation situation: a new scale. *Personality and Individual Differences*, 10, 535–40.

Gudjonsson, G. H. (1991). Suggestibility and compliance among alleged false confessors and resisters in criminal trials. *Medicine, Science and the Law*, 31, 147–51.

Gudjonsson, G. H. (1992a). *The Psychology of Interrogations, Confessions and Testimony*. Chichester: Wiley.

Gudjonsson, G. H. (1992b). The admissibility of expert psychological and psychiatric evidence in England and Wales. *Criminal Behaviour and Mental Health*, 2, 245–52.

Gudjonsson, G. H. (1993). The implications of poor psychological evidence in court. *Expert Evidence*, 2, 120–4.

Gudjonsson, G. H. (1995a). The vulnerability of mentally disordered witnesses. *Medicine, Science and the Law*, 35, 101–6.

Gudjonsson, G. H. (1995b). Psychology and assessment. In R. Bull and D. Carson (eds), 55–66.

Gudjonsson, G. H. (1995c). The effects of interrogative pressure on strategic coping. *Psychology, Crime and Law*, 1, 309–18.

Gudjonsson, G. H. (1996). Forensic psychology in England: one practitioner's experience and viewpoint. *Legal and Criminological Psychology*, 1, 131–42.

Gudjonsson, G. H. and Adlam, K. R. C. (1982). Factors reducing occupational stress in police officers: senior officers' view. *Police Journal*, 55, 365–9.

Gudjonsson, G. H. and Bownes, I. (1992). The reasons why suspects confess during custodial interrogation: data for Northern Ireland. *Medicine, Science and the Law*, 32, 204–12.

Gudjonsson, G. H., Clare, C., Rutter, S. and Pewarse, J. (1994). Persons at risk during interviews in police custody: the identification of vulnerabilities. *Research Bulletin*, No. 35, 31–2. London: Home Office Research and Planning Unit.

Gudjonsson, G. H. and Clark, N. K. (1986). Suggestibility in police interrogation: a social psychological model. *Social Behavior*, 1, 83–104.

Gudjonsson, G. H. and Hilton, M. (1989). The effects of instructional manipulation on interrogative suggestibility. *Social Behavior*, 4, 189–93.

Gudjonsson, G. H. and Lebegue, B. (1989). Psychological and psychiatric aspects of a coerced-internalized false confession. *Journal of the Forensic Science Society*, 29, 261–9.

Gudjonsson, G. H. and McKeith, J. A. C. (1988). Retracted confessions: legal, psychological and psychiatric aspects. *Medicine, Science and the Law*, 28, 187–94.

Gudjonsson, G. H. and Petursson, H. (1991). Custodial interrogation: why do suspects confess and how does it relate to their crime, attitude and personality? *Personality and Individual Differences*, 12, 295–306.

Gudjonsson, G. H. and Sartory, G. (1983). Blood-injury phobia: a 'reasonable excuse' for failing to give a specimen in case of suspected drunken driving. *Journal of Forensic Sciences Society*, 23, 197–201.

Gudjonsson, G. H. and Sigurdson, J. F. (1994). How frequently do false confessions occur? An empirical study among prison inmates. *Psychology, Crime and Law*, 1, 21–6.

Haaga, D. A. F. (1989). Mood-state-dependent retention using identical or non-identical mood induction at learning and recall. *British Journal of Clinical Psychology*, 28, 75–83.

Hagan, J. (1975). Law, order and sentencing: a study of attitude in action. *Sociometry*, 38, 374–84.

Hagan, J. (1977). Finding discrimination: a question of meaning. *Ethnicity*, 4, 167–76.

Hagan, J. and Bernstein, L. N. (1979). Conflict in context: the sanctioning of draft resisters, 1963–76. *Social Problems*, 27, 109–22.

Hagen, A. M. (1991). Note: tolling the statute of limitations for adult survivors of childhood sexual abuse. *Iowa Law Review*, 76, 355.

Hain, P. (1976). *Mistaken Identity: The Wrong Face of the Law*. London: Quartet Books.

Halevy, T. (1995). Racial discrimination in sentencing? A study with dubious conclusions. *Criminal Law Review*, 267–71.

Ham, P. (1996). You must remember this … and this … and this. *Australian Magazine*, 26–31.

Hamlyn-Harris, S. (1992). The limits of expert evidence. In I. Freckelton et al. (eds), 79–93.

Hammersley, R. and Read, J. D. (1985). The effect of participation in a conversation on recognition and identification of the speakers' voices. *Law and Human Behavior*, 9, 71–81.

Hammersley, R. and Read, J. D. (1995). Voice identification by humans and computers. In S. L. Sporer, R. C. Malpass and G. Köhnken (eds), *Suspect Identification: Psychological Knowledge, Problems and Perspective* (pp. 117–52). Hillside, NJ: Lawrence Erlbaum.

Hamond, N. R. and Fivush, R. (1990). Memories of Mickey Mouse: young children recount their trip to Disneyworld. *Cognitive Development*, 6, 433–48.

Hampel, His Honour Justice G. (1993). Preface. In T. A. Mauet and L. A. McCrimmon.

Hampton, R. E. (1979). Sexual sentencing in children's court. *Australian and New Zealand Journal of Criminology*, 12, 24–32.

Hand, L. (1901). Historical and practical considerations regarding expert testimony. *Harvard Law Review*, 15, 40–58.

Haney, C. (1980). Psychology and legal change: on the limits of factual jurisprudence. *Law and Human Behavior*, 4, 147–99.

Haney, C. (1993). Psychology and legal change: the impact of a decade. *Law and Human Behavior*, 17, 371–98.

Haney, C., Sontag, S. and Costanzo, S. (1994). Deciding to take a life: capital juries, sentencing instructions, and the jurisprudence. *Journal of Social Issues*, 50, 149–76.

Hans, V. P. (1992). Jury decision-making. In D. K. Kagehiro and W. S. Laufer (eds), 56–76.

Hans, V. P. (1995a). Jury decision-making in complex trials. In R. Bull and D. Carson (eds), 527–41.

Hans, V. P. (1995b). How juries decide death: the contributions of the capital jury project. *Indiana Law Journal*, 70, 1233–40.

Hans, V. P. and Lofquist, W. S. (1992). Jurors' judgements of business liability in tort cases: implications for the litigation explosion. *Law and Society Review*, 26, 85–115.

Hans, V. P. and Vidmar, N. (1982). Jury selection. In N. L. Kerr and R. M. Bray (eds), 39–82.

Hans, V. P. and Vidmar, N. (1986). *Judging the Jury*. New York: Plenum.

Hans, V. P. and Vidmar, N. (1991). The American jury at twenty-five years. *Law and Society Inquiry*, 16, 323–51.

Harding, R. (1988). Jury performance in complex cases. In M. Findlay and P. Duff (eds), 74–94.

Hare, R. D. (1970). *Psychopathy: Theory and Research*. New York: Wiley.

Harlow, R. E., Darley, J. M. and Robinson, P. H. (1995). The scaling of intermediate penal sanctions: a psychophysical scaling approach for obtaining community perceptions. *Journal of Quantitative Criminology*, 11, 71–95.

Harman, H. and Griffith, J (1979). *Justice Deserted: The Subversion of the Jury*. London: National Council for Civil Liberties.

Harnon, E. (1982). Evidence obtained by polygraph: an Israeli perspective. *Criminal Law Review*, 340–8.

Harrison, A., Halem, M. and Raney, D. F. (1978). Cue to deception in an interview situation. *Social Psychology*, 4, 156–61.

Harry, B. (1986). A diagnostic study of the criminal alias. *Journal of Forensic Sciences*, 31, 1023–8.

Harsch, N. and Neisser, U. (1989). Substantial and irreversible errors in flashbulb memories of the Challenger explosion. Paper presented at the meeting of the Psychonomic Society, Atlanta, GA.

Hartshorne, H. and May, M. A. (1928). *Studies in Deceit*. New York: Macmillan.

Hasher, L. and Zacks, R. (1979). Automatic and effortful processes in memory. *Journal of Experimental Psychology*, General, 108, 356–88.

Hastie, R. (ed.) (1993a). *Inside the Juror: The Psychology of Juror Decision-Making*. New York: Cambridge University Press.

Hastie, R. (1993b). Introduction. In R. Hastie (ed.), 3–41.

Hastie, R. (1993c). Algebraic models of juror decision-making. In R. Hastie (ed.), 84–115.

Hastie, R., Penrod, S. D. and Pennington, N. (1983). *Inside the Jury*. Cambridge, MA: Harvard University Press.

Hastings, P. (1923). *Cases in Court*. London: Heinemann.

Haugaard, J. J. and Crosby, C. (1989). Children's definitions of the truth and their competency as witnesses in legal proceedings. Paper presented at the Southeastern Psychological Association Conference, Washington, DC.

Havatny, N. and Strack, F. (1980). The impact of a discredited key witness. *Journal of Applied Social Psychology*, 10, 490–509.

Haward, L. R. C. (1979). The psychologist as expert witness. In D. P. Farrington et al. (eds), 44–53.

Haward, L. R. C. (1981a). Expert opinion based on evidence from forensic hypnosis and lie-detection. In S. M. A. Lloyd-Bostock (ed.), 107–18.

Haward, L. R. C. (1981b). *Forensic Psychology*. London: Batsford.

Hazlehurst, K. M. (1988). Racial tension, policing, and public order: Australia in the eighties. In I. Freckelton and H. Selby (eds), *Police in Our Society* (pp. 8–25). Sydney: Butterworths.

Heaton-Armstrong, A. (1995a). Editorial: eyewitness testimony and judicial studies. *Medicine, Science and the Law*, 35, 93–4.

Heaton-Armstrong, A. (1995b). Recording and disclosing statements by witnesses – law and practice. *Medicine, Science and the Law*, 35, 136–43.

Hecker, M. H., Stevens, K. N., von Bismarck, G. and Williams, C. E. (1968). Manifestations of task-induced stress in the acoustic speech signal. *Journal of the Acoustical Society of America*, 44, 993–1001.

Hedderman, C. (1987). *Children's Evidence: The Need for Corroboration.* Home Office Research and Planning Unit, Paper No. 41. London: Home Office.

Hedderman, C. (1994). Decision-making in court: observing the sentencing of men and women. *Psychology, Crime and Law*, 1, 165–73.

Heider, F. (1958). *The Psychology of Interpersonal Relations.* New York: Wiley.

Heilbrun, K. (1992). The role of psychological testing in forensic assessment. *Law and Human Behavior*, 16, 257–72.

Henning, T. (1995). Psychological explanations in sentencing women in Tasmania. *Australian and New Zealand Journal of Criminology*, 28, 298–322.

Herkov, M. J., Myers, W. C. and Burket, R. C. (1994). Children's reactions to serial murder. *Behavioral Sciences and the Law*, 12, 251–9.

Hermann, D. and Gruneberg, M. (1993). The need to expand the horizons of the practical aspects of memory movement. *Applied Cognitive Psychology*, 7, 553–65.

Hernandez-Fernaud, E. and Alonso-Quecuty, M. (1995). The cognitive interview and lie detection: a new magnifying glass for Sherlock Holmes? Paper presented at European Psychology and Law Conference, Budapest, Hungary.

Hessing, D. J., Elffers, H. and Wigel, R. H. (1988). Exploring the limits of self-reports and reasoned action: an investigation of tax evasion behavior. *Journal of Personality and Social Psychology*, 54, 405–13.

Heuer, L. and Penrod, S. (1988). Increasing jurors' participation in trials: a field experiment with jury note taking and question asking. *Law and Human Behavior*, 12, 231–61.

Heuer, L. and Penrod, S. D. (1989). Instructing jurors: a field experiment with written and preliminary instructions. *Law and Human Behavior*, 13, 409–30.

Heuer, L. and Penrod, S. (1994a). Juror note taking and question asking during trials: a national field experiment. *Law and Human Behavior*, 18, 121–50.

Heuer, L. and Penrod, S. (1994b). Trial complexity, its meaning and effects. *Law and Human Behavior*, 18, 29–51.

Heuer, L. and Penrod, S. (1995). Jury decision-making in complex trials. In R. Bull and D. Carson (eds), 527–41.

Heuer, F. and Reisberg, D. (1990). Vivid memories of emotional events: the accuracy of remembered minutiae. *Memory and Cognition*, 18, 496–506.

Hilgendorf, L. and Irving, B. (1978). False positive identification. *Medicine, Science and the Law*, 18, 255–62.

Hill, P. and Hill, S. (1987). Videotaping children's testimony: an empirical view. *Michigan Law Review*, 85, 809–33.

Himelein, M., Nietzel, M. T. and Dillehay, R. C. (1991). Effects of prior juror experience on jury sentence. *Behavioral Sciences and the Law*, 9, 97–106.

Hindley, G. (1990). *The Book of Magna Carta.* London: Constable & Co.

Hinsz, V. B. (1990). Cognitive and consensus processes in group recognition memory performance. *Journal of Personality and Social Psychology*, 59, 715–18.

Ho, R. and Venus, M. (1995). Reactions to a battered woman who kills her abusive spouse: an attributional analysis. *Australian Journal of Psychology*, 47, 153–9.

Hodgkinson, T. (1990). *Expert Evidence: Law and Practice.* London: Sweet & Maxwell.

Hoffman, H. G., Loftus, E. F., Greenmun, C. N. and Dashiell, R. L. (1992). The generation of misinformation. In F. Lösel et al. (eds), 292–301.

Hoffmann, J. L. (1995). Where's the buck? – juror misperception of sentencing responsibility in death penalty cases. *Indiana Law Journal*, 70, 1137–60.

Hogarth, J. (1971). *Sentencing as a Human Process.* Toronto: University of Toronto Press.

Holdaway, S. (1983). *Inside the British Police.* Oxford: Blackwell.

Holdsworth, Sir W. A. (1903). *A History of English Law*, vol. 1, 7th edn. London: Methuen.

Hollien, H. (1980). Vocal indicators of psychological stress. In F. Wright, C. Bahn and R. W. Rieber (eds), *Forensic Psychology and Psychiatry: Annals of the New York Academy of Sciences* (vol. 347). New York: Academy of Sciences.

Hollien, H., Bennett, G. and Gelfer, M. P. (1983). Criminal identification comparison: aural versus visual identifications resulting from a simulated crime. *Journal of Forensic Sciences*, 28, 208–21.

Hollin, C. R. (1989). *Psychology and Crime: An Introduction to Criminological Psychology.* London: Routledge.

Hollin, C. R. (1995). *Clinical Approaches to Working With Young Offenders.* Chichester: Wiley.

Hollin, C. R. (ed.) (1996). *Working With Offenders: Psychological Practice in Offender Rehabilitation.* Chichester: Wiley.

Hollinger, R. C. and Clark, J. P. (1983). *Theft by Employees.* Lexington, MA: Lexington Books.

Holst, V. F. and Pezdek, K. (1992). Scripts for typical crimes and their effects on memory for eyewitness testimony. *Applied Cognitive Psychology*, 6, 573–87.

Home Office Research and Statistics Department (1994). Research Bulletin, vol. 35, special edn. Research undertaken for the Royal Commission on Criminal Justice. London.

Honts, C. R. and Perry, M. V. (1992). Polygraph admissibility: changes and challenges. *Law and Human Behavior*, 16, 357–78.

Honts, C. R. and Raskin, D. C. (1988). A field study of the validity of the directed lie control question. *Journal of Police Science and Administration*, 16, 373–85.

Honts, C. R., Raskin, D. C. and Kircher, J. C. (1994). Mental and physical countermeasures reduce the accuracy of polygraph tests. *Journal of Applied Psychology*, 79, 252–9.

Hood, R. (1962). *Sentencing in Magistrates' Court.* London: Stevens.

Hood, R. (1972). *Sentencing the Motoring Offender: A Study of Magistrates' Views and Practices.* London: Heinemann.

Hood, R. (1992). *Race and Sentencing: A Study in the Crown Court.* A Report for the Commission for Racial Equality. Oxford: Oxford University Press.

Hood, R. (1995). Race and sentencing: a reply. *Criminal Law Review*, 272–9.

Hood, R. and Sparks, R. (1970). *Key Issues in Criminology.* London: World University Library.

Horgan, J. J. (1979). *Criminal Investigation* (2nd edn). New York: McGraw Hill Book Co.

Horne, J. A. (1992). Stay awake, stay alive. *New Scientist*, 4, 20–4.

Horne, J. A. and Ostberg, O. (1976). A self-assessment questionnaire to determine morningness–eveningness in human circadian rhythms. *International Journal of Sociology*, 4, 97–110.

Horowitz, M., Wilner, M. and Alvarez, W. (1979). Impact of event scale: a measure of subjective stress. *Psychosomatic Medicine*, 41, 209–18.

Horvath, F. (1979). Effect of different motivational instructions on detection of deception with the psychological stress evaluator and the galvanic skin response. *Journal of Applied Psychology*, 64, 323–30.

Hosch, H. (1994). Individual differences in personality and eyewitness identification. In D. F. Ross et al. (eds), 328–47.

Hosch, H. M., Bothwell, R. K., Sporer, S. L. and Saucedo, C. (1990). The accuracy of witness choice: facial recognition ability, reaction time and confidence. Southwestern Psychological Association, Houston, TX.

Hosch, H. M., Bothwell, R. K., Sporer, S. L. and Saucedo, C. (1991). Assessing eyewitness identification accuracy: an individual differences approach. Southeastern Psychological Association, New Orleans, LA.

Hosch, H. M. and Cooper, S. D. (1982). Victimization as a determinant of eyewitness accuracy. *Journal of Applied Psychology*, 67, 649–52.

Hosch, H. M., Leippe, M. R., Marchione, P. M. and Cooper, D. S. (1984). Victimization, self-monitoring, and eyewitness identification. *Journal of Applied Psychology*, 69, 280–8.

Hosch, H. M. and Platz, S. J. (1984). Self-monitoring and eyewitness accuracy. *Personality and Social Psychology Bulletin*, 10, 289–92.

House of Commons Employment Committee (1985). Third Report from the Employment Committee Session 1984–1985. *The Implications for Industrial Relations and Employment of the Introduction of the Polygraph*. Together with the Proceedings of the Committee. London: HMSO.

Houston, T. C. (1980). Reporting and nonreporting of observed crimes: moral judgement of the act and actor. *Journal of Applied Social Psychology*, 10, 56–70.

Houts, M. (1963). *From Evidence to Guilt*. Springfield IL: Charles C. Thomas.

Howels, K. and Blackburn, R. (1995). Clinical psychology and offenders: Part I, an introduction. *Psychology, Crime and Law*, 2, 1–4.

Howels, K. (1994). Child sexual abuse: Finkelhor's precondition model revisited. *Psychology, Crime and Law*, 1, 201–14.

Howels, T. H. (1983). A study of ability to recognize faces. *Journal of Abnormal and Social Psychology*, 123, 173–4.

Hudson, B. (1989). Discrimination and disparity: the influence of race on sentencing. *New Community*, 16, 23–34.

Hudson, J. A. (1986). Memories are made of this: general event knowledge and the development of autobiographic memory. In K. Nelson (ed.), 97–118.

Hudson, J. A. (1990). The emergence of autobiographic memory in mother–child conversations. In R. Fivush and J. A. Hudson (eds), *Knowing and Remembering in Young Children* (pp. 166–96). New York: Cambridge University Press.

Hudson, J. A. and Fivush, R. (1987). As time goes by: sixth graders remember a kindergarten experience. *Emory Cognition Project Report No. 13*, Emory University, Atlanta.

Huff, C. R., Rattner, A. and Sagarin, E. (1986). Guilty until proven innocent: wrongful conviction and public policy. *Crime and Delinquency*, 32, 518–44.

Huffman, M. L. (1995). Can CBCA discriminate between accurate and false reports of preschoolers? A validation attempt. Manuscript submitted for publication.

Humphrey, G. F. (1992). Scientific fraud: the McBride case. *Medicine, Science and the Law*, 32, 199–203.

Hunt, R. R. and Einstein, G. O. (1981). Relational and item-specific information in memory. *Journal of Verbal Learning and Verbal Behavior*, 20, 497–514.

Hunter, I. M. L. (1957). *Memory: Facts and Fallacies*. Harmondsworth: Penguin.

Hunter, I. M. L. (1968). *Memory*. Harmondsworth: Penguin.

Hurvich, L. M. (1981). *Color Vision*. Sunderland, MA: Sinaner Associates.

Hurwitz, D., Wiggins, N. and Jones, L. (1975). Semantic differential for facial attributions: the face differential. *Bulletin Psychonomic Science*, 6, 370–2.

Hurwitz, S. D., Miron, M. S. and Johnson, B. T. (1992). Source credibility and the language of expert testimony. *Journal of Applied Social Psychology*, 22, 1909–39.

Hutchins, R. and Slesinger, D. (1928). Some observations on the law of evidence: spontaneous exclamations. *Columbia Law Review*, 28, at 432.

Hyman, R. (1989). The psychology of deception. *Annual Review of Psychology*, 40, 133–54.

Iacono, W. G. (1995). Offender testimony: detection of deception and guilty knowledge. In N. Brewer and C. Wilson (eds), 155–71.

Iacono, W. G., Cerri, A. M., Patrick, C. J. and Fleming, J. A. E. (1987). The effect of anti-anxiety drugs on the detection of deception. *Psychophysiology*, 24, 594.

Iacono, W. G., Cerri, A. M., Patrick, C. J. and Fleming, J. A. E. (1992). Use of anti-anxiety drugs as countermeasures in the detection of guilty knowledge. *Journal of Applied Psychology*, 77, 60–4.

Inbau, F. E., Reid, J. E. and Buckley, J. P. (1986). *Criminal Interrogation and Confessions* (3rd edn). Baltimore: Williams & Wilkins.

Ingram, R. E. and Reed, M. (1986). Information encoding and retrieval processes in depression: findings, issues and future directions. In R. E. Ingram (ed.), *Information Processing Approaches to Clinical Psychology* (pp. 131–50). Orlando, FL: Academic Press.

Irving, B. and Hilgendorf, L. (1980). Police interrogation: the psychological approach. Royal Commission on Criminal Procedure (Research Study No. 1). London: HMSO.

Irving, B. and McKenzie, B. (1988). *Regulating Custodial Interviews*. London: Police Foundation.

Isenberg, D. J. (1986). Group polarisation: a critical review and meta-analysis. *Personality and Social Psychology*, 50, 1141–51.

Izzett, R. and Leginski, W. (1974). Group discussion and the influence of defendant characteristics in a simulated jury setting. *Journal of Social Psychology*, 93, 271–9.

Jack, M. and Yeo, T. (1992). Foreword. *Memorandum of Good Practice on Video Recorded Interviews with Child Witnesses for Criminal Proceedings*. Home Office in conjunction with department of Health. London: HMSO.

Jackson, R. (1959). *The Chief: a Biography of Lord Hewitt, Lord Chief Justice, 1922–40*. London: Harrap.

Jackson, J. (1994). Trial by jury and alternative modes of trial. In J. McConville and L. Bridges (eds), *Criminal Justice in Crisis* (pp. 255–63). London: Edward Elgar.

Jackson, J. (1995). Evidence: legal perspective. In R. Bull and D. Carson (eds), 163–77.

Jackson, L. A. and Ervin, K. S. (1992). Height stereotypes of women and men: the liability of shortness for both sexes. *Journal of Social Psychology*, 132, 433–45.

Jacobs, B. A. (1993a). Getting narced: neutralization of undercover identity discreditation. *Deviant Behavior: An Interdisciplinary Journal*, 14, 187–208.

Jacobs, B. A. (1993b). Undercover detection clues: a case of restrictive deterrence. *Criminology*, 31, 281–99.

Jalbert, N. L. and Getting, J. (1992). Racial and gender issues in facial recognition. In F. Lösel et al. (eds), 309–16.

James, W. (1890). *The Principles of Psychology*, vol. 2. New York: Holt.

Jastrow, J. (1900). *Fact and Fable in Psychology*. Cambridge, MA: Riverside Press.

Jefferson, T. and Walker, M. A. (1992). Ethnic minorities in the criminal justice system. *Criminal Law Review*, 83–95.

Jenkins, C. D., Zyzanski, S. J. and Rosenman, M. D. (1979). *Jenkins Activity Survey Manual* (Form C). New York: Psychological Corporation.

Jobe, J. B., Tourangeau, R. and Smith, A. F. (1993). Contributions of survey research to the understanding of memory. *Applied Cognitive Psychology*, 7, 567–84.

Joffe, R. (1992). Criteria-based content analysis: an experimental investigation with children. Unpublished doctoral thesis, University of British Columbia, Vancouver, British Columbia.

Johnson, M. K. (1983). A multiple-entry modular memory system. In G. H. Bower (ed.), *The Psychology of Learning and Motivation*, vol. 17, 81–123. New York: Academic Press.

Johnson, M. K., Hashtroudi, S. and Lindsay, D. S. (1993). Source monitoring. *Psychological Bulletin*, 114, 3–28.

Johnston, E. (1991). *National Report of the Royal Commission into Aboriginal Deaths in Custody*, vol. 2. Canberra: Australian Government Publishing Service.

Jonas, K., Eagly, A. H. and Stroebe, W. (1995). Attitudes and persuasion. In M. Argyle and A. M. Colman (eds), *Social Psychology* (pp. 1–19). London: Longman.

Joyce, D. (1993). How comprehensible are PACE Codes of Practice to the majority of persons who might wish to read them? *Issues in Criminological and Legal Psychology*, No. 20, 70–4.

Judd, J. J., Judd, F. K. and Burrows, G. D. (1994). Hypnosis and the Australian legal process. In B. J. Evans and R. O. Stanley (eds), 71–9.

Jung, C. G. (1905). Die psychologische diagnoses des Tatbestands Schweizerische Zeitschrift für Strafrecht, 18, 368–408.

Kadane, J. B. (1993). Sausages and the law. In R. Hastie (ed.), 229–34.

Kagan, J., Rosman, B. L., Day, D., Albert, J., and Phillips, W. (1964). Information processing in the child: significance of analytic and reflective attitudes. *Psychological Monographs*, 78 (Whole No. 578).

Kagehiro, D. K. and Laufer, W. S. (eds) (1992). *Handbook of Psychology and Law*. New York: Springer.

Kalbfleisch, P. J. (1985). Accuracy in deception detection: a quantitative review. Unpublished PhD dissertation, Michigan State University, East Lansing. Cited by G. R. Miller and J. B. Stiff, *Deceptive Communication*. New York: Sage.

Kalven, H. and Zeisel, H. (1966). *The American Jury*. Chicago: University of Chicago Press.

Kanovitz, J. (1992). Hypnotic memories and civil sexual abuse trials. *Vanderbilt Law Review*, 45, 1185.

Kapardis, A. (1984). *A Psychological Study of Magistrates' Decision-Making*. PhD dissertation, Institute of Criminology, Cambridge University.

Kapardis, A. (1985). *Sentencing by English Magistrates as a Human Process*. Nicosia, Cyprus: Asselia Press.

Kapardis, A. (1988). *They Wrought Mayhem: An Insight into Mass Murder*. Melbourne: River Seine Press.

Kapardis, A. (1989). One-Hundred Armed Robbers in Melbourne: Myths and Reality. In D. Challinger (ed.), *Armed Robbery* (pp. 37–47). Canberra: Australian Institute of Criminology.

Kapardis, A. (1990a). Stranger homicides in Victoria, January 1984–December 1989. *Australia and New Zealand Journal of Criminology*, 23, 241–58.

Kapardis, A. (1990b). *Firearms Training in the Victoria Police Force: A Consultancy Report*. Melbourne: Police Headquarters.

Kapardis, A. (1993). Killed by a Stranger in Victoria, January 1990–April 1992. In H. Strang (ed.), *Homicide: Patterns, Prevention and Control* (pp. 121–32). Canberra: Australian Institute of Criminology.

Kapardis, A. (in preparation). Police and computer composite images of real criminals' faces: a survey of 1,636 crime victim/witnesses and a follow-up of 200 composites.

Kapardis, A. and Cole, B. (1988). Characteristics of homicide in Victoria. *Australia Police Journal*, 42, 130–2.

Kapardis, A. and Farrington, D. P. (1981). An experimental study of sentencing by magistrates. *Law and Human Behavior*, 5, 107–21.

Kargon, R. (1986). Expert testimony in historical perspective. *Law and Human Behavior*, 10, 15–27.

Kassin, S. M. (1985). Eyewitness identification: retrospective self-awareness and the accuracy–confidence correlation. *Journal of Personality and Social Psychology*, 49, 88–93.

Kassin, S. M., Ellsworth, P. C. and Smith, V. L. (1989). The 'general acceptance' of psychological research on eyewitness testimony: a survey of experts. *American Psychologist*, 44, 1089–98.

Kassin, S. M., Ellsworth, P. C. and Smith, V. L. (1994). *Déjà vu* all over again: Elliott's critique of eyewitness experts. *Law and Human Behavior*, 18, 203–10.

Kassin, S. M. and Wrightsman, L. S. (1983). The construction and validation of juror bias scale. *Journal of Research in Personality*, 17, 423–42.

Kassin, S. M. and Wrightsman, L. S. (1988). *The American Jury on Trial*. New York: Hemisphere.

Keil, T. J. and Vito, G. F. (1990). Race and the death penalty in Kentucky murder trials: an analysis of post-Gregg outcomes. *Justice Quarterly*, 7, 189–207.

Kelley, H. H. (1967). Attribution theory in social psychology. In *Nebraska Symposium on Motivation* (pp. 192–238). Lincoln, Nebraska: University of Nebraska Press.

Kennedy, L. W. and Silverman, R. A. (1990). The elderly victim of homicide: an application of the routine activities approach. *Sociological Quarterly*, 31, 307–19.

Kerkoff, G. (1985). Interindividual differences in the human circadian system: a review. *Biological Psychology*, 20, 83–112.

Kerr, J. F. (1987). *A Presumption of Wisdom: An Expose of the Jury System of Injustice*. Sydney: Angus & Robertson.

Kerr, N. L. (1993). Stochastic models of juror decision-making. In R. Hastie (ed.), 116–35.

Kerr, N. L. and Bray, R. M. (eds) (1982). *The Psychology of the Courtroom.* London: Academic Press.

Kerr, N. L. and MacCoun, R. J. (1985). The effects of jury size and polling method on the process and product of jury deliberation. *Journal of Personality and Social Psychology,* 48, 349–63.

Kidd, R. F. (1985). Impulsive bystanders: why do they intervene? In D. P. Farrington and J. Gunn (eds), *Reactions to Crime: The Public, the Police, Courts and Prisons* (pp. 21–39). Chichester: Wiley.

King, M. (1986). *Psychology In and Out of Court.* Oxford: Pergamon Press.

Kirby, Justice M. D. (1981). Psychology and evidence law reform. Paper presented at the second Australian Congress of Psychiatry Psychology on Law in Melbourne on 6 November 1981.

Kircher, J. C. and Raskin, D. C. (1988). Human versus computerized evaluations of polygraph data in a laboratory setting. *Journal of Applied Psychology,* 73, 291–302.

Kleck, G. (1985). Life support for ailing hypotheses, modes for summarizing the evidence for racial discrimination in sentencing. *Law and Human Behavior,* 9, 271–84.

Kleck, R. and Rubenstein, C. (1975). Physical attractiveness, perceived attitude similarity and interpersonal attraction in an opposite-sex encounter. *Journal of Personality and Social Psychology,* 31, 107–14.

Knittel, E. and Seiler, D. (1972). The merits of trial by jury. *Cambridge Law Journal,* 56, 223–8.

Kogan, N. (1971). Educational implications of cognitive styles. In G. S. Lesser (ed.), *Psychology and Educational Practice* (pp. 242–92). Glenview, IL: Scott, Foresman.

Kogan, N. and Wallach, M. A. (1967). Risk taking as a function of the situation, the person, and the group. In G. Mandler, P. Mussen, N. Kogan and M. A. Wallach (eds), *New Directions in Psychology III* (pp. 111–278) New York: Holt, Rinehart & Winston.

Köhnken, G. (1992). The cognitive interview: a meta-analysis. Paper presented at the Third European Conference on Psychology and Law, Oxford.

Köhnken, G. and Brockman, C. (1987). Unspecific postevent information, attribution of responsibility and eyewitness performance. *Applied Cognitive Psychology,* 1, 197–207.

Köhnken, G., Finger, M. and Nitschke, N. (1991). Statement validity analysis and the cognitive interview with child witnesses. Unpublished manuscript, Germany: University of Kiel.

Köhnken, G. and Maass, A. (1988). Eyewitness testimony: false alarms on biased instructions? *Journal of Applied Psychology,* 73, 363–70.

Konečni, V. J. and Ebbesen, E. B. (1979). External validity of research in legal psychology. *Law and Human Behavior,* 3, 39–70.

Konečni, V. J. and Ebbesen, E. B. (1982). *The Criminal Justice System: A Social Psychological Analysis.* San Francisco: W. H. Freeman and Co.

Konečni, V. J. and Ebbesen, E. B. (1992). Methodological issues in research on legal decision-making, with special reference to experimental simulation. In F. Lösel et al. (eds), 413–23.

Konečni, V. J., Ebbesen, E. B. and Hock, R. R. (1996). Factors affecting simulated jurors' decisions in capital cases. *Psychology, Crime and Law,* 2, 269–90.

Koocher, G. P., Goodman, G. S., White, C. S., Friedrich, W. N., Sivan, A. B. and Reynolds, C. R. (1995). Psychological science and the use of anatomically detailed dolls in child sexual-abuse assessment. *Psychological Bulletin*, 118, 199–222.

Kopelman, M. D. (1987). Amnesia: organic and psychogenic. *British Journal of Psychiatry*, 150, 428–42.

Kramer, H. T., Buckhout, R. and Euginio, P. (1990). Weapon focus, arousal and eyewitness memory. *Law and Human Behavior*, 14, 167–84.

Kramer, G. P., Kerr, N. L. and Carroll, J. S. (1990). Pretrial publicity, judicial remedies and jury bias. *Law and Human Behavior*, 14, 409–38.

Krauss, Stanton D. (1995). Thinking clearly about guilt, juries and jeopardy. *Indiana Law Journal*, 70, 921–7.

Krauss, Stephen J. (1995). Attitudes and the prediction of behavior: a meta-analysis of the empirical literature. *Personality and Social Psychology Bulletin*, 21, 58–75.

Kraut, R. E. and Poe, D. (1980). Behavioral roots of person perception: the deception judgements of custom inspectors and laymen. *Journal of Personality and Social Psychology*, 39, 784–98.

Kroes, W. H. (1985). *Society's Victim – The Policeman – An Analysis of Job Stress in Policing*. New York: Charles C. Thomas.

Kuehn, L. L. (1974). Looking down a gun barrel: person perception and violent crime. *Perception and Motor Skills*, 39, 1159–64.

Ladefoged, P. (1981, April). Expectation affects identification by listening. Paper presented at the 94th meeting of the Acoustical Society of America. New York.

Lamb, M. E. (1994). The investigation of child sexual abuse: an interdisciplinary consensus statement. *Expert Evidence*, 2, 151–6.

Lamb, M. E., Strenberg, K. and Esplin, P. (1995). Making children into competent witnesses: reactions to the amicus brief in *re Michaels*. *Psychology, Public Policy, and Law*, 1, 438–49.

Landry, K. and Brigham, J. (1992). The effects of training in Criteria-Based Content Analysis on the ability to detect deception in adults. *Law and Human Behavior*, 16, 663–76.

Landsman, S. (1995). Of witches, madmen, and products liability: an historical survey of the use of expert testimony. *Behavioral Sciences and the Law*, 13, 131–57.

Landy, D. and Aronson, E. (1969). The influence of the character of the criminal and his victim on decisions of simulated jurors. *Journal of Experimental Social Psychology*, 5, 141–52.

Landy, F. J. (1992). Hugo Münsterberg: victim or visionary? *Journal of Applied Psychology*, 77, 6, 787–802.

Lass, N. J., Hughes, K. R. and Bowyer, M. D. (1976). Speaker sex identification from voiced, whispered and filtered isolated vowels. *Journal of the Acoustical Society of America*, 59, 675–8.

Lasswell, H. D. (1948). The structure and function of communication in society. In L. Bryson (ed.), *The Communication of Ideas: Religion and Civilization Series* (pp. 37–51). New York: Harper & Row.

Laster, K. (1989). Infanticide: a litmus test for feminist criminological theory. *Australian and New Zealand Journal of Criminology*, 22, 151–66.

Latane, B. and Darley, J. M. (1970). *The Unresponsive Bystander: Why Doesn't He Help?* New York: Appleton-Century-Crofts.

Latane, B. and Naida, S. (1981). Ten types of research on group size and helping. *Psychological Bulletin*, 89, 308–24.

Laughery, K. R., Alexander, T. and Lane, A. (1971). Recognition of human faces: effects of target exposure time, target position, and type of photograph. *Journal of Applied Psychology*, 55, 477–83.

Laughery, K. R. and Wogalter, M. S. (1989). Forensic applications of facial memory research. In A. W. Young and H. D. Ellis (eds), 519–55.

Law Reform Commission of Victoria (1985). *The Jury in a Criminal Trial*. Melbourne.

Law Reform Commission of Western Australia (1991). *Report on Evidence of Children and Other Vulnerable Witnesses*. Project No. 87, Perth.

Law Society (1994). *Police Station Skills for Legal Advisers*. London: Law Society.

Lawrence, J. and Homel, R. (1987). Sentencing in Magistrates' Courts: the magistrate as professional decision-maker. In I. Potas (ed.), *Sentencing in Australia: Issues, Policy and Reform* (pp. 151–90). Canberra: Australian Institute of Criminology.

Lawrence, Judge T. (1993). Judicial appointments – a system fit for change? *Medicine, Science and the Law*, 33, 279–84.

Lecont, P. (1988). Les rhythmicités de l'efficience cognitive. *L'Année Psychologique*, 88, 215–36.

Lee, T. and Geiselman, R. E. (1994). Recall of perpetrator height as a function of eyewitness and perpetrator ethnicity. *Psychology, Crime and Law*, 1, 11–19.

Leeman-Conley, M. and Crabtree, J. (1989). Providing assistance to victims of bank hold-ups. In D. Challinger (ed.), *Armed Robbery* (pp. 101–9). Canberra: Australian Institute of Criminology.

Legge, D. (1975). *An Introduction to Psychological Science*. Sydney: Methuen.

Legge, G. E., Grossman, C. and Pieper, C. M. (1984). Learning unfamiliar voices. *Journal of Experimental Child Psychology*, 10, 298–303.

Leiken, L. S. (1970). Police interrogation in Colorado: the implementation of *Miranda*. *Denver Law Review*, 47, 1–53.

Leippe, M. R. (1980). Effects of integrative and memorial cognitive processes on the correspondence of eyewitness accuracy and confidence. *Law and Human Behavior*, 4, 261–74.

Leippe, M. R. (1985). The influence of eyewitness non-identifications on mock-jurors' judgements of a court case. *Journal of Applied Social Psychology*, 15, 656–72.

Leippe, M. R. (1994). The appraisal of eyewitness testimony. In D. F. Ross et al. (eds), 385–418.

Leippe, M. R., Manion, A. P. and Romanczyk, A. (1993). Discernablity or discrimination? Understanding jurors' reactions to accurate and inaccurate child and adult witnesses. In G. S. Goodman and B. L. Bottoms (eds), 169–202.

Leippe, M. R., Romanczyk, A. and Manion, A. P. (1991). Eyewitness memory for a touching experience: accuracy differences between child and adult witnesses. *Journal of Applied Psychology*, 76, 267–379.

Leo, R. A. (1994). Police interrogation and social control. *Social and Legal Studies*, 3, 93–120.

Leo, R. A. (1996). *Miranda*'s revenge: police interrogation as a confidence game. *Law and Society Review*, 30, 259–88.

Lerner, R. M. and Korn, S. J. (1972). The development of body-build stereotypes in males. *Child Development*, 43 (3), 908–20.

Lester, D. (1980). The personalities of English and American police. *Journal of Social Psychology*, 111, 153–4.

Lester, D. (1983). The selection of police officers: an argument for simplicity. *Police Journal*, 56, 53–5.

Lester, D., Babcock, S. D., Cassisi, J. P. and Brunetta, M. (1980). Hiring despite the psychologist's objections. *Criminal Justice and Behavior*, 7, 41–9.

Levine, F. and Tapp, J. (1971). The psychology of criminal identification: the gap from Wade to Kirby. *University of Pennsylvania Law Review*, 121, 1079–132.

Levine, J. P. (1992). *Juries and Politics*. Pacific Grove, CA: Brooks/Cole Publishing Co.

Levine, M. L. (ed.) (1995). *Law and Psychology*. Aldershot: Dartmouth.

Liggett, J. (1974). *The Human Face*. London: Constable.

Light, L. H. (1991). Memory and aging: four hypotheses in search of data. *Annual Review of Psychology*, 42, 333–76.

Lilli, W. (1989) The perception of social events and behavior consequences. In H. Wegener et al. (eds), 216–27.

Lind, E. A. and Ke, G. Y. (1985). Opening and Closing Statements. In S. M. Kassin and L. S. Wrightsman (eds), *The Psychology of Evidence and Trial Procedure* (pp. 229–52). Beverly Hills, CA: Sage.

Lindsay, D. S. (1994). Memory source monitoring and eyewitness testimony. In D. F. Ross et al. (eds), 27–55.

Lindsay, D. S. and Read, J. D. (1994). Psychotherapy and memories of child-hood sexual abuse: a cognitive perspective. *Applied Cognitive Psychology*, 8, 281–338.

Lindsay, R. C. L. (1986). Confidence and accuracy of eyewitness identification from line-ups. *Law and Human Behavior*, 10, 229–39.

Lindsay, R. C. L. (1994a). Expectations of eyewitness performance: jurors' verdicts do not follow their beliefs. In D. F. Ross et al. (eds), 362–83.

Lindsay, R. C. L. (1994b). Biased line-ups: where do they come from? In D. F. Ross et al. (eds), 182–200.

Lindsay, R. C. L. and Harvie, V. L. (1988). Hits, false alarms, correct and mistaken identification: the effects of method of data collection on facial memory. In M. Gruneberg et al. (eds), *Practical Aspects of Memory: Current Research and Issues* (pp. 47–52). Chichester: Wiley.

Lindsay, R. C. L. and Johnson, M. K. (1987). Reality monitoring and sug-gestibility: children's ability to discriminate among memories from different sources. In S. J. Ceci, M. P. Toglia and D. F. Ross (eds) *Children's Eyewitness Memory* (pp. 92–121). New York: Springer-Verlag.

Lindsay, R. C. L., Lea, J. A., and Fulford, J. A. (1991a). Sequential line-up presentation: technique matters. *Journal of Applied Psychology*, 76, 741–5.

Lindsay, R. C. L., Lea, J. A., Nosworthy, G. J., Fulford, J. A. et al. (1991b). Biased line-ups: sequential presentation reduces the problem. *Journal of Applied Psychology*, 76, 796–802.

Lindsay, R. C. L., Martin, R. and Webber, L. (1994a). Default values in eyewitness descriptions: a problem for the match-to-description line-up foil selection strategy. *Law and Human Behavior*, 18, 527–41.

Lindsay, R. C. L., Nosworthy, G. J., Martin, R. and Martynuck, C. (1994b). Using mugshots to find suspects. *Journal of Applied Psychology*, 79, 121–30.

Lindsay, R. C. L., Wallbridge, H. and Drennan, D. (1987). Do the clothes make the man? An exploration of the effect of line-up attire on eye-witness identification accuracy. *Canadian Journal of Behavioral Science*, 19, 463–78.

Lindsay, R. C. L. and Wells, G. L. (1980). What price justice? Exploring the relationship of line-up fairness to identification accuracy. *Law and Human Behavior*, 4, 303–14.

Lindsay, R. C. L. and Wells, G. L. (1983). What do we really know about cross-race eyewitness identification? In S. M. A. Lloyd-Bostock and B. R. Clifford (eds), 219–33.

Lindsay, R. C. L. and Wells, G. L. (1985). Improving eyewitness identifications from line-ups: simultaneous versus sequential line-up presentation. *Journal of Applied Psychology*, 70, 556–64.

Lindsay, R. C. L., Wells, G. L. and Rumpel, C. (1981). Can people detect eyewitness identification accuracy within and across situations? *Journal of Applied Psychology*, 66, 79–89.

Ling, J. and Blades, M. (1995). Children's memory for colour. *Forensic Update*, Issue 41, April, 23–9.

Lipovsky, J. A., Tidwell, R., Crisp, J., Kilpatrick, D. G., Saunders, B. E. and Dawson, V. L. (1992). Child witnesses in criminal courts: descriptive information from three southern states. *Law and Human Behavior*, 16, 635–50.

Lipton, J. P. (1977). On the psychology of eyewitness testimony. *Journal of Applied Psychology*, 66, 79–89.

Lisman, S. A. (1974). Alcoholic 'blackouts': state-dependent learning. *Archives of General Psychiatry*, 30, 46–53.

List, J. (1986). Age and schematic differences in the reliability of eyewitness testimony. *Developmental Psychology*, 22, 50–7.

Lloyd-Bostock, S. M. A. (ed.) (1981a). *Psychology In Legal Contexts: Applications and Limitations*. London: Macmillan.

Lloyd-Bostock, S. M. A. (ed.) (1981b). Psychology and law: a critical review of research and practice. *British Journal Law and Society*, 8, 1–28.

Lloyd-Bostock, S. M. A. (ed.) (1984). *Children and the Law*. Oxford: Centre for Socio-Legal Studies.

Lloyd-Bostock, S. M. A. (1988). *Law in Practice: Applications of Psychology to Legal Decision-making and Legal Skills*. London: Routledge/British Psychological Society.

Lloyd-Bostock, S. M. A. (1994). Research and teaching in legal psychology: an outline of British developments. *Psychology, Crime and Law*, 1, 159–64.

Lloyd-Bostock, S. M. A. and Clifford, B. R. (eds) (1983). *Evaluating Witness Evidence: Recent Psychological Research and New Perspectives*. Chichester: Wiley.

Loftus, E. F. (1974). Reconstructing memory: the incredible witness. *Psychology Today*, 8, 116–19.

Loftus, E. F. (1976). Unconscious transference in eyewitness identification. *Law and Psychology Review*, 2, 93–8.

Loftus, E. F. (1979). *Eyewitness Testimony*. Harvard, MA: Harvard University Press.

Loftus, E. F. (1980). Impact of expert psychological testimony on the unreliability of eyewitness identification. *Journal of Applied Psychology*, 65, 9–15.

Loftus, E. F. (1981). Eyewitness testimony: psychological research and legal thought. In M. Tonry and N. Morris (eds), *Crime and Justice: An Annual Review of Research*, vol. 3 (pp. 105–51). Chicago, IL: University of Chicago Press.

Loftus, E. F. (1993). The reality of repressed memories. *American Psychologist*, 48, 518–37.

Loftus, E. F., Banaji, M. R., Schooler, J. W. and Foster, R. A. (1987c). Who remembers what? Gender differences in memory. *Michigan Quarterly Review*, xxvi, 64–85.

Loftus, E. F. and Burns, T. E. (1982). Mental shock can produce retrograde amnesia. *Memory and Cognition*, 10, 318–23.

Loftus, E. F. and Doyle, J. M. (1987). *Eyewitness Testimony: Civil and Criminal.* New York: Kluwer Law Book Publishers.

Loftus, E. F., Greene, E. L. and Doyle, J. M. (1989). The psychology of eyewitness testimony. In D. C. Raskin (ed.), 3–45.

Loftus, E. F. and Ketcham, K. E. (1983). The malleability of eyewitness accounts. In S. M. A. Lloyd-Bostock and B. R. Clifford (eds), 159–71.

Loftus, E. F. and Ketcham, K. E. (1991). *Witness for the Defense.* New York: St Martin's Press.

Loftus, E. F., Loftus, G. R. and Messo, J. (1987a). Some facts about 'weapon focus'. *Law and Human Behavior*, 11, 55–62.

Loftus, E. F., Miller, D. G. and Burns, H. J. (1978). Semantic integration of verbal information into a visual memory. *Journal of Experimental Psychology: Human Learning and Memory*, 4, 19–31.

Loftus, E. F. and Palmer, J. C. (1974). Reconstruction of automobile destruction: an example of the interaction between language and memory. *Journal of Verbal Learning and Verbal Behavior*, 13, 585–9.

Loftus, E. F., Schooler, J. W., Booye, S. M. and Kline, D. (1987b). Time went by so slowly: overestimation of event duration by males and females. *Applied Cognitive Psychology*, 1, 3–13.

Loftus, E. F. and Zanni, G. (1975). Eyewitness testimony: the influence of the wording of a question. *Bulletin of the Psychonomic Science*, 5, 86–8.

Logie, R., Wright, R. and Decker, S. (1992). Recognition memory performance and residential burglary. *Applied Cognitive Psychology*, 6, 109–23.

Lord, C. G., Ross, L., and Lepper, M. R. (1979). Biased assimilation and attitude polarization: the effects of prior theories on subsequently considered evidence. *Journal of Personality and Social Psychology*, 37, 2098–109.

Lösel, F. (1992). Psychology and law: overtures, crescendos and reprises. In F. Lösel et al. (eds), 3–21.

Lösel, F., Bender, D. and Bleisener, T. (eds) (1992a). *Psychology and Law: International Perspectives.* New York: Walter de Gruyter.

Lösel, F., Bender, D. and Bleisener, T. (1992b). International perspectives on psychology and law: an introduction. In F. Lösel et al. (eds), vii–xvii.

Lovegrove, A. (1984). An empirical study of sentencing disparity among judges in an Australian criminal court. *International Review of Applied Psychology*, 33, 161–76.

Lubert, S. (1993). *Modern Trial Advocacy: Analysis and Practice.* Notre Dame, Indiana: National Institute of Trial Advocacy.

Luginbuhl, J. and Howe, J. (1995). Discretion in capital sentencing: guided or misguided? *Indiana Law Journal*, 70, 1161–85.

Luntz, H. and Hambly, A. D. (1992). *Torts: Cases and Commentary* (3rd edn). Sydney: Butterworths.

Luus, C. A. E. and Wells, G. L. (1991). Eyewitness identification and the selection of distractors for line-ups. *Law and Human Behavior*, 15, 43–57.

Luus, C. A. and Wells, G. L. (1994a). Eyewitness identification confidence. In D. F. Ross et al. (eds), 348–61.

Luus, C. A. E. and Wells, G. L. (1994b). The malleability of eyewitness confidence: co-witness and perseverance effects. *Journal of Applied Psychology*, 79, 714–23.

Lykken, D. T. (1959). The GSR in the detection of guilt. *Journal of Applied Psychology*, 43, 385–8.

Lykken, D. T. (1988). The case against polygraph testing. In A. Gale (ed.), 111–25.

Lyon, T. D. (1995). False allegations and false denials in child sexual abuse. *Psychology, Public Policy and Law*, 1, 429–37.

Maass, A. and Köhnken, G. (1989). Eyewitness identification: simulating the 'weapon effect'. *Law and Human Behavior*, 13, 397–408.

MacCoun, R. (1990). The emergence of extralegal bias during jury deliberation. *Criminal Justice and Behavior*, 17, 303–14.

MacDowell, D. M. (1978). *The Law in Classical Athens*. London: Thames & Hudson.

Mackay, R. D. (1993). The consequences of killing very young children. *Criminal Law Review*, 21–30.

MacLeod, M. D. (1987). Psychological dynamics of the police interview. Unpublished PhD thesis, University of Aberdeen.

MacLeod, M. D., Frowley, J. N., and Shepherd, J. W. (1994). Whole body information: its relevance to eyewitnesses. In D. F. Ross et al. (eds), 125–43.

MacLeod, M. D. and Shepherd, J. W. (1986). Sex differences in eyewitness reports of criminal assaults. *Medicine, Science and the Law*, 26, 311–18.

Macmillan, Lord (1952). *Law and Other Things*. London: Macmillan.

Magistrates' Association (1993). *Sentencing Guidelines*. London.

Magner, E. (1991). Wigmore confronts Münsterberg: present relevance of a classic debate. *Sydney Law Review*, 13, 121–37.

Magner, E. (1995). Recovered memories: the Australian position. *Expert Evidence*, 3 (4), 157.

Magner, E. S. (1995). Improving witness memory: an interdisciplinary research agenda. *Current Issues in Criminal Justice*, 7, 25–35.

Mair, G. (1986). Ethnic minorities, probation and the courts. *British Journal of Criminology*, 26, 147–55.

Malpass, R. S. (1981). Effective size and defendant bias in eyewitness identification. *Law and Human Behavior*, 5, 299–309.

Malpass, R. S. and Devine, P. G. (1981). Realism and eyewitness identification research. *Law and Human Behavior*, 4, 347–58.

Malpass, R. S. and Devine, P. G. (1983). Measuring the fairness of eyewitness identification line-ups. In S. M. A. Lloyd-Bostock and B. R. Clifford (eds), 81–102.

Mandler, G. (1975). *Mind and Emotion*. New York: Wiley.

Mann, V., Diamond, R. and Carey, S. (1979). Development of voice recognition: parallels with face recognition. *Journal of Experimental Child Psychology*, 27, 153–65.

Mannheim, H. et al. (1957). Magisterial policy in the London courts. *British Journal of Delinquency*, 8, 13–33, 119–39.

Manolias, M. (1986). The psychologist as an agent for change. In J. C. Yuille (ed.), 347–51.

Manolias, M. (1991). Police stress. *International Criminal Police Review*, 13–17.

Manstead, A. S. R. and Lee, J. S. (1979). The effectiveness of two types of witness appeal signs. *Ergonomics*, 22, 1125–40.

Margolick, D. (1995). Strain of Simpson trial takes toll on one juror; asks judge to be removed from the case. *New York Times*, 21 April, 144, A8, A14.

Mark, Sir R. (1973). Minority verdict. Dimbleby Lecture, British Broadcasting Corporation, 8–14.

Marshall, G. (1975). The judgement of one's peers: some aims and ideals of jury trial. In N. D. Walker and A. Pearson (eds), *The British Jury System: Papers Presented at the Cropwood Round-Table Conference*, December 1974. Cambridge: Institute of Criminology.

Marshall, J. (1969). *Law and Psychology in Conflict*. New York: Doubleday-Anchor. (Original work published in 1966.)

Marx, G. T. (1988). *Undercover: Police Surveillance in America*. Berkeley, CA: University of California Press.

Marxsen, D., Yuille, J. C. and Nisbett, M. (1995). The complexities of eliciting and assessing children's statements. *Psychology, Public Policy, and Law*, 1, 450–60.

Mason, M. A. (1991). A judicial dilemma: expert witness testimony in child sexual abuse cases. *Journal of Psychiatry and Law*, 19 (3–4), 185–219.

Mather, L. M. (1979). *Plea Bargaining on Trial*. Lexington, MS: Lexington Books.

Mauet, T. A. and McCrimmon, L. A. (1993). *Fundamentals of Trial Techniques. Australian Edition*. Melbourne: Longman.

Mauro, R. (1991). Tipping the scales toward death: the biasing effects of death qualification. In P. Suedfeld and P. E. Tetlock (eds), *Psychology and Social Policy* (pp. 243–54). New York: New York Publishing Corporation.

Mawby, R. I. (1977). Sexual discrimination and the law. *Probation Journal*, 24, 38–43.

Mayer, J. D. and Bower, G. H. (1986). Detecting mood-dependent retrieval. In P. H. Blainey (chair), *Mood and Memory: Current Research Issues*. Symposium conducted at the meeting of the American Psychological Association, Washington, DC.

McCabe, S. (1975). Discussions in the jury room: are they like this? In N. D. Walker (ed.), *The British Jury System* (pp. 22–8). Cambridge: Institute of Criminology.

McCabe, S. and Purves, R. (1972a). By-passing the jury: a study of changes of plea and directed acquittals in higher courts. Oxford University Penal Research Unit, Occasional Paper 3.

McCabe, S. and Purves, R. (1972b). The jury at work: a study of jury trials in which the defendant was acquitted. Oxford University Penal Research Unit, Occasional Paper 4.

McCabe, S. and Purves, R. (1974). *The Jury at Work*. Oxford: Blackwell.

McCann, J. T. (1992). Criminal personality profiling in the investigation of violent crime: recent advances and future directions. *Behavioral Sciences and the Law*, 10, 475–81.

McCarthy, B. R. and Smith, B. L. (1986). The conceptualization of discrimination in the juvenile justice process: the impact of administrative factors and screening decisions on juvenile court dispositions. *Criminology*, 24, 42–64.

McCarty, D. (1929). *Psychology for the Lawyer*. Englewood Cliff: Prentice-Hall.

McCloskey, M. and Egeth, H. (1983). Eyewitness identification: what can a psychologist tell the jury? *American Psychologist*, 38, 573–5.

McCloskey, M., Egeth, H. and McKenna, J. (1986). The experimental psychologist in court: the ethics of expert testimony. *Law and Human Behavior*, 10, 1–13.

McCloskey, M., Wible, C. G. and Cohen, N. J. (1988). Is there a special flashback memory mechanism? *Journal of Experimental Psychology*, 117, 171–81.

McCloskey, M. and Zaragoza, M. (1985). Misleading postevent information and memory for events: arguments and evidence against memory impairment hypothesis. *Journal of Experimental Psychology*, 114, 1–16.

McConkey, K. M. (1992). The social sciences, the humanities and science and technology in economic development: the place of psychology. *Bulletin of the Australian Psychological Society*, 14, 3–6.

McConkey, K. (1995). Hypnosis, memory and the ethics of uncertainty. *Australian Psychologist*, 30, 1–10.

McConkey, K. M. and Roche, M. (1989). Knowledge of eyewitness memory. *Australian Psychologist*, 24, 377–84.

McConkey, K. M. and Sheehan, P. W. (1988). Forensic hypnosis: current legislation and its relevance to practice. *Australian Psychologist*, 23, 323–34.

McConville, M. and Mirsky, C. (1995). Guilty plea courts: a social disciplinary model of criminal justice. *Social Problems*, 42, 216–34.

McDowell, D. M. (1978). *The Law in Classical Athens*. London: Thames & Hudson.

McEwan, J. (1988). Child evidence: more proposals for reform. *Criminal Law Review*, 813–22.

McEwan, J. (1990). In the box or on the box? The Pigot report and child witnesses. *Criminal Law Review*, 363–70.

McEwan, J. (1995). Adversarial and inquisitorial proceedings. In R. Bull and D. Carson (eds), 495–608.

McGehee, F. (1937). The reliability of the identification of the human voice. *Journal of General Psychology*, 17, 249–71.

McGehee, F. (1944). An experimental study of voice recognition. *Journal of General Psychology*, 31, 53–65.

McGeoch, J. A. (1932). Forgetting and the law of disuse. *Psychological Review*, 39, 352–70.

McGinley, G. and Waye, V. (1994). *Evidence Handbook*. Sydney: Law Book Company.

McGough, L. S. (1995). For the record: videotaping investigative interviews. *Psychology, Public Policy and Law*, 1, 370–86.

McGuire, W. J. (1972). Attitude change: the information processing paradigm. In C.G. McClintock (ed.), *Experimental Social Psychology* (pp. 108–41). New York: Holt, Rinehart & Winston.

McGuire, W. J. (1985). Attitudes and attitude change. In G. Lindzey and E. Aronson (eds), *The Handbook of Social Psychology*, vol. 2, (pp. 233–346). New York: Random House.

McGurk, T., Platton, T. and Gibson, R. L. (1994). Detectives: a job and training needs analysis. *Issues in Criminological and Legal Psychology*, 21, 24–31.

McIntosh, J. A. and Prinz, R. J. (1993). The incidence of alleged sexual abuse in 603 family court cases. *Law and Human Behavior*, 17, 95–101.

McKenzie, I. (1995). Psychology and legal practice: fairness and accuracy in identification parades. *Criminal Law Review*, 200–8.

McLean, M. (1995). Quality investigation? Police interviewing of witnesses. *Medicine, Science and the Law*, 35, 116–22.

McMahon, M. and Knowles, A. (1995). Confidentiality in psychological practice: a decrepit concept? *Australian Psychologist*, 30, 164–8.

McNair, D. M., Lorr, M. and Drappelman, M. (1971). *Manual for the Profile of Mood States (POMS)*. San Diego: Educational and Industrial Testing Service.

Medical Research Council Applied Psychology Unit (1986). *Fraud Trials Committee: Improving the Presentation of Information to Juries in Fraud Trials*. London: HMSO.

Mehrabian, A. and Williams, M. (1969). Nonverbal concomitants of perceived and intended persuasiveness. *Journal of Personality and Social Psychology*, 13, 37–58.

Mellers, B. A. and Baron, J. (eds) (1993). *Psychological Perspectives on Justice: Theory and Applications*. New York: Cambridge University Press.

Melton, G. B., Monahan, J. and Saks, M. J. (1987). Psychologists as law professors. *American Psychologist*, 42, 502–9.

Memon, A. and Bull, R. (1991).The cognitive interview: its origins, empirical support and practical implications. *Journal of Community and Applied Psychology*, 1, 291–307.

Memon, A., Bull, R. and Smith, M. (1995). Improving the quality of the police interview: can training in the use of cognitive techniques help? *Policing and Society*, 5, 53–68.

Memon, A., Cronin, O., Eaves, R. and Bull, R. (1993). The cognitive interview and child witnesses. *Issues in Criminological and Legal Psychology*, No. 20, 3–9.

Memorandum of Good Practice on Video-Recorded Interviews with Child Witnesses for Criminal Proceedings. Home Office in conjunction with Department of Health, 1992. London: HMSO.

Messick, S. and Damarin, F. (1964). Cognitive styles and memory for faces. *Journal of Abnormal and Social Psychology*, 69, 313–18.

Metcalfe, J. (1990). Composite holographic associative recall model (CHARM) and blended memories in eyewitness testimony. *Journal of Experimental Psychology: General*, 119, 145–60.

Meudell, P. R., Hitch, G. J. and Kirby, P. (1992). Are two heads better than one? Experimental investigations of the social facilitation of memory. *Applied Cognitive Psychology*, 6, 525–43.

Michon, J. A. and Pakes, F. J. (1995). Judicial decision-making: a theoretical perspective. In R. Bull and D. Carson (eds), 509–25.

Milgram, S. (1974). *Obedience to Authority*. London: Tavistock.

Miller, A. G. (1970). Role of physical attractiveness in impression formation. *Psychonomic Science*, 19, 241–3.

Miller, A. G., Ashston, W. and Mishal, M. (1990). Beliefs concerning features of constrained behaviour: a basis for the fundamental attribution error. *Journal of Personality and Social Psychology*, 59, 635–50.

Miller, G. R. and Stiff, J. B. (1993). *Deceptive Communication*. Newbury Park: Sage Publications.

Miller, N., Maruyama, G., Beaber, R. and Valone, K. (1976). Speed of speech and persuasion. *Journal of Personality and Social Psychology*, 34, 615–24.

Miller, R. J., Chino, A. F., Haney, M. K., Haines, D. A. and Saavedra, R. L. (1986). Assignment of punishment as a function of the severity and consequences of the crime and the consequences of the defendant. *Journal of Applied Social Psychology*, 16, 77–91.

Milne, R. and Bull, R. (1995). Children with mild learning disability: the cognitive interview and suggestibility. Paper presented at the Fifth European Psychology and Law Conference, Budapest, Hungary, September 1995.

Milne, R., Bull, R., Köhnken, G. and Memon, A. (1994). The cognitive interview and suggestibility. Paper presented at the Fourth European Conference on Law and Psychology, Barcelona.

Milne, R., Bull, R., Köhnken, G. and Memon, A. (1995). The cognitive interview and suggestibility. *Issues in Criminological and Legal Psychology*, 22, 21–7.

Mirrles-Black, C. (1992). Using psychometric personality tests in the selection of firearms officers. Paper 68. London: Home Office Research and Planning Unit.

Mitchell, B. (1983). Confessions and police interrogations of suspects. *Criminal Law Review*, 596–604.

Moloney, L. (1986). Cross-examination of social workers and psychologists in the Family Court. *Australian Psychologist*, 21, 377–87.

Monahan, J. and Loftus, E. F. (1982). The psychology of law. *Annual Review of Psychology*, 33, 441–75.

Monahan, J. and Walker, L. (1985). *Social Science in Law: Cases and Materials.* Mineola, New York: The Foundation Press.

Montaya, J. (1995). Lessons from Akiki and Michaels on shielding child witnesses. *Psychology, Public Policy and Law*, 1, 340–69.

Moore, L. E. (1973). *Tool of Kings, Palladium of Liberty.* Cincinnati: W. H. Anderson.

Morgan, J. and Zedner, L. (1992a). The victim's charter: a new deal for child victims? *Howard Journal*, 31, 294–307.

Morgan, J. and Zedner, L. (1992b). *Child Victims: Crime, Impact and Criminal Justice.* Oxford: Clarendon Press.

Morgan, M. (1995). *How to Interview Sexual Abuse Victims, Including the Use of Anatomical Dolls.* Thousand Oaks, CA: Sage.

Morgan, R. and Clarkson, C. (1995). The politics of sentencing reform. In C. Clarkson and R. Morgan (eds), *The Politics of Sentencing Reform* (pp. 1–16). Oxford: Clarendon Press.

Morgan, P., Moxon, D. and Tarling, R. (1987). The implications of sentencing for the criminal justice system. In D. C. Pennington and S. M. A. Lloyd-Bostock (eds), 159–70.

Morris Committee (1965). Jury Service. Cmnd 2627. London: HMSO.

Morse, C. K., Woodward, E. M. and Zweigenhaft, R. L. (1993). Gender differences in flashbulb memories elicited by the Clarence Thomas hearings. *Journal of Social Psychology*, 133, 453–8.

Morse, W. and Beattie, R. H. (1932). A study of the variances in sentences imposed by circuit judges. In J. R. Klonoski and R. I. Mendelsohn (eds), *The Politics of Local Justice* (pp. 175–86). Boston: Little Brown & Co.

Mortimer, A. (1991). 'A case of . . .': patterns in police officers' perceptions of offences. *Issues in Criminological and Legal Psychology*, 18, 13–29.

Morton, A. (1978). *Literary Detection: How to Prove Authorship in Literature and Documents.* London: Bowker.

Morton, A. and Michaelson, S. (1990). *The Qsum Plot.* Department of Computer Science, University of Edinburgh.

Morton, J., Hammersley, R. H. and Bekerian, D. (1985). Headed records: a model for memory and its failures. *Cognition*, 20, 1–23.

Moston, S. (1990). How children interpret and respond to questions: situation sources of suggestibility in eyewitness interviews. *Social Behavior*, 5, 155–67.

Moston, S. and Engelberg, T. (1992). The effect of social support on children's testimony. *Applied Cognitive Psychology*, 6, 61–75.

Moston, S., Stephenson, G. and Williamson, T. M. (1992). The effects of case characteristics on suspect behaviour during police questioning. *British Journal of Psychology*, 32, 23–40.

Mugford, S. and Gronfors, M. (1978). Racial and class factors in the sentences of first offenders. *Australian and New Zealand Journal of Sociology*, 14, 58–61.

Müller, D. E., Blackman, D. E. and Chapman, A. J. (eds), (1984). *Psychology and Law*. Chichester: Wiley.

Mulroy, T. M. (1993). How to examine a psychologist in a custody case. *American Journal of Family Law*, 7, 65–72.

Mungham, G. and Bankowski, Z. (1976). The jury in the legal system. In P. Carlen (ed.), *The Sociology of Law* (pp. 202–25). Sociological Review Monograph 23, University of Keele, UK.

Mungham, G. and Thomas, P. A. (1979). Advocacy and the solicitor–advocate in Magistrates' Courts in England and Wales. *International Journal of the Sociology of Law*, 7, 169–95.

Munkman, J. H. (1951). *The Technique of Advocacy*. London: Steven & Sons.

Munkman, J. H. (1986). *The Technique of Advocacy*. London: Sweet Maxwell.

Münsterberg, H. (1908). *On the Witness Stand: Essays on Psychological Crime*. New York: Clark Boardman.

Murphy, K. R. (1995). Integrity testing. In N. Brewer and C. Wilson (eds), 205–28.

Myers, J. E. B. (1993). The competence of young children to testify in legal proceedings. *Behavioral Sciences and the Law*, 11, 121–33.

Nagel, S. S. (1961). Political party affiliation and judges' decisions. *American Political Science Review*, 55, 844–50.

Narby, D. J. and Cutler, B. L. (1994). Effectiveness of *voir dire* as a safeguard in eyewitness cases. *Journal of Applied Psychology*, 79, 274–9.

Nathanson, H. S. (1995). Strengthening the criminal jury: long overdue. *Criminal Law Quarterly*, 38, 217–48.

National Committee on Violence (1990). *Violence: Directions for Australia*. Canberra: Australian Institute of Criminology.

Navon, D. (1990a). How critical is the accuracy of an eyewitness' memory? Another look at the issue of line-up diagnosticity. *Journal of Applied Psychology*, 75, 506–10.

Navon, D. (1990b). Ecological parameters and non-line-up evidence: a reply to Wells and Luus. *Journal of Applied Psychology*, 75, 517–20.

Naylor, B. (1989). The child in the witness box. *Australian and New Zealand Journal of Criminology*, 22, 82–94.

Neisser, U. (1967). *Cognitive Psychology*. New York: Appleton-Century Crofts.

Neisser, U. (1982). Snapshots or benchmarks? In U. Neisser (ed.), *Memory Observed* (pp. 43–8). San Francisco: W. H. Freeman & Co.

Neisser, U. (1986). Nested structure of autobiographical memory. In D. C. Rubin (ed.), *Autobiographical Memory* (pp. 71–81). Cambridge: Cambridge University Press.

Neisser, U. and Harsch, N. (1992). Phantom flashbulbs: false recollections of hearing the news about Challenger. In E. Winograd and U. Neisser (eds).

Nelson, J. F. (1992). Hidden disparities in case processing: New York State, 1980–1986. *Journal of Criminal Justice*, 20, 181–200.

Nelson, K. (ed.) (1986). *Event Knowledge: Structure and Function in Development*. Hillsdale, NJ: Lawrence Erlbaum.

Nelson, K., Fivush, R., Hudson, J. and Lucariello, J. (1983). Scripts and the development of memory. In M. Chi (ed.), *Current Trends in Memory Research* (pp. 52–69). New York: Springer-Verlag.

Neubauer, D. W. (1974). Confessions in prairie city: some causes and effects. *Journal of Criminal Law and Criminology*, 65, 103–12.

New South Wales Law Reform Commission (1985). *The Jury in a Criminal Trial*. Discussion paper, No. 12. Sydney.

New South Wales Law Reform Commission. (1996). *Sentencing.* Discussion paper, No. 33. Sydney.

Newman, S. A. (1994). Assessing the quality of expert testimony in cases involving children. *Journal of Psychiatry and Law,* 22, 181–234.

Nietzel, M. T. and Hartung, C. M. (1993). Psychological research on police: an introduction to a special section on the psychology of law enforcement. *Law and Human Behavior,* 17, 151–5.

Nightingale, N. N. (1993). Juror reaction to child victim witnesses: factors affecting trial outcome. *Law and Human Behavior,* 17, 679–700.

Nijboer, H. (1995). Expert evidence. In R. Bull and D. Carson (eds), 555–64.

Nisbett, R. E. and Wilson, T. D. (1977). Telling more than we can know: verbal reports of mental processes. *Psychological Review,* 84, 231–59.

Noon, E. and Hollin, C. R. (1987). Lay knowledge of eyewitness behaviour: a British survey. *Applied Cognitive Psychology,* 1, 143–53.

North, C. S. et al. (1989). Short-term psychopathology in eyewitnesses to mass murder. *Hospital and Community Psychology,* 40, 1293–5.

Nosworthy, G. J. and Lindsay, R. C. L. (1990). Does nominal line-up size matter? *Journal of Applied Psychology,* 75, 358–61.

O'Barr, W. M. (1982). *Linguistic Evidence: Language, Power and Strategy in the Courtroom.* New York: Academic Press.

Odubekum, L. (1992). A structural approach to differential gender sentencing. *Criminal Justice Abstracts,* 24, 343–60.

Office of Technology Assessment, US Congress (1983). *Scientific Study of Polygraph Testing: A Research Review and Evaluation.* Washington, DC: US Printing Office.

Office of Technology Assessment, US Congress (1990). *The Use of Integrity Tests for Pre-Employment Screening* (OTA-SET-442). Washington, DC: US Government Printing Office.

Ofshe, R. (1989). Coerced confessions: the logic of seemingly irrational action. *Cultic Studies Journal,* 6, 1–15.

Ofshe, R. and Christman, K. (1986). A two-process theory of social behavior. In A. R. Harris (ed.), *Rationality and Collective Belief.* New Jersey: Ablex Publishing Corporation.

Ogloff, J. R. P. (1992). *Law and Psychology: The Broadening of the Discipline.* Durham, North Carolina: Academic Press.

Ogloff, J. R. P. and Vidmar, N. (1994). The impact of pretrial publicity on jurors: a study to compare the relative effects of television and print media in a child sex abuse case. *Law and Human Behavior,* 18, 507–25.

Oligny, M. (1994). Burnout in the police environment. *International Criminal Law Review,* 22–5.

O'Neil, M. J. (1992). Juridical situation of child witnesses in Canada. In F. Lösel et al. (eds), 399–410.

Ones, D. S., Viswesvaran, C. and Schmidt, F. L. (1993). Meta-analysis of integrity testing. Findings and implications for personnel selection and theories of job performance. Monograph. *Journal of Applied Psychology,* 78, 679–703.

Orchard, T. L. (1993). Factors affecting voice identification accuracy. Unpublished Master's thesis, University of Guelph, Ontario, Canada.

Orne, M. T. (1979). The use and misuse of hypnosis in court. *International Journal of Clinical and Experimental Hypnosis,* 27, 311–41.

Orne, M. T., Soskis, D. A., Dinges, D. F. and Orne, E. C. (1984). Hypnotically induced testimony. In G. Wells and E. F. Loftus (eds), 171–213.

Osborne, Y. H., Rappaport, N. B. and Meyer, R. G. (1986). An investigation of persuasion and sentencing severity with mock juries. *Behavioral Sciences and the Law*, 4, 339–49.

Osner, N., Quinn, A. and Crown, G. (eds) (1993). The Royal Commission on Criminal Justice. *Criminal Justice Systems in Other Jurisdictions*. London: HMSO.

Ostrom, T. M., Werner, C. and Saks, M. (1978). An integration theory analysis of jurors' presumption of guilt or innocence. *Journal of Personality and Social Psychology*, 36, 436–50.

Oswald, M. E. (1992). Justification and goals of punishment and the attribution of responsibility in judges. In F. Lösel et al. (eds), 424–34.

Otani, H. and Hodge, M. H. (1991). Does hypermnesia occur in recognition and cued recall? *American Journal of Psychology*, 104, 101–16.

O'Toole, D. M. (1988). Crime under the influence: the effects of alcohol intoxication during a crime on subsequent physiological detection of deception. Unpublished doctoral dissertation, University of British Columbia, Vancouver, cited by D. C. Raskin (1989b).

Ouston, J. (1984). Delinquency, family background and educational attainment. *British Journal of Criminology*, 24, 2–26.

Overton, D. A. (1964). State-dependent or dissociated learning procedure with pentobarbital. *Journal of Comparative Physiological Psychology*, 57, 3–12.

Oxford, T. (1991). Spotting a liar. *Police Review*, 15 February, 328–9.

Paley, B. and Geiselman, R. E. (1989). The effects of alternative photospread instructions on suspect identification performance. *American Journal of Forensic Psychology*, 7, 3–13.

Palmiotto, M. J. (1983). An historical review of lie-detection methods used in detecting criminal acts. *Canadian Police College Journal*, 7 (3), 206–16.

Palys, T. S. and Divorski, S. (1986). Explaining sentencing disparity. *Canadian Journal of Criminology*, 28, 347–62.

Pannell, W. K., Hosch, H. M. and Sands, S. (1992). Self-monitoring and event-related potentials as predictors of facial recognition. Manuscript submitted for publication.

Pannick, D. (1992). *Advocates*. New York: Oxford University Press.

Parker, E. S., Birnbaum, I. M., Weingartner, H., Hartley, J. T., Stillman, R. C. and Wyatt, R. J. (1980). Retrograde enhancement of human memory with alcohol. *Psychopharmacology*, 69, 219–22.

Parker, J. F. and Carranza, L. E. (1989). Eyewitness testimony of children in target-present and target-absent line-ups. *Law and Human Behavior*, 13, 133–49.

Parker, J. F. and Ryan, V. (1993). An attempt to reduce guessing behavior in children's and adults' eyewitness identifications. *Law and Human Behavior*, 17, 11–26.

Parker, K. D. and Ray, M. C. (1990). Fear of crime: an assessment of related factors. *Sociological Spectrum*, 10, 29–40.

Parkinson, P. (1991). The future of competency testing for child witnesses. *Criminal Law Journal*, 15, 186–92.

Parrick, C. J. and Iacono, W. G. (1989). Psychopathy, threat and polygraph test accuracy. *Journal of Applied Psychology*, 74, 347–55.

Parrick, C. J. and Iacono, W. G. (1991). Validity of the control question polygraph test. The problem of sampling bias. *Journal of Applied Psychology*, 76, 229–38.

Parry, E. A. (1923). *The Seven Lamps of Advocacy*. London: Unwin.

Patchett, K. W. and McClean, J. D. (1965). Decision-making in juvenile cases. *Criminal Law Review*, 699–710.

Payne, D. G. (1987). Hypermnesia and reminiscence in recall: a historical and empirical review. *Psychological Bulletin*, 101, 5–27.

Pennington, D. C. and Lloyd-Bostock, S. M. A. (eds) (1987). *The Psychology of Sentencing: Approaches to Consistency and Disparity*. Oxford: Centre for Socio-Legal Studies.

Pennington, N. and Hastie, R. (1986). Evidence evaluation in complex decision-making. *Journal of Personality and Social Psychology*, 51, 242–58.

Pennington, N. and Hastie, R. (1990). Practical implications of psychological research on juror and jury decision-making. *Personality and Social Psychology Bulletin*, 16 (1), 90–105.

Pennington, N. and Hastie, R. (1993). The story model for juror decision-making. In R. Hastie (ed.), 192–221.

Penrod, B. L. and Cutler, S. D. (1995a). *Mistaken Identification: The Eyewitness, Psychology, and Law*. New York: Cambridge University Press.

Penrod, B. L. and Cutler, S. D. (1995b). Assessing the accuracy of eyewitness identifications. In R. Bull and D. Carson (eds), 193–213.

Penrod, S., Loftus, E. F. and Winkler, J. D. (1982). The reliability of eyewitness testimony: a psychological perspective. In N. L. Kerr and R. M. Bray (eds), 119–68.

Penrod, S. D., Solomon, M., Fulero, J. D. and Cutler, B. L. (1995). Expert psychological testimony on eyewitness reliability before and after *Daubert*: the state of the law and science. *Behavioral Sciences and the Law*, 13, 229–59.

Perlman, N. B., Erickson, K. I., Esses, V. M. and Isaacs, B. (1994). The developmentally handicapped witness: competency as a function of question format. *Law and Human Behavior*, 18, 171–87.

Perrott, S. B. and Taylor, D. M. (1995). Attitudinal differences between police constables and their supervisors: potential influences of personality, work environment, and occupational role. *Criminal Justice and Behavior*, 22, 326–39.

Perry, N. W. and Wrightsman, L. (1991). *The Child Witness: Legal Issues and Dilemmas*. Newbury Park, CA: Sage.

Peters, D. P. (1985). A naturalistic study of earwitness evidence: does the addition of a voice to a line-up influence accuracy and/or confidence? Paper presented at the annual meeting of the Eastern Psychological Association.

Peters, D. P. (1987). The impact of naturally occurring stress on children's memory. In S. J. Ceci, M. P. Toglia and D. F. Ross (eds), *Children's Eyewitness Memory*, 122–41, New York: Springer-Verlag.

Peters, D. P. (1991). Confrontational stress and children's testimony: some experimental findings. In J. Doris (ed.), 60–76.

Peterson, C. C., Peterson, J. L. and Seeto, D. (1983). Developmental changes in ideas about lying. *Child Development*, 54, 1529–35.

Petty, R. E. and Cacioppo, J. T. (1984). The effects of issue involvement on responses to argument quantity and quality: central and peripheral routes of persuasion. *Journal of Personality and Social Psychology*, 46, 69–81.

Petty, R. E., Cacioppo, J. T. and Goldman, R. (1981). Personal involvement as a determinant of argument-based persuasion. *Journal of Personality and Social Psychology*, 41, 847–55.

Phillips, J. (1985). *Advocacy With Honour*. Sydney: Law Book Co.

Phillpots, G. J. and Lancucki, L. B. (1979). *Previous Convictions, Sentence and Reconviction: A Statistical Study of a Sample of 5000 Offenders Convicted in January 1971*. Research Study, No. 53. London: Home Office.

Piaget, J. (1972). *Judgement and Reasoning in the Child*. (M. Warden, trans.) Totawa, NJ: Littlefield, Adams. (Originally published 1924.)

Pickel, K. L. (1995). Inducing jurors to disregard inadmissible evidence: a legal explanation does not help. *Law and Human Behavior*, 19, 407–24.

Pigot, His Honour Judge (1989, December). *Report of the National Advisory Group on Video Evidence*. London: Home Office.

Pigott, M. A. and Brigham, J. C. (1985). Relationship between accuracy of prior description and facial recognition. *Journal of Applied Psychology*, 70, 547–55.

Pike, G. and Kemp, R. (1995). Turning heads. *Forensic Update*, Issue 40, 23–7.

Piliavin, I. and Briar, S. (1964). Police encounters with juveniles. *American Journal of Sociology*, 70, 206–14.

Piliavin, J. A., Dovidio, J. F., Gaertner, S. L. and Clark, R. D. (1981). *Emergency Intervention*. New York: Academic Press.

Pillemer, D. and White, S. H. (1989). Childhood events recalled by children and adults. In H. W. Reese (ed.), *Advances in Child Development and Behavior* vol. 22, (pp. 297–346). New York: Academic Press.

Pipe, M. E. and Goodman, G. S. (1991). Elements of secrecy: implications for children's testimony. *Behavioral Science and the Law*, 9, 33–41.

Pitchert, J. W. and Anderson, R. C. (1977). Taking perspectives on a story. *Journal of Educational Psychology*, 69, 309–15.

Ploscowe, M. (1951). The court and the correctional system. In P. Tappan (ed.), *Contemporary Correction*. New York: McGraw-Hill.

Podlesny, J. A. and Raskin, D. C. (1977). Physiological measures and the detection of deception. *Psychological Bulletin*, 84, 782–99.

Podlesny, J. A. and Raskin, D. C. (1978). Effectiveness of techniques and physiological measures in the detection of deception. *Psychophysiology*, 15, 344–58.

Pogrebin, M. R. and Poole, E. D. (1991). Police and tragic events: the management of emotions. *Journal of Criminal Justice*, 19, 395–403.

Pogrebin, M. R. and Poole, E. D. (1993). Vice isn't nice: a look at the effects of working undercover. *Journal of Criminal Justice*, 21, 383–94.

Police and Criminal Evidence Act (1984). Codes of Practice, Revised edn, effective 1 April 1991. London: HMSO, 1992.

Policy Studies Institute (1983). *Police and People in London*. London: Policy Studies Institute.

Polk, K. and Tait, D. (1988). The use of imprisonment by the Magistrates' Courts. *Australian and New Zealand Journal of Criminology*, 21, 31–44.

Pope, C. E. (1975). *The Judicial Processing of Assault and Burglary Offenders in Selected California Counties*. Utilization of Criminal Statistics Project, Analytic Report 7, US Department of Justice Law Enforcement Assistance Administration.

Popper, K. R. (1939). *The Logic of Scientific Discovery*. London: Hutchinson.

Porter, S. and Yuille, J. C. (1995). Credibility assessment of criminal suspects through statement analysis. *Psychology, Crime and Law*, 1, 319–31.

Potas, I. and Rickwood, D. (1984). *Do Juries Understand?* Canberra: Australian Institute of Criminology.

Powel, M. B. and Thomson, D. M. (1994, March). A study of children's memory about a specific episode of a recurring event. Paper presented by Powel at the First National Conference on Child Sexual Abuse, Radisson Hotel, Melbourne.

Power, D. J. (1977). Memory, identifications and crime. *Medicine, Science and the Law*, 17, 132–9.

Powers, P. A., Andriks, J. L. and Loftus, E. F. (1979). Eyewitness account of females and males. *Journal of Applied Psychology*, 64, 339–47.

Pynes, J. and Bernardin, H. J. (1992). Entry-level police selection: the assessment center as an alternative. *Journal of Criminal Justice*, 20, 41–52.

Pynoos, R. and Eth, S. (1984). The child as witness to homicide. *Journal of Social Issues*, 40, 87–108.

Quattrone, G. A. and Jones, E. E. (1980). The perception of variability with in-groups and out-groups: implications for the law of small numbers. *Journal of Personality and Social Psychology*, 38, 141–52.

Queensland Criminal Justice Commission (1991). *Report of an Investigative Hearing into Alleged Jury Interference*. Brisbane.

Rabbitt, P. M. A. (1981). Applying human experimental psychology to legal questions about evidence. In S. M. A. Lloyd-Bostock (ed.), 3–18.

Ragg, M. (1995). Proof positive or negative? *Bulletin*, 13 June, 14–17.

Rapaport, E. (1991). The death penalty and gender discrimination. *Law and Society Review*, 25, 367–83.

Raskin, D. C. (ed.) (1989a). *Psychological Methods in Criminal Investigation and Evidence*. New York: Springer-Verlag.

Raskin, D. C. (1989b). Polygraph techniques for the detection of deception. In D. C.'Raskin (ed.), 247–95.

Raskin, D. C. and Esplin, P. W. (1991). Assessment of children's statements of sexual abuse. In J. Doris (ed.), 153–64.

Raskin, D. C. and Yuille, J. C. (1989). Problems in evaluating interviews of children of sexual abuse. In S. Ceci, D. Ross, and M. Toglia (eds), *Perspectives on Children's Testimony* (pp. 184–207). New York: Springer-Verlag.

Rattner, A. (1988). Convicted but innocent: wrongful conviction and the criminal justice system. *Law and Human Behavior*, 12, 283–94.

Ray, J. J. (1972). A new balance F scale and its relation to social class. *Australian Psychologist*, 7, 155–66.

Read, J. D. and Lindsay, D. S. (1994). Moving toward a middle ground on the 'false memory debate': reply to commentaries on Lindsay and Read. *Applied Cognitive Psychology*, 8, 407–35.

Read, J. D., Tollestrup, P., Hammersley, R., McFazden, E. and Christensen, A. (1990). The unconscious transference effect: are innocent bystanders ever misidentified? *Applied Cognitive Psychology*, 4, 3–31.

Read, J. D., Yuille, J. C. and Tollestrup, P. (1992). Recollections of a robbery: effects of arousal and alcohol upon recall and person identification. *Law and Human Behavior*, 16, 425–46.

Rector, N. A. and Bagby, R. M. (1995). Criminal sentence recommendations in a simulated rape trial: examining juror prejudice in Canada. *Behavioral Sciences and the Law*, 13, 113–21.

Redmayne, M. (1994). The Royal Commission's proposals on expert evidence. *Expert Evidence*, 2, 157–63.

Reich, A. and Duke, J. (1979). Effects of selected vocal disguises upon speaker identification by listening. *Journal of the Acoustical Society of America*, 66, 1023–8.

Reid, J. and Associates (1986). *The Reid Technique of Interviewing and Interrogation*. Chicago, IL: Reid & Associates.

Reifman, A., Gusick, S. M. and Ellsworth, P. C. (1992). Real jurors' understanding of the law in real cases. *Law and Human Behavior*, 16, 539–54.

Reinke, R. (1977). *Selection Through Assessment Centers*. Washington, DC: Police Foundation.

Reisberg, D., Heuer, F., Maclean, J. and O'Shaughnessy, M. (1988). The quantity, not the quality, affect predicts memory vividness. *Bulletin of the Psychonomic Society*, 26, 100–3.

Reiser, M. (1989). Investigative hypnosis. In D. C. Raskin (ed.), 151–90.

Reiser, M. and Klyver, N. (1987). Consulting with the police. In I. B. Weiner and H. K. Hess (eds), 437–59.

Report of the Inquiry into Child Abuse in Cleveland (1987). London: HMSO.

Report of the Royal Commission on Criminal Procedure (1981). London: HMSO.

Reskin, B. F. and Visher, C. A. (1986). The impacts of evidence and extralegal factors in jurors' decisions. *Law and Society Review*, 20, 423–38.

Rezdek, K. (1994). The illusion of illusory memory. *Applied Cognitive Psychology*, 8, 339–50.

Rhodes, W. M. (1977). A study of sentencing in the Hennepin County and Ramsay County District Courts. *Journal of Legal Studies*, 6, 333–53.

Richardson, G. (1991). A study of interrogative suggestibility in an adolescent forensic population. M.Sc dissertation, University of Newcastle Upon Tyne.

Richardson, G. and Kelly, T. P. (1995). The relationship between intelligence, memory and interrogative suggestibility in young offenders. *Psychology, Crime and Law*, 1 (4), 283–90.

Roberts, H. and Glasgow, D. (1993). *Issues in Criminological and Legal Psychology*, No. 20, 10–14.

Robertson, B., Vignaux, G. A. and Egerton, I. (1994). Stylometric evidence. *Criminal Law Review*, 645–9.

Rock, P. (1991). Witness and space in a Crown Court. *British Journal of Criminology*, 31, 266–79.

Rose, G. (1965). An experimental study of sentencing. *British Journal of Criminology*, 5, 314–19.

Rosen, J. (1992). Jury mandering: a case against peremptory challenges. *New Republic*, 30 November, 15–16.

Rosenbaum, D. (1989). Prayer was a turning point, a juror says. *New York Times*, 5 May, A.19.

Rosenfeld, J. P., Angell, A., Johnson, M. and Qian, J. (1991). An ERP-based, control-question lie detector analog: algorithms for discriminating within individuals' average waveforms. *Psychophysiology*, 28, 319–55.

Rosenthal, R. (1995). S*tate New Jersey v. Margaret Kelly Michaels*: an overview. *Psychology, Public Policy and Law*, 1, 246–71.

Roskill, Lord P. C. (1986). *Fraud Trials Committee Report*. London: HMSO.

Ross, D. F., Ceci, S. J., Dunning, D. and Toglia, M. P. (1994b). Unconscious transference and line-up identification: toward a memory blending approach. In D. F. Ross et al. (eds), 80–100.

Ross, D. F., Ceci, S. J., Dunning, D. and Toglia, M. P. (1994c). Unconscious transference: when a witness misidentifies a familiar but innocent person. *Journal of Applied Psychology*, 79, 918–30.

Ross, D. F., Dunning, D., Toglia, M. P. and Ceci, S. (1990). The child in the eyes of the jury: assessing mock jurors' perceptions of the child witness. *Law and Human Behavior*, 14, 5–23.

Ross, D. F., Hopkins, S., Hanson, E., Lindsay, R. C. L., Hazen, K. and Eslinger, T. (1994d). The impact of protective shields and videotape testimony on conviction rates in a simulated trial of child sexual abuse. *Law and Human Behavior*, 18, 553–66.

Ross, D. F., Read, J. D. and Toglia, M. P. (eds) (1994a). *Adult Eyewitness Testimony: Current Trends and Developments*. New York: Cambridge University Press.

Royal Commission on Civil Liability and Compensation for Personal Injury (The Pearson Commission, Chairman, Lord Pearson) (1978). Cmnd. 7054–1. London: HMSO.

Royal Commission on Criminal Procedure (1984). London: HMSO.

Royal Commission on Criminal Justice (1993). *Report*. (Chair: Lord Runciman) Cmnd 2263. London: HMSO.

Royal Commission on Gambling (1978). Final Report (The Rothschild Report). Cmnd 7200. London: HMSO.

Ruck, M. D. (1996). Why children think they should tell the truth in court: developmental considerations for the assessment of competency. *Legal and Criminological Psychology*, 1, 103–16.

Rudy, L. and Goodman, G. S. (1991). Effects of participation on children's reports: implications for children's testimony. *Developmental Psychology*, 27, 527–38.

Rue, L. (1994). *By the Grace of Guile: The Role of Deception in Natural History and Human Affairs*. New York: Oxford University Press.

Runciman, Lord (1993). Report of the Royal Commission on Criminal Justice. Cmnd 2263. London: HMSO.

Russell, J. A. (1995). Facial expression of emotion: what lies beyond minimal universality? *Psychological Bulletin*, 118, 379–91.

Russell, K. (1986). Polygraph use in the United Kingdom. *Yearbook of Law Computers and Technology*, 126–9.

Sackett, P. R. (1985). Honesty research and the person-situation debate. In W. Terris (ed.), *Employee Theft*. Chicago, IL: London House Press.

Sackett, P. R., Burris, L. R. and Callahan, C. (1989). Integrity testing for personnel selection: an update. *Personnel Psychology*, 42, 491–529.

Saks, M. (1977). *Jury Verdicts: The Role of Group Size and Social Decision Rule*. Heath, Mass.: Lexington.

Saks, M. and Hastie, R. (1978). *Social Psychology in Court*. London: Van Nostrand.

Saks, M. J. (1986). The law does not live by eyewitness-testimony alone. *Law and Human Behavior*, 10, 279–80.

Saks, M. J. (1992). Normative and empirical issues about the role of expert witnesses. In D. K. Kagehiro and W. S. Laufer (eds), 185–203.

Sales, B.D. (ed.) (1977). *Perspectives in Law and Psychology*, vol. 1, The Criminal Justice System. New York: Plenum.

Sales, B. D., Shuman, D. W. and O'Connor, M. (1994). In a dim light: admissibility of child sexual abuse memories. *Applied Cognitive Psychology*, 8, 399–406.

Sallmann, P. and Willis, J. (1984). *Criminal Justice in Australia*. Melbourne: Oxford University Press.

Sanborn, J. B. (1993). The right to a public jury trial: a need for today's juvenile court. *Judicature*, 76, 230–8.

Sanders, A. (1987). Constructing the case for the prosecution. *Journal of Law and Society*, 14, 229–53.

Sanders, G. S. (1986). On increasing the usefulness of eyewitness research. *Law and Human Behavior*, 10, 333–5.

Sanders, G. S. and Warnick, D. H. (1981). Truth and consequences: the effects of responsibility on eyewitness behavior. *Basic and Applied Social Psychology*, 12, 67–79.

Sandys, M. (1995). Cross overs – capital jurors who change their minds about the punishment: a litmus test for sentencing guidelines. *Indiana Law Journal*, 70, 1183–221.

Sandys, M. and Dillehay, R. C. (1995). First-ballot votes, predeliberation dispositions, and final verdicts in jury trials. *Law and Human Behavior*, 19, 175–95.

Sapir, A. (1991). Scientific content analysis course presentation. March 1992. Detroit, Michigan.

Sapir, A. (1993). SCAN advanced workshop. 1–3 June, Washington, DC.

Sarat, A. (1995). Violence, representation and responsibility in capital trials: the view from the jury. *Indiana Law Journal*, 70, 1103–39.

Saslove, H. and Yarmey, A. D. (1980). Long-term auditory memory: speaker identification. *Journal of Applied Psychology*, 65, 111–16.

Sattar, G. and Bull, R. (1994). Preparing the child witness. *Policing*, 11 (3), 155–70.

Saunders, W. (1984). *Alcohol Use in Britain: How Much is Too Much?* Edinburgh.

Saywitz, K. J. (1987). Children's testimony: age-related patterns of memory errors. In S. J. Ceci, M. P. Toglia and D. F. Ross (eds), *Children's Eyewitness Memory* (pp. 36–52). New York: Springer-Verlag.

Saywitz, K. J., Geiselman, R. E. and Bornstein, G. K. (1993). Effects of cognitive interviewing and practice on children's recall performance. *Applied Psychology*, 77, 744–56.

Saywitz, K. J., Goodman, G. S., Nicholas, E. and Moan, S. (1991a). Children's memories of physical examinations involving genital touch: implications for reports of child sexual abuse. *Journal of Consulting and Clinical Psychology*, 59, 682–91.

Saywitz, K. J., Moan, S. and Lamphear, V. (1991b, August). The effect of preparation on children's resistance to misleading questions. Paper presented at the annual meeting of American Psychological Association, San Francisco, CA.

Saywitz, K. J. and Snyder, L. (1991, April). Preparing child witnesses: the efficacy of comprehension monitoring training. Paper presented at the biennial convention of the Society for Research on Child Development, Seattle, WA., cited by K. J. Saywitz and L. Snyder (1993).

Saywitz, K. J. and Snyder, L. (1993). Improving children's testimony with preparation. In G. S. Goodman and B. L. Bottoms (eds), 117–46.

Saywitz, K. J., Snyder, L. and Lamphear, V. (1990, August). Preparing child witnesses: their efficacy of memory strategy training. Paper presented at the annual convention of the American Psychological Association, Boston, MA.

Scarman, Rt. Hon. Lord (1981). *The Brixton Disorders, 10–12 April 1981: Report of an Enquiry by Rt. Hon. Lord Scarman*. Cmnd 8427. London: HMSO.

Schacter, L., Kagan, J. and Leichtman, M. D. (1995). True and false memories in children and adults: a cognitive neuroscience perspective. *Psychology, Public Policy and Law*, 1, 411–28.

Schare, M. L., Lisman, S. A. and Spear, N. E. (1984). The effects of mood variation on state-dependent retentions. *Cognitive Therapy Research*, 8, 387–408.

Scheflin, A. W. (1994). Forensic hypnosis and the law: the current situation in the United States. In B. J. Evans and R. O. Stanley (eds), 25–48.

Schiff, W., Banka, L. and Bordes Galdi, G. (1986). Recognising people seen in events via dynamic 'mugshots'. *American Journal of Psychology*, 99, 219–31.

Schill, T. (1966). Effects of approval motivation and varying conditions of verbal reinforcement on incidental memory for faces. *Psychological Reports*, 19, 55–60.

Schneider, D. J. (1995). Attribution of social cognition. In M. Argyle and A. M. Colman (eds), *Social Psychology* (pp. 38–56). London: Longman.

Schooler, J. W. and Engstler-Schooler, T. Y. (1990). Verbal overshadowing of visual memories: some things are better left unsaid. *Cognitive Psychology*, 22, 36–71.

Schor, D. P. and Sivan, A. B. (1989). Interpreting children's labels for sex-related body parts of anatomically explicit dolls. *Child Abuse and Neglect*, 13, 523–31.

Schubert, G. (1959). *Quantitative Analysis of Judicial Behavior*. Glucoe, IL: The Free Press.

Schum, D. A. (1993). Argument structuring and evidence evaluation. In R. Hastie (ed.), 175–91.

Schwalb, B. L. (1991). Child abuse trials and the confrontation of traumatized witnesses: defining 'confrontation' to protect both children and defendants. *Harvard Civil Rights – Civil Liberties Law Review*, 26, 185–217.

Scrivner, E. and Safer, M. A. (1988). Eyewitnesses show hypermnesia for details about a violent event. *Journal of Applied Psychology*, 73, 371–7.

Scrivner, E. M. (1986). Assessment strategy for special unit assignments: an alternative to psychological tests. In J. C. Yuille (ed.), 251–5.

Sealy, A. P. (1975). What can be learned from the analysis of simulated juries? In N. D. Walker (ed.), 12–21.

Sealy, A. P. (1989). Decision processes in the jury room. In H. Wegener et al. (eds), 163–80.

Sealy, A. P. and Cornish, W. R. (1973). Juries and the rules of evidence. *Modern Law Review*, 208–23.

Seltzer, R., Venuti, M. A. and Lopes, G. M. (1991). Juror honesty during *voir dire. Journal of Criminal Justice*, 19 (5), 451–62.

Sentencing Committee [Victoria]. (1988). *Report of the Victorian Sentencing Committee*, vol. 1. Melbourne: Attorney-General's Department.

Severance, L. J., Goodman, J. and Loftus, E. F. (1992). Inferring the criminal mind: toward a bridge between legal doctrine and psychological understanding. *Journal of Criminal Justice*, 20, 107–20.

Shakoor, B. H. and Chalmers, D. (1991). Co-victimization of African–American children who witness violence: effects on cognitive, emotional, and behavioral development. *Journal of the National Medical Association*, 83, 233–8.

Shapiro, P. N. and Penrod, S. (1986). Meta-analysis of facial identification studies. *Psychological Bulletin*, 100, 139–56.

Shapland, J. (1987). Who controls sentencing? Influences on the sentencer. In D. C. Pennington and S. M. A. Lloyd-Bostock (eds), 77–87.

Sheehan, P. W. (1989). Response to suggestions of memory distortions in hypnosis: sampling cognitive and social factors. In V. A. Gheorgiu et al. (eds), *Suggestion and Suggestibility: Theory and Research* (pp. 295–303). Berlin: Springer.

Sheehan, P. W. (1994). Issues in forensic hypnosis. In B. J. Evans and R. O. Stanley (eds), 61–79.

Sheehan, P. W. and McConkey, K. (1994). Lying in hypnosis: a conceptual analysis of the possibilities. In B. J. Evans and R. O. Stanley (eds), 125–33.

Sheingold, K. and Tenney, Y. J. (1982). Memory for a salient childhood event. In U. Neisser (ed.), *Memory Observed* (pp. 201–2). San Francisco: W. H. Freeman & Co.

Sheldon, D. H. and MacLeod, M. D. (1991). From normative to positive data: expert psychological evidence re-examined. *Criminal Law Review*, 811–20.

Sheldon, W. H. (1942). *The Varieties of Temperament: A Psychology of Constitutional Differences*. New York: Harper.

Shepherd, E. (1991a). Resistance in interviews: the contribution of police perceptions and behaviour. *Issues in Criminological and Legal Psychology*, 18, 5–11.

Shepherd, E. (1991b). Ethical interviewing. *Issues in Criminological and Legal Psychology*, 18, 46–55.

Shepherd, E. (1995). Representing and analysing the interviewee's account. *Medicine, Science and the Law*, 35, 122–35.

Shepherd, J. W., Ellis, H. D. and Davies, G. M. (1982). *Identification Evidence: A Psychological Evaluation*. Aberdeen: University Press.

Sherman, S. J. (1995). The capital jury project: the role of responsibility and how psychology can inform the law. *Indiana Law Journal*, 70, 1241–8.

Shoemaker, D., South, D. and Lowe, J. (1973). Facial stereotypes of deviants and judgements of guilt or innocence. *Social Forces*, 51, 427–33.

Shuman, D. W., Hamilton, J. A. and Daley, C. E. (1994). The health effects of jury service. *Law and Psychology Review*, 18, 267–307.

Siegal, M. and Peterson, C. C. (1995). Memory and suggestibility in conversations with children. *Australian Journal of Psychology*, 47, 38–41.

Sigall, H. and Ostrove, N. (1975). Beautiful but dangerous: effects of offender attractiveness and nature of the crime on juridic judgements. *Journal of Personality and Social Psychology*, 31, 410–14.

Simon, R. J. (1967). *The Jury and the Defence of Insanity*. Boston: Little Brown & Co.

Skinner, J. and Berry, K. (1993). Anatomically detailed dolls and the evaluation of child sexual abuse. *Law and Human Behavior*, 18, 399–421.

Skyrme, Sir T. (1979). *The Changing Image of the Magistracy*. London: Macmillan.

Slind-Flor, V. (1992). Counties begin to help jurors cope afterward. *National Law Journal*, 20 January, 14, 3.

Slora, K. B. (1989). An empirical approach to determining employee deviance base rates. Paper presented at the 97th annual convention of the American Psychological Association, New Orleans, LA.

Slovenko, R. (1993). The 'revival of memory' of childhood sexual abuse: is the tolling of the statute of limitations justified? *Journal of Psychiatry and Law*, 21, 7–34.

Small, M. A. (1993). Advancing psychological jurisprudence. *Behavioral Sciences and the Law*, 11, 3–16.

Small, M. A. and Melton, G. B. (1994). Evaluation of child witnesses for confrontation with criminal defendants. *Professional Psychology: Research and Practice*, 25, 228–33.

Smith, A. D. and Winograd, E. (1978). Adult age differences in remembering faces. *Developmental Psychology*, 14, 443–4.

Smith, D. (1994). Race, crime and criminal justice. In M. Maguire, R. Morgan and R. Reiner (eds), *The Oxford Handbook of Criminology*. Oxford: Clarendon Press.

Smith, V. L. and Ellsworth, P. C. (1987). The social psychology of eyewitness accuracy: misleading questions and communicator expertise. *Journal of Applied Psychology*, 72, 294–300.

Smith, V. L., Kassin, S. M. and Ellsworth, P. C. (1989). Eyewitness accuracy and confidence: within- versus between-subjects' correlation. *Journal of Applied Psychology*, 74, 356–9.

Snel, B. (1978). Observation in the courtroom. *Netherlands Journal of Sociology*, 14, 173–90.

Snyder, M. (1979). Self-monitoring processes. In L. Berkowitz (ed.), *Advances in Experimental Social Psychology*, vol. 12 (pp. 85–128). New York: Academic Press.

Snyder, M. (1987). *Public Appearance/Private Realities*. New York: W. H. Freeman & Co.

Softley, P., Brown, D., Forde, B., Mair, G. and Moxon, D. (1980). *Police Interrogation: An Observational Study in Four Police Stations*. London: HMSO.

Solimine, M. E. and Wheatley, S. E. (1995). Rethinking feminist judging. *Indiana Law Journal*, 70, 891–920.

Spencer, J. and Flin, R. (1990). *The Evidence of Children: The Law and the Psychology*. London: Blackwell.

Spencer, J. and Flin, R. (1993). *The Evidence of Children: The Law and the Psychology* (2nd edn). London: Blackwell.

Spiegel, R. (1989). *Psychopharmacology: An Introduction*. Chichester: Wiley.

Spielberger, C. D., Gorsuch, R. L., Lushene, R. E., Vagg, P. R. and Jacobs, G. A. (1983). *State-Trait Anxiety Inventory Manual*. Palo Alto, CA: Consulting Psychologists Press.

Spohn, C. (1992). An analysis of the 'jury trial penalty' and its effect on black and white offenders. *Justice Professional*, 7, 93–112.

Spohn, C. and Cederblom, J. (1991). Race and disparities in sentencing: a test of the liberation hypothesis. *Justice Quarterly*, 8, 305–27.

Spohn, C., Gruhl, J. and Welch, S. (1981–82). The effect of race on sentencing: a re-examination of an unsettled question. *Law and Society Review*, 16, 72–88.

Sporer, S. L. (1989). Verbal and visual process in person identification. In H. Wegener et al. (eds), 303–24.

Sporer, S. L. (1993). Eyewitness identification accuracy, confidence and decision times in simultaneous and sequential line-ups. *Journal of Applied Psychology*, 78, 22–33.

Sporer, S. L., Penrod, S., Read, D. and Cutler, B. (1995). Choosing, confidence, and accuracy: a meta-analysis of the confidence–accuracy relation in eye-witness identification studies. *Psychological Bulletin*, 118, 315–27.

Spreutels, J. P. (1980). Giving reasons for sentence at the Crown Court. *Criminal Law Review*, 486–95.

Squire, L. R., Knowlton, B. and Musen, G. (1993). The structure and organiz-ation of memory. *Annual Review of Psychology*, 44, 453–95.

Stalans, L. J. and Finn, M. A. (1995). How novice and experienced officers interpret wife assaults: normative and efficiency frames. *Law and Society Review*, 29, 287–321.

Steblay, N. M. (1992). A meta-analytic review of the weapon focus effect. *Law and Human Behavior*, 16, 413–24.

Steele, C. M. and Josephs, R. A. (1990). Alcohol myopia: its prized and dangerous effects. *American Psychologist*, 45, 921–33.

Steffensmeier, D. J. and Terry, R. M. (1973). Deviance and respectability: an observational study of reactions to shoplifting. *Social Forces*, 51, 417–26.

Steffensmeier, D. J., Kramer, J. and Streifel, C. (1993). Gender and imprisonment decisions. *Criminology*, 31, 411–46.

Stein, F. M. (1986). Helping young policemen cope with stress and manage conflict situations. In J. C. Yuille (ed.), 301–5.

Steller, M. and Boychuk, T. (1992). Children as witnesses in sexual abuse cases: investigative interview and assessment techniques. In H. Dent and R. Flin (eds), 47–71.

Steller, M. and Köhnken, G. (1989). Criteria-based statement analysis. In D. C. Raskin (ed.), 217–45.

Stephenson, G. M. (1992). *The Psychology of Criminal Justice.* Oxford: Blackwell.

Stephenson, G. M. (1995). Looking to the future: a psychologist's comments on Richard Abel's *Contested Communities. Journal of Law and Society,* 22, 133–9.

Stephenson, G. M., Abrams, D., Wagner, W. and Wade, G. (1986a). Partners in recall: collaborative order in the recall of police interrogation. *British Journal of Social Psychology,* 25, 341–3.

Stephenson, G. M., Brandstatter, H. and Wagner, W. (1982). An experimental study of social performance and delay on the testimonial validity of story telling. *European Journal of Social Psychology,* 13, 175–91.

Stephenson, G. M., Clark, N. K. and Kniveton, B. H. (1989). Collaborative testimony by police officers: a psycho-legal issue. In H. Wegener et al. (eds), 254–70.

Stephenson, G. M., Clark, N. K. and Wade, G. S. (1986b). Meetings make evidence? An experimental study of collaborative and individual recall of a simulated police interrogation. *Journal of Personality and Social Psychology,* 50, 1113–22.

Stephenson, G. M., Kniveton, B. H. and Wagner, W. (1991). Social influences on remembering: intellectual, interpersonal and intergroup components. *European Journal of Social Psychology,* 21, 463–75.

Stephenson, G. M. and Moston, S. J. (1991). Attitudes and assumptions of police officers when questioning criminal suspects. *Issues in Criminological and Legal Psychology,* 18, 30–6.

Stephenson, G. M. and Moston, S. J. (1994). Police interrogation. *Psychology, Crime and Law,* 1, 151–7.

Stern, L. B. and Dunning, D. (1994). Distinguishing accurate from inaccurate eyewitness identifications: a reality monitoring approach. In D. F. Ross et al. (eds), 273–99.

Stern, L. W. (1910). Abstracts of lectures on the psychology of testimony and on the study of individuality. *American Journal of Psychology,* 21, 270–82.

Stern, L. W. (1939). The psychology of testimony. *Journal of Abnormal and Social Psychology,* 34, 3–20.

Stevens, P. and Willis, C. F. (1979). *Race, Crime and Arrests.* Study No. 58. London: Home Office.

Steward, M. (1992). Preliminary findings from the University of California – Davis, child memory study. *Advisor,* 5, 11–13.

Stewart, J. E. (1980). Defendant's attractiveness as a factor in the outcome of criminal trials: an observational study. *Journal of Applied Social Psychology,* 10, 348–61.

Stiff, J. B. and Miller, G. R. (1986). 'Come to think of it': interrogative probes, deceptive communication, and deception detection. *Human Communication Research,* 12, 339–57.

Stone, E. F. and Stone, D. L. (1990). Privacy in organizations: theoretical issues, research findings, and protection mechanisms. In G. Ferris and K. Rowland (eds), *Research in Personnel and Human Resources Management,* vol. 8, (pp. 349–411). Greenwich, CT: JAI Press.

Stone, M. (1991). Instant lie detection? Demeanour and credibility in criminal trials. *Criminal Law Review,* 821–30.

Stone, R. W. (1990). Commentary: twelve good men (or women) and true. *Police Journal*, 63, 283–5.

Strodtbeck, F. L., James, J. and Hawkins, C. (1957). Social status in jury deliberations. *American Sociological Review*, 22, 713–19.

Stuesser, L. (1992). Admitting prior inconsistent statements for their truth. *Canadian Bar Review*, 71, 48–76.

Sue, S., Smith, R. E. and Gilbert, R. (1974). Biasing effects of pretrial publicity on judicial decisions. *Journal of Criminal Justice*, 2, 163–71.

Swanson, C. R., Chamelin, N. and Territo, L. (1988). *Criminal Investigation* (4th edn). New York: Random House.

Sweeney, L. T. and Haney, C. (1992). The influence of race on sentencing: a meta-analytic review of experimental studies. *Behavioral Sciences and the Law*, 10, 179–95.

Szasz, J. S. (1957). Psychiatric expert testimony: its court meaning and social function. *Psychiatry*, 20, 313–16.

Tanford, S. and Penrod, S. (1986). Jury deliberations: discussion, content and influence processes in jury decision-making. *Journal of Applied Social Psychology*, 16, 322–47.

Tanford, S., Penrod, S. and Collins, R. (1985). Decision-making in joined criminal trials: the influence of charge similarity, evidence similarity and limiting instructions. *Law and Human Behavior*, 9, 319–37.

Tapp, J. L. (1976). Psychology and the law: an overture. In M. L. Rosenzweig and L. W. Porter (eds), *Annual Review of Psychology*, vol. 27. Palo Alto, CA: Annual Reviews.

Tapp, J. L. and Levine, F. J. (eds) (1977). *Law, Justice and the Individual in Society*. Holt, Rinehart & Winston.

Taylor, P. J. and Kopelman, M. D. (1984). Amnesia for criminal offences. *Psychological Medicine*, 14, 581–8.

Taylor, S. E. and Crocker, J. (1980). Schematic basis of social information processing. In E. T. Higgins et al., *Social Cognition, The Ontario Symposium*, vol. 1. Hillside, NJ: Lawrence Erlbaum.

Teahan, J. E. (1975). A longitudinal study of attitude shifts among black and white police officers. *Journal of Social Issues*, 31, 47–56.

Terr, L. (1991). *Too Scared to Cry*. New York: Harper & Row.

Terry, W. C. (1981). Police stress: the empirical evidence. *Journal of Police Science and Administration*, 9, 61–75.

Thomas, D. (1979). *Principles of Sentencing*. London: Heinemann.

Thomas, D. (1987). Sentencing: some current questions. In D. C. Pennington and S. M. A. Lloyd-Bostock (eds), 13–23.

Thomas, D. (1979). *Principles of Sentencing* (2nd edn). London: Heinemann.

Thomas, G. C. and Pollack, B. S. (1992). Rethinking guilt, juries and jeopardy. *Michigan Law Review*, 91, 1–33.

Thomassin, L. and Michael, A. (1990). Performance of eyewitnesses when giving evidence and making eyewitness identification. *Canadian Police College Journal*, 14, 233–46.

Thompson, C. P. (1985a). Voice identification: speaker identification and a correction of the record regarding sex effects. Human Learning. *Journal of Practical Research and Applications*, 4, 19–28.

Thompson, C. P. (1985b). Voice identification: attempted recovery from a biased procedure. Human Learning. *Journal of Practical Research and Applications*, 4, 213–24.

Thompson, C. P. (1987). A language effect in voice identification. *Applied Cognitive Psychology*, 1, 121–31.

Thompson, W. C. (1989). Are juries competent to evaluate statistical evidence? *Law and Contemporary Problems*, 52, 9–41.

Thomson, D. M. (1981). Person identification influencing the outcome. *Australian and New Zealand Journal of Criminology*, 14, 49–54.

Thomson, D. M. (1984). Towards a more efficient judicial system – observations of an experimental psychologist. In M. Nixon (ed.), *Issues in Psychological Practice* (pp. 107–32). Melbourne: Longman Cheshire.

Thomson, D. M. (1988). A matter of justice: protecting the rights of the victim and the accused in child sexual abuse cases. In H. Dent and R. Flin (eds), 2.1–2.18.

Thomson, D. M. (1991). Reliability and credibility of children as witnesses. In J. Vernon (ed.), 43–52.

Thomson, D. M. (1995a). Eyewitness testimony and identification tests. In N. Brewer and C. Wilson (eds), 121–53.

Thomson, D. M. (1995b). Allegations of childhood sexual abuse: Repressed memories or false memories? *Psychiatry, Psychology and Law*, 2, 97–106.

Thornton, P. (1995). The admissibility of expert psychiatric and psychological evidence: judicial training. *Medicine, Science and the Law*, 35, 143–9.

Tickner, A. and Poulton, E. (1975). Watching for people and actions. *Ergonomics*, 18, 35–51.

Toch, H. (1961). *Legal and Criminal Psychology*. New York: Holt, Rinehart & Winston.

Todd, C. and Perlmutter, M. (1980). Reality recalled by preschool children. In M. Perlmutter (ed.), *New Directions for Child Development, No. 10: Children's Memory* (pp. 69–86). San Francisco: Jossey-Bass.

Tollestrup, P. A., Turtle, J. W. and Yuille, J. C. (1994). Actual victims and witnesses to robbery and fraud: an archival analysis. In D. F. Ross et al. (eds.), 144–60.

Tooley, V., Brigham, J. C., Maass, A. and Bothwell, R. K. (1984). Facial recognition: weapon effect and attentional focus. Unpublished manuscript, Florida State University, Tallahassee.

Tooley, V., Brigham, J. C., Maass, A. and Bothwell, R. K. (1987). Facial recognition: weapon effect and attentional focus. *Journal of Applied Social Psychology*, 17, 845–9.

Torpy, D. (1994). You must confess. *Issues in Criminological and Legal Psychology*, 21, 21–3.

Tousignant, D. D. (1991). Why suspects confess. *FBI Law Enforcement Bulletin*, 60 (3), 14–18.

Trankell, A. (1972). *The Reliability of Evidence: Methods of Analysing and Assessing Witness Statements*. Stockholm: Beckmans.

Traverso, G. and Manna, O. (1992). Law and psychology in Italy. In F. Lösel, D. Bender and T. Bliesener (eds), 535–45.

Treadway, M. and McCloskey, M. (1987). Cite unseen: distortions of the Allport and Postman study in the eyewitness testimony literature. *Law and Human Behavior*, 11, 19–25.

Treadway, M. and McCloskey, M. (1989). Effects of racial stereotypes on eyewitness performance: implications of the real and rumored Allport and Postman studies. *Applied Cognitive Psychology*, 3, 53–64.

Tremper, C. R. (1987a). Sanguinity and disillusionment where law meets social science. *Law and Human Behavior*, 11, 267–76.

Tremper, C. R. (1987b). Organized psychology's efforts to influence judicial policy-making. *American Psychologist*, 42, 496–501.

Triplett, N. (1900). The psychology of conjuring deceptions. *American Journal of Psychology*, 11, 439–510.

Tronk, K. and Dearden, I. (1993). *Advocacy Basics for Solicitors*. Sydney: Law Book Co.

Tucker, A., Mertin, P. and Luszcz, M. (1990). The effect of a repeated interview on young children's eyewitness memory. *Australian and New Zealand Journal of Criminology*, 23, 117–24.

Tulving, E. (1974). Cue-dependent forgetting. *American Scientist*, 62, 74–82.

Tulving, E. (1983). *Elements of Episodic Memory*. Oxford: Oxford University Press.

Tuohy, A. P., Wrennall, M. J., McQueen, R. A. and Stradling, S. G. (1993). Effect of socialization factors on decisions to prosecute. *Law and Human Behavior*, 17, 167–81.

Turnbull, D. G. and Thomson, D. M. (1984, May). Eyewitness testimony: photographic versus live line-ups. Paper presented at the Experimental Psychology Conference, Deakin University, Geelong, Australia.

Turnstall, O., Gudjonsson, G., Eysenck, H. and Howard, L. (1982). Professional issues arising from psychological evidence presented in court. *Bulletin of the British Psychological Society*, 35, 329–31.

Turtle, J. W. and Yuille, J. C. (1994). Lost but not forgotten: repeated eyewitness recall leads to reminiscence but not hypermnesia. *Journal of Applied Psychology*, 79, 260–71.

Twining, W. (1983). Identification and misidentification in legal processes: redefining the problem. In S. M. A. Lloyd-Bostock and B. R. Clifford (eds), 255–84.

Tzeng, O. J. L. and Cotton, B. (1980). A study-phase retrieval model of temporal coding. *Journal of Experimental Psychology*, 6, 705–16.

Underwood, G. and Milton, H. (1993). Collusion after a collision: witnesses' reports of a road accident with and without discussion. *Applied Cognitive Psychology*, 7, 11–22.

Undeutsch, U. (1982). Statement reality analysis. In A. Trankell (ed.), *Reconstructing the Past: The Role of Psychologists in Criminal Trials* (pp. 27–56). Stockholm: P. A. Norsted and Sons.

Unnever, J. D., Frazier, C. E. and Henretta, J. C. (1980). Race differences in criminal sentencing. *Sociological Quarterly*, 21, 197–206.

Van Wallandael, L. R., Surace, A., Parsons, D. B. and Brown, M. (1994). Earwitnesses' voice recognition: factors affecting accuracy and impact on jurors. *Applied Cognitive Psychology*, 8, 661–77.

Vandermaas, M. O., Hess, T. M. and Baker-Ward, L. (1993). Does anxiety affect children's reports of memory for a stressful event? *Applied Cognitive Psychology*, 7, 109–27.

Verinis, J. S. and Walker, V. (1970). Policemen and the recall of criminal details. *Journal of Social Psychology*, 81, 217–21.

Vernon, J. (ed.) (1991). *Children as Witnesses*. Canberra: Australian Institute of Criminology.

Victoria Law Reform Committee (1995). *Jury Service in Victoria*. Issue Paper No. 2. Melbourne.

Victoria Law Reform Commission (1985). *The Role of the Jury in Criminal Trials*. Background Paper No. 1. Melbourne: Parliament of Victoria.

Visher, C. A. (1987). Juror decision-making: the importance of evidence. *Law and Human Behavior*, 11, 1–17.

von Hirsch, A. (1995). Proportionality and parsimony in American sentencing guidelines. In C. Clarkson and R. Morgan (eds), *The Politics of Sentencing Reform* (pp. 149–67). Oxford: Clarendon Press.

Vrij, A. and Winkel, F. W. (1992). Police–citizen interaction and non-verbal communication: the impact of culturally determined smiling and gestures. In F. Lösel et ál. (eds), 240–52.

Vrij, A. and Winkel, F. W. (1993). Objective and subjective indicators of deception. *Issues in Criminological and Legal Psychology*, No. 20, 51–7.

Vrij, A. and van Wijngaarden, J. J. (1994). Will truth come out? Two studies about the detection of false statements expressed by children. *Expert Evidence*, 3, 78–83.

Vrij, A., Van Fer Steen, J. and Koppelaar, L. (1995). The effects of physical effort on police officers' perception and aggression in simulated shooting incidents. *Psychology, Crime and Law*, 1, 301–8.

Wagenaar, W. A. (1988). *Identifying Ivan. A Case Study in Legal Psychology*. London: Harvester-Weatsheaf.

Wagenaar, W. A. and Boer, H. P. A. (1987). Misleading postevent information: testing parameterised models of integration in memory. *Acta Psychologica*, 66, 291–306.

Wagenaar, W. A. and van der Scrier, J. (1994, April). Face recognition as a function of distance and illumination: a practical test for use in the courtroom. Paper presented at the Fourth European Conference on Law and Psychology, Barcelona.

Wagenaar, W. A. and Veefkind, N. (1992). Comparison of one-person and six-person line-ups. In F. Lösel et al. (eds), 275–85.

Waid, W. M., Orne, E. C., Cook, M. R. and Orne, M. T. (1981). Meprobamate reduces accuracy of physiological detection of deception. *Science*, 212, 71–3.

Waight, P. K. and Williams, C. R. (1995). *Evidence: Commentary and Materials* (4th edn). Sydney: Law Book Company.

Wakefield, H. and Underwager, R. (1991). Sexual abuse allegations in divorce and custody disputes. *Behavioral Sciences and the Law*, 9, 451–68.

Wakefield, H. and Underwager, R. (1992). Recovered memories of alleged sexual abuse: lawsuits against parents. *Behavioral Sciences and the Law*, 10, 485–507.

Walker, A. G. (1993). Questioning young children in court: a linguistic study. *Law and Human Behavior*, 17, 59–81.

Walker, J. and McDonald, D. (1995). The over-representation of indigenous people in custody in Australia. *Trends and Issues in Crime and Criminal Justice*, No. 47. Canberra: Australian Institute of Criminology.

Walker, N. D. (1975). *The British Jury System*. Cambridge: Institute of Criminology.

Walker, N. D. (1980). *Punishment, Danger and Stigma: The Morality of Criminal Justice*. Oxford: Blackwell.

Walker, N. D. (1987). *Crime and Criminology: A Critical Introduction*. Oxford: Oxford University Press.

Walker, T. G. (1972). A note concerning partisan influences on trial-judge decision-making. *Law and Society Review*, 6, 645–9.

Wallace, J. G. (1956). Some studies of perception in relation to age. *British Journal of Psychology*, 67, 283–97.

Walsh, A. (1991). Race and discretionary sentencing: an analysis of 'obvious' and 'non-obvious' cases. *International Journal of Offender Therapy and Comparative Criminology*, 35, 7–19.

Wardlaw, G. (1984). The psychologist in court: some guidelines on the presentation of psychological evidence. In M. Nixon (ed.), *Issues in Psychological Practice* (pp. 133–43). Melbourne: Longman Cheshire.

Wark, L., Memon, A., Holley, A., Köhnken, G. and Bull, R. (1994). Children's memory for a magic show: use of the cognitive interview. Paper presented at the Fourth European Conference on Law and Psychology, Barcelona.

Warner, K. (1988). Child witnesses in sexual assault cases. *Criminal Law Journal*, 286–306.

Warner, S. B. and Cabot, H. B. (1936). *Judges and Law Reform*. Harvard, Mass.: Harvard University Press.

Warren, A., Hulse-Trotter, K. and Tubbs, E. C. (1991). Inducing resistance to suggestibility to children. *Law and Human Behavior*, 15, 273–85.

Warren, A. and Swartwood, J. N. (1992). Developmental issues in flashbulb memory research: children recall the Challenger event. In E. Winograd and U. Neisser (eds), 95–120.

Watkins, J. G. (1993). Dealing with the problem of 'false memory' in clinic and court. *Journal of Psychiatry and Law*, 21, 297–317.

Watkins, M. J. (1990). Mediationism and the obfuscation of memory. *American Psychologist*, 45, 328–35.

Wexler, P. (1983). *Critical Social Psychology*. London: Routledge.

Weaver, III, C. A. (1993). Do you need a 'flash' to form a flashbulb memory? *Journal of Experimental Psychology: General*, 122, 39–46.

Wegener, H., Lösel, F. and Haisch, J. (eds) (1989). *Criminal Behavior and the Justice System: Psychological Perspectives*. New York: Springer-Verlag.

Weinberg, H. A. and Baron, R. S. (1982). The discredible witness. *Personality and Social Psychology Bulletin*, 8, 60–7.

Weiner, B. (1979). A theory of motivation for some classroom experiences. *Journal of Educational Psychology*, 71, 3–25.

Weiner, B. (1980). *Human Motivation*. New York: Holt, Rinehart & Winston.

Weiner, I. B. and Hess, A. K. (eds) (1987). *Handbook of Forensic Psychology*. New York: Wiley.

Weiner, R. L. and Small, M. A. (1992). Social cognition and tort law: the roles of basic science. In D. K. Kagehiro and W. S. Laufer (eds), 433–54.

Weingardt, K. R., Toland, H. K. and Loftus, E. F. (1994). Reports of suggested memories: do people truly believe them? In D. F. Ross et al. (eds), 3–26.

Weingartner, H., Miller, H. and Murphy, D. L. (1977). Mood-state-dependent retrieval of verbal associations. *Journal of Abnormal Psychology*, 86, 276–94.

Weir, J. A. and Wrightsman, L. S. (1990). The determinants of mock jurors' verdicts in a rape case. *International Journal of Applied Psychology*, 20, 901–19.

Weisberg, R. (1983). Deregulating death. *Sup. Ct. Review*, 305–95.

Wellborn III, O. G. (1991). Demeanor. *Cornell Law Review*, 1075–105.

Wells, G. L. (1978). Applied eyewitness research: system variables and estimator variables. *Journal of Personality and Social Psychology*, 36, 1546–57.

Wells, G. L. (1984). How adequate is human intuition for judging eyewitness testimony? In G. L. Wells and E. F. Loftus (eds), 256–72.

Wells, G. L. (1984). The psychology of line-up identifications. *Journal of Applied Social Psychology*, 14, 89–103.

Wells, G. L. (1985). The eyewitness. In S. Kassin and L. S. Wrightsman (eds), *The Psychology of Evidence and Trial Procedure* (pp. 43–66). Beverly Hills, CA: Sage.

Wells, G. L. (1988). *Eyewitness Identification*. Toronto: Carswell.

Wells, G. L. (1993). What do we know about eyewitness identification? *American Psychologist*, 48, 553–71.

Wells, G. L. and Cutler, B. L. (1990). The right to counsel at videotaped line-ups: an emerging dilemma. *Connecticut Law Review*, 22, 373–95.

Wells, G. L., Leippe, M. R. and Ostrom, T. M. (1979). Guidelines for empirically assessing the fairness of a line-up. *Law and Human Behavior*, 3, 285–93.

Wells, G. L. and Lindsay, R. C. L. (1980). On estimating the diagnosticity of eyewitness identifications. *Psychological Bulletin*, 88, 776–84.

Wells, G. L., Lindsay, R. C. L. and Ferguson, T. J. (1979). Accuracy, confidence and juror perceptions in eyewitness identification. *Journal of Applied Psychology*, 64, 440–8.

Wells, G. L. and Loftus, E. F. (eds) (1984). *Eyewitness Testimony: Psychological Perspectives*. New York: Cambridge University Press.

Wells, G. L. and Luus, C. A. E. (1990a). Police line-ups as experiments: social methodology as a framework for properly conducted line-ups. *Personality and Social Psychology Bulletin*, 3, 285–93.

Wells, G. L. and Luus, C. A. E. (1990b). The diagnosticity of a line-up should not be confused with the diagnostic value of non-line-up evidence. *Journal of Applied Psychology*, 75, 511–16.

Wells, G. L. and Murray, D. M. (1984). Eyewitness confidence. In G. L. Wells and E. F. Loftus (eds), 155–70.

Wells, G. L., Rydell, S. M. and Seelau, E. P. (1993). The selection of distractors for eyewitness line-ups. *Journal of Applied Psychology*, 78, 835–44.

Wells, G. L., Seelau, E. P., Rydell, S. M. and Luus, C. A. E. (1994). Recommendations for properly conducted line-up identification tasks. In D. F. Ross et al. (eds), 223–44.

Wells, G. L. and Turtle, J. W. (1986). Eyewitness identification: the importance of line-up models. *Psychological Bulletin*, 99, 320–9.

Wells, W. (1988). *Evidence and Advocacy*. Sydney: Butterworths.

Werner, C. M., Strube, M. J., Cole, A. M. and Kagehiro, D. K. (1985). The impact of case characteristics and prior jury experience on jury verdicts. *Journal of Applied Social Psychology*, 15, 409–27.

Wertheimer, M. (1906). Experimentelle Untersuchungen zur Tatbestandsdiagnostik. *Archiv für die gesamte Psychologie*, 6, 59–131.

Westcott, H. L. (1995). Children's experiences of being examined and cross-examined: the opportunity to be heard. *Expert Evidence*, 4, 1319.

Westcott, H. L., Davies, G. M. and Clifford, B. R. (1991). Adults' perceptions of children's videotaped truthful and deceptive statements. *Children and Society*, 5, 123–35.

Whipple, G. M. (1909). The observer as reporter: a survey of the 'psychology of testimony'. *Psychological Bulletin*, 6, 153–70.

Whipple, G. M. (1918). The obtaining of information: psychology of observation and report. *Psychological Bulletin*, 15, 217–48.

Wickland, R. A. and Brehm, J. W. (1976). *Perspectives in Cognitive Dissonance*. Hillside, NJ: Lawrence Erlbaum.

Wigmore, J. H. (1974). *Evidence*. Boston: Little Brown.

Wilbanks, W. (1986). Are female felons treated more leniently by the criminal justice system? *Justice Quarterly*, 3, 517–29.

Wilczynski, A. and Morris, A. (1993). Parents who kill their children. *Criminal Law Review*, 31–6.

Williams, F. P. and McShane, M. D. (1990). Inclinations of prospective jurors in capital cases. *Sociology and Social Research*, 74, 85–94.

Williams, G. L. (1963). *The Proof of Guilt: A Study of the English Criminal Trial.* 3rd edn. London: Stevens.

Williams, K. D., Loftus, E. F. and Deffenbacher, K. A. (1992). Eyewitness evidence and testimony. In D. K. Kagehiro and W. S. Laufer (eds), 141–66.

Williamson, D., Chalk, M. and Knepper, P. (1993). Teen court: juvenile justice for the 21st century? *Federal Probation,* 57, 54–8.

Willis, J. (1983). Jury disagreements in criminal trials – some Victorian evidence. *Australian and New Zealand Journal of Criminology,* 20, 20–30.

Willis, J. (1995). New wine in old bottles: the sentencing discount for pleading guilty. In A. Kapardis (ed.), *Sentencing. Law in Context* (Special Issue), 13, 39–78.

Wilson, C. H. (1995). Developmental issues concerning testing children's evidence in court. *Expert Evidence,* 4, 20–4.

Winkel, F. W. and Koppelaar, L. (1992). Perceived credibility of the communicator: studies of perceptual bias in police officers conducting rape interviews. In F. Lösel et al. (eds), 219–33.

Winograd, E. and Neisser, U. (eds) (1992). *Affect and Accuracy in Recall: Studies of 'Flashbulb' Memories.* New York: Cambridge University Press.

Winograd, E. and Soloway, R. M. (1985). Reminding as a basis for temporal judgements. *Journal of Experimental Psychology: Learning, Memory and Cognition,* 11, 262–71.

Wippich, W. (1989). Remembering social events and activities. In H. Wegener et al. (eds), 228–41.

Witkin, H. A., Dyke, R. B., Faterson, H. F., Goodenough, D. R. and Karp, S. A. (1962). *Psychological Differentiation.* New York: Wiley.

Wolfgang, M. E. and Reidel, M. (1975). Rape, race and the death penalty in Georgia. *American Journal of Orthopsychiatry,* 45, 658–68.

Wood, W. (1982). Retrieval of attitude relevant information from memory: effects on susceptibility to persuasion and on intrinsic motivation. *Journal of Personality and Social Psychology,* 42, 798–810.

Wooley, R. M. and Hakstian, A. R. (1992). An examination of the construct validity of personality-based and overt measures of integrity. *Educational Psychological Measurement,* 52, 475–89.

Wooton, B. (1959). *Social Science and Social Pathology.* London: Allen & Unwin.

Worden, A. P. (1993). The attitudes of men and women in policing: testing conventional and contemporary wisdom. *Criminology,* 31, 203–41.

Wortley, K. R. and Homel, R. J. (1995). Police prejudice as a function of training and outgroup contact: a longitudinal investigation. *Law and Human Behavior,* 19, 305–31.

Wright, D. B. (1993). Recall of the Hillsborough disaster over time: systematic biases of 'flashbulb' memories. *Applied Cognitive Psychology,* 7, 129–38.

Wright, P. (1991). *The Spycatcher's Encyclopedia of Espionage.* Melbourne: Heinemann.

Wrightsman, S. L. (1987). *Psychology and the Legal System.* Pacific Grove, CA: Brooks Cove Publishing.

Yanagihara, T. and Petersen, R. C. (eds) (1991). *Memory Disorders: Research and Clinical Practice.* New York: Dekker.

Yarmey, A. D. (1979). *The Psychology of Eyewitness Testimony.* New York: Free Press.

Yarmey, A. D. (1986a). Perceived expertness and credibility of police officers as eyewitnesses. *Canadian Police College Journal,* 10, 31–52.

Yarmey, A. D. (1986b). Verbal, visual, and voice identification of a rape suspect under different conditions of illumination. *Journal of Applied Psychology*, 71, 363–70.

Yarmey, A. D. (1990). *Understanding Police and Police Work*. New York: New York University Press.

Yarmey, A. D. (1991). Voice identification over the telephone. *Journal of Applied Social Psychology*, 21, 1868–76.

Yarmey, A. D. (1994). Earwitness evidence: memory for a perpetrator's voice. In D. F. Ross et al. (eds), 101–24.

Yarmey, A. D. (1995). Earwitness and evidence obtained by other senses. In R. Bull and D. Carson (eds), 261–73.

Yarmey, A. D. and Jones, H. P. T. (1983). Accuracy of memory of male and female eyewitnesses to a criminal assault and rape. *Bulletin of the Psychonomic Society*, 21, 89–92.

Yarmey, A. D. and Kent, J. (1980). Eyewitness identification by elderly and young adults. *Law and Human Behavior*, 4, 359–71.

Yarmey, A. D. and Matthys, E. (1992). Voice identification of an abductor. *Applied Cognitive Psychology*, 6, 367–77.

Yarmey, A. D. and Pauley, T. (1993). The effects of weapon focus and perceived violence on voice identification. Unpublished manuscript, University of Guelph, Ontario.

Yarmey, A. D. and Tressillian Jones, H. P. (1982). Police awareness of the fallibility of eyewitness identification. *Canadian Police College Journal*, 6, 113–24.

Yarmey, A. D., Yarmey, A. L. and Yarmey, M. J. (1994). Face and voice identifications in showups and line-ups. *Applied Cognitive Psychology*, 8, 453–64.

Yerkes, P. M. and Berry, C. S. (1909). The association reaction time method of mental diagnosis. *American Journal of Psychology*, 20, 22–37.

Yerkes, R. M. and Dodson, J. D. (1908). The relation of strength of stimulus to rapidity of habit-information. *Journal of Comparative Neurology of Psychology*, 18, 459–82.

Yeschke, C. L. (1993). *Interviewing: A Forensic Guide to Interrogation* (2nd edn). Springfield, IL: Charles C. Thomas.

Young, A. W. and Ellis, H. D. (1989). *Handbook of Research on Face Recognition*. Amsterdam: North Holland.

Yuille, J. C. (ed.) (1986). *Police Selection and Training: The Role of Psychology*. Dordecht: Martinus Nijhoff.

Yuille, J. C. (1986). Meaningful research in the police context. In J. C. Yuille (ed.), 225–43.

Yuille, J. C. (1988). *Credibility Assessment*. The Netherlands: Kluwer Academic.

Yuille, J. C. (1992). Psychologists and the police. In F. Lösel et al. (eds), 205–11.

Yuille, J. C., and Cutshall, J. L. (1986). A case study of eyewitness memory for a crime. *Journal of Applied Psychology*, 71, 291–301.

Yuille, J. C. and Cutshall, J. L. (1988). Analysis of the statements of victims, witnesses and suspects. In J. C. Yuille (ed.), 175–91.

Yuille, J. C., Davies, G. M., Gibling, F., Marxsen, D. and Porter, S. (1994). Eyewitness memory of police trainees for realistic role plays. *Journal of Applied Psychology*, 79, 931–6.

Yuille, J. C., Hunter, R., Joffe, R. and Zaparniuk, J. (1993). Interviewing children in sexual abuse cases. In G. S. Goodman and B. L. Bottoms (eds), 95–115.

Yuille, J. C. and Kim, C. K. (1987). A field study of the forensic use of hypnosis. *Canadian Journal of Behavioral Science*, 193, 418–35.

Yuille, J. C., Marxsen, D. and Menard, K. (1993). Report to the Ministry of Social Services of British Columbia on the Systematic Interviewing Project. Vancouver, BC: Authors.

Yuille, J. C. and McKewan, N. H. (1985). Use of hypnosis as an aid to eyewitness testimony. *Journal of Applied Psychology*, 70, 389–400.

Yuille, J. C. and Tollestrup, P. A. (1990). Some effects of alcohol on eyewitness memory. *Journal of Applied Psychology*, 75, 268–73.

Yuille, J. C. and Tollestrup, P. A. (1992). A model of the direct effects of emotion on eyewitness memory. In S. A. Christianson (ed.), *The Handbook of Emotion and Memory: Research and Theory* (pp. 201–15). Hillsdale, NJ: Lawrence Erlbaum.

Yuille, J. C. and Wells, G. L. (1991). Concerns about the application of research findings: the issue of ecological validity. In J. Doris (ed.), 118–28.

Zander, M. (1974). Why I disagree with Sir Robert Mark. *Police*, April, 16.

Zander, M. and Henderson, P. (1994). The Crown Court study. Royal Commission on Criminal Justice, Study No. 19. *Research Bulletin*, No. 35, 46–8. London: Home Office Research and Statistics Department.

Zaparniuk, J., Yuille, J. C., and Taylor, S. (1995). Assessing the credibility of true and false statements. *International Journal of Law and Psychiatry*, 18, 343–52.

Zaragoza, M. S., Graham, J. R., Hall, G. C. N., Hirschman, R. and Ben-Porath, Y. S. (1995). *Memory and Testimony in the Child Witness*. Thousand Oaks, CA: Sage.

Zaragoza, M. S., Jamis, M. and McCloskey, M. (1987). Misleading postevent information and recall of the original event: further evidence against the memory impairment hypothesis. *Journal of Experimental Psychology: Learning, Memory and Cognition*, 13, 36–44.

Zaragoza, M. S. and Koshmider, III, J. W. (1989). Misled subjects may know more than their performance implies. *Journal of Experimental Psychology: Learning, Memory and Cognition*, 15, 246–55.

Zeisel, H. and Diamond, S. S. (1987). Convincing empirical evidence on the six-member jury. In L. S. Wrightsman, S. M. Kassin and C. E. Willis (eds), *In the Jury Box: Controversies in the Courtroom* (pp. 193–208). Newbury Park, CA: Sage.

Zerman, M. (1977). *Call the Final Witness: the People vs. Mather as Seen by the 11th Juror.* New York: Harper & Row.

Zigmond, A. S. and Smith, R. P. (1983). The hospital anxiety and depression scale. *Acta Psychiatrica Scandinavica*, 67, 361–70.

Zimbardo, P. G. and Leippe, M. R. (1991). *The Psychology of Attitude and Social Influence.* New York: McGraw-Hill.

Zuckerman, M. and Driver, R. (1985). Telling lies: verbal and non-verbal correlates of deception. In A. W. Siegman and S. Feldstein (eds), *Nonverbal Communication: An Integrated Perspective* (pp. 129–47). Hillsdale, NJ: Lawrence Erlbaum.

Author Index

Subject Index

378